EQUITY AND ADEQUACY IN EDUCATION FINANCE

Issues and Perspectives

Helen F. Ladd, Rosemary Chalk, and Janet S. Hansen, *Editors*

Committee on Education Finance

Commission on Behavioral and Social Sciences and Education

National Research Council

NATIONAL ACADEMY PRESS
Washington, D.C. 1999

NATIONAL ACADEMY PRESS • 2101 Constitution Avenue, N.W. • Washington, D.C 20418

NOTICE: The project that is the subject of this volume was approved by the Governing Board of the National Research Council, whose members are drawn from the councils of the National Academy of Sciences, the National Academy of Engineering, and the Institute of Medicine. The members of the committee responsible for the volume were chosen for their special competences and with regard for appropriate balance.

This volume was supported by Contract No. RF95194001 between the National Academy of Sciences and the U.S. Department of Education. Any opinions, findings, conclusions, or recommendations expressed in this publication are those of the author(s) and do not necessarily reflect the view of the organizations or agencies that provided support for this project.

Library of Congress Cataloging-in-Publication Data

Equity and adequacy issues in education finance : issues and
perspectives / Helen F. Ladd, Rosemary Chalk, and Janet S. Hansen,
editors ; Committee on Education Finance, Commission on Behavioral
and Social Sciences and Education, National Research Council.
     p. cm.
Includes bibliographical references and index.

    ISBN 0-309-06563-1 (cloth)
    1. Education—United States—Finance. 2. Educational
equalization—United States. I. Ladd, Helen F. II. Chalk, Rosemary
A. III. Hansen, Janet S. IV. National Research Council (U.S.).
Committee on Education Finance.
    LB2825 .E68 1999
    379.1'1'0973—dc21

                98-51230

Additional copies of this volume are available from:
National Academy Press
2101 Constitution Avenue N.W.
Washington, D.C. 20418
Call 800-624-6242 or 202-334-3313 (in the Washington Metropolitan Area).

This volume is also available on line at **http://www.nap.edu**

Contents

TABLES

BOXES

Preface

In the mid-1990s, the U.S. Congress requested a major study of the U.S. system of elementary and secondary education finance. In response to this request, the National Research Council (NRC) set up the Committee on Education Finance to undertake the study. The committee was established within the NRC's Commission on Behavioral and Social Sciences and Education.

This volume of background papers was prepared in connection with one part of the committee's study. The volume includes eight papers commissioned by the committee to inform its discussions about equity and adequacy in education finance, two of the issues it was specifically charged to address.

The preparation of this volume and the conduct of the larger study are supported by funds from the U.S. Department of Education that were appropriated as part of the legislation for the Departments of Education, Labor, and Health and Human Services in 1994 (P.L. 103-333). The study is being carried out under a contract with the National Institute on Educational Governance, Finance, Policy Making, and Management, part of the Department of Education's Office of Educational Research and Improvement. The views expressed by the authors are theirs alone and do not reflect the opinions of the Committee on Education Finance or the U.S. Department of Education.

The committee acknowledges the valuable contributions of the authors, who prepared and revised their papers within relatively short time periods, as well as the committee members and reviewers who provided thoughtful advice and criticism to the authors.

The papers in this volume have been reviewed in draft form by individuals chosen for their diverse perspectives and technical expertise, in accordance with procedures approved by the NRC's Report Review Committee. The purpose of this independent review is to provide candid and critical comments that will assist the institution in making the published volume as sound as possible and to ensure that the volume meets institutional standards for objectivity and evidence. The review comments and draft manuscript remain confidential to protect the integrity of the process.

We wish to thank the following individuals for their participation in the review of this volume: John Augenblick, Augenblick & Myers, Denver, Colorado; Dominic Brewer, RAND, Santa Monica, California; William Buss, College of Law, University of Iowa; David Figlio, Department of Economics, University of Oregon; Eric Hanushek, Department of Economics, University of Rochester; David Monk, Department of Education, Cornell University; Richard Murnane, Graduate School of Education, Harvard University; Lawrence Picus, School of Education, University of Southern California; Andrew Reschovsky, Robert N. Lafollette Institute of Public Affairs, University of Wisconsin; Julie Underwood, Department of Education, Miami University; and Arthur Wise, National Council on Accreditation of Teacher Education, Washington, D.C. Although these individuals have provided constructive comments and suggestions, it must be emphasized that responsibility for the final content of this volume rests entirely with the contributing authors and the NRC.

Several staff members also made important contributions to this work: Rosemary Chalk, a coeditor, was instrumental in shepherding the papers through the production process and providing oversight and editorial guidance during the preparation of the volume, Anne Marie Finn conducted extensive reference checks for each paper, and Nat Tipton and Sharon Vandivere ably assisted the authors by producing multiple iterations of the papers with technical efficiency.

This volume of background papers does not represent the committee's findings and conclusions about the equity or adequacy of school finance in the United States. Those conclusions must await the 1999 publication of the committee's final report. In the interim, the Committee on Education Finance hopes that the insights and perspectives presented in the following papers will be useful to all who are concerned with the challenges of achieving fairness in school finance and establishing equal educational opportunity for all students.

Helen F. Ladd, *Cochair*
Janet S. Hansen, *Study Director*
Committee on Education Finance

EQUITY AND
ADEQUACY IN
EDUCATION
FINANCE

Introduction

The U.S. system of education finance is characterized by large disparities in funding and opportunities for K-12 education among schools, local school districts, and states. These disparities have historical, constitutional, and social origins: states play a major role in financing education, local school districts bear significant responsibility for raising revenue for schools, the property tax is the primary source of local revenue for school districts, and property wealth varies significantly between districts within a state. As a result, districts with small property tax bases typically find it harder than those with large property tax bases to generate local revenue for schools. Compounding the problem, districts with more-costly-to-educate youngsters are often not the ones with the large property tax bases. Although the effects of low wealth or concentrations of costly-to-educate students have been partially offset by small amounts of aid from the federal government and larger amounts from state governments, significant disparities remain both within and between states.

Spending disparities, especially those within states, have inspired education finance reform efforts for decades. These reform efforts were initially driven by the belief that it was inequitable to have high levels of spending in some districts and low levels in others and, significantly, were quite separate from other reform efforts dealing with broader areas of educational policy. In recent years, however, questions about finance reform have increasingly been linked to questions about improving school performance. This linkage has taken on new importance in light of widespread dissatisfaction with the quality of American education, skepticism about the ways in which educational funds are used and distributed within the public school system, and growing awareness of the economic and social disadvantages facing individuals whose educational achievement is low. One manifestation of this broader concern has been the emergence of the comparatively new legal paradigm of educational adequacy which emphasizes the adequacy, rather than the distribution, of resources available to districts and schools and of the educational outcomes they produce. This new paradigm of educational adequacy has spread rapidly in recent years and now serves as the foundation for many current court cases and legislative deliberations.

Finance inequities and the linkages among education finance, school performance, and academic achievement were among the concerns that led Congress to ask the National Research Council to study the theory and practice of financing elementary and secondary education by federal, state, and local governments in the United States. The National Research Council responded by establishing the Committee on Education Finance. The key question posed to the committee was: How can education finance systems be designed to assure that all students achieve high levels of learning and that education funds are raised and used in the most efficient and effective manner possible?

Although funding disparities and the adequacy of funding levels, which are the central concern of this volume, are one part of the puzzle requiring examination, they must be considered in connection with other important questions about the education system. For example, while more equal funding across schools and school districts might be desirable, it does not assure that funds would be directed productively toward the goal of academic achievement, that students from advantaged and disadvantaged backgrounds would have equal opportunities, or that the educational opportunities for all students would be adequate to achieve the desired outcome of their full participation in the civil and economic life of the community. Efforts to equalize spending in order to enhance educational opportunities for disadvantaged students have also raised other concerns, such as how much funding for education is sufficient for a state to meet its educational obligations.

In developing our study, the committee had to consider an extensive amount of research literature on educational finance and educational reform. To help with this task, we have commissioned a number of papers. This volume presents a selected subgroup of these papers, ones that focus explicitly on issues pertaining to equity and adequacy in the U.S. education system. The authors examine the legal, economic, and political forces that influence the response of the education finance systems to shifting social concerns about racial discrimination, tax reform, wealth differences, and the problems of inner cities in American society.

The committee has chosen to publish these eight papers in advance of its final report so they may assist not only us but also the policymakers and scholars who grapple continuously with questions of equity and adequacy of school finance formulas. The papers make a significant and timely contribution to the literature on school finance reform by revealing important trends in the long struggle to reduce disparities and equalize educational opportunities. They suggest that we are beginning to understand how state education finance systems respond to court-ordered reforms and political forces within individual states. They reveal the complex dynamics of how school spending and school districts adapt to changes in state educational finance systems. They trace the evolution of finance reform based on concerns about funding equity and indicate some of the possibilities and pitfalls facing policy makers as equity-based reforms become increasingly concerned with the adequacy of the educational opportunities provided to children.

The "shift toward adequacy" in school finance, as the papers in this volume suggest, begins to make explicit the link between the funding of schools and their educational performance. Yet these papers do not address in a direct way crucial questions about how the financing system does or could influence the behavior and effectiveness of schools. These questions are of central concern to the Committee on Education Finance, however, and will be addressed in our final report, scheduled for publication in late 1999.

Each paper in this volume represents only the views of the individual authors. The papers were commissioned to inform the committee's deliberations and were not designed to provide a comprehensive review of all issues related to equity and adequacy in education finance or to reflect the committee's positions on these issues. Among other things, these papers do not address issues such as the impact of efforts to equalize funds on student outcomes, the relationship between spending and student performance, or the performance or behavioral incentives set up by general or categorical funding with the educational system. Signs of disagreement also exist within the papers, such as the strength of the relationship between the landmark equity cases in California (the *Serrano* cases) and the passage of Proposition 13 in that state (see, for example, comments by Minorini and Sugarman in Chapter 2 and by Evans, Murray, and Schwab in Chapter 3 of this volume). We recognize that many other critical concerns about educational finance are not addressed, such as the plight of disadvantaged students, the concentration of poverty in urban areas, the impacts of the growth and diversity of student populations, or the introduction of new technologies on the financing of U.S. education. These issues, and others, will be considered in our final report.

The eight papers in this volume trace the history and current status of efforts to foster fairness in educational finance systems. The first paper, authored by Robert Berne and Leanna Stiefel, seeks to clarify and define concepts of school finance equity and to provide a firm conceptual framework for the papers that follow. Two lawyers, Paul A. Minorini and Stephen D. Sugarman, then examine the historical evolution, impact, and future of school finance litigation designed to foster equity in the allocation of educational resources among advantaged and disadvantaged districts.

The catalytic role of the courts is documented in the third paper by economists William N. Evans, Sheila E. Murray, and Robert M. Schwab. They show that states facing court orders were more likely to reduce within-state disparities than states where reform was initiated by the legislature rather than the courts. Moreover they show that two-thirds of the current disparities in per pupil funding differences are attributable to cross-state differences rather than the within-state differences that can be addressed by court orders.

Understanding why states differ in their ability to engage in successful finance reform requires the political perspective brought by Melissa C. Carr and Susan H. Fuhrman. In Chapter 4, they describe the changing political landscape of education finance reform during the past 30 years and report on case studies of four states that highlight differences across states in their political environments and hence their ability to reduce disparities. The fifth paper, by economist Margaret E. Goertz and sociologist Gary Natriello, explores how finance reform is likely to affect spending for specific purposes. Three conclusions emerge from their analysis: (1) changes in school finance formulas increased local district spending levels; (2) changes in formulas equalized spending somewhat (which is consistent with the findings by Evans, Murray, and Schwab in Chapter 3 of this volume); and (3), perhaps most importantly, school districts used new money pretty much the way they used old money.

In tracing the origins of adequacy in education finance, Paul Minorini and Stephen Sugarman have prepared a second paper in this volume (Chapter 6) that explains how the adequacy strategy developed in school finance litigation, how it has been used in state courts, and how state courts have interpreted adequacy to date. Their paper emphasizes that although the courts can be powerful influences, they have limited power to determine the nature of state education systems. The fashioning of acceptable finance strategies is commonly left to state legislators, who must determine the goals and purpose of their state educational system and the resource allocations that are necessary to provide a fair and adequate education to children from both advantaged and disadvantaged backgrounds.

The seventh paper, by James W. Guthrie and Richard Rothstein, who specialize in education and public policy, describes the conceptual and technical challenges involved in operationalizing an adequacy standard and provides examples of how several states are addressing these challenges. A key problem for the states is how to determine how much money a district would need to provide an adequate level of education. Guthrie and Rothstein describe and assess three approaches being pioneered by policy analysts and researchers. The final paper by William Duncombe and John Yinger, from the fields of public administration and economics, presents a technical analysis of one of these approaches, one that focuses on the differential costs of adequacy for different groups of students. The authors use a compelling metaphor to clarify the factors that affect the costs of education, that of providing comfortable shelter under varying weather conditions. But a tough question, which is beyond the scope of this paper, is whether the "technology" of education (input-output relationships) is as well defined as the technology of providing comfortable shelter. The Guthrie/Rothstein and

Duncombe/Yinger papers differ in their assessments of the strengths and weaknesses of efforts to define the costs of adequacy, reflecting the fact that these inquiries are in their infancy. Greater consensus about methods and magnitudes ought to grow as the efforts mature.

Drawing on the fields of economics, education, law, political science, public administration, public finance, and sociology, the collection of papers suggests the breadth of ongoing dialogues about ways to understand and measure the significance and impact of selected forces in the educational environment. The multidisciplinary analyses within this volume provide a rich context for identifying key themes that shape discussions of equity and adequacy in education finance and influence the decisions of economic, political, legal, and educational institutions. The Committee on Education Finance hopes that the insights and perspectives presented in the following papers will be useful to all who are concerned with the challenges of achieving fairness in school finance, establishing high standards of educational performance, and assuring equal educational opportunity for all students.

1

Concepts of School Finance Equity: 1970 to the Present

Robert Berne and Leanna Stiefel

INTRODUCTION

The idea of "America as a land of opportunity" captures an essential part of our national spirit and heritage, and public education is often viewed as the institution that can transform that idea into a reality. Thus, to many, an equitable system of education is one that offsets those accidents of birth that would otherwise keep some children from having an opportunity to function fully in the economic and political life of the community.

The idea of providing opportunity by using education as a vehicle has occupied social scientists and educational policy makers throughout the twentieth century, with the work of Ellwood P. Cubberley often cited as the first to link the method of finance with the fairness of the education system (Guthrie et al., 1988:133). Early school finance work focused on the resources available to children (inputs), although the authors of this work implicitly assumed that equalizing resources would also equalize performance and life outcomes. We now know that the linkages between inputs and outputs are complicated. While a common statement among experts in education is that changing resource allocation can lead to improvements in outputs if schools use their funds productively, the enormous literature on education production functions is not conclusive about which specific resources, under which particular circumstances, will affect outputs and outcomes (Hanushek, 1986; Ferguson and Ladd, 1996; Mosteller et al., 1996).[1]

In addition to conceptual issues about the extent to which finance inputs are related to improving performance, fairness in financing also runs headlong into the particular American way of funding and delivering public primary and secondary education. All 50 states create public school systems that are generally organized into local school districts and rely heavily on financing from local property taxes. Property taxes in turn are based on property values that are unequally distributed across school districts and across states. Beginning at the turn of the century, the traditional policy response to inequities caused by unequal property tax bases has been to restructure state financing systems to mitigate the disequalizing effects within states while still maintaining the 50-state system.

Several key realities describe the challenge faced by Americans as they strive to provide opportunity through public education, all within the context of a federal system of state and local control. First, a well-accepted equity concept such as equal opportunity includes many specific, different definitions. Some of these differences, especially more recent ones, have their origin in whether student performance or resource access is the ultimate goal of a finance system. The different definitions then lead to different opinions among legislators, lawyers, advocates, and the public about specific goals they are trying to achieve. Second, unlike most other countries, in the United States the federal government provides a relatively small share of public primary and secondary education funding, around 7 percent. State and local governments share roughly equally the remaining 93 percent. Third, the reliance on individual states means that there are actually 50 separate and different public education systems with substantial variation in finance, governance, and instruction. Fourth, equity in education has been affected by litigation and court decisions, not at the federal level for broad-based equity concerns, but instead at the state level, largely based on state constitutions. Fifth, the popular press and journalists are active participants in the discourse about education equity.[2] While these factors have influenced school finance over the past century, the most recent changes since 1970 have been dramatic and important.

The 1970s mark the beginning of a significant period to examine school finance equity, comparable to other times when major events changed the direction of K-12 finance legislation or law.[3] The early 1970s were watershed years, most dramatically marked by the California Supreme Court's decision against the state in *Serrano v. Priest I*. This landmark case declared that "the quality of education may not be a function of wealth other than the wealth of the state as a whole" and ushered in a series of court cases, academic studies, and legislative changes focused on the equity of state school financing systems (Guthrie et al., 1988:201).

This chapter provides a framework for other chapters in this volume written on more specific topics, such as the effects on school finance equity of litigation, politics, legislation, and new concepts such as adequacy. This chapter begins with an analysis of the development of major concepts of school finance equity from 1970 to the present, including definitions of each concept. Subsequent sections describe how the concepts have been shaped over time by the courts,

research, legislation, data availability, and school reform, and analyze five different concepts of school finance equity that have been prominent since the 1970s.
Finally, we conclude with thoughts about the relevance of the concepts to today's
challenges in school finance.

DISTINCTIONS IMPLICIT IN ANALYZING
SCHOOL FINANCE EQUITY

Above all, the idea of equity involves value judgments about how to determine fairness in the financing of K-12 education. As such, there are many
different ways to approach a definition of equity. During the last quarter century,
as ideas about equity have evolved, several important distinctions have been
made. In some cases, these distinctions have emerged as part of the judicial or
advocacy processes that have played such an important role in school finance
equity since 1970.

In order to facilitate the presentation in this chapter, we first identify and
define these distinctions. Although not every distinction is important to every
concept of equity, different combinations apply to each and we discuss the
distinctions in enough detail to be able to use them in the sections on equity
concepts.[4]

The distinctions characterize differences among equity concepts as applied
to school finance systems. A school finance system is a set of formulas and rules
for using publicly collected revenues to pay for K-12 education.[5] In the United
States, each state is responsible for K-12 education within its borders and thus the
school finance system is established in state law, often supplemented by state
department of education regulations. Revenues to finance K-12 education come
almost equally from state and local sources (about 93 percent of the total) and
only in a small percentage from federal sources (about 7 percent of the total).
State revenues are derived from each state's general tax and other revenues,
consisting in most states primarily of sales and income taxes. Local revenues are
derived mostly from property taxes and, to a lesser extent, from local sales and
income taxes. States usually delegate responsibility for provision of K-12 education to local school districts and then design complex formulas to govern how
state funds will be distributed to those districts. A general formula often applies
to all students, with varying numbers of special formulas for different types of
students (e.g., at-risk, gifted, handicapped), for specific types of spending (e.g.,
transportation, buildings), and for differences among districts in costs and size.
In addition, state legislators often design some of the formulas to provide more
money to poorer districts and/or to match local spending more generously for
poorer districts. The federal government's aid to states and local school districts
is almost entirely for special needs students such as economically disadvantaged
or at-risk (Title I) or disabled (P.L. 94-142).

Once the formulas are in place, school districts "respond" to them by deciding how much to spend per pupil. Increasingly over the last 30 years, voters in states have placed limits on how much can be spent from local sources and sometimes state sources as well. With this background in mind, we describe distinctions important to analyses of the equity of school finance systems.[6]

Child Versus Taxpayer Perspectives

When equity is approached out of a concern for opportunity, in many people's minds the child or student perspective is paramount. Thus, school-age children are most often the subject of an equity definition in school finance. Because we are discussing the financing of education with public funds, however, taxpayers are sometimes brought into definitions along with the children. Occasionally, the interests of both groups are served simultaneously in the same definition.

When children are the subject of equity definitions, differences among the children, such as whether they speak English as a second language, are mildly or severely handicapped, have learning disabilities, or are poor or minority, become important. Resources made available to different groups of children are often the principal concern of equity discussions, sometimes with the emphasis on fairness of access, but increasingly with an eye toward how differing resources relate to the costs of bringing each group of children to an acceptable (or adequate) performance level.

The school finance and public finance conceptions of taxpayer equity do not always conform to one another. From a school finance perspective, a system would be judged fair to taxpayers if every taxpayer was assured that a given tax rate would translate into the same amount of spending per pupil regardless of where the taxpayer lived. From a public finance perspective, on the other hand, a system would be judged fair to taxpayers on the basis of either the ability to pay or the benefit principle. The ability to pay principle enables one to judge how fairly tax burdens change as ability to pay changes.[7] Tax burdens are defined as reductions in welfare, usually measured by changes in income, and ability to pay is usually measured by annual or average lifetime income. Thus, while school finance taxpayer equity compares tax rates to spending per child, public finance taxpayer equity compares tax burdens to ability to pay.[8]

The benefit principle states that, where possible, taxation should relate to the value of the services that the tax provides. This idea can only apply when a direct relationship exists between a particular tax and a service (e.g., tolls and highway maintenance) and when the service does not involve a significant public goods aspects. While some have tried to link local property taxation and K-12 education in this way, it is difficult to do in states that finance large shares of K-12 education through general state taxes.

In general, neither the courts nor advocates nor researchers in school finance have focused on the public finance concepts of equity; rather, they have based taxpayer equity on the idea of fairness of tax rates faced by or effort exerted by districts. Some exceptions to this are the occasional discussion of whether commercial or utility property should be made a statewide asset for school finance purposes or whether a major change in the school finance system will result in such large changes in residential property values as to undo the intended direction of equity (i.e., will changes be capitalized into property values in ways that make unclear the direction of change for taxpayers' real tax burdens?). But aside from these occasional discussions of commercial property or capitalization, the vast majority of school finance work on taxpayer equity has not used public finance ideas.[9]

The Unit of Analysis

States, districts, schools, and students grouped by socioeconomic or other characteristics have all been used as units of analysis in school finance equity analyses. The federal government and analysts have often compared and ranked states according to their school finance equity. Common questions using the state as the unit of analysis are (1) Is state A more equitable than state B? and (2) Has equity improved in state C? For any given state, the unit in most instances is the district because the financing and provision of public education are carried out largely through local school districts. Within districts, schools have been important in two court cases and, in urban districts with large numbers of schools, researchers and policy makers are increasingly interested in intra-district equity. In addition, the school reform movement that emphasizes school-based decision making, including budgetary decisions, potentially elevates the school to a position of particular interest.[10] Although the individual student is rarely the unit of analysis, groups of students (e.g., poor versus rich, minority versus non-minority, handicapped versus non-handicapped) have been used in some analyses. The unit of analysis issue is often resolved with at least one eye on data availability and another on the politics of school finance, the latter focusing on where the power to change lies, which is often with the state or district. Political issues involved in equity of school financing are discussed by Carr and Fuhrman (Chapter 5 of this volume).

Inputs, Processes, Outputs, and Outcomes

One way to understand different approaches to school finance equity is to examine the varying emphases on different stages in the "production" of education. Some definitions of equity focus on inputs—labor, equipment, capital—in their dollar or raw unit forms. That is, the ideal is to have these inputs distributed equitably, which is not necessarily equally. Sometimes the discussion ends here with an assertion that it is inputs, measured in dollars, that should be the focus of school finance equity. In other cases the idea of equity goes beyond inputs to something further along in the education production process. For example, concern about issues such as what occurs in the classroom, what courses students take, or educational tracking can be seen as a focus on equitable processes.

More recently, attention is turning to outputs (e.g., what schools produce, such as types of achievement and graduates) and outcomes (e.g., lifetime accomplishments, such as earnings or health status) that are variously related to what schools do. This output focus is consistent with the attention paid over the past 15 years to the quality of the U.S. education system in general and in comparison with other nations. Focusing on output equity invariably leads to questions about what levels and uses of inputs and processes are required to achieve desired distributions or levels of outputs. As we will discuss later in the chapter, these distinctions begin to hint at how the concepts of equity and adequacy interact.[11] Of course, specifying how processes relate to outputs within a school is very difficult, both because of variations in factors outside the school environment as well as uncertainties about the ways in which dollars and resources are currently used or could be used more effectively within schools. Chapter 4 of this volume, by Goertz and Natriello, explores some of these issues by reviewing what is known about the patterns of personnel usage and service provision that result from school finance reforms. Guthrie and Rothstein (see Chapter 7 in this volume), Duncombe and Yinger (see Chapter 8 in this volume), and Minorini and Sugarman (see Chapter 6 in this volume) explore ideas of adequacy and its relationship to inputs, outputs, and processes.

Alternative Groups of Special Interest

The connections between education equity and opportunity have oriented the discourse around those who are most in need of enhanced opportunities. Low-income, minority, and disabled students are often the most targeted groups in this context, and the same general focus has been applied to low-wealth or low-income taxpayers. Many court cases since the 1970s have focused on property-poor school districts. This latter emphasis has proved problematic in some instances because the correlation between poor districts and poor children is not high. The chapter on equity by Minorini and Sugarman (Chapter 2 of this volume) discusses this issue when it addresses the United States Supreme Court's consideration of school finance.

Ex Ante Versus Ex Post Concepts

Ex ante concepts outline the conditions for equity in the statutory formulas of K-12 financing systems. Ex ante concepts analyze the equity of statutory design elements such as the way a formula provides aid for poor versus rich districts or the way a formula is designed to provide additional funding for at-risk students. Ex post concepts are used to analyze actual outcomes that result from behavioral changes of school districts as they respond to the design elements of a school finance system. These observed outcomes may or may not differ from the intended, ex ante ones. For example, legislators might design a school finance formula that matches spending in a property-poor local school district at some multiple of the matching rate of a property-rich local district. Such a formula would have elements of ex ante equity with respect to property-poor and -rich districts. Ex post, however, as property-poor school districts respond to the matching rate, they might or might not spend equally per child compared to property-rich districts. For example, property poor districts might spend less per child for any number of reasons, including that the matching rate was not high enough or that other factors (e.g., tastes or income levels of residents) were working in the direction of lower per pupil spending.

Ex post concepts in school finance equity are often measured using statistical analyses of actual data. In some cases ambiguity is introduced because the conceptual approach is ex ante while the empirical measurement is ex post. Chapter 3 of this volume, by Evans, Murray, and Schwab, explores ex post results by reviewing studies of the impact of reform of school finance systems on aggregate and average spending as well as on spending and input disparities.

EQUAL OPPORTUNITY

The idea that public policy can be designed to improve or equalize the opportunity for some Americans, coupled with the belief in education as one of the most effective institutions in this regard, makes the concept of equal opportunity the logical place to start a discussion of equity concepts. But while it may be the right starting point and the most widely held value, our review of the history of concepts of school finance equity since 1970 suggests that it is perhaps among the more ambiguous concepts of equity.

In positive terms, the general idea of equal opportunity is that all students should have an equal chance to succeed, with actual observed success dependent on certain personal characteristics, such as motivation, desire, effort, and to some extent ability. In negative terms, the idea of equal opportunity is that success should not depend on circumstances outside the control of the child, such as the financial position of the family, geographic location, ethnic or racial identity, gender, and disability. "Success" has been defined in many different ways, including ability to obtain resources (often measured in dollars) while in school, access to high-level curricular offerings, achievement on tests, and accomplishments in life.

Equal opportunity is defined both ex ante and ex post. The ex ante idea is that education should provide access to opportunity or a fair starting line, especially for students who are poor, minority, female, or disabled. An ex ante question to be answered in order for equal opportunity to be achieved is: Are the conditions set up to allow the possibility for all to "succeed"?

Equal opportunity is harder to define ex post than ex ante because the ex ante definitions can be general while the ex post ones must be specific in order to give exact guidance to empirical work.[12]   One common ex post conceptualization of equal opportunity assesses whether low-income and high-income pupils (or other groups) have the same access to the education system, in terms of inputs (e.g., dollars of expenditures), processes (e.g., advanced placement classes), or outputs (e.g., high achievement levels).   There is some evidence that school finance equity concerns regarding equal opportunity are moving farther along the production process continuum, with output analyses appearing with greater frequency.

Another explicitly ex post equal opportunity equity definition in school finance focuses on the relationship between education available to students and the property wealth (or fiscal capacity) of their school district. This idea is so prominent in earlier court cases and legislation that it has a name of its own—wealth (or fiscal) neutrality. In Chapter 2 of this volume, Minorini and Sugarman summarize equity litigation using the wealth neutrality concept.

Part of the ambiguity in the concept of equal opportunity is the intermingling of educational and legal concepts within the courts. Equal educational opportunity is an educational concept, while the similar idea of equal protection is a legal concept that extends to a wide array of public services. It is possible that efforts to move the legal concepts of equal protection, and now adequacy, further into educational outcomes and processes (as opposed to just inputs) will encourage the courts to address, with more specificity, the types of curriculum, program, teacher quality, or technology that constitute "equal educational opportunity" or "an adequate education."[13]

The equal opportunity concept is much broader in application to education than in school finance issues per se. School finance equity has stressed one particular formulation of equal opportunity—wealth neutrality—which we explore more fully in the next section of the chapter. Nevertheless, some of the more general thinking about equal opportunity in education has been influential in the school finance area. One court case and three early books have been particularly influential. *Brown v. Board of Education* (1954) riveted the nation's attention to inequality in educational opportunity, focusing on inequalities due to differences in racial composition of schools. Although the Supreme Court did not tie its findings in the *Brown* case to financing of schools, the subsequent remedies to the findings involved additional financial resources, which quickly affected school finance. Arthur Wise (1968) and more recently Peter Enrich (1995) cite the theme of race in the *Brown* decision as one of three particular themes in court cases that are important historically to the evolution of legal ideas about school finance equity.[14]

Equality of Educational Opportunity (Coleman et al., 1966), written for the U.S. Office of Education to fulfill a legislative mandate of the 1964 Civil Rights Act, surveyed principals and teachers about students and schools in an effort to understand variations in school resources as well as their effects on student achievement. Its conclusions, the most controversial of which indicated that students' family and other background characteristics were more important than school resources in determining school achievement, set off an academic and public debate that continues today.[15] Production functions relating inputs to outputs have been reestimated using alternative units of analysis, measures of inputs, outputs, controls, and functional forms. The continuing lack of consensus among social science researchers about "whether money matters" has influenced the development of concepts of school finance equity. With the controversy over how outputs are influenced by increasing resources for schools, litigators appear to be reluctant to argue too strenuously for output or outcome equity and perhaps, until recently, academics are also reluctant to try harder to measure output equity. The area of school finance equity is truly one where the major actors (courts, legislators, academics, and the public) are influenced by one another's work.

Christopher Jencks and co-authors followed Coleman et al. with a major collaborative study, culminating in the publication of *Inequality* (1972). *Inequality*'s most broad finding was that reducing disparity in income among adults was most effectively brought about by attacking the problem head-on rather than by trying to change personal characteristics, such as education levels. Income redistribution programs (including more progressive taxation systems) would work better than changing inequality in education services. The last paragraph of *Who Gets Ahead* (Jencks et al., 1979) makes the same point: "But *Inequality* also argued that past efforts at equalizing the personal characteristics known to affect income had been relatively ineffective. This assertion, sad to say, remains as true as ever. Thus, if we want to redistribute income, the most effective strategy is probably still to redistribute income" (1979:307).

Jencks et al.'s conclusions about education's effect on the broader social goal of income equality were even more pessimistic than the Coleman Report conclusions. The latter emphasized that individual characteristics, not school resources, were the primary determinants of one type of schooling success. Jencks et al. went further to say that making education more equal would not make incomes more equal.[16]

The work of Coleman et al. and of Jencks et al. occurred at the beginning of a long line of research on education production functions and in the middle of a body of work on investment in human capital, both of which continue today (Burtless, 1996). These works of the 1960s and 1970s that questioned the link between resources and effects in education may have had a very particular influence on the development of school finance equity concepts by convincing those working with school finance equity to stick more closely to inputs and processes, waiting for more definitive, less controversial findings on the link to outputs before using output concepts. More recent work is indeed beginning to challenge the findings of the 1960s. For example, Ferguson and Ladd (1996) argue that inadequate measures of resources may have influenced earlier findings and their work provides an example of how more meticulous measures of inputs can lead to findings of positive effects of resources on outputs. As we will discuss below, several other factors have contributed recently to an evolution of school finance concepts away from an exclusive focus on inputs.

Arthur Wise's *Rich Schools, Poor Schools: The Promise of Equal Educational Opportunity* (1968), based on his doctoral dissertation at the University of Chicago, was more directly targeted to equity in the financing of schools than were the works of Coleman et al. and Jencks et al., and as such it had a more immediate impact on the development of school finance equity concepts. His purpose, in his own words, was "to determine whether the absence of equal educational opportunity within a state, as evidenced by unequal per-pupil expenditures, may constitute a denial by the state of the equal protection of its laws" (1968:4). Wise began his thinking on this issue in the mid-1960s, and a large number of his ideas found their way into early court cases. For example, his theoretical standard became a central argument in *Serrano*-type cases: "the quality of a child's education in the public schools of a state should not depend upon where he happens to live or the wealth of his local community" (1968:xi).

While Wise's in-depth analyses of possible legal arguments applying the equality of educational opportunity concept to school finance were highly influential in the 1970s, his analyses also raised many of the issues we still wrestle with today. For example, he explored the meaning of the Coleman Report's results and concluded that "nonetheless, even in the absence of a demonstrated relationship between inputs and outputs, the burden remains of defending the current variation in educational spending" (Wise, 1968:141). He explored 10 alternative definitions of equal educational opportunity, many of which we still use. Most prescient is his minimum-attainment definition, which reads quite like the contemporary definitions of adequacy: "the minimum-attainment definition of equality of educational opportunity asserts that resources shall be allocated to every student until he reaches a specified level of achievement" (Wise, 1968:151).

The number of direct quotations from Wise in the last two paragraphs shows how he both influenced and foresaw much of the evolution and debate about school finance equity. His major contribution, however, lies with application of the equal opportunity concept to school finance in the law and especially his development of the wealth neutrality concept.

WEALTH NEUTRALITY

Wealth neutrality as a school finance equity concept specifies that no relationship should exist between the education of children and the property wealth (or other fiscal capacity) that supports the public funding of that education. Alternatively, it specifies that taxpayers should be taxed at equal rates to fund equal education per child (generally defined as equal spending per child).

Wealth neutrality has been formulated both ex ante and ex post. The idea argued in the *Serrano* court cases, that no child's education should depend on the wealth of his neighbors, can be thought of as an ex ante idea.[17]   It led to the formulation of the guaranteed tax base (GTB) formula for distributing state aid to school districts, which, in its pure form, is constructed so that districts that levy the same tax rates will spend the same amount of money per pupil.[18]   GTB has also been used as a way to achieve ex ante taxpayer equity based on the idea that potential tax rate equity is a good measure of taxpayer equity.[19]

A large amount of school finance research as well as legislative and court activity has focused on the ex post definitions of wealth neutrality. Ex post analysts look for statistical relationships (associations) between education, usually measured in dollars, and school district wealth. They ask whether or not there is an actual association between educational inputs and ability to pay. Much of the earlier work focused on district-level inputs (per-pupil dollars or per-pupil resources, such as staff or teachers) and per-pupil property wealth.

The unit of analysis for wealth neutrality has been the state and its districts. It is not a relevant concept at the school level because schools do not have the authority to levy taxes, but rather districts and/or states levy taxes for the schools within them.[20]   At the beginning of the period, the focus was on inputs; now, in addition, users are interested in outputs and outcomes.

In *Private Wealth and Public Education* (1970), Coons et al. set the stage for court and legislative activity in the 1970s in three ways: by establishing an ex ante principle that could be used to argue for judicial intervention on the basis of the Fourteenth Amendment (or its state constitutional versions), by demonstrating that the specifics of current state financing systems violated the principle both ex ante and ex post, and by proposing a new system that would remedy the problem. Their ex ante principle was that a child's education should not depend on his neighbor's wealth, and their analyses showed that current financing systems did not prevent such dependence. They proposed the district power equalizing finance formula (DPE, also known as guaranteed tax base or GTB) as a way to make a child's education depend on local effort not wealth. Explicit in their work was an emphasis on inputs[21] and a remedy that preserved local choice.[22]

Trite but true, the rest is history. *Private Wealth and Public Education* wrote the script for *Serrano* and many cases that followed, such as *Levittown* (1982) and *Abbott v. Burke* (1985).[23]   It also stimulated analytical, legislative, and legal work. Martin Feldstein (1975) showed that the power-equalizing formula does not in theory sever the relationship between a community's expenditures per pupil and its wealth per pupil. School districts make decisions about spending per pupil based on their local tax price, income levels of residents, and other taste and socioeconomic factors. Feldstein demonstrated that district power equalizing does not correctly offset the effects of DPE's tax price and other wealth-related factors and, therefore, districts do not respond in ways that break the positive wealth-spending relationship.[24]

Berne and Stiefel's *The Measurement of Equity in School Finance* (1984) presented a variety of ex post measures of wealth neutrality, including correlations, slopes, elasticities, and adjusted relationship measures from regressions of objects per child on full value of property wealth per child. Applications of these measures by numerous researchers in the years that followed demonstrated the lack of wealth neutrality in the states, whether or not they had adopted a form of power equalizing.[25] Some state legislatures did change their systems to a form of power equalizing, although none moved to a fully implemented system. In 1986-87, six states used some form of this system, although by 1993-94 the number had dropped to two (Gold et al., 1995).

Research using the wealth neutrality concept continues to this day. Using 1991-92 data, the U.S. General Accounting Office recently completed a study that concluded that fiscal neutrality has not been achieved in most states: "Although most states pursued strategies to supplement the local funding of poor school districts, wealthier districts in 37 states had more total (state and local combined) funding than poor districts in the 1991-92 school year. This disparity existed even after adjusting for differences in geographic and student need-related education costs" (1997:2).[26]

Some economists advocate the use of broader tax bases to fund education in order to make it more fiscally neutral and more acceptable to taxpayers (Strauss, 1995). Legal scholars are moving to new arguments in the face of defeats in state courts and perhaps a desire to look at outputs, as described by Minorini and Sugarman in their discussion of adequacy in Chapter 6 of this volume.

HORIZONTAL EQUITY

Horizontal equity, as a children's concept, specifies that equally situated children should be treated equally.[27] A challenge to users of the concept is how to identify students who are "equally situated." When analyzing inputs, researchers have usually defined general education, at-risk (or educationally disadvantaged), and special education students as separate groups. Intra-group equality of inputs is a reasonable criteria to apply to these groups. When the focus moves to outputs, however, horizontal equity is more difficult to apply. Nobody argues that outputs (such as achievement scores or graduation rates) should be the same (perfectly horizontally equitable) for all students. On the other hand, we do not use distinctions such as at-risk or disabled students to justify differences in outputs.[28] Perhaps the idea of a sufficiently high level of achievement for all (one possible version of the adequacy idea) is a more meaningful concept for outputs than is horizontal equity.

The concept of horizontal equity has been used both ex ante and ex post, although most school finance research work and evidence submitted in court cases is ex post. Historically, analysts have applied the horizontal equity criterion to states and their districts, but increasingly schools are being compared this way as well. The concept with respect to inputs is well suited to school-level analysis, since funds targeted and students served by general education programs (as opposed to funds and students in compensatory or special education) often can be separated using school-level data, allowing intra-group analyses of equity.

Interestingly, the courts, even in the early 1980s when defendants were using the wealth neutrality concept, often heard testimony about the degree of ex post horizontal equity. States, including California, made arguments that their systems were improving in equity on the basis of measures of horizontal equity. Horizontal equity is a useful concept if it is measured correctly, as intra-group equality, with equally situated groups identified and separated in an analysis. On the other hand, the concept is less useful when analysts apply horizontal equity with no distinctions to all students and all funding streams, as has often been the case in legal analyses.

Extensive research exists on horizontal equity using a variety of inputs and alternative statistical measures. The statistical work has evolved from use of the simple range to use of other measures that are identified with different values. For example, the McLoone index is often used when there is interest in the bottom of the distribution; the coefficient of variation is used when there is interest in the whole distribution. The Theil measure is useful when the existing variation needs to be separated into parts, such as the part due to variation between states versus the part due to variation within states, in a national study.

Berne and Stiefel (1984) summarized their earlier work in a book that discussed several concepts of equity and alternative ways to measure them quantitatively. Among the 11 horizontal equity measures they review are the federal range ratio, the coefficient of variation, the McLoone index, the Gini coefficient, and Theil's measure.

Data from Michigan and New York in the late 1970s were used to illustrate what could be concluded, quantitatively, about ex post equity, including horizontal equity. Many studies in the *Journal of Education Finance* subsequently followed the book's methods, applying them to other states. Three important studies used data from most of the 50 states to compare various kinds of ex post equity across those states (Schwartz and Moskowitz, 1988; Wyckoff, 1992; Hertert et al., 1994). These cross-state studies were important because many states previously had resisted such comparisons, insisting that their systems of financing were unique, that the data across states were not comparable, or that such studies would lead to unwanted federal intervention into a state function.

In 1995, the National Center for Education Statistics went a step beyond the cross-state studies and quantified horizontal (and vertical) equity, using several statistical measures, at the district level, across the entire United States (Parrish et al., 1995). This study set a new precedent for using large amounts of district data, but it did not clearly indicate how the omission of the state as a unit of analysis was or was not important to the purpose of equity measurement. Evans et al. (1997) also studied horizontal equity in all districts in the nation, with the express purpose of looking for the effects on equity of state legislative action and court-ordered reform. These authors used the Theil measure to quantify horizontal equity and did not measure vertical equity or wealth neutrality. They concluded that reforms did improve (horizontal) equity.

Most recently, horizontal equity has been studied at the school level. Berne and Stiefel (1994) looked at general education funding in New York City elementary and middle schools. Rubenstein (1998), Moser (1996), and Sherman (1996) assessed the degree of horizontal equity in three other cities as part of a study of school-level budgeting in large cities.

The staying power of the concept of horizontal equity is unusual, especially since it could not reasonably be applied to outputs or outcomes. It is most useful as a concept for inputs that involve equally situated students. Such application requires that funding streams meant for compensatory or other purposes (such as gifted programs) be separated from streams meant for all students so that intra-group equality can be measured. To the extent that horizontal equity has been used extensively by analysts, lawyers, and legislators, it is important to evaluate the effects of trying to achieve it, as reviewed by Evans et al. in Chapter 3 of this volume.

VERTICAL EQUITY

Vertical equity, a children's concept that has been used both ex ante and ex post, specifies that differently situated children should be treated differently. Analogous to the challenge for users of horizontal equity, users of vertical equity must identify "differently situated" students. This identification is usually done, implicitly or explicitly, by identifying groups of students who differ in their needs for quality or use of inputs to achieve defined levels of outputs. Thus, in concept, vertical equity ties input equity to output equity. When inputs are "adjusted" for the costs of educating various groups of children, as is often done when vertical equity is measured, the adjustment is meant to indicate the amount of additional resources that are needed (higher costs that are incurred) to bring some students to given output levels. Such adjustments are empirically difficult to execute. For example, many might agree that learning disabled students need more resources, but how much more is not clear. One must define the outputs that are the goal (e.g., minimum competency, maximum potential, sufficient level, the point where the value of the marginal gain in output equals the marginal cost of resources), and all require knowledge of the quantitative relationship between inputs and outputs. Often we do not know enough about these quantitative relationships to know how to adjust resources.

The state and its districts have been the traditional units of analysis for vertical equity analyses. Now, as with horizontal equity, school-level data that allow students and funds to be separated into general education, special education, and other streams are resulting in an application of the concept at the school level, where the separate streams can be linked to the "differently situated" students.

Berne and Stiefel (1984) developed a conceptual definition of vertical equity and then, in applications to district-level data in Michigan and New York, used weights for students of various types to adjust for differences among the students. They also assessed the effects of inter-district price-level differences.[29] In *Disparities in Public School District Spending: 1989-90* (Parrish et al., 1995), the authors used cost of education indexes, estimated by McMahon and Chang (1991)[30] for all districts in the United States, and weights, based on studies of special education students (weight equals 2.3), average federal Title I allocations for poor children (weight equals 2.0), and limited English proficient (LEP) students (weight equals 1.2). School finance legislation in the states has addressed vertical equity by weighting students according to needs or costs (37 states in 1993-94), by funding special needs programs categorically, or both (Gold et al., 1995).

Recent empirical work by several economists has resulted in cost indexes based on the economic definition of costs—resources that are consumed to produce given levels of outputs (Downes and Pogue, 1994; Duncombe et al., 1996; Ladd and Yinger, 1989, 1994). The researchers have estimated district-level cost functions that control (or statistically hold constant) outputs such as test scores and dropout rates (and sometimes efficiency levels as well).[31] These empirically estimated cost functions then indicate the additional resources needed to achieve output levels due to external (or environmental) factors outside a district's control (such as percentages of students in poverty, with disabilities, with limited English proficiency, or living in single-parent households).[32] The cost functions in turn can be converted to cost indexes, usually with a statewide average of 1.0, showing relative costs by district. Such indexes are empirical efforts to adjust expenditures for costs of obtaining given outputs and are thus useful in the measurement of vertical equity. The chapter by Duncombe and Yinger (Chapter 8 of this volume) is an example of this method.

Vertical equity is an appealing concept to many analysts because it takes into account differences among pupils and (implicitly) outputs. Federal legislation, such as Title I and the Individuals with Disabilities Education Act, is based on a vertical equity idea. Beyond some basic agreements that some children need more resources, however, there is little agreement on how much more. This absence of agreement goes back to the research findings on production functions, which have not been able to pinpoint exactly where and how more resources will result in more achievement.

ADEQUACY

A Nation at Risk (National Commission on Excellence in Education, 1983) changed the nature of the debate about the goals of public education, shifting it for several years from its preoccupation with equity to concern about achievement, especially achievement of U.S. students compared to those in other countries with developed economies. Later in the 1980s a more balanced public concern emerged, with both equity and excellence as goals. The increased focus on outcomes, the continued appeal of equal opportunity, and the shift in legal strategies as described by Enrich (1995) have increased the use of the concept of adequacy in educational analyses.

Adequacy could be defined in a number of ways. One definition specifies a level of resources that is sufficient to meet defined or absolute, rather than relative, output standards. In the words of William Clune (1995a:481), "adequacy refers to resources which are sufficient (or adequate) to achieve some educational result, such as a minimum passing grade on a state achievement test."

Lawyers generally make a distinction between adequacy and equity. To us the most useful distinction between adequacy and equity concepts is the focus on sufficient and absolute levels in adequacy and on relative levels or distributions in equity.

There is an ex ante definition of adequacy that involves specifying the kinds of outputs that must be achieved and even how they will be measured. The Kentucky court went the furthest in a legal specification by listing seven capacities that were defined absolutely and not relatively.[33] In other court cases, such as *Harper v. Hunt* in Alabama, lawyers used state and national input and output regulations and standards to argue that Alabama's system, by comparison, was inadequate. The regulations and standards were ex ante ones, while the evidence from Alabama was ex post. Thus, adequacy is also an ex post idea, lending itself to quantification of results on various kinds of outcomes, such as test scores, graduation rates, attendance rates, college enrollment rates, etc. Sometimes the ex post measures are relative (to national ones for example), thus confusing a conceptual distinction between adequacy as absolute, external levels and equity, as relative distributions of levels.

The most recent New Jersey court case (*Abbott v. Burke*) and its remedy point the way in which the courts, through the concept of adequacy, may possibly join outputs, inputs, and processes. In New Jersey, the remedy has focused on resources, curricular offerings, and support services available to poor districts versus wealthy ones. While the idea is to provide an adequate education for children in poor districts, the method for achieving this involves a focus on details of programs, teacher quality, and technology. The New Jersey court has wrestled with the concept of adequacy since its first court case in the 1970s (*Robinson v. Cahill*).

Adequacy is a child-based concept. Conceptually, the unit could be the individual child, but litigators in state school finance cases have thus far used it as a district-level concept. The concept's unit would probably follow the funding patterns, so if funding were to go to schools, then the schools would be assessed for their adequacy on the basis of levels of achievement of students in those schools.

A distinction between adequacy and the way some equity concepts have been conceived historically is adequacy's emphasis on outputs. The definition of adequacy begins with the idea of adequate performance by students, which requires specifications of performance in various kinds of output dimensions. But we believe that it is conceptually most useful to maintain the distinction between absolute levels (adequacy) and relative distributions of levels (equity). It is entirely possible for inputs, outputs, and outcomes to be equitable or inequitable, and it is possible for inputs, outputs, and outcomes to be adequate and inadequate.

Lawyers and judges have used the adequacy concept to apply to all districts in some cases (e.g., Kentucky, Massachusetts) and to poor, urban districts in others (e.g., New Jersey). William Clune is the most prominent advocate of using the idea to apply, in particular, to urban, poor districts.[34] His writing on the topic has evolved from a description of adequacy that includes all children to one that targets poor children. He has even ventured a rough guestimate of the cost of adequate education in high-poverty schools: "the national average spending is about $5,000 per pupil, and the total adequacy package is about $5,000 per pupil above the typical budget of a high-poverty school, suggesting a total budget of $10,000 per pupil per year" (1993:391).

In a volume of the *University of Michigan Journal of Law Reform*, edited by Clune (1995b), several lawyers looked at applications of adequacy in three states—Alabama, Oklahoma, and Kentucky (Morgan et al., 1995; Grossman 1995; Trimble and Forsaith, 1995). Julie Underwood, in the same volume, interprets adequacy as a form of vertical equity, which is an interesting way to link the previous equity work with the current legal concept of adequacy: "adequacy from the perspective of 'vertical equity,' meaning that different students should be treated differently based on their special educational needs" (1995:493). Clune's definition, when targeted to high-poverty students, could be interpreted as a form of output vertical equity where differences among students are based on their family income.

Robert Berne's article, in the volume he co-edited on *Outcome Equity in Education* (1994), illustrates how outputs are related to poverty (and race) in one of the largest states. This article has been used as "evidence" by some for the need for adequacy-driven reform.

Legislators have also begun to use the concept of adequacy as they consider remedies, even in cases where the court's decision involved equity.[35] Clune has outlined a research agenda that would help implement the adequacy concept (Clune, 1997), and some ongoing research on production functions and educational evaluation research of programs, such as Accelerated Schools and Success for All, is helpful to his framework, although not necessarily carried out with adequacy in mind.

Clune and others say that adequacy is a different concept from equity because it changes the focus from inputs to outputs and because it leaves behind the idea of equal resources for all. As we note above, in a broader view of equity, neither of these distinctions is essential, since outputs and outcomes can be accommodated in equity concepts and because fiscal neutrality, vertical equity, and equal opportunity concepts of school finance equity do not require equal inputs or resources per pupil. The use of minimum, albeit high levels of outputs, rather than the use of the idea of relative levels (distributions) of outputs, does help distinguish adequacy from equity. Whether people would be content to see vast disparities in educational outcomes, once adequacy was achieved, is a matter of speculation. And certainly one can think of equitable situations (condensed distributions) that are inadequate. Perhaps California or some of the low-spending and low-achieving Southern states fall into this latter category.

SCHOOL FINANCE EQUITY AS WE ENTER THE TWENTY-FIRST CENTURY

Equity is a concept that is steeped in values and requires conceptual clarity to avoid spinning conceptual and empirical wheels and talking past one another. Our review of school finance equity concepts since 1970 suggests that several ideas seem to be reasonably well accepted among researchers, lawyers, and policymakers. First, there are alternative concepts of equity, and no single concept serves the purposes of all users, in part because people have different values and in part because people use the concepts for different purposes (to argue court cases, to design school finance systems, etc.). Second, children and taxpayers each have a legitimate perspective from which to view equity. Third, we should continue to examine inputs even as we move to using concepts of output equity because many users (e.g., lawyers, the public) find input equity meaningful. And, fourth, given the American structure of primary and secondary education, states and school districts are important units of analysis.

Moreover, several recent trends are apparent. First, analysts are paying greater attention to outputs throughout the broader field of educational policy, and this attention can be seen in school finance equity discussions. Second, while the school district remains an important unit of analysis, the school is increasingly used as well, especially in areas such as governance, accountability, and finance, that involve large, urban school districts. Decentralization, site-based decision making, and school-based budgeting all foster a focus on the school rather than exclusive attention on the district. Third, policy makers and lawyers now frequently use concepts of adequacy. Fourth, the courts continue to be used to achieve change that is not possible through the political process and in the state legislatures. And, fifth, more detailed data bases permit greater differentiation of pupil characteristics and funding streams, and this leads to greater use of vertical equity, rather than the traditional reliance on horizontal equity alone.

The fifth point, which involves data availability and conceptual measurement, deserves particular attention. Throughout the past 25 years, data availability has been an important factor in determining how school finance equity concepts and even court case remedies are formulated. For example, in the 1970s, many states were reluctant to measure within-state, intra-district, horizontal equity because of the incompatibility of how expenditures, revenues, and pupils were counted. Researchers pushed ahead with data that were available and now the Department of Education produces data with standard definitions for all states (Common Core of Data from the National Center for Education Statistics). Likewise, the relationships between financing inputs and student performance have both driven and been driven by the kinds of data available. Twenty years ago, most researchers could access cross-section, district-level data, with very imperfectly measured inputs. Currently, the federal government sponsors several student-level surveys that follow students over several years (e.g., High School and Beyond and the National Education Longitudinal Study). In addition, many states collect and use student-level data for their performance systems. These student-level data allow researchers interested in production functions to refine their approaches. Remedies to court cases 25 years ago focused little on student performance, but as states have begun to produce numerous measures of performance by district (and often by school), these measures have been picked up by lawyers to help define and monitor adequacy of school finance systems. The importance of education to Americans, the large percentage of government expenditures devoted to it, and the constant attention of researchers, legislators, and lawyers have created pressures on state education departments and federal departments to provide better data. Whatever the direction of causality, it seems true that measures of school finance equity are intimately intertwined with the data that can be accessed by analysts.

If equity remains an important value, and adequacy continues to grow in its importance, then the research that links inputs to outputs will remain at the center of debates over school finance equity. Individual studies confirm that under some circumstances resources affect outcomes (Ferguson and Ladd, 1996; Mosteller et al., 1996; Krueger, 1997). If that research, combined with the extensive literature that already exists on the subject, can be interpreted to mean that when resources are used well they affect outcomes and when they are used poorly they do not, then we have a strong incentive to understand when effective use occurs.

Although it is reasonably safe to maintain that the financing of primary and secondary education in America will remain public, we can be less sure about the constancy of public provision in the traditional form of public schools organized in local school districts. Various changes that are being debated today, such as voucher schemes and charter schools, may lead to significant structural changes. How concepts of equity that developed within the framework of the traditional school district and public school will or will not fit with these newer arrangements remains to be seen.

In some ways, we have come full circle to the problems and issues that were addressed three decades ago. Whether we look across states, within states across districts, within districts across schools, or within schools across groups of students, it is hard to argue that we have achieved equity in education or in the larger American society. Wide differences in property bases still persist and often lead to inequities in finance; educational outputs and lifetime outcomes are still highly related to socioeconomic status, race, ethnicity, and gender; and inequality in income and wealth continues at high levels. In addition, there are serious and widespread concerns that schools are not meeting society's needs for an educated workforce and citizenry as we enter the next century. Concepts of equity are likely to be at the center of these issues that, unfortunately, do not appear to be close to resolution.

NOTES

1.   Review of the education production function literature is outside the domain of this chapter.

2.   Jonathon Kozol's (1991) book about education was a best-seller. The *New York Times* devoted a week's worth of articles (e.g., Hartocollis, 1997) to the controversy stirred up by parental donations for a teacher's salary at a local public school and the debate about whether the practice was fair to other schools with less affluent parents. The event made national news as well.

3.   Other significant years in the history of K-12 education equity policy and law are 1923 (publication of Strayer and Haig's foundation plan for school finance), 1954 (*Brown v. Board of Education* Supreme Court decision), 1965 (passage of the federal Elementary and Secondary Education Act [ESEA] with Title I funding for poor children), and 1975 (passage of the federal Education for All Handicapped Children Act, P.L. 94-142).

4.   In previous work (Berne and Stiefel, 1984), we develop a series of questions that highlight the values inherent in equity concepts. These questions, briefly, are who, what, how, and how much. "Who" asks which groups are the focus of the equity concept. The usual two choices are children and taxpayers. "What" asks what objects will be used in the analysis, the choices being inputs (dollars and/or real resources), processes, outputs, or outcomes. "How" identifies the equity concept, which can include horizontal equity, vertical equity, and equal opportunity. "How much" focuses on the statistical measure used to quantify the other choices. We identify a large number of measures and specify the values inherent in choosing each of them. One of the questions (How?) involves choosing a concept. In this chapter, we put the emphasis on the concepts themselves and broaden the discussion to include other authors who have taken different cuts at equity ideas. Although decisions involving values must be made about all four questions, the broader community of scholars and the public think first of the concept. Thus the emphasis here is on concepts.

5.   See Gold et al. (1995) for detailed descriptions of each state's school finance system and Odden and Picus (1992: Chapters 7 and 8) for a more technical explanation of alternative finance formulas.

6. See Berne and Stiefel (1979) for more detail on how to apply equity concepts to state finance plans.

7. Generally this is done by calculating tax burdens as a percentage of ability to pay, although researchers have also used other measures such as regression coefficients relating burden to ability to pay or Gini type coefficients.

8. Economists use three alternative concepts of incidence or burden—absolute, balanced budget, and differential. We are discussing absolute burden here. See Rosen (1992:277) for the differences among the three alternatives.

9. If the courts or legislatures used public finance ideas, the remedies proposed or legislated for taxpayers would be quite different. Equal tax rates for equal spending (a school finance principle) does not translate into particular patterns of public finance incidence such as progressive, regressive, or proportional tax burden, and each proposed school finance formula would have to be studied from the public finance viewpoint. Such linkages of school finance equity to public finance equity are beyond the scope of this chapter.

10. Advocates of school-based budgeting have suggested that states fund schools directly rather than through the intermediary of districts. Some charter school funding works this way.

11. Kenneth Strike argues that the shift to outputs, combined with research findings that much of the variation in outputs is due to factors outside the school environment, results in an equity concept that is built on the schools compensating for outside-the-school factors in order to reach adequacy. (See Strike, 1988, and personal communication.)

12. For example, Coleman et al. defined five alternative ways to measure equal opportunity in his *Equality of Educational Opportunity* report (Coleman et al., 1966). They note that "as a consequence, in planning the survey it was obvious that no single concept of equality of educational opportunity existed and that the survey must give information relevant to a variety of concepts" (Coleman, 1968:16-17). This chapter is a review of school finance equity since 1970. Our objective is not to define or redefine equal opportunity, but to analyze what others have written.

13. We thank an anonymous reviewer for this idea.

14. The other two themes cited by both Wise and Enrich as important historically are wealth in criminal justice rights cases (the indigent criminal) and mathematically equivalent treatment in legislative reapportionment cases (voter equality).

15. One of the most famous and controversial findings of the report was ". . . that schools bring little influence to bear on a child's achievement that is independent of his background and general social context; and that this very lack of an independent effect means that the inequalities imposed on children by their home, neighborhood, and peer environment are carried along to become the inequalities with which they confront adult life at the end of school" (Coleman et al., 1966:325).

16. Christopher Jencks, in a personal communication, now believes there is evidence to support the view that education can change outcomes for disadvantaged students; see also Jencks and Phillips (1998).

17. When it comes to empirical measurement in *Serrano* litigation, ex post measurement is common.

18. It can be mathematically equivalent to a percentage equalizing funding system, which had existed before in impure forms in states such as New York, for example, but GTB was seen as new in the 1970s.

19. As this paragraph implies, wealth neutrality is both a child and taxpayer concept. It began with the child in Coons et al. (1970), but developed to include taxpayers as well. Sometimes it seems to be aimed at both at the same time. For the child, analysts look at the relationship of the child's education to the wealth of the school district. For the taxpayer, the concept specifies equal tax rates for equal spending per pupil.

20. The concept could be reconstrued to apply to schools if family income of students attending the schools were substituted for community property wealth.

21. Coons et al. (1970:25): "Having chosen the objective standard, the measure of quality becomes not what is achieved but *what is available. . . .* What is available becomes whatever goods and services are purchased by school districts to perform their task of education. Quality is the sum of district expenditures per pupil; quality is money."

22. Coons et al. (1970:xxii): "We have a strong preference, and that preference is for balance . . . we find equally offensive the current efforts to use the Constitution as a battering ram for uniformity or even for compensatory education. There are less polarized and destructive ways to approach the problem of fiscal equity through the courts."

23. See Sugarman and Minorini in Chapter 2 of this volume for more detail on the court cases based on the principle of wealth neutrality.

24. In fact, using empirical estimates from the then-existing Massachusetts's education finance system, Feldstein showed that: "the estimated elasticities therefore indicate that the widely advocated district power equalizing form of percentage equalization grant, which has a price-wealth elasticity of 1, would not be wealth neutralizing but is more likely to result instead in an inverse relation between local wealth and local educational spending" (Feldstein, 1975:88).

25. See the *Journal of Education Finance* in the years after 1984 for empirical studies of ex post wealth neutrality (for example, Kearney et al., 1990; Sample and Hartman, 1990; and Johnson and Pillainayagam, 1991).

26. The authors of the GAO report devised a new measure, "the implied foundation level" to quantify the degree of fiscal neutrality in a site. This measure simulated the minimum total funding per pupil each state could support for all its school districts, assuming all districts were taxed at the same tax rate, that the state share of funding remained constant, and that total state plus local spending remained constant. The report uses per-capita income as a measure of fiscal

capacity because of the lack of property wealth numbers for districts in all the states.

27. Horizontal (and vertical) equity are traditional public finance taxpayer equity concepts that are used to judge the relationship between tax burdens and income. We do not discuss them here as taxpayer concepts because they have not been used extensively to date in school finance taxpayer equity analyses.

28. For example, if at-risk students have been treated equally to one another throughout their schooling (and have been provided more resources than other students), we would expect (hope) that the students would perform equally to other students who are not at-risk by the end of their K-12 education (or even before that).

29. Price adjustments are often part of horizontal equity analyses because they are meant to adjust the nominal dollars to reflect differences in prices of constant quality inputs across districts. Student weights are used in vertical equity analyses to reflect differences in costs of educating pupils. Following the publication of Berne and Stiefel's book, many district-level vertical equity analyses have been performed and reported in the *Journal of Education Finance*.

30. Since the publication of Parrish et al.'s *Disparities in Public School District Spending: 1989-90*, Chambers (1997) has estimated new cost-of-education indexes for all districts in the United States.

31. Duncombe et al. (1996) use Data Envelopment Analysis (DEA) as a way to construct an efficiency index to include in their cost functions.

32. Downes and Pogue (1994) also estimate indirect cost functions or expenditure functions as a way to empirically derive cost indexes.

33. See Trimble and Forsaith (1995:606-607) for a quote from *Rose v. Council for Better Education*.

34. Clune (1995a:658): "The rest of this article is an effort to point toward the direction of true educational adequacy for economically poor children."

35. "The education debate riveting the Statehouse abruptly has shifted gears, U-turning from how much to tax Ohioans to what to give them in return. . . . As a result, lawmakers over the next two weeks are likely to enact sweeping reforms aimed at improving student performance and holding schools accountable for the money they spend and results they achieve" (Hallet and Marrison, 1997).

ACKNOWLEDGMENTS

We wish to thank Helen Ladd, Kenneth Strike, Amy Ellen Schwartz, and two anonymous reviewers for helpful comments on earlier drafts of this chapter. The authors alone are responsible for the content of the final version of the chapter.

REFERENCES

Berne, R.
   1994   Educational input and outcome inequities in New York state. Pp.1-23 in *Outcome Equity in Education*, R. Berne and L.O. Picus, eds. Thousand Oaks, CA: Corwin Press.
Berne, R., and L. Stiefel
   1979   Concepts of equity and their relationship to state school finance plans. *Journal of Education Finance* 5(2):109-132.
   1984   *The Measurement of Equity in School Finance*. Baltimore: Johns Hopkins University Press.
   1994   Measuring equity at the school level: The finance perspective. *Educational Evaluation and Policy Analysis* 16(4):405-421.
Burtless, G., ed.
   1996   *Does Money Matter? The Effect of School Resources on Student Achievement and Adult Success*. Washington, DC: The Brookings Institution.
Chambers, J.
   1997   Geographic Variations In Public Schools' Costs. Unpublished manuscript. American Institutes for Research, Washington, DC.
Clune, W.H.
   1993   The shift from equity to adequacy in school finance. *The World and I* 8(9):389-405.
   1995a   Accelerated education as a remedy for high-poverty schools. *University of Michigan Journal of Law Reform* 28(3):481-491.
   1995b   Editor. *University of Michigan Journal of Law Reform* 28(3).
   1997   The empirical argument for educational adequacy, the critical gaps in the knowledge base, and a suggested research agenda. Pp. 101-124 in *Selected Papers in School Finance, 1995*, W.J. Folwer, Jr., ed. Washington, DC: National Center for Educational Statistics, U.S. Department of Education.
Coleman, J.S.
   1968   The concept of equality of educational opportunity. *Harvard Educational Review* 58(1):7-22.
Coleman, J.S., E.Q. Campbell, C.J. Hobson, J. McPartland, A.M. Mead, F.D. Weinfeld, and R.L. York
   1966   *Equality of Educational Opportunity*. Washington, DC: U.S. Department of Health, Education and Welfare.
Coons, J.E., W.H. Clune, and S.D. Sugarman
   1970   *Private Wealth and Public Education*. Cambridge, MA: Harvard University Press.
Downes, T.A., and T.F. Pogue
   1994   Adjusting school aid formulas for the higher cost of educating disadvantaged students. *National Tax Journal* 47(1):89-110.
Duncombe, W., J. Ruggiero, and J. Yinger
   1996   Alternative approaches to measuring the cost of education. Pp. 327-356 in *Holding Schools Accountable*, H.F. Ladd, ed. Washington, DC: The Brookings Institution.
Enrich, P.
   1995   Leaving equality behind: New directions in school finance reform. *Vanderbilt Law Review* 48:101-194.
Evans, W., S. Murray, and R. Schwab
   1997   Schoolhouses, courthouses, and statehouses after Serrano. *Journal of Policy Analysis and Management* 16(1):10-31.

Feldstein, M.
 1975   Wealth neutrality and local choice in public education. *American Economic Review* 61(1):75-89.
Ferguson, R.F., and H.F. Ladd
 1996   How and why money matters: An analysis of Alabama schools. Pp. 265-298 in *Holding Schools Accountable*, H.F. Ladd, ed. Washington, DC: The Brookings Institution.
Gold, S., D. Smith and S. Lawton, eds.
 1995   *Public School Finance Programs of the United States and Canada, 1993-94, Volume One*. Albany, NY: American Education Finance Association and The Nelson A. Rockefeller Institute of Government.
Grossman, M.S.
 1995   Oklahoma school finance litigation: Shifting from equity to adequacy. *University of Michigan Journal of Law Reform* 28(3):521-557.
Guthrie, J.W., W.I. Garms, and L.C. Pierce
 1988   *School Finance and Education Policy: Enhancing Educational Efficiency, Equality, and Choice*, 2nd edition. Englewood Cliffs, NJ: Prentice-Hall.
Hallett, J., and B. Marrison
 1997   Legislators say schools must do a better job. *The Cleveland Plain Dealer* (July 11):1A, 10A.
Hanushek, E.A.
 1986   The economics of schooling: Production and efficiency in public schools. *Journal of Economic Literature* 24(3):1141-1177.
Hartocollis, A.
 1997   At a public school, parents rally with money to keep a teacher. *New York Times* (October 20):B4.
Hertert, L., C. Busch, and A. Odden
 1994   School financing inequities among the states: The problem from a national perspective. *Journal of Education Finance* 19(3):231-255.
Jencks, C., M. Smith, H. Acland, M.J. Bane, D. Cohen, H. Gintis, B. Heynes, and S. Michelson
 1972   *Inequality: A Reassessment of the Effect of Family and Schooling in America*. New York: Harper and Row.
Jencks, C., S. Bartlett, M. Corcoran, J. Crouse, D. Eaglesfield, G. Jackson, K. McClelland, P. Mueser, M. Olneck, J. Schwartz, S. Ward, and J. Williams
 1979   *Who Gets Ahead? The Determinants of Economic Success in America*. New York: Basic Books.
Jencks, C., and M. Phillips
 1998   *The Black-White Test Score Gap*. Washington, DC: The Brookings Institution.
Johnson, G., and M.G. Pillainayagam
 1991   A longitudinal equity study of Ohio's school finance system 1980-1989. *Journal of Education Finance* 17(1):66-82.
Kearney, C., L. Chen, and P. Chen
 1990   Race and equity of opportunity: A school finance perspective. *Journal of Education Finance* 15(3):333-350.
Kozol, J.
 1991   *Savage Inequalities: Children in America's Schools*. New York: Crown.
Krueger, A.B.
 1997   Experimental Estimates of Education Production Functions. Working Paper #379 (May). Princeton, NJ: Princeton University Industrial Relations Section.

Ladd, H F., and J.M. Yinger
    1989   *America's Ailing Cities: Fiscal Health and the Design of Urban Policy.* Baltimore:
            Johns Hopkins University Press.
    1994   The case for equalizing aid. *National Tax Journal* 47(1):211-224.
McMahon, W.W., and S. Chang
    1991   *Geographical Cost of Living Differences: Interstate and Intrastate Update 1991,*
            MacArthur/Spencer Series Number 20. Normal, IL: Center for the Study of Educational
            Finance, Illinois State University.
Morgan, M.I., A.S. Cohen, and H. Hershkoff
    1995   Establishing education program inadequacy: The Alabama example. *University of Michi-
            gan Journal of Law Reform* 28(3):559-598.
Moser, M.
    1996   *School-Based Budgeting in Rochester, New York.* Part of Final Report to Andrew W.
            Mellon Foundation for Study of Resource Allocation in Urban Public Schools. New
            York: Robert F. Wagner Graduate School of Public Service.
Mosteller, F., R.J. Light, and J. Sachs
    1996   Sustained inquiry in education: Lessons from skill grouping and class size. *Harvard
            Educational Review* 66(4):797-842.
National Commission on Excellence in Education
    1983   *A Nation at Risk: The Imperative for Educational Reform.* Washington, DC: U.S. Gov-
            ernment Printing Office.
Odden, A.R., and L.O. Picus
    1992   *School Finance: A Policy Perspective.* New York: McGraw-Hill.
Parrish, T., C. Matsumoto, and W. Fowler, Jr.
    1995   *Disparities in Public School District Spending: 1989-90.* Washington, DC: National
            Center for Education Statistics, U.S. Department of Education.
Rosen, H.
    1992   *Public Finance.* Homewood, IL: Irwin.
Rubenstein, R.
    1998   Resource equity in the Chicago public schools: A school-level approach. *Journal of
            Education Finance* 23(4):468-489.
Sample, P.R., and W.T. Hartman
    1990   An equity simulation of Pennsylvania's school finance system. *Journal of Education
            Finance* 16(1):49-69.
Schwartz, M., and J. Moskowitz
    1988   *Fiscal Equity in the United States 1984-85.* Washington, DC: Decisions Resource Cor-
            poration.
Sherman, J.
    1996   School-Based Budgeting in Fort Worth, Texas. Part of Final Report to Andrew W.
            Mellon Foundation for Study of Resource Allocation in Urban Public Schools. New
            York: Robert F. Wagner Graduate School of Public Service.
Strauss, R.P.
    1995   Reducing New York's reliance on the school property tax. *Journal of Education Finance*
            20(1):123-164.
Strike, K.A.
    1988   The ethics of resource allocation in education. Pp. 143-180 in *Microlevel School Fi-
            nance,* D.H. Monk and J.K. Underwood, eds. Cambridge, MA: Ballinger.
Trimble, C.S., and A.C. Forsaith
    1995   Achieving equity and excellence in Kentucky education. *University of Michigan Journal
            of Law Reform* 28(3):599-653.

Underwood, J.K.
   1995   School finance adequacy as vertical equity. *University of Michigan Journal of Law Reform* 28(3):493-519.
U.S. General Accounting Office
   1997   *School Finance: State Efforts to Reduce Funding Gaps Between Poor and Wealthy Districts.* GAO/HEHS-97-31. Washington, DC: U.S. General Accounting Office.
Wise, A.
   1968   *Rich Schools, Poor Schools: The Promise of Equal Educational Opportunity.* Chicago: University of Chicago Press.
Wyckoff, J.H.
   1992   The interstate equality of public primary and secondary education resources in the U.S., 1980-1987. *Economics of Education Review* 11(1):19-30.

2

School Finance Litigation in the Name of Educational Equity: Its Evolution, Impact, and Future

Paul A. Minorini and Stephen D. Sugarman

INTRODUCTION

Since the 1960s in America, individuals and groups seeking an increased level or share of valued public benefits have often turned to courts for assistance, hoping thereby to achieve their goals outside the traditional political process. Courts have been especially receptive to these pleas when they are made by the politically powerless and deal with matters of fundamental importance.

As this new judicial activism started taking hold, lawyers and scholarly advocates turned their attention to the financing of our public schools. They focused on the way in which most states have historically relied on local property taxes as a substantial source of funding public education (Enrich, 1995). Those early advocates (and many subsequent legal scholars) viewed equity as an essential component of the principle of basic fairness. Yet, traditional school finance arrangements, they argued, created grave inequities for children in the availability of educational resources and opportunities. In light of the enormous importance of education, it is not surprising, therefore, that those inequities have been the subject of intense litigation.

What is surprising, however, is the predominantly state law and state court character of this litigation. Federal courts and federal law have played the central role in lawsuits concerning other aspects of public education such as school desegregation, student rights to free expression, and the needs of the disabled and pupils with limited English proficiency. But the federal constitutional challenges to school finance inequalities that were brought in the late 1960s and early 1970s were ultimately unsuccessful.

Nevertheless, school finance litigation has flourished in state courts. In these cases, challengers have relied on equal protection clauses[1] and/or education clauses[2] contained in state constitutions. By now, lawsuits challenging the legality of state systems of public school finance under state constitutions have been brought in at least 43 states. In 19 states, courts have declared school funding systems unconstitutional and have ordered reforms—with varying degrees of specificity and success. Court decisions in 24 states have rejected school finance claims. In 9 of those latter states, however, challengers subsequently sought relief under a different legal theory, and most of those cases are currently pending. If history is any guide, school finance litigation promises to remain active well into the next century, at least in those states with perceived educational "haves and have nots."

This chapter examines the origins, evolution, achievements, and future directions of school finance litigation. Despite dramatic state-to-state differences, the courts across the nation increasingly have become a voice in the school finance debate. As will be seen below, however, the final resolution of complex school finance issues in nearly all states continues to be determined largely through the legislative and executive processes.

EARLY THINKING: WEALTH-BASED DISCRIMINATION AND THE FEDERAL CONSTITUTION

During the late 1960s, several scholars and lawyer activists began examining America's system of school finance, in which, everywhere but in Hawaii (which has a single statewide system) and the District of Columbia, money raised by local school districts through local property taxes was the heart of the scheme. These newcomers to the world of school finance learned what experts in the field had long known—that, by giving local governments the primary power and responsibility to raise funds and set spending levels in public schools, states had created systems that substantially advantaged some children over others. Notwithstanding the publication of the Coleman Report (1966), which raised doubts about how much money really mattered in improving student outcomes, these scholars and activists found a great deal unfair about the funding of the nation's public schools.

These early reformers put forward new legal theories, which in turn had major implications for the role taken by judges and legislatures in changing the way public schools would be financed. In other words, although each claimed that the existing system violated the requirement of the Fourteenth Amendment to the United States Constitution that states not deny individuals "equal protection of the law," they differed greatly as to what equal protection required.

Arthur Wise was one of the first to lay his ideas out in print (Wise, 1968). For Wise, the problem was that school spending varied dramatically from school district to school district within most states. Indeed, in many states high-spending districts were able to lavish two, three, and in some cases even four or more times as much per pupil on their students than what low-spending districts were able to spend on their students.

The legal challenge he developed drew upon two important judicial developments in the 1960s—the school desegregation cases and the reapportionment cases. Based on the school desegregation cases, Wise argued that public education was a "fundamental interest" for equal protection purposes and thus could not be distributed unequally within any state absent a "compelling state interest" for doing so (and, he argued, there was no such compelling interest).[3] Drawing on the "one man-one vote" principle of the reapportionment cases,[4] Wise advanced a similar standard for public school finance: one scholar-one dollar. In short, under Wise's theory, the federal equal protection clause required an end to unequal spending from district to district. This push for dollar equity is what some scholars have referred to as horizontal equity (see Berne and Stiefel, Chapter 1 in this volume).

Looking at the same spending patterns, UCLA law professor Harold Horowitz turned to a different area of the law from which he developed the principle of geographic uniformity (Horowitz, 1966; Horowitz and Neitring, 1968). He argued that, like a state's law governing murder, school spending could not vary within a state based on geography alone. To many, the implication of this argument appeared to be the same as would follow from Wise's principle—uniform per-pupil spending statewide. But this was not necessarily so. Under Horowitz's theory, a legislature might decide, for example, to spend more money on disabled or at-risk children. If it turned out that more of those children resided in some school districts than in others, then more per pupil on average would be spent there. Such district-to-district differences would be acceptable under Horowitz's principle because those differences would be based on student need and not geography. By contrast, it was not entirely clear just how Wise's "one dollar-one scholar" principle might, if at all, accommodate differential spending based on different pupil needs.

Some legal-aid lawyers who tackled the issue found both the Wise and Horowitz principles ill-suited to their purposes. They developed an alternative theory that focused primarily on unequal student need and the resulting imperative, as they saw it, to spend more than average on the schooling of low-achieving children from low-income families, many of whom lived in urban areas. Wise's equal spending rule would clearly not suffice. Horowitz's geographic uniformity theory only permitted, but did not mandate, what these advocates sought to have the courts require.

The basic thrust of the legal-aid lawyers' "needs-based" constitutional claim was that rich and poor children had a right to have their educational needs "equally" met. This principle, which some scholars have termed vertical equity, required unequal spending (see Berne and Stiefel, Chapter 1 in this volume). The legal-aid lawyers and their clients got to court first.

A central difficulty with the needs-based claim existed, however. How much spending does any child, or class of children, "need"? If "need" implies a level of school spending necessary to achieve some sort of educational "outcome" standard, then exactly what outcome? And if "need" is not about outcomes, what does it involve that a court could address? Would a court order whatever spending education experts thought is "needed"? But which experts? And "needed" for what? In other words, the problem lay in identifying an acceptable constitutional principle for courts to announce that contained the certainty and clarity that seemed necessary (at least at the time) before the claimants had any hopes of winning an equal protection case.

Federal courts were indeed troubled by just such questions when faced with early needs-based claims, and these suits were promptly dismissed.[5] *McInnis v. Shapiro,* a 1968 Illinois case, was first. The federal district court panel rejected the claimants' theory precisely on the ground that it could not discern judicially manageable standards to gauge what students' needs were and whether they were being met. A similar conclusion was soon reached by a federal district court panel in Virginia in *Burrus v. Wilkerson* (1969). The *Burrus* court concluded that "courts have neither the knowledge, nor the means, nor the power to tailor the public moneys to fit the varying needs of these students throughout the State" (*Burrus,* 1969:574). Both *McInnis* and *Burrus* were appealed to the United States Supreme Court, where they were affirmed without comment. Advocates would have to wait several years for the nation's highest court to opine on the merits of school finance challenges.

In addition to the Wise, Horowitz, and needs-based approaches, a fourth legal strategy for attacking school finance inequities emerged in the late 1960s (Coons et al., 1969, 1970). Working at Northwestern University Law School, Professor John Coons and two students, William Clune and Stephen Sugarman, developed a theory that combined a concern about poverty with the idea that education was a constitutionally fundamental interest. In this respect, their legal strategy was not unlike that of the legal-aid lawyers. But the Coons team cast the shortcoming of America's school finance systems in a different way. To them, the constitutional evil was that the "poor" school districts had little property wealth to tax in order to support their local schools, whereas "rich" districts had lots of it. Although states offset some of the rich districts' wealth advantage through a variety of state aid formulas designed to assure all pupils some minimum level of spending, enormous wealth advantages remained. Furthermore, the poor districts tended to impose on themselves higher tax rates per dollar of assessed value of property than did their wealthy counterparts. Yet despite the greater "effort" made through higher tax rates (and notwithstanding the state aid they received), property-poor districts had less money per pupil to spend.

This wealth discrimination, argued the Coons team, was unconstitutional. They dubbed their core legal principle "Proposition I (later referred to as the theory of "fiscal neutrality"): the quality of public education, measured most commonly by looking at dollar inputs, may not be a function of wealth other than the wealth of the state as a whole.

Since Proposition I attacked the formal structure of school finance systems, it would be relatively easy for the courts to apply, unlike the needs-based theory of the legal-aid advocates. Moreover, so long as the amount of resources available to a pupil was not determined by the amount of the district's local wealth, it left room for the state to choose among several finance options. Under Proposition I, states could adopt Wise's one dollar-one scholar idea. States also could elect to spend more on educationally needier poor children than on children from other families—the goal of the legal-aid lawyers. Moreover, in contrast to Horowitz's theory, Proposition I allowed geographic-based differences in spending. For example, if two districts were equally wealthy, it would not be unconstitutional for one to choose to spend more than the other by taxing itself more. Put differently, the Coons team sought to end the long-existing politics of school finance, in which the poor districts were pitted against the rich ones, and to replace it with a politics that concerned itself more with educational objectives.

To demonstrate how a new school finance scheme could meet their principle of fiscal neutrality and yet tolerate geographically different spending levels, Coons and his colleagues developed a mechanism that they called "district power equalizing." That system sought, through the use of a state aid formula, to make every district effectively equally wealthy. Once that was assured, the state might permit districts to tax as high or low as they wished; the resulting geographic inequalities would be allowed under Proposition I because they would reflect differences in tax effort, not wealth. Coons and his colleagues emphasized this remedy because they recognized the traditional importance of local control over education and anticipated the reluctance of the federal judiciary to override that control.

Significantly, under the Coons team's theory, the objectionable discrimination on the basis of poverty was based on school district poverty, rather than personal poverty, and was measured by the assessed value of property per pupil that a district could tax. Low property wealth per pupil might have been a good proxy for concentrations of family poverty in some districts, and indeed the low-wealth districts tended to be home to lower-income families. But this certainly was not the case in every district. In fact, many large cities were relatively "wealthy," often containing some well-to-do families and valuable commercial property. As a result, despite having many poor residents, large cities often spent more on their students than the statewide average per pupil, although usually considerably less than was spent in nearby wealthy suburbs. This made the Coons team's theory unattractive to some legal-aid advocates for poor children living in large urban centers, whose goal was to achieve "equity" in opportunity for the pupils they represented even if that meant more unequal state spending.

But unlike the claims of the lawyers who brought the earlier needs-based cases, the Coons team's legal theory was soon embraced in two important cases:

by the California Supreme Court in *Serrano v. Priest* (more on that in the following section) and by a lower Texas federal court panel in *Rodriguez v. San Antonio
Independent School District*.[6] As a result, it appeared for a short time that the
federal Constitution—and the Coons team's Proposition I—would indeed play a
central role in shaping America's school finance system.

The lower court ruling in *Rodriguez* was appealed to the United States Supreme Court, and in 1973, in a narrow 5-4 decision, the Court rejected the Coons
team's theory. This decision dashed the advocates' hopes for a federal remedy to
school finance inequities (*Rodriguez*, 411 U.S. 1, 1973).

The plaintiffs in *Rodriguez* consisted of a class of children throughout the
state of Texas living in districts with low per-pupil property valuations. In line
with the Coons team's theory, they claimed that the Texas school finance system's
reliance on local property taxation unfairly favored more affluent districts, creating substantial inter-district disparities that violated the equal protection clause of
the Fourteenth Amendment. The plaintiffs asserted—and the lower court
agreed—that, as a matter of federal constitutional law, education was a "fundamental interest" and wealth was a "suspect classification," thus requiring the
application of "strict judicial scrutiny" to the state's wealth-based school finance
scheme. With no "compelling interest" in discriminating against low-wealth
districts, the Texas plan (and by implication the school finance plans of virtually
every state) would have to change.

The Supreme Court majority found several things wanting in the plaintiffs'
case. First, the Court rejected the plaintiffs' invitation to treat wealth generally as
a "suspect classification" (as it had treated race, for example), thereby triggering
the need to justify unequal treatment with a compelling reason.[7] Moreover, the
Court distinguished within a group of prior decisions upon which the Coons team
relied. The two most important cases involved states denying people access to
divorce and to an appeal of a criminal conviction. But the Court emphasized that
in those other cases a class of indigent persons were completely precluded from
enjoying the desired benefit (*Rodriguez*, 1973:20).

By contrast, the plaintiffs in *Rodriguez* could not demonstrate to the Court's
satisfaction that the Texas school finance system disadvantaged any class of
persons fairly definable as indigent or with incomes below any designated poverty line. On the contrary, the primary basis for the plaintiffs' claims was discrimination based on district, not personal wealth. And, as the Court observed,
there was no necessary correlation between the two.

Unlike the prior cases, *Rodriguez* did not involve an absolute deprivation of
any benefits since all of the plaintiff children were receiving a free public education and their districts were assured at least some minimal level of funding.

The Court also decided that it would not treat education, as it had treated the
right to travel for example,[8] as a "fundamental interest" any infringement of
which was subject to strict judicial scrutiny. The Court acknowledged the "grave
significance of education both to the individual and to society" but nevertheless

concluded that the importance of a government service to society does not determine that the service is fundamental for purposes of an equal protection analysis
(*Rodriguez,* 1973:30). For the Court, a right was fundamental only if either
explicitly or implicitly guaranteed by the Constitution, and neither was the case
with respect to education. Nearly a decade later, in *Plyler v. Doe* (487 U.S. 202,
1982), the Court arguably came out the other way on the question of whether
education is a constitutionally fundamental interest, but that case, unlike
Rodriguez, involved an absolute denial—illegal immigrant children were barred
from school entirely.

Recognizing that the Court might take a narrow view of education as a
constitutionally fundamental right, the Coons team, as friend of the court, argued
more broadly that education was fundamental because it enabled people to exercise effectively their right to vote and their First Amendment right to free speech.
The Court, however, sidestepped that First Amendment argument. Again, because Texas guaranteed pupils at least a minimum level of spending, the Court
expressed doubts that the differential spending levels alleged by the plaintiffs
interfered with First Amendment rights, both as a constitutional matter and empirically (*Rodriguez,* 1973:36, 42).

Having rejected the application of the strict scrutiny test, the Court's majority next asked whether Texas had a "rational basis" for its finance scheme. The
tradition of local control over education easily provided such a basis.

Three justices dissented in *Rodriguez,* broadly endorsing the Coons team's
legal theory. A fourth, Justice White, dissented on narrower grounds, concluding
that the Texas school finance system effectively denied local control to poor
districts and thus was irrational. As he saw it, property-poor school districts did
not have control over their inability to raise revenues for education, and in fact
were often forced to tax their meager resources at rates much higher than the
wealthier districts.

The *Rodriguez* majority's reluctance to involve the federal courts in state
school finance issues was driven by important concerns about federalism. As the
Court observed, "it would be difficult to imagine a case having a greater potential
impact on our federal system than the one now before us, in which we are urged
to abrogate systems of financing public education presently in existence in virtually every state" (*Rodriguez,* 1973:44). The Court expressed further concern
about the delicacies of the state/federal relationship, noting that "the judiciary is
well advised to refrain from imposing on the states inflexible constitutional re-
straints that could circumscribe or handicap the continued research and experimentation so vital to finding even the partial solutions to educational problems
and keeping abreast of ever changing conditions" (*Rodriguez,* 1973:43).

These early school finance cases, as well as most subsequent ones, were in
no respect cast as matters of racial discrimination. The decision to leave race out
was partly based on the fact that, with the end of the system of separate black and
white schools in the wake of *Brown v. Board of Education,* no formal structural

discrimination existed against blacks in the funding of public schools. It also was partly a matter of uncertainty as to whether blacks as a class would be helped by successful school finance litigation. Advocates believed that black children living in low-spending districts would benefit, but many African-Americans were increasingly living in cities where the school finance problems were more complex than simply having a low property tax base and, as a result, spending less per pupil than elsewhere in the state.

Rodriguez abruptly cut off efforts to reform unequal state school finance systems through federal litigation based on the United States Constitution,[9] but it certainly did not end the school finance litigation reform effort.

TURNING TO STATE CONSTITUTIONS

Overview

With the door to federal courts closed by *Rodriguez*, and faced with the persistence of large disparities in the availability of educational resources and opportunities, advocates turned to state courts for relief. State court litigation has continued since the early 1970s and has reflected the variety of legal theories initially advanced by reformers in the late 1960s (see Tables 2-1 through 2-6). In 19 states, as noted above, state school funding systems—and in some cases the entire education system—have been declared unconstitutional. While results in the state cases have been mixed (24 cases rejected the plaintiffs' claims, with 9 of

TABLE 2-1 Overview of Litigation Involving State Education Finance Systems

Plaintiffs won at state supreme court level[a]	19
Plaintiffs lost at supreme court level; no further complaints filed or further complaints also lost[b]	12
Plaintiffs lost in prior action; further complaints have been filed	9
Litigation is present; no supreme court decision has been rendered	3
No litigation is present or case is dormant	7

[a]Some of these decisions stopped short of declaring entire finance systems unconstitutional, but instead established certain entitlements to educational services for all students or declared parts of systems unconstitutional.

[b]Not all of these decisions ruled that the state finance systems were constitutional. Some rejected plaintiffs challenges on the ground that the asserted claims were not supported under state law.

SOURCE: Authors' calculations.

TABLE 2-2 Plaintiffs Won at State Supreme Court Level (19)[a]

State	Decision	Year(s)	Notes
Alabama	*Harper v. Hunt*	1993, 1997	1993 trial court ruled system unconstitutional— not appealed and therefore final; 1997 high court ruling gave legislature one year to develop remedy
Arizona	*Roosevelt Elem. Sch. Dist. 66 v. Bishop*	1994, 1997	
Arkansas	*Dupree v. Alma Sch. Dist.*	1983	1983 lower court ruled
	Lake View v. Arkansas	Filed 1994	system unconstitutional —not appealed
California	*Serrano v. Priest*	1971, 1977	
Connecticut	*Horton v. Meskill*	1977	
	Sheff v. O'Neill	1996	
Kentucky	*Rose v. The Council*	1989	
Massachusetts	*McDuffy v. Secretary of Educ.*	1993	
Missouri	*The Committee v. Missouri and Lee's Summit P.S.U. v. Missouri*	1996	High court upheld legislation passed in response to a 1993 lower court decision declaring finance system unconstitutional
Montana	*Helena Sch. Dist. v. Montana*	1989	
	Montana Rural Educ. Assoc. v. Montana	Filed 1993	
New Hampshire	*Claremont v. Gregg*	1997	High court found that education clause requires funding for adequate education
New Jersey	*Robinson v. Cahill*	1973, 1976	
	Abbott v. Burke	1990, 1994, 1997, 1998	
North Carolina	*Leandro v. North Carolina*	1997	Supreme Court overturned dismissal and remanded for trial on merits
Ohio	*DeRolph v. Ohio*	1997	
Tennessee	*Tennessee Small Sch. Systems v. McWherter*	1993, 1995	
Texas	*Edgewood v. Kirby*	1989, 1991, 1992, 1995	
Vermont	*Lamoille Co. v. Vermont*	1997	
	Brigham v. Vermont	1997	

TABLE 2-2 *(continued)*

State	Decision	Year(s)	Notes
Washington	*Seattle v. Washington*	1978	
	Tronson v. Washington	1991	
West Virginia	*Pauley v. Kelly*	1979, 1984	
	Pauley v. Bailey	Filed 1994	
Wyoming	*Washakie v. Herschler*	1980	
	Campbell v. Wyoming	1995	

[a]Some of these decisions stopped short of declaring entire finance systems unconstitutional, but instead established certain entitlements to educational services for all students or declared parts of systems unconstitutional.
SOURCE: Modified from Hickrod et al. (1997).

those states embroiled in new legal actions), the litigation certainly has been a force in shaping school finance debates nationwide. (One has to be cautious when using any "scorecard" of these cases. In some states, litigation never reached the state's highest court. In other states, such as Missouri and Oklahoma, the mere threat of filing a lawsuit has been enough to bring about some school finance reform. A court decision subsequently upholding the reformed system would mean something very different from a defense victory in other states.)

Many of the state court decisions striking down their state's school finance scheme rely on the state constitution's equal protection clause.[10] Early on, it became clear that, despite similar wording, a state court might interpret its own state constitution's equal protection clause differently than the federal Constitution's. For one thing, the state court might declare education to be a fundamental interest and/or school district wealth a suspect classification for purposes of state constitutional law, even if these propositions do not apply in federal constitutional litigation.[11] In that event, the state court would likely follow the reasoning expressed by the group of three dissenters in *Rodriguez*. Alternatively, a state court could follow the lead of Justice White and find its state school finance system irrational.[12]

Many other state courts have relied in whole or in part on state constitutional provisions specific to education in deciding school finance cases. Some of those decisions use the state constitution's education clause to buttress the equal protection analysis, relying in part on the presence and content of the education clause to support treating education as a fundamental right (Enrich, 1995). Others, however, interpret the education clause independently—as itself requiring some degree of equity in educational funding or opportunity (Underwood, 1995; Enrich, 1995).

In reviewing state school finance cases, both the particular state constitutions

TABLE 2-3 Plaintiffs Lost at Supreme Court Level; No Further Complaints
Filed or Further Complaints Also Lost (12)[a]

State	Decision	Year(s)	Notes
Alaska	*Matanuska-Susitna Borough v. Alaska*	1997	
Florida	*Coalition v. Childs*	1996	High court ruled that no cause of action presented
Georgia	*McDaniels v. Thomas*	1981	
Idaho	*Thompson v. Engelking*	1975	
	Idaho Schools for Equal Educ. Oppty	1993	
Kansas	*Unified Sch. Dist. 229, et al. v. Kansas*	1992	
	Unified Sch. Dist. 244, Coffey Co., et al. v. Kansas	1994	
	Unified Sch. Dist. 217, Rolla, et al. v. Kansas	1994	
Maine	*M.S.A.D. #1 v. Leo Martin*	1995	
Michigan	*East Jackson Public Sch. v. Michigan*	1984	
Nebraska	*Gould v. Orr*	1993	High court ruled that no cause of action presented
North Dakota	*Bismarck Public Schools v. North Dakota*	1994	Majority (3) ruled in favor of plaintiff, but North Dakota requires four justices to declare a statutory law unconstitutional
Oklahoma	*Fair School v. Oklahoma*	1987	
Rhode Island	*City of Pawtucket v. Sundlun*	1995	
Virginia	*Scott v. Virginia*	1994	

[a]Not all of these decisions ruled that the state finance systems were constitutional. Some rejected
plaintiffs challenges on the ground that the asserted claims were not supported under state law.
SOURCE: Modified from Hickrod et al. (1997).

on which the courts rely and the tradition of judicial review in the particular state
should be considered. Many state constitution education clauses provide that the
state shall provide for a "thorough and efficient" system of public schools, others
merely require "efficient," still others call for "ample," and so on. Moreover,
beyond its words, each state constitution has its own political history and its own
prior history of judicial interpretation.[13] Hence, while some scholars (McUsic,
1991; Thro, 1993) have attempted to categorize state education clauses based

TABLE 2-4 Plaintiffs Lost in Prior Action; Further Complaints Have Been Filed (9)

State	Decision	Year(s)	Notes
Colorado	*Lujan v. State Bd. of Educ.,*	1982	
	New case filed	1998	
Illinois	*Committee v. Edgar*	1996	
	New case filed	1997	
Maryland	*Hornbeck v. Somerset Co*	1983	
	Bradford v. Maryland St. Bd. of Educ.	Filed 1994	
Minnesota	*Skeen v. Minnesota*	1993	Win for plaintiffs at district court on motion to dismiss
	NAACP v. Minnesota	Filed 1996	
	St. Paul Sch. Dist. v. Minnesota	Filed 1996	
New York	*Board of Educ. v. Nyquist*	1982, 1987	1993, 1995 win for plaintiffs at high court on motion to dismiss; remanded for trial on merits
	Reform Educational Financing Inequities Today (R.E.F.I.T.) v. Cuomo	1991, 1995	
	Campaign for Fiscal Equity v. New York State	1993, 1995	
Oregon	*Olsen v. Oregon*	1976	
	Coalition for Ed. Equity v. Oregon	1991	
	Withers v. Oregon	1997	
Pennsylvania	*Danson v. Casey*	1979, 1987	
	Pennsylvania Assoc. of Rural and Sm. Sch. v. Casey	Filed 1991	
South Carolina	*Richland v. Campbell*	1988	1993 lower court dismissed case in 1996, appeal pending
	Lee Co. v. South Carolina	Filed 1993	
Wisconsin	*Kukor v. Grover*	1989	
	Vincent v. Voight	Filed 1995	

SOURCE: Modified from Hickrod et al. (1997).

TABLE 2-5 Litigation Is Present; No Supreme Court Decision Has Been Rendered (3)

State	Decision	Year	Notes
Louisiana	*Charlet v. Legislature of State of Louisiana*	1992	Intermediate appellate court dismissed suit 3/97
New Mexico	*Alamagordo v. Morgan*	1995	
South Dakota	*Bezdichek v. South Dakota*	1991	Win for defendants at trial court on merits

SOURCE: Modified from Hickrod et al. (1997).

upon their wording so as to be able to predict results in school finance cases, there appears to be little correlation between the language per se and the likelihood of success in a given suit (Underwood, 1995).

Plaintiffs in a traditional state constitutional school finance equity case— whether grounded in the equal protection clause, the education clause, or both— typically allege that a state's method for funding public schools is inequitable because the amount of resources available to local school districts is a function of the property wealth located in that district. This reflects the predominance gained by the Coons team's theory described above. Plaintiffs focus their evidence in such cases on disparities in the tax bases and financial resources available to schools in high-property-wealth and low-property-wealth school districts and the resulting disparities in educational opportunities available to students.

Some other state court advocates have sought primarily to eliminate the spending gap between high-wealth and low-wealth school districts. For example, they oppose the district power equalizing scheme developed by the Coons team arguing that a child's education should not depend upon the willingness of voters

TABLE 2-6 No Litigation Is Present or Case Is Dormant (7)

State	Decision	Year	Notes
Delaware			
Hawaii			
Indiana	*Lake Central v. Indiana*	1987	Case withdrawn
Iowa			
Mississippi			
Nevada			
Utah			

SOURCE: Modified from Hickrod et al. (1997).

in the community to make a certain tax effort in support of education. As a result, these advocates appear to favor legal remedies that more reflect Wise's theory.

More recently, however, advocates have begun pursuing state law claims that differ from those advanced by either the Coons team or Wise. These cases are focused on ensuring that all students in a state have equitable access to adequate educational opportunities that are reasonably designed to allow them to achieve expected educational outcomes.[14] Such cases rely primarily on a state constitution's education clause, with the plaintiffs' evidence typically focusing on the inadequacy of educational opportunities offered in one or more school districts in a state as demonstrated in part by the inability of students in that district to meet state or other contemporary education standards.

An "adequacy" claim does not complain about disparities in funding among school districts per se, but instead alleges that one or more districts lack the resources necessary to provide students with adequate educational opportunities. In effect, these advocates charge that schools are failing their clients, that more money is needed to serve them properly, and that the state constitution requires that increased spending. Because the legal remedies sought typically ask that the state provide complaining school districts with the resources necessary to afford students the opportunity to achieve desired educational outcomes, it matters not that such additional resources may result in those districts receiving higher levels of resources than other districts. Quite plainly, the new "adequacy" approach is an important revival, in state court, of the legal-aid lawyers' "needs-based" claims of the late 1960s.

As discussed below, several themes have emerged from cases both accepting and rejecting constitutional challenges to school funding schemes, and those themes highlight the strengths and limitations of the various legal theories. In the end, however, regardless of the litigation theory pursued, the fate of a plaintiffs' school funding challenge seems to be determined by whether a court takes a broad or narrow view of the rights bestowed by its state constitution.

Serrano and the 1970s

The decade of the 1970s was marked by the first successful state school finance equity lawsuits in California and New Jersey. The California case, *Serrano v. Priest*, perhaps the most famous school finance lawsuit, embraced the theory of the Coons team (indeed, Coons and Sugarman participated in the oral argument of the case before the California Supreme Court).[15] The New Jersey case, which originally resembled an equity case based on the Coons team's theory, has been reshaped in several directions over the years of its seemingly unending litigation (more on this below). West Virginia and Washington decisions from the 1970s are also significant because they moved in the direction of opportunity and outcomes-based standards of equity that laid the foundation for the current adequacy movement.

During this same decade, courts in several other states rejected plaintiffs' claims, referring the reformers to the legislative process to cure the school finance system's alleged ills.[16] Like the United States Supreme Court in *Rodriguez,* these decisions reflected the reluctance of some courts to get involved in difficult and complex social policy issues relating to public school finance.

California

The first successful state court case, *Serrano v. Priest,* 487 P.2d 1241 (1971) (*Serrano I*), was filed in California by a class of Los Angeles County public schoolchildren and their parents. The plaintiffs alleged that the California school funding system was unconstitutional because it created wide disparities in the quality and availability of resources and educational opportunities across the state. Plaintiffs' evidence demonstrated that in the 1969-70 school year, elementary school districts' expenditures ranged from $407 to $2,586, while high school districts' expenditures ranged from $722 to $1,761 (Franklin, 1987). Such disparities, plaintiffs alleged, were the consequence of the finance system's heavy reliance on local property taxes as a primary source of funding for public schools. The plaintiffs claimed that the finance system violated the equal protection clauses of both the United States Constitution and the California constitution.

The California Supreme Court embraced the Coons team's Proposition I, holding that the state's school "funding scheme invidiously discriminated against the poor because it made the quality of a child's education a function of the wealth of his parents and neighbors" (*Serrano I,* 1971:1244). The court recognized that the right to an education was a fundamental interest that could not be conditioned on wealth, and could identify no compelling state purpose that necessitated the present method of financing.

The court squarely rejected the defendants' assertion that a compelling interest promoted local control over the financing and operation of schools. According to the court, local control was a "cruel illusion" for property-poor districts, where, because of the lack of taxable wealth, residents effectively had no control over how much to spend on their schools (*Serrano I,* 1971:1261).

It appeared initially that the *Serrano I* decision relied primarily on the United States Constitution's Fourteenth Amendment in reaching its holding, as the lawyers had urged. But a few additional words were put in the opinion noting that the California constitution's equal protection clause also was applicable (*Serrano I,* 1971:1249, note 11). Later, in its 1976 decision evaluating the sufficiency of the legislature's response to *Serrano I,* the California Supreme Court explicitly held that the federal equal protection analysis it had advanced in *Serrano I* was equally applicable to the California constitution's equal protection clause (*Serrano II,* 1976:951). The United States Supreme Court, of course, had decided *Rodriguez* during the time between the first and second *Serrano* decisions. But by redirecting the focus of the California court's analysis and embracing a wider and independent view of the California constitution, the California Supreme Court was able to hold firm to its prior decision.

In *Serrano II* (557 P.2d 929, 1976), the court held that the school finance legislation passed in response to *Serrano I* was insufficient. The court noted that even under the new plan, "local wealth is the principal determinant of revenue" (*Serrano II*, 1976:938-39). *Serrano II* went on to offer the state a host of alternative school funding schemes that would avoid the pitfalls of the then current system including the Coons team's district power equalizing plan. The *Serrano II* decision indicated what would suffice to meet the constitutional requirement by affirming the trial court's order requiring that, by September 1980, the legislature implement a school funding formula that reduced wealth-related disparities in per-pupil expenditures, exclusive of categorical aids and special needs programs, to less than $100 (*Serrano II,* 1976:940, note 21).

Shortly after *Serrano II*, the legislature enacted a comprehensive school finance package that essentially adopted the Coons team's district power equalization plan. Under that plan, a school district, no matter how poor, was guaranteed a certain amount of revenue if it taxed itself at a specified rate.

Before the legislative scheme went into effect, however, the voters of California passed Proposition 13, which limited property tax rates to 1 percent of the cash value of real property subject to taxation. Proposition 13 also required a two-thirds vote of the legislature to increase state taxes and absolutely prohibited the imposition of a statewide property tax. The passage of Proposition 13 required a totally new method of school funding skewed toward state funding. In other words, Proposition 13 essentially nullified the district power-equalizing plan adopted by the legislature.

In its place, the legislature passed a school funding formula that relied more upon state revenue sources. This plan tried to achieve the equalization required by *Serrano II* by allowing for minimal increases in high-spending districts, while providing low-revenue districts with larger increases. Indeed, the revised system narrowed the gap in the amount of money per pupil available to school systems around the state to a level that the California Court in *Serrano III* found to be constitutionally acceptable. Over time, however, the impact of Proposition 13 has been to slow considerably the overall growth in spending on public schools in California, with the result that California, which used to be one of the highest spenders on elementary and secondary education, is now well below the national average.

The California saga is sometimes pointed to as an example of how states will be forced to level spending down in higher-wealth districts in response to school finance equity suits. However, that criticism is oversimplistic and overstated. The California experience with school finance reform and property tax relief seems to have been a unique episode because of Proposition 13. It is unclear whether the *Serrano I* and *II* decisions substantially influenced the passage of Proposition 13. Similarly, it is unclear to what extent the *Serrano* decisions contributed to California's relative decline in statewide spending, as compared to national averages.

New Jersey

The concepts of equity and fiscal neutrality embraced in *Serrano I* spread beyond California to both Texas and Minnesota where lower federal courts adopted *Serrano's* federal constitutional analysis.[17] This momentum, of course, was halted by *Rodriguez*. But the state constitutional branch of *Serrano* also proved fertile. Perhaps most importantly, the New Jersey Supreme Court in 1973 found that the state's school funding system—which, like California, resulted in property-poor districts spending half as much per pupil as wealthy districts— violated the New Jersey constitution.

Unlike *Serrano*, the New Jersey court based its decision exclusively on the state's education clause whose wording guaranteed to all students a "thorough and efficient system" of public education (*Robinson v. Cahill*, 303 A.2d 273, 1973, *Robinson I*). Although the central concept underlying equal protection of the law is a clear notion of equal treatment, state constitution education clauses are more amorphous and open-ended. Exactly what, for example, makes a system "thorough and efficient"? Initially, this difference in the choice of relevant state constitutional provisions was not self-evidently important, because the New Jersey court in *Robinson I* seemed to treat the education clause as imposing the same equity norms that the California Supreme Court found in its state equal protection clause. For advocates at the time, therefore, this opened up a new ground in which to anchor their legal claims to school finance equity. Subsequently, however, state constitution education clauses have turned out to be sources of new notions of equity and ultimately school finance adequacy cases (more on this below).

New Jersey school finance litigation has carried on for more than 20 years, and remains unresolved. Over the years, the New Jersey Supreme Court's focus has not been constant. The roots of this instability may be seen in *Robinson I*. The court announced that the education clause required the state to afford every pupil "educational opportunit[ies] that will equip [him] for his role as citizen and as competitor in the labor market" (*Robinson I*, 1973:293). Yet despite its embrace of this qualitative notion, the court focused its analysis of the state's compliance with that standard exclusively on quantitative measures of dollar inputs. "We deal with the problem in those terms because dollar input is plainly relevant and because we have been shown no other viable criterion for measuring compliance with the constitutional standard" (*Robinson I*, 1973:295).

Three years after its decision in *Robinson I*, the court reviewed the constitutionality of the legislature's response. The revised school funding legislation relied in part on the adoption of a version of the Coons team's district power-equalization scheme, under which "each district retained the authority to set its own school tax rate, while the state supplied aid sufficient to provide each district with the revenues it would have reaped from its chosen tax rate had its property wealth equalized 135 percent of the statewide average property wealth per student" (Enrich, 1995:132). This suggests that the legislature understood the principle of fiscal neutrality used by the court. At the same time, however, the revised school law also established a mechanism for the state to adopt education standards and monitor students' success in meeting those standards.

When these reforms reached the New Jersey Supreme Court they were found to have brought the state into compliance (*Robinson V*, 355 A.2d 129, 1976). But this time, the majority and concurring opinion focused more on the substantive education goals and opportunities outlined in the new legislation than on the finance provisions. To the extent that the finance provisions were addressed at all, the inquiry was whether they would afford sufficient financial support for the education system, not on inter-district inequities. Put differently, the structure of this 1976 New Jersey decision was to look first to the quality of educational opportunities as a constitutional requirement, and then back into finance as a means of assuring that all students have access to those opportunities.

Litigation in New Jersey during the late 1980s and 1990s has incorporated both the educational opportunity strand and the strict dollar equalization strand of the *Robinson* era decisions. The *Abbott v. Burke* litigation, filed on behalf of a group of the state's poorest urban school systems, has made several trips to the New Jersey Supreme Court over the last decade. Two results have emerged. First, the court has required that the state equalize the spending in the poorest districts to that of the wealthiest districts. Second, the court has also required that the state provide additional funding to the poorer districts to account for the extra educational needs of children from disadvantaged backgrounds (*Abbott*, 643 A.2d 575, 1994). The court's most recent decision in 1998 (*Abbott v. Burke,* N.J. Sup. Ct. May 1998) moves further in the direction of constitutionally required educational quality, directing the state to implement a broad-based education reform package. Interestingly, those sweeping reforms were largely recommended to the lower court by the State Commissioner of Education. Now that they have been incorporated into the state supreme court's order, they take on the force of law and will bind the state government. At long last, after more than two decades of litigation, the New Jersey battle over school finance equity appears to be over.

Washington and West Virginia

While fiscal neutrality (the Coons team's Proposition I) dominated the school finance literature and the scholarly and policy debates of the early 1970s, two other state court decisions moved toward a different notion of equity during this same period. This notion might be called equity in access to adequate educational opportunities. Those two decisions established the conceptual precursor for today's educational adequacy movement. Adequacy broadens the notion of equity from one predominantly focused on financial inequalities arising from the structure of the school finance system, to one focused on equally providing all students what is required for them to have a fair opportunity to achieve desired educational outcomes (see Chapter 6 for a fuller discussion of the adequacy movement).

This way of thinking about equity first crept into the Washington Supreme Court's 1978 school finance ruling, which held that the state's school funding system violated the Washington Constitution's education clause (*Seattle v. State of Washington*, 585 P.2d 71, 1978). Plaintiffs in the case were the Seattle School District, parents, and educational advocates. They contended that the state school finance system's reliance on "special excess levy funding" by local school systems—which required voter approval and had failed in the last two local elections—deprived the city school district of the funds necessary to provide students with educational opportunities in compliance with state statutes and regulations.

In 1979, the West Virginia Supreme Court expanded the notion of equal and adequate educational opportunities (*Pauley v. Kelly*, 255 S.E.2d 859, 1979) and identified a set of broad goals for a constitutionally valid education system. The high court then remanded the case back to the trial court for further hearings. The lower court outlined the basic elements of a "thorough and efficient" educational system as mandated by the constitution. Those elements were classified into broad categories of curriculum, personnel, facilities, and materials and equipment. The court found that the systems in existence in the plaintiff school district and other property-poor districts around the state were "woefully inadequate." The court also found that the state system of financing education was discriminatory, favoring property-wealthy districts over property-poor districts. Lastly, the court found positive correlation between the quality of a county's education system and the wealth of real and personal property (Franklin, 1987).

Consistent with the historical role of other courts in such cases, the trial judge left the design of the plan to the legislature. In 1983, the trial court approved the Master Plan for Education developed by the state legislature and State Department of Education. The plan included the development of education standards and curricula geared to those standards, improved facilities, and a revised school finance plan. The programmatic remedies sparked by the high court's decisions went beyond mere tinkering with the state school finance formula, and instead restructured the entire state education system.

On the school finance side, the Master Plan first established a time line and procedure for equalizing teacher salaries around the state. In addition, revenue was earmarked to fund fully current operations expenses in all counties. In conjunction with the new education standards developed under the plan, the state was to conduct an analysis of the additional costs that would be associated in each county with meeting the standards. Lastly, several features sought to address the disparities in revenue availability that resulted from variations in local property tax bases, including a move to statewide excess levies and some provisions that would recapture revenues raised in wealthy districts for use in poorer ones.

Like the New Jersey litigation, however, the West Virginia litigation has returned to court. In April 1997, the West Virginia Supreme Court found that the State had failed to fully implement and abide by the terms of the Master Plan. The court ordered that the full implementation of the Master Plan be achieved during 1998.

To reemphasize the point, the Washington and West Virginia cases expanded the notion of equity that previously had dominated school finance litigation. Equity arguments in the late 1960s and early 1970s focused on disparities in taxable wealth and per-pupil expenditures, whereas some courts in the late 1970s shifted the focus toward achieving equity in the educational opportunities and student outcomes in particular districts. This shift changed not only the focus of the arguments and evidence in school finance cases, but as the West Virginia case illustrates, it also called for legislative remedies directed specifically at educational programs and services, not just revenues and expenditures.

State Victories

Many of the lawsuits brought on behalf of school finance equity in the 1970s were unsuccessful. Courts in Oregon, Idaho, Ohio, and Pennsylvania all rejected challenges to their state school funding systems.[18] Those decisions relied on rationales that would prove fatal to many other school finance challenges in the coming decades.

Some courts essentially adopted the outlook of the United States Supreme Court in *Rodriguez*. For example, the Idaho Supreme Court in *Thompson v. Engelking* (1975) expressed concern about judicial intrusion into matters traditionally reserved for the legislature. As the court noted, agreeing with the plaintiffs' contentions "would be an unwise and unwarranted entry into the controversial area of public school financing, whereby this court would convene as a 'super-legislature,' legislating in a turbulent field of social, economic and political policy" (*Thompson*, 1975:640). That separation-of-powers concern was echoed in many decisions rejecting school funding equity challenges in the 1980s and 1990s.

The Idaho court also expressed some doubt as to whether equal funding had a significant relationship to educational quality:

> Assuming, arguendo, that the Idaho Constitution requires that our public school students receive equal educational opportunities, we cannot adopt the ultimate conclusion advanced by respondents, *i.e.*, that unless a substantially equal amount of funds are expended per-pupil throughout the state, subject only to natural variations such as sparsity of population, students in those districts receiving less than that district with the greatest expenditure per student are denied equal educational opportunities (*Thompson*, 1975:341-42).

That issue of whether and how much money matters continues to be a significant point of contention in most school finance cases today.

The Oregon Supreme Court's 1979 decision in *Olsen v. State* picked up on a different theme from *Rodriguez*. It rejected a school finance challenge primarily on the ground that the state's asserted interest in promoting local control justified the disparities in funding produced by the finance system. Unlike the *Serrano* court, the Oregon court held that the fact that some districts in the state may have less local control over spending because they have access to fewer resources does not necessarily lead to a conclusion that the state equal protection clause has been violated. Among other things, the Oregon court feared that if disparities in local governments' ability to raise revenue for education led to an equal protection violation, that same logic might be used to attack disparities in resource availability for other government functions, such as police and fire protection.

In *Danson v. Casey* (1979), the City School District of Philadelphia alleged that the state's heavy reliance on locally generated revenues to fund schools, and the city school district's inability to raise such revenues, had led to a budget crisis in the school district requiring dramatic cutbacks in the educational programs offered to students.[19] The plaintiffs contended that the finance system violated the Pennsylvania constitution's education clause, which required the state to provide for the "maintenance and support of a thorough and efficient system of public education to serve the needs of the Commonwealth" (Pa. Const. art. 3, sec. 14).

The *Danson* court rejected the plaintiffs' claims in large part due to the district's position of relative wealth in the state as a whole. Like many urban school systems, Philadelphia spent more per pupil than a large proportion of the other school districts in the state (*Danson,* 1979: 365, note 10). That position of relative "wealth" obviously bothered the court and led it to question the plaintiffs' alleged injury. In other words, so far as Philadelphia was concerned, its pupils appeared to be winners, not losers, if one were to apply the Coons team's Proposition I.

To be sure, a case might be made that at least two adjustments should be made in ascertaining a large urban district's "wealth" (its available assessed value of property per pupil). First, urban areas faced higher costs to deliver the same product (primarily because of higher wages in the cities resulting from higher living costs). Second, because urban areas had to deliver so many noneducational services to their population, their "municipal overburden" reduced the amount of the tax base available for schools. The Coons team discussed both of these ideas in their writings, recognizing that to take them into account threatened the easy judicial manageability of a simplified application of Proposition I.

Even these adjustments would not satisfy the Philadelphia plaintiffs, however, because they essentially sought to replay the legal-aid lawyers' early needs-based theory under the state constitution. In any event, the Pennsylvania court conceded only that its state "thorough and efficient" clause might assure pupils some sort of "minimum" or "basic" level of educational opportunities. But the plaintiffs failed to allege that this basic level of educational opportunity had been denied.

In sum, during the 1970s, by means of a variety of theories and demands, several state courts aggressively trod into the school finance fray that the United States Supreme Court declined to enter. The plaintiffs' success in about half of the decided cases created a genuine school finance litigation industry.

The 1980s: If It Ain't Broke, Don't Fix It

From 1980 through 1988, two state high court decisions invalidated their school finance systems,[20] while eight upheld systems as constitutional.[21] Plaintiffs in these 10 cases relied almost exclusively on traditional finance equity claims. More or less relying on the Coons team's Proposition I, their evidence and arguments focused primarily on the disparities in resource availability between wealthy and poor school districts that resulted from the systems' reliance on local property tax revenue as a chief source of public school funding.

Judicial restraint and deference to the legislative process—the *Rodriguez* perspective—characterized most decisions of this decade. When faced with state equal protection clause challenges, most courts took the view that education was not a fundamental right entitled to strict scrutiny under their state constitution (Underwood, 1995). Applying the more deferential rational basis test, those courts upheld their finance systems—and the local control they fostered.

So too, in response to arguments based on education clauses, most courts during this period took a very narrow view of what those provisions required of the state legislatures (Underwood, 1995). Courts often held that the education clauses did not require the state to adopt a particular school funding system, and certainly did not preclude a reliance on locally generated revenue as a source of funding for schools. Moreover, those courts did not view the education clauses as embodying notions of equity, and thus did not view the disparities in the availability of financial resources for schools as a problem of constitutional significance.

In rejecting traditional equity claims, many of the decisions of the 1980s also expressed frustration that plaintiffs did not allege what they considered to be sufficient injury. Several criticized plaintiffs for failing to demonstrate that, merely by having less money spent on them, students in property-poor school districts were denied their constitutional rights.[22]

Nonetheless, decisions rejecting finance equity claims often left the door open to possible future cases alleging that the state was failing to afford districts sufficient resources to provide students with the basic, minimum, or adequate educational opportunity required by state's education clause (Verstegen, 1995; Enrich, 1995).[23] As a result, despite initial school finance litigation failures in Maryland, Minnesota, New York, North Carolina, and Wisconsin, plaintiffs in each of those states later initiated "adequacy" suits and already have been successful in two of them. Most strikingly, the North Carolina Supreme Court ruled in 1997 that although the state constitution does not require equality in the distribution of educational resources, it does require that all students have access to adequate educational opportunities.

The two plaintiff victories in the 1980s—the Wyoming and Arkansas challenges—reflected the equity concept embodied in the Coons team's theory. Both state supreme courts struck down their school finance systems on the grounds that the property wealth located in a district largely determined the amount of revenue that was available to finance education. Such wealth-based disparities were found in both cases to be offensive to the state constitutions, although in the Wyoming case the court relied primarily upon the equal protection guarantees, while in Arkansas the court rested its decision upon both the state constitution's education and equal protection clauses.

Into the 1990s

A turning point in school finance litigation occurred in 1989. In that year alone, courts in Texas, Montana, and Kentucky declared their state systems of finance—and in the case of Kentucky the entire state education system—to be inequitable and unconstitutional.[24]

Texas

In Texas, the court relied on a traditional finance equity rationale (*Edgewood v. Kirby*, 777 S.W.2d 391, 1989), embracing the Coons team's fiscal neutrality theory in the very state in which the United States Supreme Court had rejected it. The plaintiffs' evidence focused on the glaring disparities in property wealth between the wealthiest and poorest communities in the state—disparities that reflected an astounding 700 to 1 ratio—and the resulting disparities in per-pupil expenditures, ranging from $2,112 to $19,333 (*Edgewood*, 1989:392).

The Texas Supreme Court agreed that the wealth-based disparities in funding for public schools were illegal and had to be corrected by the state legislature. Hence, the poor Texas school districts were able to achieve through state law what they had earlier failed to achieve in *Rodriguez*. Unlike the California experience, however, the new Texas decision was not based on the equal protection requirements of the state constitution.

Instead, the court relied on the state constitution's education clause, which required that the state make "suitable" provision for an "efficient" system of free public schools allowing for a "general diffusion of knowledge." The bottom line conclusion was much the same, however. The Texas Supreme Court concluded that the Texas school funding system "provide[d] not for a diffusion of knowledge that is general, but for one that is limited and unbalanced" (*Edgewood*,

1989:396). According to the court, the disparities created by the school finance system were antithetical to the constitution's commands of efficiency and equity.

The court deferred to the legislature to devise a constitutionally acceptable system. Solutions acceptable to the court were not easy to come by, however. Just as the New Jersey case returned to court several times during the 1970s, the Texas case appeared before the state supreme court four times in the 1990s, with the court repeatedly having to judge the constitutionality of the legislature's revised school finance plans. Finally, in 1995, the court found that the legislature had devised a constitutionally "efficient" plan, and ended the long-standing litigation battle (*Edgewood*, 1995 WL 36074, 1995).

The legislative scheme that the court finally approved was quite innovative in its approach to achieving fiscal equity. In essence, Texas modified its existing two-tier school finance structure. Tier 1 (similar to conventional "foundation plans") provides a guaranteed base level of spending per pupil for each district in the state that taxes itself at a state-determined minimum. Tier 2 is a guaranteed yield system (similar to district power equalizing) that provides each district with the opportunity to supplement the basic program at a level of its own choosing. To accomplish that objective, for every cent of additional tax effort beyond that amount required to qualify for Tier 1 funding, the state guaranteed a yield of $20.55 per weighted student.

The controversial part of the new plan involves a form of state recapture of part of the revenue generated by wealthy districts. The plan requires the Commissioner of Education each year to review the tax base per pupil of every school district in the state. Any district with more than $280,000 per pupil may elect one of five options to bring its taxable property under the cap (*Edgewood*, 1995:4): (1) total consolidation with another property poor district, (2) detachment of territory for taxable valuation purposes, (3) purchase of average daily attendance credits from a property-poor district, (4) contracting for the education of nonresident students, or (5) tax base consolidation with another property-poor district. Options 1 and 2 can be exercised by agreement of two school districts, while options 3, 4, and 5 require voter approval. The new plan was to be phased in gradually, and allowed districts flexibility so as not to require that their expenditures drop below certain levels.

The Texas legislation included many nonfinance reforms, comparable to the wake of the earlier West Virginia and New Jersey school finance decisions. The state set education goals and established a series of assessments to measure districts' progress in meeting those goals. While not mandated by the court's rulings, these programmatic reforms to the education system reflect the aspiration of the Coons team noted earlier. That is, when state school finance politics is freed from its conventional rich-district/poor-district battles, the legislature is more likely to focus on more systemic educational reforms. Where this happens, the legislature may voluntarily embrace the same approach that other legislatures are forced to adopt through "adequacy" cases.

Kentucky

The Kentucky decision is perhaps most important of the recent series of "adequacy" cases. As noted earlier, and as foreshadowed in the Washington and West Virginia cases, the meaning of "equity" in "adequacy" cases is very different—that all children should have equitable access to adequate educational opportunities.

In 1989, the Kentucky Supreme Court found that the entire Kentucky system of education violated the mandates of the state constitution's education clause (see Minorini and Sugarman, Chapter 6 in this volume). The court ordered the state to overhaul the entire system of education to bring it into compliance (*Rose v. Council for Better Educ.*, 790 S.W.2d 186, 1989). The court found that the education clause's "efficiency" language required that the state afford all students with equal access to adequate educational opportunities (Heise, 1995).

The Kentucky court provided broad guidelines to the legislature that included a list of seven items that characterized an adequate education (see Minorini and Sugarman, Chapter 6 in this volume). This approach deals with the same problems addressed by the legal-aid lawyers' needs-based theory. The court itself supplied the answer to the question of "needed for what educational result?" This list of seven items is not contained in the Kentucky constitution. It is a list that the court largely made up. But it is hardly an objectionable list, and it reflects the same pronouncements included in prominent national or international reports about what sort of education children "need" in our postindustrial contemporary society.

The hard part, of course, comes next. Do all children, or nearly all, actually have to reach those educational objectives? That appears not to be the case, and those who view the "adequacy" theory as insisting upon certain outcomes may have misinterpreted the idea. Rather, the courts and "adequacy" theorists seem to believe only that the educational finance system be structured and delivered so as to provide all children with a fair opportunity to achieve those outcomes (Clune, 1993; Underwood, 1995).

Even so, the task of restructuring the education finance system is tossed back to experts and the legislature. In other words, the policymakers and the educators should decide how much to spend and how to spend it, not the court itself. In a case like Kentucky the court seems to be saying that it is confident that the challenged scheme fails to provide all pupils with a fair opportunity to succeed. If nothing else, the system is manifestly not designed with that in mind. Instead, it is a hodge-podge of state mandates packaged together with a funding mechanism that encourages local autonomy.

One issue remains uncertain in this approach: What will constitute compliance? Once a system is found "inadequate," then until all (or nearly all) children in the state demonstrate high achievement, should the system remain under the court's supervision? We suspect, however, that there will be a different answer to this question. We anticipate that the system will be deemed in compliance when the legislature, in good faith and with steadfast purpose, has enacted a scheme designed to provide pupils with a fair opportunity to succeed. Yet, the sort of scheme that will pass this test remains rather elusive. Must it have certain minimum school finance and spending fairness features, and if so, which ones? Must it have certain governance, accountability, and curricular features, and if so, which? Will this turn out to be a procedural requirement? To return to an earlier theme, perhaps the court will be looking for evidence that the political process abandoned the conventional fight between rich and poor school districts and instead focused its attention on what would be educationally best for the children in the state. Because the "adequacy" approach is so new, its future remains uncertain.

In Kentucky, the legislature responded to the court's decision by enacting a sweeping and comprehensive statewide education reform package—the Kentucky Education Reform Act (KERA; Trimble and Forsaith, 1995). On the school funding side, KERA established a new foundation program that substantially increased the guaranteed minimum per-pupil expenditure statewide.[25] In addition to the funding reforms, KERA mandated a new statewide performance-based assessment system tied to new content-education standards, statewide curriculum frameworks, an accountability system with rewards and sanctions for schools tied to the achievement of high academic standards and the new assessments, as well as school-based decisionmaking statewide. While some debate whether and how much that reform has improved (or is likely to improve) student achievement, few question the sweeping nature of the reforms. Moreover, on the money side, a state that prior to 1990 was one of the lowest spending on public education in the country is now near the middle. Whether the Kentucky Supreme Court will be asked to pass on these reforms and, if so, what it might say, remains uncertain.

The 1990s: New Approaches and Mixed Results

Overview

The impact of the Kentucky decision and the legislature's response has been felt in many state courts across the country. Since 1989, courts in Alabama and Massachusetts have directly followed the Kentucky precedent. They have declared their education systems to be constitutionally inadequate under state law and have specifically relied on the Kentucky Supreme Court's definition of an adequate education when providing guidance to the state legislatures as they craft remedies (*Alabama Coalition for Equity v. Hunt*, reprinted in Appendix to Opinion of the Justices, 624 So.2d 107, 1993; *McDuffy v. Secretary of Educ.*, 615 N.E.2d 516, 1993).

Five other state courts[26] have also found that their state constitutions require the systems of education to afford students adequate opportunities to achieve broad educational outcomes, but those courts have relied on more general statements of what is constitutionally required.

Not every state's high court, however, has been receptive to adequacy arguments. In Illinois, where the state constitution's education clause explicitly requires the state to "provide for an efficient system of high quality public educational institutions and services," the Illinois Supreme Court rejected attempts by plaintiffs to involve the judiciary in determining whether the quality of education offered in the plaintiff districts met the constitutional standard. According to the court, "questions relating to the quality of education are solely for the legislative branch to answer" (*Committee for Educational Rights v. Edgar*, 672 N.E.2d 1178, Ill. 1996). The high courts in Rhode Island and Florida relied on a similar rationale in rejecting adequacy-based claims.[27]

As in the 1980s, several court decisions in the 1990s in Maine, Virginia, and Minnesota have rejected traditional finance equity challenges, while at the same time leaving the door open to future arguments that the state system of education must meet a standard of adequacy.[28] These decisions reveal the ambiguities and tensions between states and school districts in moving to an adequacy standard: states may simply provide enough aid for an adequate education (some or all of which the district may use for tax relief) or compel the districts to spend as much on education as required to provide an adequate education as defined by the legislature. These states are fertile ground for future court cases alleging that the state system of education is not providing students with a constitutionally adequate education. In fact, such a case was filed in 1996 in Minnesota.

Wyoming

The migration by state courts away from requiring only fiscal equity to insisting on more is nicely demonstrated by developments in Wyoming. In 1980, the Wyoming Supreme Court had found that the state education funding system violated the state constitution's equity requirement, primarily because the system did not achieve equality of financing (*Washakie v. Herschler*, 606 P.2d 310, Wyo. 1980). Fifteen years later, the court ordered the state legislature to determine the cost of the "proper" educational package for each Wyoming student (see Minorini and Sugarman, Chapter 6 in this volume). In response to this latest decision, the Wyoming legislature promptly formed several task forces charged with the duty to respond to the court's mandate.

The Wyoming court did emphasize that, once having decided what sort of education system is proper, the legislature would have to find a way to pay for it. The decision seems to require that the legislature place education funding above all other social and governmental services in its budgetary process. Of course, in Kentucky too the court presumably would be dissatisfied with a legislative response that specified what was needed to meet the court's broad guidelines but then candidly conceded that insufficient funds were appropriated to implement the new system. Moreover, it is politically naive to expect the Wyoming legislators to be blind to what things cost and what they think the state can afford as they go about deciding what a "proper educational package" for all Wyoming students should be. Nonetheless, the thrust of the Wyoming court's decision is to try to change the political dynamics of its legislature's approach to school finance and education more generally.

Events since the court's decision, however, illustrate the intensely political nature of school funding controversies. The legislature worked diligently over the course of a year and a half to meet the court's requirements, and in June of 1997 passed a revised school funding plan. The Governor soon vetoed that bill, however, prompting both the original plaintiffs and several state legislators to return to court to compel compliance.

In the spring of 1998, the legislative and executive branches came together and worked out a reform that they hope will comply with the court's orders. The new school finance law raises school district funding from the state by $76.5 million, increasing the upcoming year's total education budget to $632.3 million. School funding is now based on a professional model of what sums ought to suffice to provide a high-quality public education for all Wyoming schoolchildren—taking into account differences among districts in both educational costs and pupil needs. The new law also establishes student assessment standards.

Vermont

While adequacy claims are now dominating the field of school finance litigation, some cases continue to be fought on traditional equity grounds. For example, a group of students and parents in property-poor school districts in Vermont filed suit challenging the constitutionality of the state school funding system, which allowed 79 percent of a school district's funds to be raised locally. The result of heavy reliance on local property taxes as a source of funding for the schools was that some wealthy districts spent twice as much per pupil as other less affluent districts. In its 1997 decision, the Vermont Supreme Court found that such disparities in resource availability, and the consequent disparities in educational opportunities throughout the state, violated the state constitution's equal protection clause (*Brigham*, No. 96—502, Vt. 1997). Reminiscent of the Coons team's theory, the Vermont decision suggests that future school finance systems in Vermont will not be able to have the wealth of a district's property base determine the educational resources and opportunities available to students.

In response to the decision, the Vermont legislature passed a new school finance, education reform, and tax reform plan during the 1997 session, which includes several components. This plan:

- creates a per-student block grant ($5,000 for 1997) that is given to each district based on its equalized pupil count; the block grant will be adjusted by annual price index; pupil count is weighted to reflect poverty, primary/secondary students, and limited English proficiency;

- appropriates additional $9.6 million for capital construction;
- allows discretionary spending by local districts above the block grant and provides for equalization of ability to raise funds for this spending;
- includes several education reforms including student standards, new assessments, school improvement grants, early childhood programs, and others;
- replaces local property taxes for schools with a statewide education property tax, setting one rate for homestead and nonresidential property; and
- finances the changes through a statewide education property tax and various tax increases.

Ohio

Recent court decisions in Ohio blur the lines between equity and adequacy. In the 1970s, an Ohio Supreme Court decision had squarely rejected a traditional equity challenge to the state's school finance system. In 1991, however, a coalition of plaintiffs filed suit claiming that the education provided in their schools was constitutionally inadequate. Following a lengthy trial, the court ruled for the plaintiffs, relying heavily on the Kentucky court's prior articulation of adequacy standards in elaborating the Ohio constitution's requirements. That trial court decision, however, was quickly appealed by the state attorney general's office.

In 1997, the Ohio Supreme Court upheld the trial court's decision, but the high court focused more on educational inputs, traditionally associated with the equity theory, than on outputs, which tend to be more of a focus in adequacy decisions (*DeRolph v. State*, 79 Oh.St.3d 297, 1997). The court criticized the heavy reliance on local property taxes to fund schools, reminded the legislature of their responsibility to support a "statewide" education system, called for a "systemic overhaul" of the funding system, and gave the legislature a year to develop a new finance system. Despite the court's emphasis on input equity, however, the state legislature's response to the court was more in keeping with the trial court's broader ruling.

Like the Wyoming legislature, the Ohio legislature attempted to determine what it would cost to provide all students in the state with an adequate and equitable education. To determine that amount, the legislature looked at the spending patterns of districts within the state that were in compliance with state input and outcome standards. Using an average spending level for those districts, and adjusting for differing costs around the state and for differing need-levels of student populations, the legislature has established a baseline level of school spending that each district will be assured. It remains to be seen whether these new arrangements will be the subject of legal challenge.

SUMMING UP: THE FUTURE OF SCHOOL FINANCE LITIGATION

As we have seen, most of the early legal theories attacking school funding arrangements emphasized equality in a way that implied either a dramatic raising up of the wealth and/or spending level of poor, low-spending districts or a leveling down of the advantaged districts (or a combination of both). The Coons team, for example, had counted on the strong commitment to high spending of many of the high-wealth/high-spending districts as a force that would promote greater educational spending across the board. Even though this did not happen in California, it does appear to be a major consequence of successful school finance "equity" cases in other states (Evans et al., 1997).

Nowadays, however, the emphasis of many school finance reformers has shifted. For one thing, restraining or bringing down spending at the top is very unpopular (in some quarters some families shift to private schools, or equity-evading tactics in wealthy communities result in the creation of community foundations that supplement the public school funding provided by government). Yet, to raise spending everywhere up to the top (even if a few outlier districts are excluded) seems too expensive in many states. At the same time, many of those who complain about the public schools seem to care less that their children (or those they represent) are relatively worse off and more that they are badly off in an absolute sense.

These factors have combined to cause legal activists to change tactics, which have been supported by some courts. Although courts in many states have by now rejected the traditional "equity" claims, other more ambitious cases demanding "adequacy" are winning.

In the end, however, these two different legal approaches—equity and adequacy—are not so far apart as some commentators have suggested (Clune, 1993; Underwood, 1995). For example, although "adequacy" candidly concerns itself with educational outcomes, its advocates are not insisting that students have a legally enforceable "right" to any particular outcome. Rather, they appear to argue that each school district must have adequate resources, given its circumstances and the nature of its pupils, to be able to offer an educational program that reasonably promises to teach at least most of them to reasonably high standards. This principle is more ambitious as a legal standard than fiscal neutrality because it focuses on more than dollar inputs. At the same time, it contains many "soft" words that courts cannot define with clarity. Nevertheless, it carries a meaning that some courts do seem comfortable with in two critical respects. First, these courts believe that they can readily tell that, at least in some states, the adequacy principle is clearly not being met; and second, they feel that they will be able to determine whether the systemic revisions developed by the legislature constitute genuine responses to the adequacy standard.

Still, even as the courts embracing the adequacy idea envision legislative responses that will include more than mere financial changes, these courts seem best able to deal with the money side. As noted above, although the New Jersey Supreme Court, has moved down the "adequacy" path, its most recent ruling is that if the wealthy communities need so many dollars per pupil to educate their children, then the poverty-ridden central cities surely need that much and more. Adequacy, in short, is anchored in some notion of spending equity.

Indeed, New Jersey is of special interest because it is traditionally among the highest spending states in the country, perhaps the highest. Even low-spending New Jersey districts currently have available to them more money per pupil than the national average. Hence, one might well have assumed that New Jersey's spending level everywhere was at least "adequate"—unless school funding arrangements are to be deemed woefully inadequate throughout virtually the entire United States (which, some would argue, is true). But since New Jersey continues to have substantial spending inequalities, the court was able to order reform on behalf of the neediest districts by casting adequacy in relative equity terms.

Although the group of successful adequacy cases employs language that generally emphasizes educational reform beyond finance, it would be a mistake to imagine that system-wide reforms are taking place only in these states. After all, since the early 1980s the country as a whole has given much greater attention to educational productivity. So, too, throughout the country today, legislatures are involved with two new powerful reform movements—(1) educational standards and (2) school choice—that also make claims about how to connect the spending of money with better educational outcomes.

Finally, and perhaps most importantly, in the end both the equity and adequacy theories depend upon the courts primarily to perform the role of striking down the traditional approaches to school finance. That is, both theories look to the legislature to provide equal educational opportunity to all of the children of the state. How the legislature does that is ultimately up to the legislature and not the court, even if the court provides the negative prod of insisting that one response or another is insufficient. We can speculate whether the courts in states like Kentucky and Wyoming will at some point involve themselves intimately in the details of their state's educational reforms. (In Kentucky, which many cite as the strongest "adequacy" case, the reform effort has been sent back to the legislature to handle without maintaining judicial supervision over the response.) Therefore, by their demands that their state provide enhanced financial backing for school districts that are unfairly disadvantaged, it is safer for the present to see those judges adopting adequacy theories as still acting in the school equity tradition.

In these newer cases the courts seem to be bolder in describing what constitutes an unfair disadvantage, and this unwillingness gives adequacy and equity different legal meanings. A different way to put the point is that the adequacy banner is a successful reemergence of the early, then unsuccessful, educational "needs" theories of the legal aid lawyers. This suggests that the relative caution exhibited by the Coons team and other early legal theorists may have been unwarranted. Or perhaps courts needed to gain experience from and comfort with the narrower equity theories before embracing a broader theory.

Whether this recent greater boldness by lawyers and judges will have significantly different consequences for children is another matter, however. That determination will require careful observation of the way school reform and school finance reform unfold in the years ahead.

In any event, what does seem clear is that litigation aimed at achieving school finance reform has not yet run its course. We should look for the filing of more "adequacy" cases. We should anticipate that some states with "adequacy" decisions against them will be hauled back into court on the ground that they have not done enough. And, we should expect that some lawyers will continue to bring some traditional "equity" cases, as exemplified by the recent Vermont case.

Moreover, once "adequacy" talk becomes more common, we might expect to see more intra-district school finance cases. In the past, this has not been viewed as a fruitful litigation target because of the absence of an obvious structural objection to the way districts distribute their money to schools. This is in contrast to the ready objection that has been mounted against the local property tax-based system for getting money to districts. Moreover, the schools with the most children from low-income families and the highest proportion of educationally-least-successful children often spend more dollars per pupil than the district average when state and federal categorical aid are counted. But as judicial concerns about need and outcomes come more to the fore, there are sure to be those whose objections may be couched in terms of how poor children in some schools within urban districts fare compared with other children in the district. Indeed, litigation of this sort is ongoing now in Los Angeles.

In conclusion, although there may be less school finance inequity today than there was 30 years ago, a substantial degree remains.[29] To the extent that states with successful school finance litigation have less inequality, and this appears broadly to be the case, reformers will have continued reason to take their battles to the courtroom. This incentive is magnified as courts show a broad willingness to respond to the widespread view that the whole public schooling enterprise is inadequate, especially in its failure to educate successfully too many of our urban poor children. Whether school finance reform alone can turn that failure around remains quite unclear. For example, no one has been able to show that the narrowed spending differentials achieved by successful school finance equity cases in the 1970s and 1980s directly led to a narrowing of educational achievement differentials. Yet advocates for judicial intervention continue to believe not only that school finance reform is required by the norm of basic fairness, but also that reform is a necessary, if not sufficient, condition for improving the educational attainment of those now served poorly by our public schools.

NOTES

1. Most state constitutions contain one or more provisions that either parallel the federal Constitution's equal protection clause or have been interpreted to afford similar protections (Williams, 1985). For typical examples, see Ill. Const., art. 1, sec. 2 (stating that "[n]o person shall . . . be denied the equal protection of the laws"); and Minn Const., art. 1, sec. 2 (stating that "[n]o member of this state shall be disenfranchised or deprived of any of the rights or privileges secured to any citizen thereof, unless by the law of the land").

2. State constitutions' education clauses vary in their language, although all impose a duty on the state government to make provision for a "system" of education. State education clauses are collected in an appendix to Hubsch (1992). A number of them require state legislatures to provide for a "thorough and efficient system" of public schools. See, e.g., N.J. Const., art. 8, sec. 4, para. 1. Others impose a duty on the state to make "ample" provisions for a "system" of education. See, e.g., Mass. Const., pt. 2, ch. 5, sec. 2.

3. For a thorough discussion of the equal protection jurisprudence at the time, see *Serrano v. Priest*, 487 P.2d 1241, 1255-59 (Cal. 1971).

4. See *Baker v. Carr*, 398 U.S. 186 (1962).

5. See *McInnis v. Shapiro*, 293 F. Supp. 327 (N.D. Il. 1968), *aff'd sub nom.*, *McInnis v. Ogilvie*, 349 U.S. 322 (1969); *Burrus v. Wilkerson*, 310 F. Supp. 572 (W.D. Va. 1969), *aff'd per curiam*, 397 U.S. 44 (1970).

6. The Coons team's theory also was accepted by a federal district court in Minnesota, *Van Dusartz v. Hatfield*, 334 F. Supp. 870 (D. Minn. 1971), but the *Rodriguez* decision soon rendered that victory moot.

7. See *Dandridge v. Williams*, 397 U.S. 471 (1970).

8. See, e.g., *U.S. v. Guest*, 383 U.S. 745 (1966); *Shapiro v. Thompson*, 394 U.S. 618 (1969); *Oregon v. Mitchell*, 400 U.S. 112 (1970) (opinion of Brennan, White, and Marshall, JJ.).

9. Litigation concerning other areas of students' rights protected by statute and the U.S. Constitution, such as special education, desegregation, and bilingual education, sometimes have had significant consequences for school finance and resource allocation in many states throughout the country. For example, as a result of school desegregation litigation in the late 1980s, the state of Missouri was compelled by the court to allocate hundreds of millions of dollars to the Kansas City school district (*Missouri v. Jenkins*, 495 U.S. 33, 1990).

10. Underwood (1995) provides a thorough discussion of the constitutional basis for state school finance decisions.

11. See *Serrano v. Priest (Serrano II)*, 557 P.2d 929, 951 (Cal. 1976), *cert. denied*, 432 U.S. 907 (1977); *Pauley v. Kelly*, 255 S.W.2d 859, 878 (W.Va. 1979); *Washakie Co. Sch. Dist. v. Herschler*, 606 P.2d 310, 340 (Wyo. 1980), *cert. denied*, 449 U.S. 824 (1980).

12. A number of state equal protection cases involving challenges to school

finance systems have proceeded to overturn those systems applying the less rigorous rational basis test. See *Dupree v. Alma Sch. Dist. No. 30*, 651 S.W.2d 90 (Ark. 1983); *Edgewood v. Kirby*, 777 S.W.2d 391 (Tex. 1989); *Tennessee Small Sch. Systems v. McWherter*, 851 S.W.2d 139 (Tenn. 1993).

13.   As the Tennessee Supreme Court observed: "The decisions of the courts in [other] jurisdictions provide little guidance in construing the reach of the education clause of the Tennessee constitution. This is true because the decisions by the courts of other states are necessarily controlled in large measure by the particular working of the constitutional provisions of those state charters regarding education and, to a lesser extent, organization and funding" (*Tennessee Sm. Sch. Sys. v. McWherter*, 851 S.W.2d 139, Tenn. 1993).

14.   See, e.g., *Rose v. The Council*, 790 S.W.2d 186 (Ky. 1989); *McDuffy v. Secretary of Education*, 615 N.E.2d 516 (Mass. 1993).

15.   Note also that the Connecticut Supreme Court embraced the Coons team's theory in a 1977 decision, *Horton v. Meskill*, 376 A.2d 359 (Conn. 1977).

16.   See *Thompson v. Engelking*, 537 P.2d 635 (Idaho, 1975*); Olsen v. State*, 554 P.2d 139 (Oreg. 1976); *Danson v. Casey*, 399 A.2d 360 (Pa. 1979).

17.   *San Antonio Indep. Sch. Dist. v. Rodriguez*, 337 F. Supp. 280 (W.D. Tex. 1971); *Van Dusartz v. Hatfield*, 333 F. Supp. 870 (D. Minn. 1971)

18.   *Thompson v. Engelking*, 537 P.2d 635 (Idaho 1975); *Olsen v. State*, 554 P. 2d 139 (Idaho 1976); *Board of Educ. v. Walter*, 390 N.E.2d 813 (Ohio 1979); *Danson v. Casey*, 399 A.2d 360 (Pa. 1979).

19.   The cutbacks included the elimination of all kindergarten classes, athletic programs, extracurricular programs, the music program, all library programs, school lunch and breakfast programs, all bussing programs except for special education, all counseling services, and approximately 536 reading teachers (*Danson*, 1979).

20.   *Washakie Co. Sch. Dist. v. Herschler*, 606 P.2d 310 (Wyo. 1980); *Dupree v. Alma Sch. Dist. No. 30*, 651 S.W.2d 90 (Ark. 1983).

21.   *McDaniels v. Thomas*, 285 S.E.2d 156 (Ga. 1981); *Levittown v. Nyquist*, 439 N.E.2d 359 (N.Y. 1982); *Lujan v. Co. Bd. of Educ.*, 649 P.2d 1005 (Col. 1982); *Hornbeck v. Somerset Co.*, 458 A.2d 758 (Md. 1983); *East Jackson v. Michigan*, 348 N.W.2d 303 (Mich. App. 1984); *Fair School v. Oklahoma*, 746 P.2d 1135 (Okla. 1987*); Britt v. North Carolina*, 357 S.E.2d 432 (N.C. 1987); *Richland v. Campbell*, 364 S.E.2d 470 (S.C. 1988).

22.   *Hornbeck v. Somerset Co. Bd. of Educ.* (1983); *Britt v. State of North Carolina* (1987); *Board of Educ. v. Nyquist* (1987); *Kukor v. Grover* (1989).

23.   For example, in Maryland the court noted that: "No evidentiary showing was made . . .—indeed no allegation was even advanced—that these [state] qualitative [education] standards were not being met in any school district, . . . or that the State's school financing scheme did not provide all school districts with the means essential to provide the basic education contemplated" by the Constitution (*Hornbeck v. Somerset Co. Bd. of Educ.*, 1983).

24. In that same year, Wisconsin's school finance plan was upheld (*Kukor v. Grover*, 1989).

25. As a result of the new legislation, revenues for all school districts increased; the poorest districts increased 25 percent and the richest increased 8 percent (Alexander, 1991).

26. *Leandro v. State of North Carolina*, No. 179PA96 (July 24, 1997) (relying on Kentucky's definition of adequate education); *Claremont Sch. Dist. v Gregg*, 635 A.2d 1375 (N.H. 1993) (state constitution required the state to create and maintain an adequate education system that "includes broad educational opportunities needed in today's society to prepare citizens for their role as participants and as potential competitors in today's marketplace of ideas"); *Tennessee Small School Systems v. McWherter*, 851 S.W.2d 139 (Tenn. 1993) ("The General Assembly shall maintain and support a system of free public schools that provides at least the opportunity to acquire general knowledge, develop the powers of reasoning and judgment, and generally prepare students intellectually for a mature life"); *Roosevelt Elem. Sch. Dist. v. Bishop*, 877 P.2d 806 (Ariz. 1994); *Campaign for Fiscal Equity v. State of New York*, 86 N.Y.2d 307 (N.Y. 1995) (state is constitutionally obligated to create and maintain an education system that provides children with: "the basic literacy, calculation, and verbal skills necessary to enable [them] to eventually function productively as civic participants capable of voting and serving on a jury . . . [and] minimally adequate physical facilities and classrooms . . . to permit children to learn").

27. See *Coalition for Adequacy v. Chiles*, 680 So.2d 400 (Fla. 1996). ("Appellants have failed to demonstrate . . . an appropriate standard for determining 'adequacy' that would not present a substantial risk of judicial intrusion into the powers and responsibilities assigned to the legislature"); *City of Pawtucket v. Sundlun*, 662 A.2d 40 (R.I. 1995) ("what constitutes an 'equal, adequate, and meaningful' [education] is 'not likely to be divined for all time even by the scholars who now so earnestly debate the issues'").

28. See, e.g., *Sch. Admin. Dist. #1 v. Commissioner of Educ., St. of Maine*, 659 A.2d 854 (Maine 1995) (plaintiffs claims focused on equity and they did not claim that they were receiving an inadequate education); *Scott v. State of Virginia*, 443 S.E.2d 138 (Va. 1994) (state education clause required that state system allow each school district to provide an educational program that meets standards of quality as determined by the legislature, and no district before the court claimed that they could not meet such standards); *Skeen v. State of Minnesota*, 505 N.W.2d 299 (Minn. 1993) (the education clause required the state to provide enough funds to ensure that each student receives an adequate education, but the plaintiff school districts before the court conceded that they were providing such an education to their students with existing resources).

29. See *School Finance: State Efforts to Reduce Funding Gaps Between Poor and Wealthy Districts*, U.S. General Accounting Office, February 1997.

The GAO report presents data as of the 1991-92 school year and hence captures no reforms undertaken since then (although it does note which states have made significant changes since 1992). By our count, the following 10 states may perhaps be said to have had successful school finance litigation an appreciable time in advance of the GAO data collection date, with the date noted representing the date of the first successful high court decision: Arkansas (1983), California (1971), Connecticut (1977), Kentucky (1989), Montana (1989), New Jersey (1973), Texas (1989), Washington (1978), West Virginia (1979), and Wyoming (1985). Of course, for some of these states reform efforts made in response to court decisions may not yet have been significantly implemented by 1991-92; in others, time has eroded the earlier impact of reform; and in several, the state was taken back to court after the GAO 1991-92 cutoff date. Nonetheless, taken as a whole, these 10 states appear generally to rate more favorably on GAO's various measures of state effort to promote equity. For example, in the GAO report, Figure 1 (p. 8) illustrates the extent to which wealthy districts (as the GAO measures them) spend more than poor districts. Six of the 10 states noted above are in the bottom third (with the least amount of inequality), and only one is in the top third (most inequality). Figure 5 (p. 17) ranks the states in terms of what they have done to equalize spending. Six of the 10 states noted above are in the top third (most equalization); only three are in the bottom third (least equalization). Table 2 (p. 20) displays which states need to do the most to maximize their equalization efforts. Six of the 10 states noted above are not on the list, and none of the 10 is in the worst category (those needing both to shift considerable funds from rich to poor and to increase funding to the poor significantly). Because of the age of the GAO data and the particular ways in which it chooses to measure equity, one should be very careful not to make too much of these findings. Nevertheless, we suggest these results are readily taken by reformers to indicate that litigation can make a difference, and as a result, we should anticipate the school finance litigation effort to continue.

REFERENCES

Alexander, K.
    1991   The common school ideal and the limits of legislative authority: The Kentucky case. *Harvard Journal of Legislation* 28(2):341-366.
Clune, W.H.
    1993   The shift from equity to adequacy in school finance. *The World and I* 8(9):389-405.
Coleman, J.S., E.Q. Campbell, C.J. Hobson, J. McPartland, A.M. Mead, F.D. Weinfeld, and R.L. York
    1966   *Equality of Educational Opportunity.* Washington, DC: U.S. Department of Health, Education and Welfare.

Coons, J.E., W.H. Clune, and S.D. Sugarman
  1969   Educational opportunity: A workable constitutional test for state financial structures. *California Law Review* 57(2):305-421.
  1970   *Private Wealth and Public Education.* Cambridge, MA: Harvard University Press.
Enrich, P.
  1995   Leaving equality behind: New directions in school finance reform. *Vanderbilt Law Review* 48:101-194.
Evans, W., S. Murray, and R. Schwab
  1997   Schoolhouses, courthouses, and statehouses after *Serrano. Journal of Policy Analysis and Management* 16(1):10-31.
Franklin, D.
  1987   The Constitutionality of the K-12 Funding System in Illinois. Illinois State University, Center for the Study of School Finance.
Heise, M.
  1995   State constitutions, school finance litigation, and the "third wave": From equity to adequacy. *Temple Law Review* 68:1151-1176.
Hickrod, G.A., L. McNeal, R. Lenz, P. Minorini, and L. Grady
  1997   Status of School Finance Constitutional Litigation, 'The Box Score': In *Illinois State University, College of Education* [online]. Available: http://www.coe.ilstu.edu/boxscore.htm [April 25, 1997].
Horowitz, H.
  1966   Unseparate but unequal: The emerging Fourteenth Amendment issue in public school education. *UCLA Law Review* 13:1147-1172.
Horowitz, H., and D. Neitring
  1968   Equal protection aspects of inequalities in public education and public assistance programs from place to place within a state. *UCLA Law Review* 15:787-816.
Hubsch, A.
  1992   The emerging right to education under state constitutional law. *Temple Law Review* 65:1325-1348.
McUsic, M.
  1991   The use of education clauses in school finance reform litigation. *Harvard Journal on Legislation* 28(2):307-341.
Thro, W.E.
  1993   The role of language of the state education clause in school finance litigation. *West's Education Law Reporter* 79:19-31.
Trimble, C.S., and A.C. Forsaith
  1995   Achieving equity and excellence in Kentucky education. *University of Michigan Journal of Law Reform* 28(3):599-653.
Underwood, J.K.
  1995   School finance adequacy as vertical equity. *University of Michigan Journal of Law Reform* 28(3):493-519.
U.S. General Accounting Office
  1997   *School Finance: State Efforts to Reduce Funding Gaps Between Poor and Wealthy Districts.* GAO/HEHS-97-31. Washington, DC: U.S. General Accounting Office.
Verstegen, D.
  1995   School Finance Reform Litigation: Emerging Theories of Adequacy and Equity. Unpublished paper presented at the American Public Policy and Management Association Annual Conference, November 3, 1995.

Wise, A.
    1968   *Rich Schools, Poor Schools: The Promise of Equal Educational Opportunity.* Chicago: University of Chicago Press.
Williams, R.F.
    1985   Equality guarantees in state constitutions. *Texas Law Review* 63:1195-1224.

3

The Impact of Court-Mandated School Finance Reform

William N. Evans, Sheila E. Murray, and Robert M. Schwab

INTRODUCTION

Through the 1960s, local governments provided the majority of funds for public primary and secondary education in the United States. Because property taxes have traditionally been the primary source of local tax revenue, the resources devoted to education were to a large extent a function of the property tax base in a community. Critics argued that this finance system was inherently unfair and, following the success of *Serrano v. Priest* (1971), repeatedly challenged the constitutionality of local funding plans in court.

Table 3-1 summarizes the status of finance reform litigation.[1] By 1998, supreme courts in 43 states had heard cases on the constitutionality of school finance systems. The courts have overturned systems in 19 states and upheld systems in 20; cases are still pending in the remaining 4. In addition, litigation has been filed in a number of states where the state supreme court had already ruled. In California, for example, there have now been three separate decisions in the *Serrano* case.

The legal grounds under which school finance systems have been challenged have varied over time. Heise (1995) has defined three "waves" of education finance cases. The first-wave cases, typified by *Serrano,* focused on the Equal Protection Clause of the United States Constitution. In 1973, the U.S. Supreme Court ruled in *San Antonio Independent School District v. Rodriguez* that local finance did not violate the U.S. Constitution and thus closed off this initial line of attack. The second wave began with a 1973 New Jersey case, *Robinson v. Cahill,* and looked to state constitutions for relief. In part, these cases appealed to state

72

TABLE 3-1   Summary of States with Court-Ordered Reforms, 1971-97[a]

Alabama[b]	1993
Arizona	1994
Arkansas	1983
California	1971
Connecticut	1977
Kansas	1976
Kentucky	1989
Massachusetts	1993
Montana	1989
New Hampshire[c]	1997
New Jersey	1973
Ohio	1997
Tennessee	1993
Texas	1989
Vermont	1997
Washington	1978
West Virginia	1979
Wisconsin	1976
Wyoming	1980

[a]Additional post-1997 reforms are discussed by Minorini and Sugarman (see Chapters 2 and 6 in this volume).

[b]The 1993 Alabama decision is a lower court decision that decided the finance system is unconstitutional. The state has indicated it will not appeal.

[c]In 1993, the New Hampshire State Supreme Court ruled that the state has a duty to fund public education.

SOURCE: Summary of Legislative and Court-Ordered Reforms; Evans, Murray, and Schwab (1997a). Journal of Public Policy Analysis and Management, Copyright © (1997). Reprinted by permission of John Wiley & Sons, Inc.

equal protection clauses and were brought in the interest of equity for school children. In addition, some also looked to state education clauses and argued that local funding violated states' constitutional responsibility to provide efficient and adequate education. The third wave began in 1989 and focused almost exclusively on education clauses in state constitutions. These provisions are often ambiguous and ambitious; the New Jersey constitution, for example, calls for a "thorough and efficient system of free public schools" (New Jersey Constitution, article 8, section 4). The courts in the third-wave cases have relied on such language to require much more sweeping reform of states' public school systems and to take far greater control of financing issues. Minorini and Sugarman (see Chapter 2 in this volume) give a thorough account of the history of school finance litigation.

We should note that although successful litigation was the impetus for many legislative reforms, some states adopted some form of finance reform without the court's prodding. For example, Utah adopted finance reform on its own without judicial intervention. Other states, including Michigan, adopted reforms even though state courts upheld their finance systems.

The remainder of this chapter has the following organization. We first examine the effect of the courts on the distribution and level of education spending per pupil. We begin by looking at the California experience in the aftermath of *Serrano* and then turn to broader empirical studies and studies that have developed simulation models. The next two sections extend the existing literature on the impact of court-ordered reform in three directions and focus on the effect of court-mandated reform on education spending. We first consider the consequences of adjusting expenditures for the costs of inputs (such as teacher salaries). We then look at the impact of successful litigation on low-income districts—as opposed to low-spending districts—and the consequences of reform for black and white students.

A final section looks at some of the other important consequences of court decisions. We begin by examining the impact of the courts on education outcomes and then turn to private contributions to public schools and the demand for private schools. Although the research on court-mandated finance reform has been extensive, clearly not all issues have been resolved, and thus we offer a brief summary and conclusions and some suggestions for future research.

EVIDENCE OF THE IMPACT OF THE COURTS ON EDUCATION FINANCE

Some of the earliest literature on court-mandated reform focused on the California experience. Broader econometric models and simulations models have addressed several implications of court-mandated reform including the effect on the distribution of resources and outcomes.[2]

California Case

The general consensus from the California work has been that the shift toward state financing of education has led to a significant decrease in spending on education. Silva and Sonstelie (1995) try to estimate what proportion of this decline should be attributed to *Serrano* and ensuing policy changes such as Proposition 13, and how much should be attributed to other factors such as changes in income and number of students.[3] They begin by estimating the determinants of education spending using data from all of the states other than California. Using this equation, they show that prior to *Serrano* in 1969-70, spending in California was similar to other states during the same period after adjusting for differences in family income and the tax price of an additional dollar of education. They found a very different story in 1989-90. Spending was significantly lower in California than they would have predicted. They conclude that roughly one-half of the decline in spending in California can be attributed to *Serrano*.

The change in spending in California in the post-*Serrano* era has been dramatic. Rubinfeld (1995) shows that in 1971-72 California spending per pupil was 98 percent of the national average and that California ranked 19th among the states; by 1991-92, California spending was only 86 percent of the national average and the state had fallen to 39th.

Broader Econometric Studies

It is difficult to know the extent to which the California experience can be generalized to all states or to any particular state. The California courts set a particularly strict standard in their definition of equality, requiring that the differences in per-pupil spending among nearly all districts be no greater than $100 (in 1971 dollars). It is quite possible that the *Serrano* decision dramatically reduced public support for education—Fischel (1989), for example, argues that *Serrano* led to the passage of Proposition 13—but that milder reform that simply required higher state support for the poorest districts would have led to a very different reaction.

Broader empirical work can address many of the shortcomings of case studies. By looking at data from many states, these empirical studies allow us to look at more general responses to school finance reform efforts. Manwaring and Sheffrin (1995) use a panel data set from 1970-90 to examine the role of equalization litigation and reform in determining the level of education funding in a dynamic model. They found that on average, successful litigation or legislative education reform raises education spending significantly. The Downes and Shah (1995) analysis is similar in some ways to the Manwaring and Sheffrin (1995) model. They show that the stringency of constraints on local discretion determines the effects of reforms on the level and growth of spending. Further, for any particular type of reform, the characteristics of a state's school population determine the direction and magnitude of the post-reform changes in spending.

We took a different approach in Murray et al. (1998). In that paper, we looked at the impact of court-ordered reform on the distribution of spending within states as well as the average level of spending across states. Our study was based on data for the more than 10,000 unified elementary and secondary school districts over the 20-year period 1972-92.[4] Table 3-2 presents some summary statistics from that paper. The first section looks at the level and sources of funding. Real resources per student grew at an average rate of 2.1 percent per year during this period.[5] The distribution of resources changed substantially over these 20 years. Revenues from state sources rose very quickly during 1972-87 and, as a consequence, the states' share of total resources increased from 38.3 percent to 49.3 percent. Revenues from the states then grew slowly during 1987-

TABLE 3-2   Summary of Current Education Expenditures, 1972-92

Measure	1972	1977	1982	1987	1992
Funding per Student ($1992)					
Local	1,923	1,881	1,799	2,163	2,621
State	1,394	1,708	1,903	2,451	2,587
Federal	325	346	297	315	368
Total	3,642	3,935	3,999	4,929	5,576
Measures of Inequality					
95/5 ratio	2.72	2.37	2.22	2.53	2.40
Coefficient of variation	30.8	28.1	25.6	29.6	29.9
Gini coefficient (×100)	16.3	15.0	13.8	15.8	15.5
Theil Index (×1000)	43.7	37.1	31.0	40.7	40.5
Theil Index Decomposition					
Within states	13.7	14.4	14.0	12.6	13.4
Between states	30.0	22.8	17.0	28.2	27.1
National	43.7	37.2	31.0	40.7	40.5
Variance Decomposition					
Within states	32.2	41.5	47.5	32.8	35.3
Between states	67.8	58.5	52.5	67.2	64.7
National	100.0	100.0	100.0	100.0	100.0

SOURCE: Funding per student from National Center for Education Statistics, *Digest of Education Statistics, 1994* (1994b). Education expenditure inequality measures are authors' calculations from Bureau of the Census, *Census of Government School System Finance File* (F-33), various years. Calculations exclude school districts from Alaska, District of Columbia, Hawaii, Montana, and Vermont.

92. Local funding increased throughout this period, including the last five years; in 1992, local governments contributed 47.0 percent of all of public education resources. The federal government played a small and shrinking role throughout 1972-92.

The second section in Table 3-2 gives several measures of inequality in district spending at the national level. Each of these measures rises when spending inequality rises.[6] The measures we chose give a bound on the effect of court-mandated reform. The ratio of the 95th percentile in per-pupil spending to the 5th percentile in spending is a simple ranking that treats transfers to the top or bottom of the distribution the same; changes in spending in the rest of the distribution change the 95th to 5th ratio. Changes throughout the distribution of spending contribute to the values of the coefficient of variation and the Gini coefficient. The Theil coefficient gives more weight to changes in the tails of the distribution.

The Theil index is attractive in part because it is relatively easy to decompose the Theil into disparity in spending between and within states.

All of the inequality measures in Table 3-2 follow a similar pattern. Spending at the 95th percentile was 2.72 times higher than spending at the 5th percentile in 1972. This ratio then fell to 2.40 in 1992, suggesting a narrowing of the differences in spending across students. The Theil index fell during the 1970s and early 1980s, rose sharply between 1982 and 1987, and then remained roughly constant. Inequality according to all four measures was higher in 1992 than in 1982 and somewhat lower than in 1972.

The next two sections of Table 3-2 break spending inequality into two components: inequality due to differences in spending within states and inequality due to differences across states. That part of Table 3-2 makes a number of interesting points. We found that between-state inequality is much larger than within-state inequality. In 1992, variation across the states represented 64.7 percent of the total variance in per-pupil spending; between-state inequality accounted for 66.9 percent of the national Theil index that year. Putting these trends together, Table 3-2 shows that more than 90 percent of the reduction in the Theil index during 1972-92 was due to a reduction in inequality between states; there was little change in inequality within states. This would suggest that the litigation that began with *Serrano* is limited in its ability to equalize the education resources available to students.

We then estimated a series of econometric models to explain state-level inequality. We used two different variables to mark the timing of reform. Initially, we included a simple indicator variable *Court Reform* that equals 1 in all years after court-ordered education finance reform, and zero otherwise. Because we suspect reform will take some time to alter inequality, we also used a second variable, *Years After Court Reform*, which equals the number of years since the state supreme court overturned a finance system. Thus, for example, this variable always equals 0 in those states without successful litigation.

We came to three main conclusions. First, court-mandated education finance reform can decrease within-state inequality significantly. Depending on the way we measure inequality, our results imply that reform in the wake of a court decision reduces spending inequality within a state by anywhere from 19 to 34 percent. Second, our results suggest that court-ordered reform reduces inequality by raising spending at the bottom of the distribution while leaving spending at the top unchanged. As a result of court-ordered reform, we found that spending would rise by 11 percent in the poorest school districts, rise by 7 percent in the median district, and remain roughly constant in the wealthiest districts. Third, finance reform leads states to increase spending for education and leave spending in other areas unchanged, and thus, by implication, states fund the additional spending on education through higher taxes. As a consequence, the state's share of total spending rises as a result of court-ordered reform.

Using our estimates of the reduction in inequality due to court-mandated reform and the average within state inequality presented in Table 3-2, we can also consider what would have happened to inequality in the absence of court-mandated reform. Our estimates imply that inequality as measured by the Theil index is 34 percent lower in reform states than in nonreform states. For the reform states we constructed a predicted Theil for each state by combining the actual Theil and the inequality lost due to reform. For the nonreform states, our predicted Theil remained the same as the actual. We then recalculated the weighted average of our within-state inequality measure. Without a court mandate, average within-state inequality would increase 9 percent (from 13.4 to 14.6) in 1992. Thus, while it is true that within-state inequality was essentially unchanged between 1972 and 1992, our estimates suggest that it would have risen sharply in the absence of court-ordered finance reform.

In Evans et al. (1997a) we tried to separate the responses of state and local governments to court mandates. We began by identifying the district at the 5th, 25th, 50th, 75th, and 95th percentile of the distribution of *local* resources in each state. We then used a district's per-pupil local, state, and total revenues as the dependent variable in a series of 30 econometric models (5 points in the distribution × 3 sources of funds × 2 reform variables).

Table 3-3 presents some of our results from that paper. We find in Table 3-3 that, following court-mandated reform, total revenues rose significantly in districts with the lowest local revenues. All of this increase represents additional funds from the state government; we find some mixed evidence that some of this additional state money replaces local revenue. We also find that revenues in the districts with highest local revenues are essentially unchanged by court-ordered reform.

Consider first the results based on *Court Reform* (the middle three columns in Table 3-3). Following reform, real revenue per student rose by $560 for the district at the 5th percentile of the distribution (16 percent of the mean expenditures for that district) and by $500 (13 percent) for the district at the 25th percentile. Local revenue fell in those districts, but the effect is not significantly different from zero, and thus all of the increase in revenues represents additional funds from the states. Estimated changes in revenues at the 75th and 95th percentile are much smaller than at the bottom of the distribution and are statistically insignificant. The results based on *Years After Court Reform* (the last three columns of Table 3-3) are similar, though there are some interesting differences. We again find large and significant increases in revenue in the lowest-revenue districts and small and insignificant changes in the highest-revenue districts. We also find that, in the districts at the 5th and 25th percentile of the distribution, increases in state revenue in part offset decreases in local revenue. Our results suggest, for example, that successful litigation will lead a state government to provide the lowest-revenue districts additional state aid of $700 per student 10 years after reform. These districts reduced local revenue by $190, and thus total revenue

TABLE 3-3 Impact of Court-Mandated Finance Reform on the Distribution of Education Resources, 1972-92

Percentile of Per-Pupil Revenues from Local Sources	Means {Standard Deviations} Per-Pupil Revenues ($1992) by Source			Coefficient {Standard Error} on *Court Reform*; Dependent Variable Per-Pupil Revenues ($1992) by Source			Coefficient {Standard Error} on *Years after Court Reform*; Dependent Variable Per-Pupil Revenues ($1992) by Source		
	Local	State	Total	Local	State	Total	Local	State	Total
5th	1,074 {584}	2,510 {1,092}	3,584 {1,173}	-152.5 {83.95}	712.45 {204.7}	559.95 {192.5}	-19.40 {6.93}	70.06 {16.88}	50.66 {16.02}
25th	1,521 {741}	2,209 {907}	3,730 {1,106}	-99.93 {95.41}	600.34 {178.6}	500.41 {193.2}	-21.07 {7.84}	101.50 {13.39}	80.44 {15.31}
50th	1,913 {907}	2,063 {815}	3,976 {1,106}	5.96 {120.2}	310.72 {155.0}	316.68 {182.1}	-8.763 {10.03}	45.71 {12.64}	36.95 {15.09}
75th	2,446 {1,195}	1,833 {836}	4,279 {1,232}	115.69 {170.7}	128.24 {163.2}	243.93 {184.1}	3.326 {14.29}	21.62 {13.56}	24.94 {15.35}
95th	3,396 {1,741}	1,622 {817}	5,018 {1,596}	136.56 {266}	135.38 {165.3}	271.94 {271.5}	-9.407 {22.24}	26.99 {13.70}	17.58 {22.72}

SOURCE: Impact of Court-Mandated Finance Reform on the Distribution of Education Resources, 1972-1992; Evans, Murray, and Schwab (1997a). Journal of Public Policy Analysis and Management, Copyright (1997). Reprinted by permission of John Wiley & Sons, Inc.

rose by $510. Court-ordered reform, according to these estimates, is in part a way of providing tax relief to the lowest-spending school districts in the state.

Card and Payne (1997) also consider the possibility that increases in state funding for education were offset by decreases in local funding. They find that this fiscal substitution effect was small, though their estimate is imprecise and they thus cannot rule out the possibility that some of the equalizing effect of state finance reform is "undone" by changes in local revenue.

Hoxby (1996) offers a very different view of the impact of court-ordered school finance reform. There are two key elements to Hoxby's approach. First, she treats school finance reform not as an event but rather as a change in the structure of school state aid. These changes in state aid change the incentives facing local schools districts. This framework allows Hoxby to exploit differences in the "price" of a $1 of education across states, across districts within states, and across time to estimate the effects of different types of reform. By price, Hoxby means the cost to the residents if they choose to increase total education spending (inclusive of state and federal aid) by $1. The econometric part of the paper then estimates total spending as a function of price, income, and demographic variables. Second, in Hoxby's paper school districts can increase spending by raising either the property tax rate or the property tax base. Changes in the structure of state aid change the optimal tax base and rate.

Hoxby's results are provocative. The paper argues that near-equality of per-pupil resources cannot be achieved without substantial decreases in the average level of per-pupil resources. In fact, it finds that districts with low income or low property value end up with lower per-pupil spending under equalization schemes that achieve near equality. These results follow directly from her estimates of the impact of price on school spending. Strong equalization plans raise the price of education for most districts and as a consequence local spending falls sharply; in many cases she finds that lower local spending more than offsets potentially higher state aid.

We have a number of concerns about this paper, in part because Hoxby's conclusion does not seem to be consistent with the spending patterns that have emerged in the aftermath of reform in most states. We discussed the evidence on this point above, but we can make this point in a somewhat more straightforward way. There were court decisions in 12 states between 1971 and 1992 (the last year of our study). Consider a simple "difference in difference calculation" where we compare the growth in expenditures per student after reform in a state to the growth in expenditures per student in the entire country. For example, the Connecticut decision was in 1977. From 1977 through 1992, expenditures per student in Connecticut rose 9.3 percent per year. For the nation as a whole, expenditures rose 7.5 percent per year during that period, and thus Connecticut expenditures rose 1.9 percentage points faster than the U.S. average following school finance litigation. If Hoxby's argument is correct, then we would expect Connecticut to be an outlier, or at the minimum we would expect to find a number of states where expenditures grew slowly or fell after a court decision. But Connecticut is not an outlier. In 10 of the 12 states we examined, expenditures rose at least as fast as the U.S. average in the aftermath of school finance litigation; California and Wyoming are the two exceptions to this rule.

We would also argue that Hoxby's characterization of reform in terms of the price of education is not completely convincing. While conceptually this framework might make sense, it is not at all clear that this sort of model could capture the impact of court-ordered reform. In general, these models rarely describe the effects of aid from higher levels of government very well. For example, this model would predict that a $1 lump-sum grant from the state would have the same effect on spending as would a $1 increase in income; in fact, grants are almost invariably found to have a much larger effect on spending than the theory would predict (the flypaper effect). Reform does not always fit neatly into the economist's view of the world. The paper's treatment of the California experience illustrates this problem. Hoxby (1996:20) assigns California the state required tax rate on the grounds that otherwise the marginal price of education would be $1. But in fact, given the rigidities of local school finance in post-*Serrano*, post-Proposition 13 California, the marginal price of education to a local district is probably infinite; districts have essentially lost all control over spending.

We are also concerned about a second conceptual issue. As we noted above, in Hoxby's paper school districts can increase spending by raising either the property tax rate or the property tax base. This notion of the districts choosing their tax base is odd. If we followed this line of reasoning to its logical limit then we would conclude that there are no property-rich or property-poor districts, only districts that find it optimal to have a large tax base and others that find it optimal to have a small tax base. There are avenues through which districts can change property values; the paper points to capitalization, for example. But as a first approximation, it seems much more sensible to take tax base as given when thinking about the price of education than to think about a district consciously trying to change its tax base in order to manipulate state aid.

This endogeneity of the tax base has important implications in Hoxby's paper for the estimated tax price. Consider, for example, district power-equalization programs (DPE).[7] The standard analysis of a DPE assumes implicitly that a school district's tax base is fixed. Under a DPE, the state would choose a tax base per student V^*. District j would then act "as if" its tax base were V^* rather than V_j (assuming for the moment that V^* is greater than V_j). That is, if it sets a tax rate t_j it will raise $t_j V_j$ from local sources, receive state aid $A_j = t_j(V^* - V_j)$, and thus spend $E_j = t_j V^*$ on education. To put things slightly differently, if a district wishes to spend E_j it would choose $t_j = E_j / V^*$ and therefore receive $A_j = E_j(1 - V_j / V^*)$. Thus, under a guaranteed tax base grant it costs local governments only V_j / V^* (which is less than 1) to raise an additional dollar of resources.[8]

In the Hoxby analysis, the community could choose (optimally) to increase

V_j in order to increase spending. But increases in V_j will lower state aid, and therefore the local price of education could be greater than $1 even if V^* is greater than V_j. Hoxby estimates that aggressive equalization programs (in her analysis, Florida, Illinois, Minnesota, New Jersey, New York, Oklahoma, Texas, and Utah) typically have prices in the range of $1.20, though those states contain districts that face very different tax prices. These estimated tax prices play a crucial role in Hoxby's paper; if we are not comfortable with this conceptual framework, then we need to consider her conclusions very cautiously.

In all, we would argue that Hoxby's paper represents an important methodological contribution to the literature. Our approach cannot capture the differences in the nature of the reforms across states. These differences were sometimes substantial; as we noted above, the California Supreme Court in the *Serrano* decision, for example, required that spending per student vary by no more than $100 per student in the vast majority of districts. Thus, our finance reform variables reflect the average effect of a court decision but cannot capture the effects of a particular decision. Hoxby's approach allows her to draw distinctions among reforms. Most of the available evidence from econometric studies of the experience of the states where the courts have overturned the system of school finance suggests that court-ordered reform has, in general, (1) raised the average level of spending and (2) successfully reduced inequality in spending. We believe that those conclusions are correct.

Simulation Models

The final source of evidence of the effects of school reforms on the level of spending and education and economic outcomes comes from simulation models. Nechyba (1997), Fernandez and Rogerson (1997), and Epple and Romano (1995) have all developed computable general equilibrium models that allow them to explore the effects of education finance reform. The Nechyba and Epple and Romano models are similar in spirit. Both models look at a metropolitan area and include housing markets, mobility, and a public sector where policy is determined as in the median voter model. In both, educational output depends on education spending and peer-group effects. The Fernandez and Rogerson model does not consider peer group effects, but does offer one important extension. It is a dynamic model, and education is not a consumption good but an investment good. The current elderly care about the current young's income, which is determined in part by education investments. All three models look at a fundamental question: What happens in a general equilibrium setting when we move from decentralized to centralized school finance?[9]

The answers these three models offer are intriguing. Fernandez and Rogerson find that a centralized education finance system could generate significant welfare gains. Centralized finance reduces heterogeneity in education spending and can change the income distribution as well as the average income in society.

Given their specification of the model and choice of parameter values, they find that centralized finance leads to higher average income in the steady state, higher average spending on education, and higher welfare. The welfare improvement from centralization is on the order of 10 percent of aggregate income. Nechyba (1997) finds that both foundation aid and district power equalization grants increase the attractiveness of lower-income communities and thus decrease segregation by income. Centralized finance systems in his model caused peer effects to lead to increased income segregation as peer groups become the only way to improve local schools.

The attraction of simulation models designed to study the impact of centralized school finance is obvious. In an ideal world from a researcher's perspective, we would like to watch a society function under a decentralized finance system, and then rerun history after the courts require more equal funding of schools. General equilibrium simulation models allow us to do that (at least on a computer).

The problem is that these models are based on some very strong assumptions. Unfortunately, sometimes we have limited knowledge about important relationships in the models, and it is therefore difficult for us to evaluate those assumptions. In the Fernandez and Rogerson (1997) model, for example, a key relationship is the impact of education on income. As we explained above, they concluded that court-mandated reform that equalized spending will decrease income inequality as well. This result turns on two assumptions: (1) current education expenditures is an important determinant of future income, and (2) there are decreasing marginal returns to education.

While both of these assumptions seem plausible, the evidence to support them is weak. Most of the evidence on the effectiveness of education expenditures focuses on the relationship between spending and education outcomes typically measured in terms of scores on standardized tests. Coleman et al. (1966) argued strongly that tests scores and spending are unrelated and that, instead, family socioeconomic status and perhaps peer groups are the key determinants of success in school. Most of the subsequent literature on education production functions has come to the same conclusion. Hanushek (1986), in his often cited review of this literature, summarized more than 150 studies that followed Coleman and concluded that "there appears to be no strong or systematic relationship between school expenditures and student performance."

There have been several recent attacks on this "money doesn't matter" argument.[10] Ferguson and Ladd (1996) show that properly specified econometric models do find that additional resources generate better outcomes. Others have argued that measures other than test scores should be considered in the debate. Murray (1995) focuses on the impact of spending on the probability of finishing high school and starting college on the grounds that the amount of education someone receives is clearly linked to wages. She finds that additional spending can substantially increase the probability that students will finish school; her results imply, for example, that a 12 percent increase in spending by the poorest 5 percent of school districts would result in a 6 percent decrease in the dropout rate. Card and Krueger (1992) provide some important direct evidence that increases in education spending raise the rate of return to education. However, Betts (1995), using data from the National Longitudinal Survey of Youth (NLSY), finds no evidence that increases in spending raise wages. In all, it seems fair to conclude that the impact of expenditures on incomes—assumption (1) we noted above—is an unresolved and important issue. Given the uncertainty surrounding the size of the marginal benefits of education spending, the rate at which those benefits decline—assumption (2) above—must certainly be regarded as an open question.

EXTENSIONS OF THE LITERATURE ON
EDUCATION FINANCE REFORM

In this section we extend the existing literature on the impact of court-ordered education finance reform in three directions: (1) adjustments for differences in the cost of inputs, (2) the impact on low-household-income districts rather than low-spending districts, and (3) the effect of reform on average spending for black and white students.

Consider first the impact of the courts on the distribution of real resources rather than simply dollars. Most court decisions have focused on dollars; the *Serrano* decision, for example, did not require that all schools have the same teacher-pupil ratio (or, for example, that schools with many students who require compensatory programs must have higher teacher-pupil ratios), but instead subsequent *Serrano* required virtually equal spending across the state.[11] Thus, if the courts equalize spending across districts, then students in high-cost metropolitan areas will receive less real aid than students in low-cost areas. As finance formulas become more centralized, it has become increasingly important to control for a local district's purchasing power. However, only a few states such as Texas, Florida, Alaska, and Ohio actually adjust for geographic differences in the cost of living or the cost of providing education.

We have tried to take a first step toward addressing this problem. We would like to adjust our data on school resources using a measure which consistently adjusts spending for differences across districts and over time. There are several alternative cost indices, but none are available before 1987. We therefore limit our investigation to the impact of these adjustments on the level and the disparity in per-pupil resources at a point in time, 1992.

We use three indices to adjust for differences in the cost of real education resources: the Barro index, Chamber's Teachers' Cost Index (TCI), and McMahon and Chang's Cost of Living index (COL). All three develop separate cost indices for urban and nonurban districts in each state; in some states, separate indices for the largest urban areas are also available. The Barro measure is an index of average teacher salaries that adjusts for teachers' education level and experience. Because a given district can influence teachers' wages by hiring only candidates with graduate degrees, this measure would overstate the adjustment necessary for purchasing power parity among districts. The TCI measure adjusts for regional variations in the cost of living and amenities. This measure removes the impact of within-state differences by adjusting for district level characteristics that, unlike average teacher's educational attainment or tenure, are not subject to district control. Finally, the McMahon and Chang index (1991) is a geographic index that only controls for the differences in housing values, income, and population growth across districts; the McMahon and Chang index yields the smallest inflation adjustment.[12]

Table 3-4 summarizes our attempts to adjust for cost differences between metropolitan and nonmetropolitan school districts in 1992. The first column gives the unadjusted estimates and the remaining columns give the estimates using the Barro, TCI, and COL indices. After controlling for the higher costs associated with urban school districts, we find a noticeable decline in our measures of inequality. For example, both the 95th to 5th ratio and the coefficient of variation decrease by 10 to 20 percent; the Theil index falls by 16 percent (COL) to 37 percent (Barro).

The second section in Table 3-4 breaks revenue inequality into inequality due to differences in revenue within states and inequality due to differences across states, and thus parallels our decomposition of expenditure inequality in

TABLE 3-4   Summary of Resources Adjusted for Cost of Living Differences, 1992

Summary Measure	Unadjusted	Cost of Living Adjustment		
		Barro Cost Index	Chamber's TCI	McMahon-Chang COL
Measures of Inequality				
95 to 5 ratio	2.47	2.07	2.08	2.19
Theil index	37.90	26.40	29.20	32.40
Coefficient of variation	30.10	24.40	25.70	27.10
Theil Index Decomposition				
Within states	12.90	12.20	12.20	12.90
Between states	25.00	14.20	17.00	19.50
National	37.90	26.40	29.20	32.40

SOURCE: Authors' calculations.

Table 3-2. The cost of living adjustments change our view of the magnitude of differences in revenue between states, but within-state Theils do not change appreciably. The cost-adjusted, between-state Theils are 20 to 40 percent lower than the unadjusted Theils. Once we account for differences in costs, we find that differences in revenue between states accounts for 53 to 60 percent of the total disparity in per-pupil resources in the United States; when we do not adjust for cost differences, between-state inequality accounts for 66 percent of total inequality.[13]

We now turn to the impact of reform on low-household-income districts. One of the key goals of the long legal battle over education finance has been to sever the link between the ability to pay for education (as measured in terms of wealth or income) and actual spending. For the most part the literature has focused on the impact of court decisions on low- and high- spending districts. This would be the right direction if spending and income were perfectly correlated. Here we offer some direct evidence on the effect of the courts on districts where the ability to pay for education is limited.

To address these issues we matched our district level resources with district level social and economic data from the 1970, 1980, and 1990 decennial census. The U.S. Bureau of the Census provides a mapping from school district boundaries to census block groups and tracts. We use the district summaries from the 1970 census (*Special Fifth Count Summary Tapes*) from the Bureau of Census (1973), the 1980 census (*Summary Tape File 3F, School Districts* Machine Readable Data file) from the Bureau of the Census (1982b), and the 1990 census (*School District Data Book* CD-ROM) from the National Center for Education Statistics (1994a). For each district in our sample, we calculate a number of important variables, including real household median income and the proportion of the district population that is black. We then match the 1970 census data with 1972 expenditure data, the 1980 census data with 1982 expenditure data, and the 1990 census data with 1992 expenditure data.

To examine the effect of the courts on the link between income and spending, we classify districts by the within-state, pupil-weighted quartile in median family income. Next, for each state/year/quartile group, we calculate the average student-weighted, per-pupil revenues from local and state sources. We then use these values as dependent variables in a series of econometric models. Let Y_{sqit} be the average per-pupil revenues from source s in income quartile q for state i in time t. The basic structure of these models is similar to the ones we employed in previous analysis, where

$$Y_{sqit} = D_{it}\alpha_q + \mu_{qi} + \eta_{qt} + \varepsilon_{sqit} \qquad (1)$$

The variable D_{it} is one of our two court-mandated reform variables, μ_{qi} and η_{qt} are the quartile-specific fixed state and year effects, respectively, and ε_{sqit} is a random error. The fixed-effect model is particularly appropriate in this context since if revenues in reform states were, on average, distributed more unequally on the basis of family income, then omitting the state fixed-effects terms would yield biased estimates of the impact of reform.

We present the estimated coefficient on *Court Reform* for each model in Table 3-5. We find in Table 3-5 that, following court-mandated reform, total revenues rose significantly in the poorest districts, those in the first quartile of household income. All of the increased revenues came from state aid, and some of the state aid provided tax relief to poor districts. Following reform, real revenue per student from state sources rose $804 for the district at the 25th percentile of household districts (20 percent of the mean expenditure for that district). These districts reduced revenues raised from their own sources by 30 percent, or $242 per student. The net effect for this district was an increase in per-pupil revenues of $562 due to court-ordered reform, an amount that is not significantly different from the average increase in per-pupil spending for all districts. It should be noted that our estimate of the impact of reform on local spending is estimated imprecisely, and we cannot reject the hypothesis (at the 5 percent level) that local revenue was unchanged.

In the final three columns of Table 3-5, we report results where the covariate of interest is *Years After Court Reform.* In these models, we again find that state resources were directed more toward districts at the bottom half of the distribution of household income, and the poorest districts (districts in the 25th percentile of household income) used these funds for some form of tax relief. For districts in the first quartile of median family income, after 10 years of reform, state revenues increased by $1,020 but 40 percent of these gains were given back to taxpayers via lower local spending. The results for the *Years After Court Reform* variable also suggest a strong relationship between changes in total revenues and median family income. Because of aggressive state redistribution of funds, students from the poorest districts had the greatest change in total spending. This effect declined monotonically as we move up the income distribution.

An implication of these results is that finance reform has reduced the covariance between income and spending in a state. This can be verified to a degree through the following model.

$$Y_{dit} = X_{dit}\alpha_{it} + I_{dit} + \beta_{it} + \varepsilon_{dit} \qquad (2)$$

Let Y_{dit} be total per-pupil revenues within district d in state i in year t. The covariance between income and spending can be estimated for each state/year pair by the simple regression where I is the median family income within a district, X is a vector of demographic characteristics, and β_{it} the correlation between revenues and income for a state/year pair. We generate estimates for the β value for 3 years and 46 states. We include in X a short list of demographic variables: the fraction of blacks in the school districts, the fraction of homes with school-aged children, and cubic terms in school enrollment. In our sample, the

TABLE 3-5 Impact of Court-Mandated Finance Reform on Per-Pupil Revenue by Source and Distribution of Household Income of Districts

Quartile of Median Household Income	Means {Standard Deviations} Per-Pupil Revenues ($1992) by Source			Coefficient {Standard Error} on Court Reform Dependent Variable: Per-Pupil Revenues ($1992) by Source			Coefficient {Standard Error} on Years after Court Reform Dependent Variable: Per-Pupil Revenues ($1992) by Source		
	Local	State	Total	Local	State	Total	Local	State	Total
First	1,640 {805}	2,367 {1,036}	4,007 {1,288}	-242 {153}	804 {214}	563 {238}	-40 {12}	102 {15}	62 {18}
Second	1,842 {924}	2,005 {848}	3,847 {1,230}	170 {206}	370 {165}	539 {262}	-2 {17}	59 {12}	56 {20}
Third	2,013 {1,021}	1912 {812}	3,926 {1,295}	173 {248}	379 {162}	552 {269}	2 {20}	49 {12}	51 {21}
Fourth	2,456 {1,436}	1,756 {735}	4,211 {1,505}	435 {345}	155 {154}	590 {332}	4 {28}	21 {12}	25 {27}

SOURCE: Authors' calculations.

mean estimate of the β_{it} overall state/year pairs is 0.027. We then use the estimates for β values as dependent variables in a regression of the form

$$\beta_{it} = D_{it}\gamma + \lambda_i + \theta_t + v_{it} \tag{3}$$

where λ and θ are state and year effects, respectively, v_{it} is a random error, and D_{it} is one of our court reform variables. When D_{it} is defined as *Court Reform*, the estimate of γ (standard error) is –0.033 (0.037), whereas when the variable is *Years after Court Reform*, the coefficient is –0.004 (0.002). Thus, the evidence here is somewhat mixed. When we use our *Court Reform* variable, the impact of the courts on the link between income and spending is negative but insignificant; when we use our *Years after Court Reform* variable, the impact is negative and statistically significant. This method and results are similar to the work of Card and Payne (1997), who also find that finance reform has weakened the link between income and spending.

We have also looked at the impact of court-mandated reform on spending for black and white students. Because black students tend to live in low-income districts, we would expect that court-mandated reform would redistribute resources toward black students. Using the distribution of black and white students in a district, we constructed race-specific shares of student enrollments. We then used these shares as weights to estimate race-specific, average per-pupil revenues for each state. We then used the average black and white per-pupil local, state, and total revenues as the dependent variables in a series of six regression models. These estimates are presented in Table 3-6.

The results in Table 3-6 on race parallel our results on income in Table 3-5. We find in Table 3-6 that, following court-mandated reform, state aid directed

TABLE 3-6   Impact of Court-Mandated Finance Reform on Per-Pupil Revenue by Source and Race

Racial Group	Mean {Standard Deviation} Per-Pupil Revenues ($1992) by Source			Coefficient {Standard Error} on *Court Reform* Dependent Variable Per-Pupil Revenues ($1992) by Source		
	Local	State	Total	Local	State	Total
Black	1,876	2,232	4,108	–216	664	448
	{882}	{922}	{1,349}	{178}	{216}	{247}
White	1,978	2,015	3,993	140	434	574
	{986}	{820}	{1,291}	{200}	{155}	{249}

SOURCE: Authors' calculations.

toward black students rose significantly. However, we find some evidence that districts substitute state aid for their own revenues. State aid directed toward black students increased by an estimated $664 per student following reform; local spending on black students fell by $216. Thus, total per-pupil revenue for black students increased by $448 per pupil while per-pupil revenue for white students increased by $574. Here again we need to interpret these results cautiously since many of the parameters in Table 3-6 are imprecise estimates.

OTHER CONSEQUENCES OF COURT-MANDATED EDUCATION FINANCE REFORM

To this point, we have focused on the impact of court-mandated reform on education spending. Here we turn to other consequences of court decisions. We look first at the effect of the courts on education outcomes. We then focus on private contributions and the demand for private schools.

Education Outcomes

There are at least two ways to approach the question of the impact of court-mandated reform on education outcomes. The first is to argue that if finance reform changes outcomes, it does so largely by redistributing resources, and therefore we can answer this question by looking at evidence of the link between resources and outcomes. Several papers have taken this approach. Husted and Kenny (1996b) use data on 1987-88 and 1992-93 SAT scores from 37 states. They conclude that the mean SAT score is higher in those states with greater within-state variation in spending. Hoxby (1996) finds that an aggressive power-equalization plan would raise the dropout rate by 3 percent and that state-financed schools would raise the dropout rate by 8 percent. In general, as we argued above, the link between spending and outcomes is a contentious issue that has received a great deal of attention but remains unresolved nonetheless.

The second approach is to look at changes in outcomes that follow court-mandated reform. This second approach has certain advantages. In particular, it captures any impacts of reform that are unrelated to changes in resources. For example, it is quite plausible to think that some of the education reforms in Kentucky following the *Rose* decision might in the end have a larger impact on outcomes than will the change in resources. On the other hand, perhaps schools will become less accountable following reform as the state role in education grows and the local role shrinks; in that case, the change in outcomes would be smaller than would be predicted based on changes in resources.

A few papers have taken this second approach. Downes (1992) looked at the California experience following *Serrano*. He found that greater equality in spending was not accompanied by greater equality in measured student performance. Downes and Figlio (1997) use individual level data from the National Longitudinal Survey of the High School Class of 1972 (NLS-72) and the National Educational Longitudinal Survey (NELS). Their evidence suggests that court-mandated school finance reforms do not significantly change either the mean level or the distribution of student performance on standardized tests of reading and mathematics. They do find, however, that legislative reforms that are not a result of a court decision lead to higher test scores in general; the estimated effect was particularly large in initially low-spending districts.

Card and Payne (1997) focus on the impact of finance reform on SAT scores. They carefully deal with an important selectivity problem that arises in any study that uses SAT scores; students who take the test are not a random sample of all students. The participation rate of high school seniors ranges from only a few percent (in states where relatively few students attend college and the SAT is not required for admission to the state university) to over 60 percent (in states where a high fraction attend college and the test is required by the state university). Moreover, students who take the SAT are far more likely to be from wealthy families and to be ranked highly in their graduating class. They conclude that the evidence points to a modest equalizing effect of school finance reforms on the test score outcomes for children from different family backgrounds (though they would agree that the evidence is not decisive). Their most precise estimates imply that, on average, court-mandated reform in 12 states over the 1980s closed the gap in average SAT scores between children of highly educated and poorly educated parents by about 10 points.

Voluntary Contributions

The demand for education spending varies across districts, in part because wealth and income vary across districts. As a consequence, almost inevitably any effort to reduce inequality in education spending will force some districts to spend less on education than they would like. How might families in those districts respond? They might try to supplement public funds with private donations. Some districts put clear limitations on such donations. New York City, for example, has what has come to be called the "Greenwich Village rule." Parents of children in P.S. 41 in Greenwich Village raised money to hire an additional fourth grade teacher. The head of New York schools, however, blocked their plan; in New York, he ruled, parents can raise money for all sorts of purposes (fixing the roof, buying new uniforms for the football team) but they cannot hire personnel.[14]

California gives parents more latitude, and Brunner and Sonstelie (1997) have shown that a number of districts have used private donations to reduce the impact of the limitations imposed by *Serrano*. They focus on the growth of local educational foundations, nonprofit organizations designed to channel voluntary contributions to local schools. There were six of these foundations in 1971 (the year of the *Serrano* decision); by 1995, there were 537. They also found that in

1992, PTAs, local education foundations, and other nonprofits raised nearly $100 million for California public schools, the bulk of which was concentrated in a few school districts that were particularly constrained by the *Serrano* spending limitations.

As Brunner and Sonstelie (1997) explain, these results are in some ways surprising. The "free rider" problem would seem to suggest that donations would be much smaller than they actually are in California. Suppose we all make decisions as to how much to contribute independently. If I contribute $1 and there are *n* children in the school, then my child will receive only $1/*n* in benefits from my contribution; for any reasonable size school, this is essentially zero. If my child will receive none of the benefits from my donation, perhaps I should donate nothing yet still enjoy the benefit of your contribution, i.e., it would make sense for me to act as a free rider. There is substantial literature that suggests that in general this free-rider problem is rarely as severe as theory suggests it should be; perhaps California families are more cooperative and are better able to avoid the free-rider trap than our textbooks tell us they should be.

It is also important to keep the Brunner and Sonstelie results in proper perspective. While contributions may have allowed wealthy parents to increase spending a bit at the margin, these contributions were far too small to undo the effects of *Serrano*. In the early 1990s, California spent approximately $24.9 billion annually on its 5.3 million public school K-12 students. Brunner and Sonstelie's $100 million thus represents spending of about $19 per student (roughly .4 percent). Even if all of the money were concentrated among the wealthiest 20 percent of all students, contributions were just $95 per student (2 percent). California PTAs would have to sell far more muffins at bake sales than they have in order to return California to a pre-*Serrano* world.

The Demand for Private Schools

How else might families respond to court-mandated spending equalization plans? They might choose to abandon the public school system entirely and send their children to private schools. As Brunner and Sonstelie (1997) explain, equalization throws some families off of their demand curve for education and thus generates a deadweight loss. Families could move back to their demand curve by choosing a private school, but of course they would then need to pay private school tuition. A family will choose private schools if the deadweight loss from equalization is greater than the additional cost of the private school.

The empirical evidence on this question is mixed. Most of the research, not surprisingly, has focused on California. The raw data suggests that *Serrano* has not led many families to choose private schools. Brunner and Sonstelie (1997) show that about 9 percent of California school children were enrolled in private schools in 1973-74, as compared to roughly 10 percent in the rest of the country. By 1992-93, private school enrollment had increased to about 10 percent in

California and 12 percent in the rest of the country. They conclude that private school enrollment in California basically followed the national trend. Downes and Schoeman (1996), however, come to a different conclusion. They argue that even if the supply of private schools did not increase, *Serrano* could account for nearly half of the actual movement from public to private schools in California over the 1970-80 period.

Husted and Kenny (1996a) have also looked at the impact of the court-ordered reform on the demand for private schools. Using data from the 1970, 1980, and 1990 census for 160 metropolitan areas, they find that as average spending per pupil rises in a state and as spending becomes more equal, private school enrollments fall.

SUMMARY AND CONCLUSIONS

The literature on the impacts of court-mandated finance reform is an important element of the research on education finance. This is not a surprising development. The passage of a quarter century since the landmark *Serrano* decision affords researchers the perspective (and data) by which court reforms can be evaluated. Since the primary emphasis of most reforms was to redistribute dollars, it is also not surprising that the vast majority of papers to date have examined whether these reforms have altered the distribution and level of education spending. We believe the bulk of the evidence suggests that court-ordered reform has achieved its primary goal of fundamentally restructuring school finance and generating a more equitable distribution of resources. In most cases, this was achieved by states' directing more resources to districts with low local revenues. This last result is however not uniform, as the experience in California points out. The California evidence suggests that greater equality was achieved by reducing spending at the top of the distribution.

In contrast, research on the other intended and unintended consequences of finance reform is just beginning to take shape. Again, this is not a surprising time line. If reform had no impact on the distribution or level of resources, there would be no need to look at many of these additional outcomes. Given the limited number of studies in this area, it is also not shocking that there is no consensus on whether court-ordered reform improved outcomes. We view research on the outcomes of finance reform to be the important next step. We realize that gains may be difficult to quantify. We may have attacked an easier set of questions through our own work simply because dollars are an easier variable to measure. More importantly, however, any change in outcomes will have to come about by a fundamental change in some characteristic of the district, such as a change in resources. Since outcomes are one more step down the causality chain, changes in these variables will obviously be more difficult to detect.

NOTES

1. In our models a state becomes a reform state when its supreme court issues its first opinion, even if the decision concerned the finance system more generally or if the decision was based on a legal issue, such as a declaratory judgment, and not on the merits of the case (declaratory judgment is a statutory remedy that allows a plaintiff to bring a suit if he is unsure of his legal rights). Others might have treated the data somewhat differently. Dayton (1996), for example, considers only state supreme court decisions that specifically address the disparity in education resources on the merits of the case. Under that definition, we would not have considered Kansas as a reform state since the Kansas decision was a declaratory judgment. Nor would we have classified Wisconsin as a reform state since the Wisconsin system was overturned in 1976 on the grounds that the state's equalization formula violated the state constitution's tax article.

2. See Evans et al. (1997b) for a further discussion of these issues.

3. Proposition 13 was an amendment to the California State Constitution that limited property tax rates and property valuations, thereby limiting local governments' access to the main source of funding for education.

4. See Murray et al. (1998) and Murray (1995) for a description of the data used in those studies.

5. Table 3-2 makes no adjustment for between-district differences in the cost of education. Thus, real resources in that table equal current dollar revenues deflated by the national Consumer Price Index. We discuss cross-section variation in costs in a later section of this paper.

6. See Berne and Stiefel (1984) for a thorough discussion of the properties of measures of equity in public school resources.

7. See Coons et al. (1970). The school finance literature sometimes draws distinctions between guaranteed tax base, guaranteed yield, and district power equalization programs. These differences are minor, and we therefore refer to all three as district power equalization programs.

8. What happens in wealthy districts where V^* is less than V_j? A pure DPE scheme includes "recapture." All districts would receive $A_j = t_j(V^* - V_j)$, which could be either positive or negative, i.e., school districts where the tax base is larger than the guaranteed base would be required to return to the state the excess tax revenue that it raised. Theoretically, DPE plans could therefore be self-financing; it is possible to set the guaranteed base so that the funds collected from the wealthy districts could be redistributed to poorer districts and therefore ΣA_j would equal 0. In practice, however, no states with DPE require recovery; in fact, in most states even the wealthiest districts receive at least some state aid (Reschovsky, 1994).

9. Epple and Romano (1995) and Nechyba (1997) are also concerned with school choice issues.

10. Burtless (1997) includes an interesting set of papers on this debate.

11. As Minorini and Sugarman (see Chapter 2 in this volume) explain, the original decision in *Serrano* allowed unequal spending, but did require that spending be uncorrelated with wealth. The California State Supreme Court established the spending rule in its third ruling in *Serrano*.

12. While these cost indices are the best available, it is not clear that they successfully capture the full difference in the costs of education across districts. Ideally, a cost index would account for the difference in wages that a central city school district would have to offer in order to attract teachers with the same qualifications, ability, and training that wealthy suburban districts attract. We suspect that these indices do not capture those differences and that it is therefore likely that they overstate the resources available to central city students. The available indices look at differences in the cost of inputs, but do not address variation in student needs; see Duncombe et al. (1996) for an important discussion of this issue.

13. We were also able to reestimate our decomposition using the individual district TCI available from the National Center of Education Statistics. The results of that decomposition are very similar to the estimates in Table 3-4; 57 percent of the overall inequality as measured by the Theil index were due to differences in resources between states.

14. In the end a "compromise" was reached; the city hired an additional teacher, and the donations were returned to the parents.

ACKNOWLEDGMENTS

This research was supported by the National Science Foundation under Grant #SPR-9409499. We thank NSF for its support. We also thank Helen Ladd, Allan Odden, and Christopher Jencks for very helpful comments on an earlier version of this chapter.

REFERENCES

Berne, R., and L. Stiefel
  1984 *The Measurement of Equity in School Finance: Conceptual, Methodological, and Empirical Dimensions.* Baltimore: The Johns Hopkins University Press.
Betts, J.R.
  1995 Does school quality matter? Evidence from the national longitudinal survey of youth. *Review of Economics and Statistics* 77:231-50.
Brunner, E., and J. Sonstelie
  1997 School Finance Reform and Voluntary Fiscal Federalism. Unpublished working paper, November.

Bureau of the Census
  1972   *Census of Government School System Finance File, (F33).* Machine readable data files. Washington, DC: U.S. Department of Commerce, Bureau of the Census and U.S. Department of Education, National Center for Education Statistics.
  1973   *Census of Population and Housing, 1970.* Special Fifth Count Summary Tapes, Technical Documentation. Washington, DC: U.S. Department of Commerce, Bureau of the Census.
  1977   *Census of Government School System Finance File, (F33).* Machine readable data files. Washington, DC: U.S. Department of Commerce, Bureau of the Census and U.S. Department of Education, National Center for Education Statistics.
  1982a   *Census of Government School System Finance File, (F33).* Machine readable data files. Washington, DC: U.S. Department of Commerce, Bureau of the Census and U.S. Department of Education, National Center for Education Statistics.
  1982b   *Census of Population and Housing, 1980.* Summary Tape File 3F, School Districts, Technical Documentation. Washington, DC: U.S. Department of Commerce, Bureau of the Census and U.S. Department of Education, National Center for Education Statistics.
  1987   *Census of Government School System Finance File, (F33).* Machine readable data files. Washington, DC: U.S. Department of Commerce, Bureau of the Census and U.S. Department of Education, National Center for Education Statistics.
  1992   *Census of Government School System Finance File, (F33).* Machine readable data files. Washington, DC: U.S. Department of Commerce, Bureau of the Census and U.S. Department of Education, National Center for Education Statistics.
Burtless, G., ed.
  1997   *Does Money Matter? The Effect of School Resources on Student Achievement and Adult Success.* Washington, DC: The Brookings Institution.
Card, D., and A.B. Krueger
  1992   Does school quality matter? Returns to education and the characteristics of public schools in the United States. *Journal of Political Economy* 100:1-40.
Card, D., and A.A. Payne
  1997   *School Finance Reform, the Distribution of School Spending, and the Distribution of SAT Scores.* Working Paper #387. Princeton, NJ: Princeton University Industrial Relations Section.
Coleman, J.S., E.Q. Campbell, C.J. Hobson, J. McPartland, A.M. Mead, F.D. Weinfeld, and R.L. York
  1966   *Equality of Educational Opportunity.* Washington, DC: U.S. Department of Health, Education and Welfare.
Coons, J.E., W.H. Clune, and S.D. Sugarman
  1970   *Private Wealth and Public Education.* Cambridge, MA: Harvard University Press.
Dayton, J.
  1996   Examining the efficacy of judicial involvement in public school funding reform. *Journal of Education Finance* 22(1):1-27.
Downes, T.A.
  1992   Evaluating the impact of school finance reform on the provision of education: The California case. *National Tax Journal* 45:405-419.
Downes, T.A., and D.N. Figlio
  1997   School Finance Reforms, Tax Limits, and Student Performance: Do Reforms Level Up or Level Down? Unpublished working paper.
Downes, T.A., and D. Schoeman
  1996   School Financing Reform and Private School Enrollment: Evidence from California. Unpublished working paper.

Downes, T.A., and M.P. Shah
  1995   The Effect of School Finance Reforms on the Level and Growth of Per-Pupil Expenditures. Unpublished working paper, March.
Duncombe, W., J. Ruggiero, and J. Yinger
  1996   Alternative approaches to measuring the cost of education. Pp. 327-356 in *Holding Schools Accountable*, H.F. Ladd, ed. Washington, DC: The Brookings Institution.
Epple, D., and R.E. Romano
  1995   Public School Choice and Finance Policies, Neighborhood Formation, and the Distribution of Educational Benefits. Unpublished working paper, July.
Evans, W., S. Murray, and R. Schwab
  1997a   Schoolhouses, courthouses, and statehouses after *Serrano*. *Journal of Policy Analysis and Management* 16(1):10-31.
  1997b   Toward increased centralization in public school finance. Pp. 139-172 in *Intergovernmental Fiscal Relations,* R.C. Fisher, ed. New York: Kluwer Academic.
Ferguson, R.F., and H.F. Ladd
  1996   How and why money matters: An analysis of Alabama schools. Pp. 265-298 in *Holding Schools Accountable*, H.F. Ladd, ed. Washington, DC: The Brookings Institution.
Fernandez, R., and R. Rogerson
  1997   Education finance reform: A dynamic perspective. *Journal of Policy Analysis and Management* 16:67-84.
Fischel, W.A.
  1989   Did *Serrano* cause Proposition 13? *National Tax Journal* 42:465-473.
Hanushek, E.A.
  1986   The economics of schooling: Production and efficiency in public schools. *Journal of Economic Literature* 24:1141-1177.
Heise, M.
  1995   State constitutional litigation, educational finance, and legal impact: An empirical analysis. *University of Cincinnati Law Review* 63:1735-1765.
Hoxby, C.M.
  1996   All School Finance Equalizations Are Not Created Equal: Marginal Tax Rates Matter. Unpublished working paper, March. Cambridge, MA: Harvard University.
Husted, T.A., and L.W. Kenny
  1996a   The Legacy of *Serrano*: The Impact of Mandated Equal Spending on Private School Enrollment. Unpublished working paper, March.
  1996b   Evidence from the States on the Political and Market Determinants of Efficiency in Education. Unpublished working paper, October.
Manwaring, R.L., and S.M. Sheffrin
  1995   Litigation, School Finance Reform, and Aggregate Educational Spending. Unpublished paper.
McMahon, W.W., and S. Chang
  1991   *Geographical Cost of Living Differences: Interstate and Intrastate Update 1991.* MacArthur/Spencer Series Number 20. Normal, IL: Illinois State University, Center for the Study of Educational Finance.
Murray, S.E.
  1995   Two Essays on the Distribution of Education Resources and Outcomes. Unpublished Ph.D. dissertation, University of Maryland, College Park, MD.
Murray, S.E., W.N. Evans, and R.M. Schwab
  1998   Education finance reform and the distribution of education resources. *American Economic Review* 88(4):789-812.

National Center for Education Statistics
  1974   *Elementary-Secondary General Information System, Part B-1 Local Education Agency Fiscal Report for Fiscal Year 1972.* Machine readable data files. Washington, DC: U.S. Department of Education, National Center for Education Statistics.
  1994a   *School District Data Book for 1990 Census Data, CD-ROM.* Washington, DC: U.S. Department of Education, National Center for Education Statistics.
  1994b   *Digest of Education Statistics, 1994.* Washington, DC: U.S. Department of Education, National Center for Education Statistics.
Nechyba, T.J.
  1997   Public School Finance in a General Equilibrium Tiebout World: Equalization Programs, Peer Effects, and Competition. Unpublished working paper.
Reschovsky, A.
  1994   Fiscal equalization and school finance. *National Tax Journal* 47:185-197.
Rubinfeld, D.L.
  1995   California Fiscal Federalism: A School Finance Perspective. Unpublished Working Paper, June.
Silva, F., and J. Sonstelie
  1995   Did *Serrano* cause a decline in school spending? *National Tax Journal* 47:199-216.

4

Court-Mandated School Finance Reform: What Do the New Dollars Buy?

Margaret E. Goertz and Gary Natriello

As states reformed their education funding systems in the 1970s and increased their share of K-12 education funding, policymakers raised several concerns about how districts would use their new state aid. The first concern was that districts would use a portion of their increased state aid for tax relief, rather than for increased education spending, thus limiting the impact of school finance reform on expenditure equity and educational program improvement. The second concern was that the dollars allocated to education would be used primarily to increase teachers' salaries. Daniel Patrick Moynihan argued that "teachers will benefit. Any increase in school expenditures will in the first instance accrue to teachers, who receive about 68 percent of the operating expenditures of elementary and secondary schools" (Moynihan, 1972:75). Finally, state legislators worried that districts receiving large aid increases, particularly urban districts, would not use these new funds efficiently. One reaction to the 1990 school finance reform in New Jersey reflected this view: "Frankly it is hard to avoid the suspicion that, at this frenzied pace, the money won't be carefully directed, but will be shoveled hastily into the bottomless pit of New Jersey's disaster areas" (Sacks, 1990:A14).

In spite of these ongoing concerns, we know little about whether and how school finance reform translates into enhanced educational services. This chapter uses data from intensive case studies of Kentucky, New Jersey, and Texas to answer three sets of questions about the impact of court-mandated school finance reforms on both education revenues and services:

1. How did low- and high-wealth districts respond to court-mandated state

school finance reforms in the 1990s? Did the level of revenues available to districts from state and local sources change? By how much and why? Did expenditure patterns change? What did the new dollars buy?

2. What factors influenced these changes in revenues and expenditure decisions? What roles did state fiscal and nonfiscal education policies, district context, and district fiscal and administrative capacities play?

3. What are the implications of these findings for school finance reform policy and for research on the impact of finance reform policies?

Although we present evidence on what the new dollars that flowed to school districts as the result of court-ordered finance reforms enabled districts to purchase, we cannot address the ultimate question of the impact of finance reforms on student performance. None of the studies considered here collected student achievement data. In New Jersey and Kentucky, changes in state testing programs during the study period make pre- and post-study period comparisons impossible.

The chapter begins with a summary of three models of district response to changes in state education aid, followed by a brief description of the methodology used in the three state case studies. The next three sections report on (1) the fiscal response of districts in the three states to their 1990 school finance reform laws, (2) how districts chose to allocate new state aid dollars, and (3) what districts bought with these new dollars. In the concluding section, we examine the implications of our findings for policy and research. Throughout, our focus is on school finance equity as it was defined in court decisions during the early 1990s; we cannot address more recent issues of finance adequacy that are emerging in these and other states. Accordingly, for the most part, we employ theories and measures developed for equity analyses.

MODELS OF DISTRICT RESPONSE TO CHANGES IN STATE AID

Researchers have developed three models that are intended to explain how school districts respond to changes in available resources: intergovernmental grant theory, expenditure models, and decision-making models. This chapter relies on intergovernmental grant theory to understand how districts respond to changes in state aid; it makes use of expenditure models and decision-making models to interpret district responses to increases in resources. Clearly, the court cases reviewed here that attempted to change the way states raise and allocate dollars to districts are only one of a number of factors that affected district expenditure patterns during the early 1990s. Although we acknowledge that other factors also affected district actions, we do not review data on how spending might have changed in the absence of court cases, and so we restrict our analyses primarily to the impact of the court cases.

Intergovernmental Grant Theory

State or federal governments provide grants to local school districts in order to change the way they allocate resources. Unrestricted general aid is designed to increase the amount that communities spend on education generally; categorical grants are used to ensure that school districts provide services deemed important by the state or federal government. Unrestricted general aid increases a school district's revenues, but districts are free to use the new dollars in any way they see fit—to supplant local revenues and thereby reduce tax rates, or to increase overall education spending, thus providing more or better services.

Past research on the effects of unrestricted intergovernmental grants for education has shown that school district spending increased by only a portion of the increase in state aid. The rest is devoted to local property tax relief. Tsang and Levin (1983) reviewed much of the research conducted in the 1960s and 1970s on district response to changes in unrestricted general education aid. By examining the different studies and different states, they found that, on average, school districts used about half of the increases in state general education aid on educational programs and about half to reduce local tax rates. Districts that received large increases in state aid as part of New Jersey's 1975 education finance reform, however, directed most of their new funds—about 85 percent on average—to education rather than to tax relief (Goertz, 1979). Districts with high levels of fiscal burden or relatively high spending levels took more tax relief than less-burdened or lower-spending communities. In her study of New York, Adams (1980) also found that high-wealth districts were more likely to use increased state aid to reduce local tax burdens than their low-wealth neighbors.

Expenditure Models

How do school districts allocate these expenditure increases? Do they use new dollars to raise teacher salaries, to increase the intensity of instructional services, to expand the "administrative blob," or for other activities? Cross-sectional analyses of districts with different spending levels (Alexander, 1974; Barro and Carroll, 1975; Hartman, 1988; Odden et al., 1979) and longitudinal studies of district response to major school finance reforms in California (Kirst, 1977) and New Jersey (Goertz, 1979) generated the following findings about how districts use increases in their education budgets.

First, expenditures for administration increased at a lower rate than total spending. Second, while districts spend a comparable percent of their budgets on instruction—around the national average of 60 percent of operating budgets—higher-spending districts purchase a different mix of instructional services than low-spending districts. As spending levels increase within a state, districts tend to use the additional money to hire more teachers and to increase nonteaching components of the budget, such as specialists and supplies and equipment. As a result, high-spending districts have lower pupil/teacher and pupil/staff ratios than their lower-spending neighbors.

Third, contrary to the Moynihan thesis, only a small portion of each additional dollar is spent on higher teacher salaries. Alexander (1974) found that less than half and Barro and Carroll (1975) found that less than one-third of increased expenditures on teachers were used to increase salaries. Kirst (1977) found that under Senate Bill (SB) 90, the increase in teachers salaries in the poorest California districts actually fell below the average increase in the state (8.24 percent versus 8.45 percent). Goertz (1979) found similar patterns in the aftermath of New Jersey's 1975 finance reform law. Salary increases in districts that received at least a 25 percent increase in state aid were lower than the statewide increase: 11.8 percent versus 13.2 percent for a two-year period.

Decision-Making Models

We know far more about *how* school districts allocate increases in state aid than *why* districts make these tax and spending decisions. Kirst (1977) examined the decision-making process of five districts in the wake of SB-90 and determined that an organizational model (rather than an economic or political model) best explained the allocation decisions in these districts. Searches for alternative uses of new dollars were limited to past expenditure patterns and current educational approaches in these and neighboring districts. The particular types of new instructional personnel and programs funded by these five California districts reflected district priorities and pent-up demands—programs that had been considered but not funded in the past.

Firestone and colleagues (1997) use a modified version of Firestone's (1989) "ecology of games" to explain how school districts use new resources generated by school finance reforms. School finance reform comprises at least four games: the court, state politics, state policy, and local administration. Each game is played on its own terms, but each depends on other games for resources, regulations, demands, and so forth. In determining how to spend new state aid dollars, districts respond to two contexts—their community and state policy. The community provides students and funding based on available property wealth and community support. The state policy context includes fiscal policy, nonfiscal policies (such as state standards and assessments), and the ways that the state administers these policies (including oversight and technical assistance). These two contexts are mediated by the school district's own context, including its administrative culture, existing spending levels and patterns, and the status of district capacities (personnel, teaching, social services, and facilities) before the school finance court decision.

These approaches are consistent with institutional theories that argue that organizational decisions are driven by a need to maintain legitimacy in the wider environment (Meyer and Rowan, 1977; Powell and DiMaggio, 1991). From this perspective, organizations such as school districts may be even more responsive to immediate external forces related to efficacy and efficiency as long as doing so does not violate the expectations and assumptions held by important elements in the external environment.

In summary, prior research has shown that some new state aid is used for tax relief. But, contrary to Moynihan's hypothesis, in the 1970s new dollars were not absorbed disproportionately by salaries for existing teachers, thereby increasing the price of existing services. Rather, it appears from these studies that low-spending districts modeled the behavior of the wealthier districts; that is, they did "more of the same" with their new state aid dollars—lowered class sizes, provided additional support services, and purchased more instructional materials and equipment. Specific district decisions, however, reflect local context.

METHODOLOGY

This chapter draws on studies of Kentucky, New Jersey, and Texas conducted by the Finance Center of the Consortium for Policy Research in Education (CPRE) and the Center for Education Policy Analysis—New Jersey (CEPA-NJ) at Rutgers University in the aftermath of these states' court-mandated school finance reforms.[1] The heart of these studies is a set of qualitative case studies that examined district response to reform in a small number of school districts in each state: two low-wealth and two high-wealth districts each in Kentucky and Texas; six low-wealth urban, two moderate-wealth suburban, and four high-wealth districts in New Jersey. The districts were selected to reflect variation in community wealth, district size, urbanicity, and geographic location within each state. Researchers interviewed district superintendents, finance officers, and other central office staff and analyzed annual financial reports and budgets in each of the study districts. District-level data were supplemented in New Jersey with interviews and surveys of staff in a sample of schools in each of the study districts.

All three studies used 1989-90 as a base year. This was the year immediately preceding the implementation of new finance laws in Kentucky and Texas, and two years preceding the implementation of New Jersey's reform law. The Kentucky and Texas cases tracked districts through 1992-93; the New Jersey research continued through 1993-94. The researchers also used statewide databases to examine changes in the overall equity of these states' funding systems between 1989-90 and 1992-93 using traditional school finance equity measures (Berne and Stiefel, 1984).

These studies have several limitations that affect the analyses presented in this chapter. First, the sample of case study districts is not representative of districts in any of the three states, so we cannot generalize from the case study data to all districts in each state. The qualitative data do provide insights, however, into how and why poor and wealthy districts respond to major changes in school funding laws. We have analyzed statewide data wherever possible to see whether these patterns hold over a larger number of districts. Second, we have limited data on the impact of finance reforms on schools in New Jersey, and none in either Kentucky or Texas. The school-level data in New Jersey are drawn primarily from a teacher survey that focused on changes in curriculum, instruction, and teaching conditions; the survey was supplemented by interviews with the school principals, in four to eight schools in each of the study districts.

IMPACT OF SCHOOL FINANCE REFORMS ON SCHOOL DISTRICT REVENUES

The school finance laws enacted in Kentucky, New Jersey, and Texas were designed to respond to their respective court mandates. Court decisions in Kentucky (*Rose v. Council for Better Education*, 1989) and New Jersey (*Abbott v. Burke*, 1990) emphasized student equity and adequacy.[2] The Kentucky court called for a funding system that was "adequate" and "substantially uniform," and that would provide "equal education opportunity" to all children, but would allow local districts to supplement the state's uniform, equal educational effort (Adams and White, 1997). The New Jersey decision focused on inequities between the state's poor urban and wealthy suburban communities, and required the legislature to equalize education spending between these two groups of school districts. In contrast, the Texas decision (*Edgewood v. Kirby*, 1989) emphasized fiscal neutrality, requiring that all districts have "substantially equal access to similar revenues per pupil at similar levels of tax effort."[3]

Table 4-1 presents the key components of the basic education funding formulas that were implemented after the court decisions and compares them to the systems in place prior to the courts' actions. Both Kentucky and New Jersey made major changes to their school funding formulas. Kentucky replaced what was essentially a flat grant system based on classroom units[4] with a cost-shared foundation formula[5] and an optional guaranteed tax base.[6] New Jersey substituted a foundation formula for a guaranteed tax base system. Texas did not make structural changes to its allocation formula but substantially increased the foundation levels, required local contribution, and guaranteed yield. The major change was the establishment of county education districts (CEDs) to raise local property taxes, essentially creating a county-level recapture provision.[7]

In addition, all three states increased their support of programs for special needs students. Kentucky and Texas included program weights for students with disabilities, at-risk students, and students with limited English proficiency (Texas only) in their foundation formulas. Kentucky also added separate categorical grant programs for extended school services, preschool for at-risk children, and family resource and youth service centers. New Jersey retained separate categorical aid formulas for special education, at-risk, and limited English proficient students but substantially increased funding of these programs.

Changes in State Aid

All three states increased state aid to education significantly between 1989-90 (pre-reform) and 1992-93 (post-reform), ranging from 31 percent in New Jersey to 35 percent in Kentucky and Texas. As shown in Table 4-2, most of the new aid was targeted on low-wealth school districts. In Kentucky, for example, the lowest-wealth quintile received, on average, $1,145 per pupil more in state aid—a 66 percent increase—compared with a $190 per pupil increase in the highest-wealth quintile (an 11 percent change). Similarly, districts in the two lowest-wealth deciles in New Jersey saw their state aid allocations increase, on average, $2,151 and $2,009 per pupil—a 46 percent and 54 percent gain, respectively. The two highest-wealth deciles lost small amounts of state aid, representing less than 5 percent of their state aid. In Texas, state aid increased $1,219 per pupil in the lowest-wealth decile, a 48 percent jump. State aid losses in the higher-wealth districts were aggravated by the loss of local property tax revenues through the county equalization system. Evans, Murray, and Schwab (Chapter 3, this volume) found similar patterns in their analysis of 16 states with court-mandated school finance reform.

Low-wealth communities were not the only winners in these states. Districts in the second and third quintiles in Kentucky and in the third through sixth deciles in New Jersey and Texas also received large dollar and percentage increases in state aid. The gains result from the operation of these states' new foundation formulas; in Kentucky and New Jersey, the post-reform foundation level was above the average spending level of the middle-wealth districts prior to reform. Middle-wealth districts in Kentucky and Texas also benefited from the guaranteed tax base (GTB) add-on provisions in their formulas.

District Response to State Formula Changes

The impact of increased state education aid on school district spending is influenced by three factors: the size of the state aid increase, local taxing decisions, and the limits imposed by tax or expenditure caps. Our review of earlier research studies showed that increases in state aid do not automatically flow to educational services for students. Other demands are made on these dollars, including a press for tax relief. Table 4-2 shows, however, that school districts in all categories of wealth in the three study states generally increased their local tax rates in response to changes in state funding formulas. Three factors account for these changes: (1) required local effort provisions in the state aid laws, (2) fiscal incentives to spend above the foundation level, and (3) demographic, cost, and programmatic pressures on school districts.

All three states enacted foundation formulas that require districts to contribute a specified amount of local revenues, often called a required local effort (RLE). Required local efforts are usually specified as minimum tax rates, which are applied to local property tax bases and, in some states, to local income wealth.

TABLE 4-1 Basic Education Funding Formulas in Effect, 1992-93: Kentucky, New Jersey, and Texas

Base	Tier 1	Tier 2
Kentucky: Kentucky Education Reform Act (1990)		
Foundation formula. Foundation level at $2,420; required local effort of 3 mills.	(optional) Up to 115% of the foundation level; equalized at 150% of property wealth. Vote required.	(optional) Up to 130% of the Base plus Tier I; no equalization.
New Jersey: Quality Education Act (1990, as amended in 1991)		
Foundation formula. Foundation level at about $6,100 per pupil (K-5); required local effort of about 11.6 mills.	(optional) Up to district budget cap; no equalization. Vote required.	
Texas: Senate Bill 351 (1991)		
Foundation formula. Foundation level at $2,400 per WADA^a (which is equal to $3,441 per ADA); required local effort of 8.2 mills.	(optional) Guaranteed yield of $22.50 per WADA ($29.24/ADA) per 0.1 mills between 8.2 and 12.7 mills. Vote required.	(optional) Between 12.7 and 15 mills. No equalization. Vote required. Recapture through County Education Districts.

WADA, weighted average daily attendance; ADA, average daily attendance.

^{a}Student counts are modified by special program (e.g., compensatory education) or instructional arrangement (e.g., grade level) weights.

The reform laws in both Kentucky and Texas increased districts' RLEs substantially: from 0 to 3 mills in Kentucky and from 3.4 to 8.2 mills in Texas. Nearly half of the school districts in Kentucky had been taxing below their RLE prior to the Kentucky Education Reform Act of 1990 (KERA). Thus, they had to raise their local tax rates to meet the new state minimum (Adams and White, 1997). The situation was different in Texas, where most districts were already taxing at close to the new effort level. Many high-wealth districts had to increase their taxes, however, to meet the requirements of the county equalization program. In New Jersey, the "fair share" requirement of the Quality Education Act (QEA), coupled with budget caps, put a floor on how much tax relief the high-taxing, poor urban districts could take.

Kentucky and Texas incorporated voluntary GTB add-ons in their new fund-

Formula It Replaced	Changes in State Aid (1989-90 to 1991-92)
Essentially a flat grant based on classroom units tied to a state minimum salary schedule.	State aid increased $541 million or 35%.
Guaranteed tax base formula. Expenditures equalized up to 65th percentile; equalized at 128% of property wealth.	State aid increased $1.02 billion or 31%.
Same formula structure with lower foundation amount ($1,477) and required local effort (about 3.4 mills), and lower Tier 1 guaranteed yield (about $18.87) and tax effort limit (between about 3.4 and 5.75 mills).	State aid increased $2.105 billion, or 35%.

SOURCES: Table compiled from data from the following: Kentucky (Adams and White, 1997; Koch and Willis, 1993); New Jersey (Goertz, 1994); Texas (Picus and Toenjes, 1994; Texas Education Agency, 1991, 1993).

ing programs as an incentive for districts to spend above the minimum foundation level. This provision was successful in both states. All but two of Kentucky's 176 school districts participated in the Tier 1 program to some degree (Koch and Willis, 1993). Many poor districts in Texas also increased their tax rates to take advantage of that state's second tier of aid (Picus and Toenjes, 1994). In fact, the level of participation in both states was so high that demands for additional state aid exceeded the funds allocated for the add-on provision.[8] This led both states to reduce funding allocations through proration. In Texas, the proration represented nearly 10 percent of state aid in 1992-93, leading many districts to raise their tax rates even higher (Picus and Toenjes, 1994).

Finally, district taxing decisions reflected the interaction of changes in state aid and local contexts. For example, high-wealth districts in New Jersey and

TABLE 4-2 Changes in State Aid per Pupil, Local Revenues per Pupil, Tax Rates (in mills), and Total Revenues per Pupil, 1989-90 to 1992-93: Kentucky, New Jersey, and Texas

Wealth Decile[c]	Kentucky[a]			
	Change in State Aid	Change in Tax Rate	Change in Local Revenue	Change in Total Revenue
1				
2	$1145	1.6	$ 211	$1355
3				
4	825	1.4	252	1077
5				
6	653	1.3	276	929
7				
8	405	1.0	385	790
9				
10	190	1.2	328	518
State average	639	1.3	288	927
Change in Property Value per Pupil	+16.7%			

[a]Data were reported in quintiles, rather than deciles. Revenues do not include transportation and categorical grant programs, such as preschool and extended school programs and include intrastate cost adjustments.

[b]Change between 1988-89 and 1992-93.

[c]Each decile (and quintile) has approximately the same number of students.

Texas that lost state aid (and in the case of Texas, lost local revenue through county equalization) raised their tax rates to offset these reductions. They raised their rates even higher to address growing enrollments, increased program costs (due to salary settlements, inflation, and the growth in the number of special needs students), and/or declining or stagnant property valuations. For example, the four high-wealth districts in the New Jersey study raised their local taxes so they could maintain growth in their school budgets (adjusted for enrollment growth) of between 2 percent and 6 percent a year (Firestone et al., 1997). One of the two high-wealth districts in the Texas sample raised its taxes 33 percent. The funds available after accounting for a shortfall in state revenues were used to support its strategic plan for school improvement. The second high-wealth district was forced to increase its taxes just to maintain its spending level (Picus, 1994).

In New Jersey, a poor economic climate in the early 1990s depressed property valuations and dampened public support of rising school budgets, especially

New Jersey				Texas[b]			
Change in State Aid	Change in Tax Rate	Change in Local Revenue	Change in Total Revenue	Change in State Aid	Change in Tax Rate	Change in Local Revenue	Change in Total Revenue
$2151	–0.3	$ 10	$2161	$1219	3.6	$ –73	$1147
2009	0.4	129	2138	940	2.8	192	987
1509	0.6	7	1516	793	2.4	–37	757
783	2.3	582	1365	500	2.4	101	601
946	2.3	608	1554	506	3.0	202	707
803	1.9	556	1359	422	2.5	28	450
415	2.7	957	1371	264	3.0	167	431
90	2.6	967	1055	–177	4.5	659	481
–18	2.6	1340	1323	–227	2.7	330	101
–69	1.8	1663	1594	–196	4.5	425	229
766	2.1	742	1507	399	3.4	201	600
–4.5%				–14.6%			

SOURCES: Table compiled from data from the following: Kentucky (Adams and White, 1997); New Jersey (Goertz, 1995; reanalysis of NJSDE data by Goertz); Texas (Texas Education Agency, 1991, 1993).

in the wealthier communities. School budgets were defeated at the polls, and many wealthy districts chose to keep their spending levels below those permitted under state budget caps (Firestone et al., 1997). In Texas, per-pupil valuations dropped nearly 15 percent between 1989 and 1992, limiting the average per-pupil increase in local revenues to $200, in spite of a 30 percent increase in tax rates. In contrast, increased state aid for most districts (and a save-harmless provision for the very wealthiest communities) coupled with growing property valuations and continued public support for education led to increased revenues across the board in Kentucky (Adams, 1994; Adams and White, 1997).

Changes in Revenues and Revenue Equity

The interaction of new finance structures, increased state aid, and rising tax rates resulted in substantially more revenues for school districts in Kentucky,

New Jersey, and Texas. Between 1989-90 and 1992-93, revenues grew an average of $600 per pupil in Texas, $927 per pupil in Kentucky, and $1,507 per pupil in New Jersey (see Table 4-2). This represented changes of 33 percent in Kentucky, 24 percent in New Jersey, and 16 percent in Texas. Low-wealth districts had the largest gains—on average, 69 percent in Kentucky (quintile 1), 36 percent to 40 percent in New Jersey (deciles 1 and 2), and 30 percent to 36 percent in Texas (deciles 1 and 2). These gains reflected the increased equalization of general operating aid and growth in programs for special-needs students, who tend to be concentrated in low-wealth communities. High-wealth districts registered smaller gains—around 16 percent in Kentucky, 20 percent in New Jersey, and less than 5 percent in Texas. Growth in the wealthy communities reflected the increased local tax effort discussed above.

Table 4-3 shows the extent to which school finance reforms in the three states equalized spending and education tax rates. The dominant pattern in 1989-90 was a positive relationship between community wealth and education revenues. Three years later, the highest-wealth districts still spent more, on average, than the lowest-wealth districts, but the extent of disparity had decreased substantially in Kentucky (from 63 percent to 12 percent) and in Texas (from 46 percent to 13 percent), and moderately in New Jersey (from 29 percent to 14 percent). In addition, the lowest-wealth communities, on average, had more resources than middle-wealth districts. Assuming that low-wealth communities serve higher concentrations of students with special needs, these three states appear to have achieved a semblance of vertical as well as horizontal equity.

Table 4-4 presents a more comprehensive set of equity measures for the three states—pre- and post-reform. The first five statistics indicate the dispersion of revenues across districts (weighted for the number of students in the districts). The *restricted range* is the difference between expenditures at the 5th and 95th percentiles of the distribution. The *federal range ratio* specifies in percentage terms how much larger the 95th percentile spending is than the 5th percentile spending. We see that the funding reforms did little to close the absolute gap between the lowest- and highest-spending districts (the restricted range), but decreased the *relative* difference between the 5th and 95th percentile districts.

The restricted range and federal range ratio statistics measure dispersion at ends of the distribution, using data from two school districts. The coefficient of variation (COV), which is the standard deviation divided by the mean, includes data from all school districts in the state and focuses on the extent of variation around average spending—both above and below the mean. A value of zero indicates that all children have access to equal amounts of education spending. The Gini coefficient is a statistic that measures the degree to which each cumulative percentage of pupils (e.g., 30 percent) receives an equal percentage of revenues (e.g., 30 percent). A completely equitable distribution of resources occurs when the index measures zero. Reductions in both the coefficients of variation and Gini coefficients are signs of greater expenditure equity in Kentucky and

Texas. New Jersey's statistics paint a mixed picture. While the coefficient of variation did not change under the QEA, the Gini coefficient improved. This probably reflects a leveling-up of resources in the state but a failure to cap growth in the higher-spending districts.

The McLoone index focuses specifically on the extent of equity in the bottom half of the distribution. A value of 1 indicates that per-pupil expenditures in the lowest-spending districts are equal to the median. The improvement in New Jersey's McLoone index does confirm more leveling-up of resources in the lowest spending districts. Surprisingly, the McLoone index shows a decline in Kentucky and minimal change in Texas, two states that also targeted state aid on their lowest-spending communities. However, the index does exceed 0.9 in these two states, which satisfies some analysts' standard for a desirable level of equity (Odden and Picus, 1992).

The sixth statistic, the *simple correlation*, measures the degree of fiscal neutrality or equal educational opportunity among districts. Here we look at the linear relationship between per-pupil education revenues and property wealth; a correlation of zero indicates no systemic relationship between these two variables. All three states show a reduction in the relationship between district wealth and education revenues, particularly in Kentucky, which replaced a flat grant system with one that is wealth-equalized. The change in New Jersey's correlation is driven by large increases in categorical aid targeted on low-wealth communities. The correlation between general operating revenues (without categorical funds) and property wealth is not only much higher (0.437) than that for all current revenues (0.291), but it did not change over the three years of this study (Goertz, 1994).

Summary

Kentucky, New Jersey, and Texas all made major changes to their funding formulas in the aftermath of court decisions declaring their school finance systems unconstitutional. These changes targeted substantially more revenues on low-wealth, low-spending school districts and provided increased funds to middle-income communities as well. Contrary to popular belief and earlier research on unrestricted education grants, most districts did not reduce their tax rates or local revenues in light of increased state aid. Formula provisions provided both mandates and incentives for districts to maintain and/or increase their local effort. Although high-spending districts in New Jersey and Texas lost state aid, they raised local taxes to offset these reductions and to address growing program costs. Thus, substantial increases in state aid, coupled with growing local revenues, yielded large increases in education revenues across the board in the three states.

Expenditure equity and fiscal neutrality improved in all three states, but especially in Kentucky and Texas. Kentucky, which historically has supported

TABLE 4-3 Distribution of Education Revenues per Pupil and Tax Rates
(in mills), 1989-90 and 1992-93: Kentucky, New Jersey, and Texas

Wealth Decile[d]	Kentucky[a]			
	Education Revenues, 1989-90	Tax Rate, 1989-90	Education Revenues, 1992-93	Tax Rate, 1992-93
1				
2	$1,956	4.0	$3,311	5.6
3				
4	2,046	3.9	3,123	5.3
5				
6	2,142	4.0	3,071	5.3
7				
8	2,281	4.5	3,071	5.5
9				
10	3,194	6.0	3,712	7.2
State Average	2,335	4.2	3,262	5.5

[a]Data were reported in quintiles, rather than deciles. Revenues do not include transportation and categorical grant programs, such as preschool and extended school programs and include intrastate cost adjustments.

[b]Revenues include those for current and capital expenses.

[c]The Texas Education Agency reports data in 20 wealth groups with equal numbers of students. We calculated the decile figures by averaging the numbers for contiguous wealth groups (e.g., wealth

nearly three-quarters of education spending through state aid, achieved greater equity by replacing a flat grant system with a more equalized funding structure and a higher foundation level. Texas, where the state share is less than 50 percent, increased equity by targeting state dollars on lower-wealth districts. This was achieved by reducing the wealth guarantee in the foundation formula at the same time it increased the foundation amount, and by raising both the second tier guarantees and tax rates that were rewarded. Attempts to improve equity in New Jersey were thwarted by the maintenance of a relatively low state share (41 percent in 1993-94), and a system of budget caps that constrained growth in low-wealth districts while insufficiently limiting growth in high-wealth communities.

WHERE DID THE NEW DOLLARS GO?

In this section we examine where local districts in Kentucky, New Jersey, and Texas chose to allocate the new dollars flowing from school finance reforms. In this analysis we use functional categories of expenditure, including instruction, administration, transportation, plant operation, maintenance, fixed costs,

New Jersey[b]				Texas[c]			
Education Revenues, 1989-90	Tax Rate, 1989-90	Education Revenues, 1992-93	Tax Rate, 1992-93	Education Revenues, 1989-90	Tax Rate, 1989-90	Education Revenues, 1992-93	Tax Rate, 1992-93
$5,925	12.1	$8,086	11.8	$3,200	8.6	$4,347	12.2
5,305	10.5	7,443	10.9	3,294	9.5	4,281	12.3
5,690	10.5	7,207	11.1	3,456	10.3	4,213	12.7
5,961	10.5	7,326	12.8	3,437	10.5	4,038	12.9
6,066	10.3	7,620	12.6	3,417	10.3	4,124	13.3
5,947	9.9	7,306	11.8	3,662	11.4	4,112	13.9
6,147	9.7	7,518	12.4	3,710	10.6	4,141	13.6
6,903	9.6	7,958	12.2	3,640	9.2	4,121	13.7
7,132	8.3	8,455	10.9	4,035	9.9	4,136	12.5
7,644	5.5	9,238	7.3	4,668	8.3	4,897	12.9
6,305	8.6	7,812	10.7	3,642	9.6	4,242	13.0

groups 1 and 2, 3 and 4, etc.). Revenues are the sum of those available under the state foundation program and from the unequalized local leeway tax rate.

[d]Each decile (and quintile) has approximately the same number of students.

SOURCES: Table compiled from data from the following: Kentucky (Adams and White, 1997); New Jersey (Goertz, 1995; reanalysis of NJSDE data by Goertz); Texas (Picus and Toenjes, 1994).

and capital outlay. As noted earlier, the literature on district decision making suggests that multiple sources drive district resource allocation decisions, some of which might cause districts to maintain previous spending patterns and others of which might cause districts to depart from those patterns. For example, districts must contend with various fixed costs of operation, including those imposed by state and federal regulations. Such costs might lead districts to maintain prior spending patterns in the relevant categories even when new funds become available. However, if spending in mandated and otherwise fixed categories caused districts to underfund areas in which they have more discretion, such as instruction, then new resources might lead to increases in the previously underfunded areas, driven by local perceptions of needs. Similarly, if districts had reacted to limited resources by maintaining instructional spending and underfunding maintenance and capital construction over the years, then new resources might lead to increases in these areas. District spending patterns in the wake of new resources appear to be driven by a combination of prior spending patterns and external regulations and expectations as well as by areas of need in individual districts resulting from prior spending patterns.

TABLE 4-4 Selected Equity Statistics, Current Revenues per Pupil, 1989-90 and 1992-93: Kentucky, New Jersey, and Texas

Statistic	1989-90	1992-93	Change	% Change
Mean				
New Jersey	$ 6,305	$ 7,812	$1,507	+23.9
Kentucky	2,835	3,806	971	+34.3
Texas[a]	3,378	4,242	864	+25.6
Restricted Range				
New Jersey	$ 4,224	$ 3,837	$ −387	−9.1
Kentucky	1,279	1,069	−210	−16.4
Texas	1,371	1,453	+82	+6.0
Federal Range Ratio				
New Jersey	0.831	0.627	−0.204	−24.5
Kentucky	0.541	0.331	−0.210	−38.8
Texas	0.490	0.399	−0.091	−18.5
Coefficient of Variation				
New Jersey	0.199	0.195	−0.004	−2.0
Kentucky	0.158	0.095	−0.063	−39.9
Texas	0.171	0.133	−0.038	−22.2
McLoone Index				
New Jersey	0.864	0.890	+0.026	+3.0
Kentucky	0.946	0.919	−0.027	−0.0[b]
Texas	0.939	0.948	+0.009	+0.1
Gini Coefficient				
New Jersey	0.106	0.090	−0.016	−15.1
Kentucky	0.083	0.054	−0.029	−34.9
Texas	0.079	0.058	−0.021	−27.6
Simple Correlation[c]				
New Jersey	0.377	0.291	−0.086	−22.8
Kentucky	0.790	0.362	−0.428	−54.2
Texas	0.729	0.506	−0.223	−30.6

[a]Mean revenues are not comparable to those reported in Table 4-2 due to different data sources.
[b]The exact figure is −0.03%.
[c]Correlation between current revenues per pupil and property wealth per pupil.

SOURCES: Table compiled from data from the following: Kentucky (Adams and White, 1997); New Jersey (Goertz, 1994); Texas (Picus and Toenjes, 1994).

Kentucky

Adams (1996) examined the changes in resource allocation following KERA. Table 4-5, taken from Adams (1996), shows the changes in per-pupil expenditures by function from 1990 to 1993 and the proportion of budgets allocated to each functional category.

First, we find that spending increased for all district functions with the exception of debt service during this period of reform. Expenditures for administration rose $37 per pupil (36 percent), those for instruction rose $680 (33 percent), those for transportation increased $53 (30 percent), those for operations and maintenance increased $70 (24 percent), those for fixed costs increased $65 (66 percent), and expenditures for capital outlay rose $117 (244 percent). Second, fixed costs, capital outlay, and expenditures on health, food, and community services all rose by more than the aggregate percentage increase of 37 percent across all functions; in contrast, administration, instruction, attendance services, transportation, plant operations, and maintenance all rose by less than the aggregate percentage.

Third, Adams notes that the spending patterns in Kentucky school districts statewide were virtually identical before and after the reform. Relative spending changed less than a percentage point in administration, attendance, health services, food services, community services, transportation, operations, maintenance, fixed costs, and debt services. In the remaining two categories, the percentage of total expenditures devoted to instruction decreased from 72.5 percent to 70.3 percent while the percentage of total expenditures devoted to capital outlay increased from 1.7 percent to 4.2 percent. Expenditure patterns remained the same or changed incrementally in the four study districts as well.

Finally, drawing on data from the *Digest of Education Statistics* (National Center for Education Statistics, 1995), Adams compared the allocation of spending in Kentucky to the nation overall. He found that school districts in Kentucky spend a greater percentage of their funds on administration (3.6 percent to 2.7 percent), instruction (70 percent to 67 percent), and transportation (5.9 percent to 4.2 percent); they spend a smaller percentage of their funds on operations and maintenance (9.3 percent to 10.3 percent) and various student services.

New Jersey

For the state of New Jersey, Firestone et al. (1997) examined the spending patterns in 12 school districts—4 high-wealth districts, 2 middle-wealth districts, and 6 of the 30 poor urban districts that were the focus of the *Abbott v. Burke* decision. Table 4-6 shows the percentage of increased expenditures between 1990-91 and 1993-94 allocated to six major spending categories.

The six expenditure categories are: (1) direct educational expense—instruction, attendance and health services; student body activities; special education and other special-needs programs; (2) plant operation and maintenance; (3) transportation; (4) fixed charges and other expenses—including administration, community services, sundry accounts, and insurance costs; (5) tuition for out-of-district placements; and (6) capital outlay. Two districts (SN6 and TR4) were excluded because budget data in line-item format were unavailable for both years.

Regardless of district type, about half the increased funds were used for direct educational expenditures. The poor urban districts, on average, put 51

TABLE 4-5 Changes in Kentucky School District Per-Pupil Expenditure
Patterns by Function, 1990 and 1993

| | 1990 | |
| | | |
Function	Per-Pupil Expenditure	As Percent of Total Budget
Administration	$103	3.6%
Instruction	2,059	72.5
Attendance Services	28	1.0
Health Services	3	0.1
Pupil Transportation	175	6.2
Plant Operations	205	7.2
Maintenance	89	3.1
Fixed Costs	99	3.5
Food Services	17	0.6
Community Services	3	0.1
Capital Outlay	48	1.7
Debt Service	12	0.4
Total	2,842	

SOURCE: Calculations based on Kentucky Form F-55 prepared by Adams (1996).

percent of new funding into direct educational expenses. The middle-wealth
districts put 65 percent and 66 percent of new funds into direct educational
expenses. The wealthy districts, on average, put 62 percent of new funds into
educational expenditures, but two districts (TR1, TF3) allocated significantly less
(54 percent and 56 percent) of new funds to this category—a figure comparable
to several of the poor urban districts—and one (TF2) spent significantly more (83
percent) of its new dollars this way. All types of districts used substantial portions of their new dollars for fixed costs: 17 percent in the poor urban districts, 10
percent in the middle-wealth districts, and 35 percent in the wealthy districts.

The districts differed in the proportions of new dollars added to operations
and maintenance, fixed charges, and capital outlay. The poor urban districts
spent an average of 9 percent of their new dollars on operation and maintenance,
17 percent on fixed charges, and another 11 percent on capital outlay. The two
middle-wealth districts kept operations and maintenance relatively stable, spending just 2 percent and 1 percent of their new dollars on this category. These
districts devoted 15 percent and 5 percent of the additional expenditures to fixed
charges and 15 percent and 13 percent to capital outlay. In contrast, two wealthy
districts (TR1, TR2) reduced operations and maintenance costs by 30 percent and
9 percent; a third wealthy district increased operations and maintenance by only
1 percent. These three districts devoted 44 percent, 18 percent, and 31 percent of

1993

Per-Pupil Expenditure	As Percent of Total Budget	Dollar Change	Percent Change	Percent of Total Dollar Change
$140	3.6%	$ 37	35.9%	3.5%
2,739	70.3	680	33.0	64.5
31	0.8	3	10.7	0.3
25	0.6	22	733.3	2.1
228	5.9	53	30.3	5.0
247	6.3	42	20.5	4.0
117	3.0	28	31.5	2.7
164	4.2	65	65.7	6.2
25	0.6	8	47.1	0.7
6	0.2	3	100.0	0.3
165	4.2	117	243.8	11.1
9	0.2	− 3	−25.0	−0.3
3,896		1,054	37.1	

additional expenditures, respectively, to fixed charges and 20 percent, 4 percent, and 5 percent of additional expenditures to capital outlay.

In dollar terms, spending on the direct education expense category increased an average of $1,350 in the poor urban districts, almost twice as much as that in the wealthy districts ($743). The foundation aid districts spent an additional $1,568 and $820 on direct education expense.

It is not surprising to find the poor urban districts increasing their investment in facilities and equipment in the early years of the QEA. Years of tight budgets had resulted in extensive deferred maintenance, hard use of school buildings, and pent-up demands for instructional equipment. SN2, for example, had already developed a wide variety of education and social support programs in the years preceding the QEA. While its students were successful on state tests, the community opposed extensive investment in education. Buildings were in poor condition, and the district had no room to house growing enrollments and expanded programs. This district made a major investment in improving its facilities. SN4 had also had a difficult time convincing its overburdened and increasingly elderly taxpayers to fund improvements to its schools. QEA dollars, along with other state funds, were used to bring schools up to the standards of the building code, modernize science laboratories, and build libraries for its elementary schools.

In summary, the six special needs districts studied by Firestone et al. (1997) used most of their new state aid to increase education expenditures. Like their

TABLE 4-6 Changes in New Jersey School District Per-Pupil Expenditures, by Category, 1990-91 to 1993-94

District	Changes in Current and Capital Expense/Pupil	Percent of Increased Expenditures Allocated to Each Category					
		Direct Education Expense[a]	Operation and Maintenance	Transportation	Fixed Charges/Other[b]	Tuition	Capital Outlay
SN1	$2,323	46	10	2	15	16	9
SN2	3,056	44	3	3	31	8	10
SN3	3,692	57	10	3	14	3	12
SN4	2,883	53	5	1	22	4	14
SN5	1,921	53	11	2	15	8	11
SN6[c]							
FN1	2,413	65	2	1	15	2	15
FN2[d]	1,243	66	1	4	5	15	13
TR1	951	56	-30	-3	44	12	20
TR2	1,443	83	-9	1	18	4	4
TR3	1,531	54	1	1	31	4	5
TR4[e]	810						

[a]Direct education expenses are defined as the sum of the following budget line items: instruction, attendance and health services, student body activities, special education and other special needs programs.

[b]Fixed charges and other are the sum of budget lines for administration, community services, sundry accounts, and insurance costs. It excludes teacher retirement and social security costs.

[c]Incomplete data available for this district.

[d]Percentages add to more than 100% due to adjustment in payments to special schools.

[e]Comparable figures were not available for this district because it uses program, rather than line item, budgeting.

SOURCE: Reprinted by permission of the publishers from Firestone et al., 1997:53. Copyright 1997 by Teachers College, Columbia University, All rights reserved.

wealthier neighbors, the poor urban districts spent about half of their new revenues on instruction, programs for special-needs students, and student support services. The urban districts also invested new state funds in facilities and equipment, addressing years of deferred spending in these areas. Some of the wealthy districts, constrained by small increases in state aid and taxpayer discontent, reduced spending on operations and maintenance to protect their instructional budgets.

Texas

Reports issued by the Texas Education Agency (1991, 1993) provide information on expenditures in Texas school districts for the 1989-90 and 1992-93 school years. These reports provide breakdowns for districts with different levels of wealth by dividing all Texas school districts into 20 wealth groups, each of which contains an approximately equal number of students. In Table 4-7 we present expenditure data for 1989-90 and 1992-93 for all districts and for the bottom three and top three groups, which each serve about 15 percent of the state's students.

As Table 4-7 reveals, all districts, on average, experienced increased spending in the wake of the finance reform. Between 1989-90 and 1992-93, the average Texas school district spent $689 or 19.6 percent more on total expenditures, while total instructional expenditures increased by $411 or 20.1 percent over the same period.

The poorest districts increased total operating expenditures substantially more, from $3,336 in 1989-90 to $4,377 in 1992-93. This increase of $1,041 represented a 31.2 percent addition. In these same districts instructional expenditures increased $567, representing a 28.6 percent addition and about 55 percent of new revenues. Expenditures grew in wealthier districts as well, but at a lower rate and with a smaller dollar amount. Per-pupil total operating expenditures grew $302, or 7.1 percent. Most of the new dollars (90 percent) were allocated to instructional functions, however, which increased $274, or 11.5 percent.

Table 4-8 presents the percentage distributions across major functions for Texas school districts in 1989-90 and in 1992-93. As in Kentucky, these distributions are very stable over time, varying by only a percentage point or two.

Summary

Overall, local districts in Kentucky, New Jersey, and Texas spent new money (from state aid and local sources) across the board in all functional categories, but generally they directed more than half of the new dollars to instructional areas. Some wealthy districts in New Jersey and Texas allocated most of their increased funds to instruction in the face of declining state aid and/or taxpayer revolts. In Kentucky and New Jersey, districts spent a disproportionate amount of new

TABLE 4-7 Spending Increases for Texas School Districts Between 1989-90 and 1992-93

Spending Level	1989-90	1992-93	$ Increase	% Increase
Statewide				
Total	$3,525	$4,214	$689	19.6
Instructional	$2,044	$2,455	$411	20.1
Poorest 15%[a]				
Total	$3,336	$4,377	$1,041	31.2
Instructional	$1,985	$2,552	$567	28.6
Wealthiest 15%[b]				
Total	$4,251	$4,553	$302	7.1
Instructional	$2,381	$2,655	$274	11.5

[a]Districts serving poorest 15 percent of students.
[b]Districts serving richest 15 percent of students.

SOURCE: Texas Education Agency, 1991, 1993.

TABLE 4-8 Percentage Expenditure Distributions Across Major Functions for Texas School Districts, 1989-90 and 1992-93

Expenditure Function	1989-90	1992-93
Expenditures		
Instructional	52	51
Central administrative	7	7
Campus administrative	5	5
Plant services	10	10
Other operating	15	15
Nonoperating	11	12
Instructional Expenditures		
Regular education	71	69
Special education	11	11
Compensatory education	10	12
Bilingual/ESL	2	3
Vocational education	4	4
Gifted and talented	1	2

SOURCE: Texas Education Agency, 1991, 1993.

money on fixed costs, such as insurance, and on capital outlay. Administration, on the other hand, received a proportionate share of the new dollars in all three states. What is most striking about these states is that the patterns of spending across functional areas remained relatively unchanged in the aftermath of the school finance reforms. These findings correspond to other research that documented the consistency of spending patterns across districts of different expenditure levels. That is, as districts increase their budgets, they continue to allocate the same portions of funds to administrative and instructional functions.

WHAT DID THE REFORM DOLLARS BUY?

The district case studies conducted in Kentucky (Adams, 1994), New Jersey (Firestone et al., 1994, 1997), and Texas (Picus, 1994) provide more detailed information on the programs and services that were purchased with new state aid dollars and provide some insights into the extent to which new dollars were used to increase teacher salaries in the immediate aftermath of the finance reforms. The results of these studies are presented by state in Table 4-9, where expenditures are organized by the five categories used in the case study reports: personnel, staff development, materials and resources, program, and facilities. We summarize the major cross-state findings below.

Staff Salaries

Districts in all three states used funds to increase staff salaries. These increases were motivated in some cases by the need to offer more competitive salaries and in other cases by the necessity of honoring prior contractual arrangements. In addition to salary increases, low-wealth districts in all three states used new dollars to add staff, to provide new services (such as counseling), and to reduce class sizes. Regardless of district wealth, many districts added staff just to keep (or attempt to keep) pace with enrollment growth. More detailed analyses of staffing data in New Jersey show that the rate of salary increases was identical, on average, in the low- and high-wealth districts in the state.

Staff Development

Low-wealth districts in all three states increased their expenditures for staff development. All the case study sites reported an increased level of professional development activities; a few districts increased the permanent staff involved in running staff development activities. Staff development activities were oriented to respond to the substance of state and national educational reforms and/or to address poor performance on statewide student testing programs.

TABLE 4-9 Major New Expenditures in Kentucky, New Jersey, and Texas, 1989-90 to 1992-93

	Kentucky
Personnel: Salaries	All four districts increased spending on teacher salaries (from 16% to 43%), but teacher salaries declined as a percentage of district expenditures. Low-wealth districts increased teacher salaries to become more competitive; one district moved from lowest in the region to average, another moved from 150th to 10th out of 176 districts statewide. High-wealth districts held the line on salaries.
Personnel: Staffing	One low-wealth district hired five new certified and eight new classified employees resulting in somewhat lower class sizes.
Staff Development	KERA provided $17 per pupil for staff development. Professional development was viewed as important in all four districts. Although the effort appeared substantial, it did not meet the huge demands generated by the reform.

New Jersey	Texas
All districts spent more of their new personnel dollars on salary increases than on new hiring; salary increases were dictated by contracts negotiated prior to the reform. The six low-wealth case study districts spent 68% of new personnel dollars on salaries compared to middle and high-wealth case study districts where personnel cuts resulted in all new personnel funds going to salary increases. Statewide, low-wealth districts spent 84% of new personnel dollars on salary increases while high-wealth districts spent 90% of such dollars on salary increases.	Three of four districts increased salaries an average of 6%. One high-wealth district had not increased salaries in the past three years and did not plan an increase; it still had one of the highest salary schedules in the state.
Three of five low-wealth districts increased staff between 4% and 9% in the first year following the reform. Staff increases were not so much "new" hiring as they were to meet enrollment growth or reinstate programs previously cut. Middle- and high-wealth districts experienced little net change in staff. Because of growing enrollments, student/teacher ratios rose in many high-wealth districts.	One low-wealth district hired new counselors for curriculum development in math, reading, and language arts. The other low-wealth district used funds to reduce its student/teacher ratio in grades K-4 to the state's 22:1 standard. One high-wealth district used funds to maintain the 22:1 class size ratio in grades K-4 and to extend music and art instruction to all students in the district. The other high-wealth district reduced the size of its teaching force with the expectation that class sizes would rise but remain at the state standard of 22:1 or lower.
Low-wealth districts increased staff development offerings. New funds were used for in-service training to support new programs, including cooperative learning, whole-language learning, site-based management, Comer School Development, and prepare for the new state high school graduation test. One low-wealth district hired a full-time staff development coordinator. There was some evidence that the quality of staff development efforts improved.	The high-wealth districts already had extensive staff development efforts. One low-wealth district expanded its staff development activities and expanded the staffing in this area with a focus on site-based management. The other low-wealth district focused on parent involvement.

TABLE 4-9 Continued

	Kentucky
Materials and Resources	One low-wealth district directed spending on equipment, supplies, and instructional materials with substantial technology purchases in response to the reform emphasis on instructional technology. This district also added a late afternoon bus to permit rural children to participate in co-curricular activities. The other low-wealth district increased spending on instructional materials from $15 to $100 per student and included major investments in technology and the purchase of new school buses.
Program	New programs in the districts responded to the mandates of the reform. One low-wealth district began a preschool program for at-risk children; the other initiated a summer school program and after school tutoring 2 days a week. One high-wealth district offered extended school services; the other offered all required categorical programs (extended school services, preschool, and family resource and youth service centers).
Facilities	The low-wealth districts devoted resources to facilities needs. One low-wealth district set aside some reform dollars to "fast-track" facilities needs and did not confine them to capital construction, including, for example, setting aside funds to make state technology grants. Another low-wealth district built new high schools and had plans to build new middle schools to replace antiquated buildings. One of the high-wealth districts used funds to build new facilities to meet enrollment growth.

SOURCE: Authors' compilation of data from Adams, 1994 (Kentucky); Firestone et al., 1997 (New Jersey); and Picus, 1994 (Texas).

New Jersey	Texas
High-wealth and middle-wealth districts reported minor delays in purchases of materials and resources. Low-wealth districts reported modest increases in the purchase of such materials. Respondents in low-wealth districts reported that they could purchase the supporting materials for new textbook series for the first time in years.	One high-wealth district deferred plans for purchasing new technology. One low-wealth district devoted about $1 million to technology improvements, partially for instructional purposes and partially for management systems. None of the districts indicated that it would use funds to purchase materials to supplement state-adopted textbooks.
Low-wealth districts added elective offerings to the curriculum, established new programs for students in need of special assistance, added more challenging programs for students who could benefit from them, and modified the curriculum to respond to the new high school graduation test. High-wealth and middle-wealth districts made less dramatic changes, at times involving minor reductions. Low-wealth districts also invested in extended day programs (e.g., after-school homework centers), extracurricular activities (e.g., high school clubs), early childhood education (e.g., full-day kindergarten, pre-kindergarten), and health and social services (e.g., parent programs, counselors, school-based health centers). High-wealth and middle-wealth districts made few or no changes in these areas.	Both low-wealth districts planned programmatic changes. One low-wealth district made organizational changes to improve the quality and quantity of staff development for teachers. The other low-wealth district was able to use new general revenues to support programs previously supported with Chapter 1 funds; the released Chapter 1 funds were used to establish a parent-involvement program. New funds were also used to establish an Instructional Monitoring Program which placed central office staff in school sites on a regular basis and to establish a year-round education program to provide remedial education to students having difficulty. One high-wealth district that experienced a funding reduction reduced central office staff and hired fewer replacement teachers. The other high-wealth district that received new money from a local property tax increase initiated curriculum improvement activities at the school site level.
One low-wealth district made facilities construction a top priority and minimized increases in other areas to build two new structures and renovate other buildings to increase space as a prerequisite to expanding programs. Two other low-wealth districts refurbished buildings, and another district improved high school science labs and established new computer labs. There were no dramatic changes in facilities in the middle-wealth and high-wealth districts.	One low-wealth district used most of its new funds to build a new middle school and to improve other facilities. The other low-wealth district did not use new money for facilities. One of the high-wealth districts used funds to upgrade school facilities.

Materials and Resources

Low-wealth districts in all three states devoted additional funds to materials and resources in support of their regular instructional programs. Expenditures for technology, an area often emphasized in state education reform efforts, were a priority in many districts. Other districts increased purchases of ancillary materials in support of new text series that incorporated new approaches to the teaching of reading, mathematics, and science.

Programs

In all three states low-wealth districts used the additional funds provided by the finance reforms to increase their program offerings. Most low-wealth districts added special programs to enhance the learning of at-risk students. These programs sometimes extended the school day and at other times extended the domains in which schools typically operated to include social and health services. District investments in programs were often in response to the mandates of state reform or changes in the state assessment program.

Facilities

Finally, low-wealth districts in all three states used some portion of their new funds to address facilities needs, including the construction of new buildings and renovation of existing buildings. These investments responded to years of deferred maintenance and unmet facilities needs, as well as a need to house new students and new programs. Districts were most likely to commit new resources to facilities when they were confronted with enrollment growth and when the present state of facilities posed barriers to the implementation of new programs and services.

Summary

Low-wealth districts in all three states used the additional resources they received to increase salaries and personnel, to augment staff development efforts, to add new technology and other resources, to implement new programs, and to refurbish old facilities and build new ones. In making these decisions, district leaders were responding to multiple forces, including enrollment growth and new state standards and requirements. At a time in the early 1990s when states were beginning to develop performance standards and loosen the regulations on how monies could be spent, we might have anticipated that the confluence of these developments would lead districts to use dollars differently to maximize performance. However, it appears that at least in this early stage the spending norms were so strong that departures from the patterns of spending evident in higher-performing neighboring districts were not seriously entertained.

IMPLICATIONS FOR POLICY AND RESEARCH

In this concluding section, we consider the implications of our findings for the design of new school finance systems, and for research on the impact of finance reform policies. We identify four key themes drawn from our analyses of finance reform in Kentucky, New Jersey, and Texas. We suggest that despite differences in local contexts, district spending patterns become more similar in the wake of reform. We note that, in addition to the level of funding, the perceived stability of funding affects spending decisions in local districts. We consider both the need for and the limitations of linkages between state education reform plans and state finance plans. Finally, we identify areas in which additional research might advance efforts to develop school finance policies that lead to school improvement.

Context and Consistency

Local district responses to finance reform can be characterized in terms of two superficially contradictory trends. Local districts in these three states were influenced by local contextual issues in distributing the additional resources made available through finance reform. At the same time, these new local allocation decisions resulted in patterns of resource utilization that were quite consistent from district to district. How can both these trends be true?

Local districts react to a host of local, state, and national contextual factors in shaping their decisions on the allocation of resources in the wake of finance reforms. District responses to increases or decreases in funding are influenced by the following: other state education policies, particularly in the areas of curriculum, assessment, and accountability; demographic trends in the districts (e.g., enrollment changes, changes in the composition of the student body); local governance structures; and the status of education programs in the districts. Although there was relative consistency in the way districts used new resources, particular allocation decisions were driven by particular local configurations of needs. For example, districts that had neglected their facilities when funds were scarce or that had experienced rapid enrollment increases identified facilities as a major priority for new expenditures. Districts with less severe and immediate facilities problems were able to devote more of the new dollars to program enhancements. At times facilities needs restricted program development, as when districts found themselves unable to offer full-day kindergarten or pre-kindergarten because they lacked physical space for more classes of students.

If districts are responding to local contextual issues in the allocation of resources, how do the district-to-district patterns of resource allocation become

quite similar? Local districts apparently share a similar model of optimal resource distribution and utilization. Districts that receive infusions of state aid
look to higher-spending/higher-performing districts for models of how to use
these new dollars. These expenditure models are very traditional: lower class
sizes; improved facilities; and increased professional development, equipment,
and instructional materials. The spending decisions of poor districts were not
capricious. One of the reasons that spending patterns appear similar in all three
states is that districts receiving new funds are modeling their spending decisions
after those of districts deemed to be more successful.

Perhaps the best explanation for this pattern of activity comes from institutional theory. The central project of the new institutionalism is to show how,
independently of efficiency demands, organizations adopt specific forms and
structures to maintain their legitimacy (Powell and DiMaggio, 1991; Rowan,
1982; Tolbert and Zucker, 1983). Regardless of their contribution to organizational effectiveness, such forms constitute legitimating myths that give organizations credence, the perception that the organization is doing the right thing, in the
outside world (Meyer and Rowan, 1977). Adoptions for legitimation can come
through three means: coercive isomorphism where pressures are brought to
bear—often through government mandates—to take on certain characteristics,
copying successful organizations in the same field, and normative pressures from
the spread of professionalism (DiMaggio and Powell, 1983). All three of these
can be observed in the case of school finance reform. State governments have
influenced local school districts in their spending patterns through mandates for
certain programs as well as through setting expectations for what constitutes
legitimate expenditures. Local districts do appear to copy well-financed and
more successful (in terms of student outcomes) counterparts in other communities. Finally, professional staff throughout local districts are influenced by national professional movements that establish standards for professional practice.
Each of these processes influences the resource allocation decisions in local
districts. However, the efficacy of poor and urban districts adopting the spending
profiles of wealthy and suburban districts remains to be determined.

Dollars and Sense

Local district responses to state finance reform are influenced not only by the
actual changes in the dollars available for education, but also by the ways that
district leaders perceive the probable future of state funding. The change embodied in each reform is a reminder of the dependency of districts, particularly poor
districts, on state actions often beyond their control. To the extent that state
revenues are perceived as unstable and unpredictable, districts avoid new expenditures with long-term commitments. Districts also were deterred from long-
term planning by the perceived instability of state funding.

District responses reflect local perceptions (and realities) of the instability of state reform dollars. Therefore, districts are more apt to spend new dollars on "one-shot" expenditures, like equipment and facilities. Local districts in Kentucky, New Jersey, and Texas experienced a significant change in state policy with the finance reforms. Consequently, district leaders questioned the stability of the newly reformed arrangements and avoided long-term resource commitments.

This cautious approach proved prescient in New Jersey and Texas, where reform laws lasted only two years. The New Jersey legislature modified the Quality Education Act between its initial passage and implementation, reducing the amount of aid targeted to the special-needs districts and requiring these districts to revise their spending plans on short notice. The major provisions of this amended QEA were in place only 2 years before politics placed the law on hold and subsequent judicial action required more changes. The Texas school finance formula was changed three times in 4 years in response to state court decisions. It is not surprising, then, that one low-wealth Texas district chose to use 80 percent of its state aid increase on facilities and technology (Picus, 1994). The perceived instability of state reforms clearly constrains local decisionmaking, and the effects of such constraints may lead to less than optimum spending decisions.

Finance Reform and Education Reform

New dollars are put to better use in districts that have a vision and plan for education reform. Strategic plans for the use of new funds are critical for obtaining the support of taxpayers (especially if a tax increase is required) and for mediating competing claims for these new resources. Not surprisingly, districts with strong leadership are more likely to develop these kinds of plans. But states can help districts identify needs and establish priorities for the use of new state aid. For example, as part of the New Jersey finance reform, each low-income district was visited by a team of outside reviewers who prepared a plan containing a list of priorities. The Kentucky education reform that accompanied that state's finance reform contained a great deal of specific guidance regarding the direction and content of district reform. Similarly, Texas districts used new dollars to respond to that state's class size and assessment and accountability policies.

Despite these examples of state actions to assist districts in shaping a vision for school reform, the relationship between finance reform and education reform remained separate at the state level in Kentucky, New Jersey, and Texas. No attempts to directly link state standards to foundation level funding emerged, even in Kentucky where education reform and finance reform occurred simultaneously. It is perhaps not surprising, then, that researchers did not find many examples of standards-driven resource allocation decisions at the local level beyond generalized responses to state and national curriculum reform standards, such as aligning curriculum and purchasing related instructional materials. Where there were some examples of linkages between finance reform and education reform, as in Kentucky, they were in response to categorical funding for things like preschool and extended day services.

As states move forward, the trade-off between linking finance reform to education reform and allowing districts sufficient discretion to make appropriate allocation decisions needs to be made more explicit. There is increasing interest in connecting finance reform to education reform and using the former to drive the latter. It is certainly possible to devise finance reform strategies that are connected to education reform goals; this is the theory behind the use of categorical grants. However, the diversity of local district conditions and contexts requires a host of resource allocation decisions to be made at the local level to insure the most efficient and efficacious use of resources. The constraints imposed by highly specified, state-level finance systems may exact a price in terms of local district efficiency. The challenge is to design state finance systems that move local districts in reform directions while allowing for the most efficient and effective distribution of resources. The danger for prescriptive state finance systems is that they might achieve control without coordination or without an appreciation of the local context.

New Dollars and New Data

There is limited research on how and where districts spend new state aid dollars in the aftermath of major school finance reforms. Further research requires the collection of quantitative data by expenditure function and object (particularly salaries) and on the numbers and type of staff districts employ. Current financial reporting procedures obscure the level and type of reform activities undertaken at the district and school level (Adams, 1994). Therefore, we must continue to rely on qualitative data collection to understand what new dollars buy programmatically, how educators use reform dollars to improve educational programs, and the factors that districts identify as influencing their resource allocation decisions. The development of better program-level accounting and of school-level finance data should help (Busch and Odden, 1997). But, because of the complexity of the factors that contribute to spending decisions, no one decision-making model can predict or explain changes in district expenditures and resource use.

Even with the collection of additional data on school district expenditures, a number of factors make the determination of "reform dollars" (i.e., dollars intended for reform) difficult. First, comprehensive finance reform involves modification of more than one aspect of a finance system and makes identification of the net effects difficult. These multiple modifications at times reinforce a particular direction and at other times operate inconsistently. Moreover, the multiple alterations to a system often have different effects in different kinds of local districts. For example, a reform that adjusts the foundation formula and restructures categorical programs may lead to very different outcomes for districts that have slightly different student populations. Second, changing local circumstances can check the intended effects of particular elements of a reform. For example, rapid changes in student enrollment can lead to very different consequences depending upon the nature of the linkage of funds to enrollments. Third, local district finance and accounting systems may not have the capacity to track income in terms of "old" and "new" dollars and so may not allow analysts to reconstruct the connection between new dollars and reform-related expenditures. All of these factors mean that the concept of "reform dollars" may be more appropriate as a rhetorical device than useful as an analytic category for tracking the impact of finance reform.

The research reported in this chapter confirms Kirst's (1977) finding that school district administrators use organizational models, rather than rational microeconomic concepts, in making resource allocation decisions. This is due, in part, to the limited applicability of these microeconomic models in education. As Jesse Burkhead noted,

> [even] if school administrators had knowledge of or interest in the marginal productivity of resource inputs . . . it could not be assumed that it would be possible to secure least-cost combinations, given the institutional rigidities of mandates and conventional practice. Neither is there a reasonable substitute for the objective function of profit maximization. Thus the optimization rationale that underlies production functions in the private sector is inapplicable for elementary and secondary education (1973:198).

Assessing the impact of changes in state funding on student outcomes will require researchers and policymakers to identify and track important intermediate outcomes, such as changes in the size and mix of educational staff, size and quality of facilities, instructional and student support services, and classroom curriculum and instruction.

At the moment, the determination that certain intermediate outcomes of finance reform are important for producing student learning rests on a foundation of assumptions with varying degrees of support from empirical research. As we discussed above, movement along the equity dimension drives poor districts to emulate wealthy districts in their spending patterns. But the determinations as to whether continued progress toward equity for poor districts will lead to the most efficient use of new dollars in these districts require consideration of several factors. First, the efficiency of spending in wealthy districts needs to be determined through empirical research. Several efforts are now underway (see Guthrie and Rothstein, Chapter 7 in this volume) to develop different models of efficient spending that can be related to a definition of adequacy in state school finance. A second fruitful line of research might be to work from the emerging models of whole-school reform to develop their implications for resource requirements and expected outcomes and to determine their relative efficacy in low-wealth districts. Such models were not available to district leaders during the early 1990s when the new funding discussed here became available. A third approach is to build on current efforts to formulate the cost differences between rich and poor districts and determine whether major variations in student or school characteristics create different models of efficiency for rich and poor districts (see Duncombe and Yinger, Chapter 8 in this volume).

At the moment, the absence of multiple studies that can yield empirical information in each of these three areas presents a major challenge to evaluations of the efficiency of current spending patterns in different types of districts. Improvements in our understanding of the variations in the nature of schools, students, and reform efforts within different states will contribute to the future models of school spending that can be used as the basis for determinations of efficiency of both current and new dollars. In the interim, we should exercise caution in assuming that all district spending patterns are driven by similar forces, especially in areas characterized by significant economic transitions, residential instability and demographic changes, or large concentrations of students with special characteristics or needs that have cost implications.

NOTES

1. The CPRE research was funded by a grant from the U.S. Department of Education, Office of Educational Research and Improvement (Grant R117-G10039). CEPA-NJ's study of New Jersey was funded by the Mellon Foundation, the Pew Charitable Trusts, and the Rockefeller Foundation.

2. See *Rose v. Council for Better Education, Inc.*, 790 S.W.2nd 186 (Ky. 1989) and *Abbott v. Burke*, 119 N.J. 287 (1990).

3. See *Edgewood Indep. Sch. Dist. v. Kirby*, No. 362, 516 (259th Dist. Ct. Tex., 1987), rev'd 761 S.W.2d 859 (Tex. Ct. App., 1988), rev'd 777 S.W.2d 391 (Tex., 1989).

4. The prior funding system used a foundation formula structure, but there was no required local effort. As a result, there was little wealth-based variation in the allocation of state aid (Koch and Willis, 1993).

5. A foundation aid formula guarantees that each student's education is supported by a state-prescribed amount of money or foundation. School districts must contribute to this foundation amount, typically by levying a state-established tax rate. State aid is the difference between the foundation amount and the district's required contribution.

6. Guaranteed tax base plans are designed to ensure that every district in a state can act as though its tax base is the same as some state-set level—a guaranteed tax base (GTB). Under this approach, the local school district chooses its tax rate for education, which is then applied to the GTB and the district's actual tax base. State aid is the difference between what would be raised with the GTB and what can actually be raised from the local tax base.

7. In 1991-92, the CED—a single or multi-county entity—replaced the local school district as the source of revenue for the required local contribution in the foundation formula. The CED generated and distributed this local revenue to each school district within its boundaries, substantially equalizing the range of property tax bases in the county. The CED provision was declared unconstitutional by the Texas Supreme Court in 1992 and was replaced with a requirement that high-wealth districts reduce their per-pupil property wealth to $280,000 (Picus and Toenjes, 1994).

8. For example, the Kentucky legislature had appropriated only $25 million for Tier 1 in 1991-92. It raised this appropriation to $150 million for the 1992-94 biennium to fully fund this program (Koch and Willis, 1993).

REFERENCES

Adams, E.K.
  1980   *Fiscal Response and School Finance Simulations: A Policy Perspective.* Report No. F80-3. Denver, CO: Education Commission of the States.
Adams, J.E., Jr.
  1994   Spending school reform dollars in Kentucky: Familiar patterns and new programs, but is this reform? *Educational Evaluation and Policy Analysis* 16(4):375-390.
  1996   Organizational Context and District Resource Allocation. Paper presented at the annual meeting of the American Educational Research Association, New York.
Adams, J.E., Jr., and W.E. White II
  1997   The equity consequences of school finance reform in Kentucky. *Educational Evaluation and Policy Analysis* 19(2):165-184.
Alexander, A.J.
  1974   *Teachers, Salaries and School District Expenditures.* Santa Monica, CA: The RAND Corporation.
Barro, S.W., and S.J. Carroll
  1975   *Budget Allocation by School Districts: An Analysis of Spending for Teacher and Other Resources.* Santa Monica, CA: The RAND Corporation.
Berne, R., and L. Stiefel
  1984   *The Measurement of Equity in School Finance.* Baltimore: The Johns Hopkins University Press.
Burkhead, J.
  1973   Economics against education. *Teachers College Record* 75:193-205.
Busch, C., and A. Odden
  1997   Introduction to the special issue: Improving educational policy and results with school-level data—A synthesis of multiple perspectives. *Journal of Education Finance* 22:225-245.
DiMaggio P.J., and W.W. Powell
  1991   Introduction. Pp. 1-40 in *The New Institutionalism in Organizational Analysis,* W.W. Powell and P.J. DiMaggio, eds. Chicago, IL: University of Chicago Press.
Firestone. W.A.
  1989   Educational policy as an ecology of games. *Educational Researcher* 18:18-24.
Firestone, W.A., M.E. Goertz, B. Nagle, and M.F. Smelkinson
  1994   Where did the $800 million go? The first year of New Jersey's Quality Education Act. *Educational Evaluation and Policy Analysis* 16(4):359-373.

Firestone, W.A., M.E. Goertz, and G. Natriello
  1997   *From Cashbox to Classroom: The Struggle for Fiscal Reform and Educational Change in New Jersey.* New York: Teachers College Press.
Goertz, M.E.
  1979   *Money and Education: How Far Have We Come? Financing New Jersey Education in 1979.* Princeton, NJ: Educational Testing Service.
  1994   The Equity Impact of the Quality Education Act in New Jersey. Paper presented at the annual meeting of the American Education Finance Association, Nashville, TN.
  1995   The Equity Impact of the Quality Education Act in New Jersey. Unpublished paper prepared for the Consortium for Policy Research in Education, Rutgers University.
Hartman, W.T.
  1988   District spending: What do the dollars buy? *Journal of Education Finance* 13(4):436-459.
Kirst, M.W.
  1977   What happens at the local level after school finance reform? *Policy Analysis* 3(3):301-324.
Koch, K., and T. Willis
  1993   The Kentucky Education Reform Act of 1990: A Review of the First Biennium. Paper presented at the annual meeting of the American Education Finance Association, Albuquerque, NM.
Meyer, J.W., and B. Rowan
  1977   Institutionalized organizations: Formal structure as myth and ceremony. *American Journal of Sociology* 83:340-363.
Moynihan, D.P.
  1972   Equalizing education: In whose benefit? *The Public Interest* 29:69-89.
National Center for Education Statistics
  1995   *Digest of Education Statistics 1995.* NCES 95-029. Washington, DC: U.S. Government Printing Office.
Odden, A., and L.O. Picus
  1992   *School Finance: A Policy Perspective.* New York: McGraw-Hill.
Odden, A., R. Palaich, and J. Augenblick
  1979   *Analysis of the New York School Finance System, 1977-78.* Denver, CO: Education Commission of the States.
Picus, L.O.
  1994   The local impact of school finance reform in four Texas school districts. *Educational Evaluation and Policy Analysis* 16(4):391-404.
Picus, L.O., and L. Toenjes
  1994   Texas School Finance: Assessing the Equity Impact of Multiple Reforms. Paper presented at the annual meeting of the American Education Finance Association, Nashville, TN.
Powell, W.W., and P.J. DiMaggio
  1991   *The New Institutionalism in Organizational Analysis.* Chicago: University of Chicago Press.
Rowan, B.
  1982   Organizational structure and the institutional environment: The case of public schools. *Administrative Science Quarterly* 27:259-279.
Sacks, D.
  1990   It will murder the middle class. *New York Times* (July 11):A14.

Texas Education Agency
  1991   *Snapshot '90: 1989-90 School District Profiles*. Austin, TX: Texas Education Agency,
          Office of Policy Planning and Evaluation.
  1993   *Snapshot '93: 1992-93 School District Profiles*. Austin, TX: Texas Education Agency,
          Office of Policy Planning and Evaluation.
Tolbert, P.S., and L.G. Zucker
  1983   Institutional sources of change in the formal structure of organizations: The diffusion of
          civil service reform, 1880-1935. *Administrative Science Quarterly* 28:22-39.
Tsang, M.C., and H.R. Levin
  1983   The impacts of intergovernmental grants on education spending. *Review of Educational
          Research* 53(3):329-367.

5

The Politics of School Finance in the 1990s

Melissa C. Carr and Susan H. Fuhrman

INTRODUCTION

Education is one of the most important investments that a state can make in the future of its individual citizens and of the society as a whole. Educational opportunities and resources, however, are unevenly distributed among rich and poor sectors in our society.[1] In the United States, a country based on the principles of equality, thousands of American children may be deprived of future opportunities because they do not receive an equal or even adequate education. Other chapters in this volume have documented the efforts in many states to reduce educational disparities, especially disparities in the amount spent per student or disparities resulting from differences in school district wealth.

Solving the problems of school finance, however, is difficult and has often required action in the courts. In addition, the politics of school finance are inherently contentious. A state's existing school finance system is a product of the legislative process and therefore reflects the state's balance of political power. Changing that system requires a shift of power relationships, and the external stimulus from the courts is often only one of many factors that determine the success of school finance reform efforts within individual states.

This chapter explores how state politics have affected the implementation of reforms that result from court orders or concerns about possible legal challenges in the area of school finance. It examines questions such as: How have state legislatures and executive branches responded to anticipated legal action and to court mandates to reform school finance systems? What coalitions formed to support or resist various approaches to equity? Do governors and state legislatures have the capacity, resources, and political will to implement the types of reforms embedded in school finance litigation?

This chapter will explore the trends in the politics of school finance from the 1970s to the present and will look specifically at four states where the courts have ordered reforms of school finance systems. Analysts of school finance litigation have argued that favorable trends in recent court decisions give cause for optimism about improved school finance equity (Thro, 1989, 1990). Political and economic analysts, on the other hand, have argued that significant challenges to school finance reform remain in many states (Reed, 1997). Using a general analysis of the issues and the evidence from these four states, we will argue that although judicial decisions in favor of finance equity are more common and more comprehensive, the political climate can impede efforts to take action based on these decisions. The political incentives for governors and legislators are such that comprehensive changes in school finance programs are not likely to come easily within a state, at least for the foreseeable future.

The analysis of school finance politics in this chapter addresses the following questions: (1) Why is school finance reform so contentious in the United States? What incentives encourage politicians to either support or oppose greater equity in school finance? (2) How were the politics of school finance in the 1970s and 1980s influenced by the trends in the courts, in state politics, and in the economy? (3) How did the political, economic, and social contexts in the 1990s differ from those of the 1970s and 1980s? (4) Are the politics of school finance in four states (Kentucky, Alabama, New Jersey,[2] and Texas) examples of the trends in the 1990s? (5) What are some of the lessons learned in school finance politics? What are some of the crucial elements for successful reform?

THE POLITICS OF SCHOOL FINANCE: ISSUES AND INCENTIVES

Issues

School finance is an inherently controversial issue in the United States because it affects two basic issues that concern most American voters: the resources available for their children's education and their state and local taxes. Education is often seen as the great equalizer, the key to success, and the most important responsibility for state and local politicians. Although most people support the idea of giving all children equal educational opportunities, problems arise when attempts are made to define equality (see Berne and Stiefel, Chapter 1 in this volume). There is no consensus about the quality of education to which every child is entitled, the extent to which each citizen should pay for that education, or the level or forms of disparities that are acceptable within a school district, state, or the nation.

Local Control

The long-standing tradition of using local property taxes to finance education has been the cause of many inequities in education and makes state reform of
school finance systems controversial. Variations in property values, local tax
rates, and costs of competing municipal services have led to large disparities in
per-pupil spending and in educational opportunity. Americans are used to the
idea that they can directly determine how much to tax themselves to fund their
local schools. Moreover, with locally determined and locally raised taxes, almost
all questions related to education—whether in the realm of finance, curriculum,
facilities, or personnel—have historically been decided and managed at the local
level. Thus, there are strong coalitions with vested interests in maintaining local
control of education funds and services. School finance reform, however, is
legislated at the state level and reduces the number of financial and, to some
extent, programmatic decisions made at the local level. Many voters are opposed
to relinquishing this local control over their taxes and education policies.

Moreover, for many people, it has become part of the American tradition to
aspire to earn more money, live in a larger house in a better community, and send
one's children to a better school than one's parents were able to do. People often
feel that they are entitled to the good public schools in their community as a
reward for their hard work. This feeling of entitlement makes people reluctant to
transfer the fruits of their labor out of their own communities. If, instead of
paying for the education of their own children, taxpayers see their money going
to students in other towns or other counties, they may feel that neither these
students nor the students' parents have earned their benefits. Similarly, since
education is considered the key to success, parents are often determined to secure
the best possible education for their children. For some people, the desire for
their own children to succeed extends into trying to maintain all possible advantages for them, even if it means unequal and unfair treatment of other children in
some other district.

Leveling-Up

In order to overcome the inequities created by the dependence on the local
property tax to finance education, states must do one or more of the following:
redistribute state and local funds, increase state revenues, or cap education expenditures in wealthy districts. Because many American voters are protective of the
local resources available for their children's education, school finance equalization has typically been a process of leveling-up. No proposal to equalize education funding throughout a state by decreasing expenditures down to the lowest
level has ever been considered politically feasible or desirable.[3] Therefore,
school finance equalization requires more money and frequently involves increased state taxes.

State officials, however, often have few incentives to raise taxes. Tax increases are always unpopular even if the program which the increased revenues support is popular. Additionally, the taxes most frequently available to states for use in supporting school finance equalization are the income tax and the sales tax. Both are hard to increase because they affect politically powerful constituencies and the state's ability to compete with other states for economic development purposes.

Demographics

In many states, demographics further complicate the school finance issue. Elderly people are often reluctant, or simply unable, to pay higher local property taxes in support of local schools. Similarly, taxpayers with no children, with grown children, or with children who attend private schools often protest paying high taxes in support of education, a state service from which they perceive little or no personal benefit. If these people are reluctant to support their local schools, they are often even less willing to pay higher taxes in support of schools outside their community. Furthermore, some would prefer to see the increased revenues applied to other programs from which they personally receive greater benefit, such as Medicaid, law enforcement, or public transportation.

To the extent that towns and school districts are segregated along racial, ethnic, religious or socioeconomic lines, corresponding prejudices often enter the politics of school finance. People in wealthy, predominantly white suburbs may oppose school finance equalization because they perceive themselves as the main losers and urban minorities as the main beneficiaries of such policies. Perceptions that equalization aid would be wasted—either by bloated administration or on children who are difficult to teach—help fuel the opposition to school finance reform.

Incentives

Considering the inherently controversial nature of school finance, what incentives exist for political actors to get involved in school finance reform and work toward school finance equalization? Education is always one of the most salient issues in state politics and educational expenditures often make up the largest share of most state budgets. Therefore, making a mark on education can make or break political careers. Traditionally, one of the best ways for governors and legislators to play a role in such a state issue is through the purse. In times of fiscal surplus, governors and legislatures often face powerful incentives to get involved in school finance reform since education aid is one of the easier methods of distributing resources to all geographic constituencies. This fact provides an incentive to get involved in school finance; it does not, however, automatically translate into an incentive to equalize educational opportunity.

Legislative Branch Incentives

Constitutional requirements vary among the states, but most state constitutions require the legislature to establish a free system of public schools that fits some quality standard such as "thorough and efficient."[4] Addressing this constitutional obligation through school finance is conceptually simpler than attempting to address it through nonmonetary criteria. Therefore, constitutional obligations sometimes provide legislatures with incentives to equalize school finance, especially when there is a court mandate for reform, a threat of litigation, or the likelihood that a court will rule that the state's educational system is constitutionally inequitable or inadequate.

Incentives for legislatures to change school finance systems exist when the risks of not acting are greater than the risks of acting. For instance, when there has been outside pressure from the court or from the community to reduce disparities in funding, some legislatures have found it in their best interest to act. These periods of legislative activity in the sphere of school finance have usually coincided with strong state economies that have decreased the necessity for, or softened the blow of, new taxes (Fuhrman, 1994b:31).

More often than not, however, legislators have been reluctant to promote school finance reform for fear of being associated with the introduction of new taxes. Legislators represent individual districts, are accountable only to those districts, and are very conscious of their district's tolerance level for taxes. Fearful of overstepping that tolerance level, legislators are often reluctant to vote for a policy that would require a tax increase even if that policy would bring benefits to some of the members of their district.

In school finance politics, representatives from poor districts are the most likely advocates of school finance equalization while representatives from other districts are protective of their portions of state aid and conscious of their voters' tolerance for new taxes. Representatives from the wealthiest districts often express their constituents' concerns: that they be allowed to spend as much as they want on education for their children and that their local money stay in their local schools rather than being put into a state pool to be redistributed to poorer districts. To the extent that poorer districts tend to be urban, their representatives have other battles to fight in the state legislature in order to secure state aid to other municipal programs. In such a scenario, representatives from suburban districts may be able to reserve more political capital for use in education debates than their colleagues from urban districts. Moreover, representatives from poor districts tend to be outnumbered by representatives from middle and wealthy districts combined. Since the 1960s, structural and legal change in state legislatures, combined with urban flight and the growth of the suburbs, have dramatically reduced the power of cities and rural areas in relation to that of the suburbs in most state legislatures (Weir, 1995).

Executive Branch Incentives

Governors are accountable to the whole state and therefore are not limited to representing local interests. This mandate makes governors more likely than members of the legislature to lead efforts for comprehensive school finance policies in the best interest of children and youth throughout the state.

Governors do, however, balance the interests of the majority with those of the minority. The fact that school finance reform is often perceived to assist children in only a few districts—albeit often the largest and most populated—at the expense of children or taxpayers in the rest of the state sometimes limits the Governor's willingness to act on this issue. Governors have a limited amount of time in office, a limited number of staff, and limited amounts of political capital. They must therefore choose cautiously the issues that they will focus on and must be careful not to use too many of these scarce resources on unpopular or contentious initiatives. As a result, gubernatorial leadership on school finance reform is unlikely without at least one of the following catalysts: outside pressure from the courts, widespread support among the population, or the existence of a fiscal surplus. An existing school finance system is, after all, the result of the legislative process and thus represents an intricate web of political compromises that reflect the state's political balance of power. Upsetting that balance is often too risky for political leaders.

Judicial Branch Incentives

Because legislatures and governors have few incentives to solve the inequities and inadequacies in school finance systems, people have often turned to the courts to break the political logjam. It is the court's duty to interpret the constitution and decide whether or not the legislated school finance system meets constitutional requirements. The court's overriding concern in school finance cases is what the state should be required, by law, to provide for students throughout the state. Some courts simply answer that question and leave the legislative and executive branches to design a solution that meets the court's standards; others have gone further by prescribing a remedy.

The court is more insulated from the political process than the legislature or the governor and is therefore most likely to advocate for the underrepresented groups in the population. It is important, however, to remember that the courts are not completely isolated from the political process. Many judges are appointed and approved by political leaders while others are elected by the population. Moreover, in deciding a school finance case, the court must always consider its willingness to enforce the decision (in some cases this has required an injunction to close the schools). Since courts really have very limited enforcement power, they run the risk of having their authority undermined if they mandate (in their decision or their prescribed remedy) a politically impossible solution that the legislature and/or governor decides not to enact or enforce.

Interest Group Incentives

The types and positions of interest groups that participate in school finance debates vary significantly over time and across states. Historically, education interest groups and state departments of education have played the key roles in determining education policy. Over the past three decades, however, their influence has decreased dramatically due to their increased fragmentation. The interest groups that have actively opposed school finance reform over the past three decades are the anti-tax groups that typically oppose school spending. On the other side of the debate, groups advocating for the poor, particularly the urban poor, have most actively argued in favor of leveling up policies and have brought many of the legal challenges to the state's system of financing education. All these interest groups play a significant role in determining the incentives facing government and legislators as they respond to court mandates for school finance reform.

Teachers unions, which in many states are traditionally politically powerful entities, have been noticeably quiet in most school finance reform debates, except to argue for increased overall spending. Frequently unions, as well as other statewide educational interest groups, have been paralyzed on the school finance issue because their members have been so divided, depending on where they live and the perceived effects of any particular policy on their district.

Competing concerns within the education community have also limited the influence of educational interest groups. Teachers, administrators, and school board associations view school finance reform proposals from different perspectives. Special education advocates, bilingual program advocates, gifted and talented program advocates, and advocates for "regular" education often compete with each other for pieces of the pie rather than forming coalitions to lobby to increase the overall amount of revenue available. Although all of these groups consistently agree that there should be more resources spent on education, they are divided by their disagreement over how these resources should be allocated.

THE POLITICS OF SCHOOL FINANCE IN THE 1970S AND 1980S

The 1970s: A Decade of School Finance Reform

The 1970s was a decade of great activity in school finance reform in all branches of state governments. During this decade, school finance litigation reached the highest court in 16 states. School finance reform emerged as an election issue in gubernatorial and legislative elections. Governors Askew of Florida, Milliken of Michigan, and Anderson of Minnesota chose to make school finance one of their top issues (Fuhrman, 1994a:57). Twenty-eight state legislatures reformed their school finance systems.[5] As a result of these reforms, the state share of education spending increased from 38 percent in 1972 (Evans et al., 1997) to 45 percent by 1979 and the state aid to elementary and secondary education doubled (Fuhrman, 1982:53). The sheer prevalence of school finance reform during this period represents more than twice the expected rate of diffusion of policy ideas from state to state (Brown and Elmore, 1982:107).[6]

The intense interest in school finance reform during the 1970s was a reflection of four emerging trends: the birth of school finance litigation, the activism of a national reform movement, changes in gubernatorial and legislative institutions, and the existence of fiscal surpluses. These factors combined to create an environment in which legislators and governors faced strong political incentives to act on the school finance issue.

Prior to the 1970s, legislative and executive participation in education policy making had been minimal (generally confined to fiscal matters) as efforts had been made to insulate education from politics. Educators, educational interest groups, and state departments of education had played united, active roles in education issues. They determined policies and simply presented them to political leaders for their approval.

In the 1970s, with school finance as the major issue in education, the role of state legislators and governors in education policy increased dramatically and began to overshadow that of the previously dominant education coalition. This trend was due in part to reforms within the legislative and executive branches, reforms that created larger professional staffs, enhanced gubernatorial veto powers, and increased budgetary control for the governors. With large professional staffs, legislators and governors could commission their own research on education issues. At the same time, conflicts between teachers and school board associations, the emergence of collective bargaining for teachers, and geographic splits between urban/rural and property-rich/property-poor districts began to fragment the once united education coalition.

During the 1970s, governors and legislatures created commissions and committees to assess equity and propose solutions. They also designed proposals to respond to anticipated or actual court mandates for school finance reform. Some even proposed tax increases and new revenue sources to increase the amount of education funding that came from the states. As a consequence of their leadership roles in school finance reforms, state legislatures and governors emerged from this decade as full-fledged education policymakers.

One of the legacies of the 1960s was an increased public awareness of social inequities and injustices. In the 1970s, this public awareness, along with the realization that desegregation efforts were not effectively providing each American child with an equal educational opportunity, helped spark a wave of successful school finance litigation, beginning with the watershed *Serrano v. Priest* case in California in 1971. In the early 1970s, people took note of the fact that education spending at the 95th percentile was 2.72 times higher than education spending at the 5th percentile and challenged these inequities in the state and federal courts.[7] The results of the first wave of cases were mixed, but they definitely succeeded in getting the issue of school finance reform on the agenda in state politics.

Although school finance litigation occurred in only 12 of the 28 states that legislated school finance reform during the 1970s, it is important not to underestimate the role that litigation had in prompting legislative and executive action in all states. The cases put the issue of school finance reform on the political agenda, dramatized the taxing and spending inequities among districts, and demonstrated to every state that its own school finance system might also be susceptible to challenge. In states where there was a school finance case, reform probably would not have occurred without litigation. In other states, the threat of school finance litigation prompted legislatures and governors to take action. Many governors and legislators therefore found school finance reform in their best interest—whether out of personal ideological conviction, in response to a court mandate, as a preemptive measure to avoid litigation, or for a combination of these reasons.

Litigation resulting in a court mandate for reform of the state school finance system did not, however, guarantee reform of school finance. Legislatures were sometimes reluctant to act, in part because of confusion over what reforms were necessary to comply with the court order. Many of the court decisions in the 1970s were narrow in scope, did not establish a clear definition of a constitutional school finance system, and did not include instructions for the legislature concerning appropriate remedies. For example, the California Supreme Court and many of the other state courts employed the principle of fiscal neutrality and declared that students should not have diminished access to resources for their education simply because they live in property-poor districts. The courts did not specify, however, whether legislatures needed to assure that the same amount of money was spent on educating each child in the state or whether they needed to equalize across districts the amount of revenue raised at any given tax rate.

The activism of the courts was encouraged and complemented by the activities of a national network of school finance reformers that emerged in the 1970s. Scholars, lawyers, government officials, citizen education groups, minority research and advocacy organizations, and national organizations such as the National Conference of State Legislators and the Education Commission of the States combined to provide research, technical assistance, and other support to the movement. The network, nurtured by the Ford Foundation's program in Education Finance and Management, helped plaintiffs make their cases about the state's constitutional responsibility to provide education for all children such that the amount of resources available to children and their schools is not dependent on where children live. Members of the network, which extended beyond the traditionally active educational interest groups, researched all aspects of school finance reform—from the technical questions regarding the best formulas to the political and economic dimensions of the issue—and then shared the results with policymakers and the public.

Not all governors and legislators, however, were eager to get involved and make the changes in school finance systems that were necessary to respond to court mandates to increase equity. The contentiousness of the issue and lack of leadership made compliance with the court mandates very slow in many states. For example, the New Jersey Supreme Court and legislature engaged in a 3-year struggle which involved seven rounds of court decisions before an equalization plan that was acceptable to the courts was finally established. After the initial *Robinson v. Cahill* decision in 1973, the New Jersey legislature defied the court order. It did not even begin to legislate a response until the court prohibited the state treasurer from disbursing state aid to education in any manner that did not comply with *Robinson*. When the legislature did pass a new formula, it stalled on enacting the taxes to pay for it. Only after the court closed the schools did the New Jersey legislature implement its first state income tax and fund a school finance plan which was found to be in compliance with *Robinson*. Similarly, in California, *Serrano v. Priest* went to the state's highest court level three times and only in the third round, 15 years after the initial decision, was the legislated school finance system upheld as constitutional.

Although court activism, the national reform network, and shifts in political roles in education policy making all provided increased incentives for gubernatorial and legislative action on school finance reform, the most crucial factor was the existence of fiscal surpluses. Pressure from the courts, the public, and their own institutions may not have been enough to force so many legislatures to act had there not been money with which to reform school finance systems. The pattern of school finance reform in the 1970s mirrors that of the economy. The high points of reform activity at the beginning and end of the decade also coincided with the years of fiscal surplus. Similarly, the middle years of the decade were a time of relative inactivity in school finance reform and a dip in the economic fortunes of the states. Reform during this period was a process of leveling-up in most states. Only three states, Montana, Utah, and Wyoming chose the politically more difficult route of equalizing school finance by redistributing funds from rich to poor districts (Odden et al., 1983:7). In the rest of the states where reform was enacted, districts with low-property wealth became eligible for increased state aid. As a result, the states added a total of over $27 billion to their share of education expenditures during the 1970s (Fuhrman, 1982:57).

It is important to note that the reforms of the 1970s were not designed, even on their surface, to fully equalize per-pupil expenditures, much less educational opportunities.[8] During the 1970s, the debate surrounding school finance reform in many states was focused on reducing property tax rates as well as equalizing education expenditures. In fact, a 1978 study found that school finance reform was accompanied by significant property tax relief in 11 of the 19 states studied. In eight of those states, tax relief appeared to have come at the expense of the educational program since those states' per-pupil expenditures declined relative to the national average (Brown and Elmore, 1982:112). Especially after *Rodriguez*, the 1973 federal court case which upheld Texas's highly inequitable school finance system as constitutional under the federal Constitution, and after the economic downturn in the mid 1970s, reforms became much more diverse in their objectives and, overall, less concerned with pure school finance equity arguments (Brown and Elmore, 1982:112-113).[9]

In the 1970s, the courts and many legislatures used the standard of fiscal neutrality. New school finance formulas did not require equalized tax rates but were designed so that districts would receive equal revenue for equal tax rates. Such formulas could only equalize revenues to the extent that districts chose to tax themselves at the same rate. In many instances, however, property-poor districts taxed themselves at relatively low rates and therefore had significantly lower amounts of revenue available for educational expenditures. Although the new formulas shrunk spending gaps and increased the proportion of the state's contribution to education expenditures, they did not equalize per-pupil expenditures (Fuhrman, 1982:57). At the time, however, these changes were enough to satisfy the courts and subdue the public pressure for equity from educational and social interest groups.

The 1980s: Excellence Replaces Equity as the Top Concern

During the 8 years from January 1981 to December 1988, only 8 school finance cases were decided in the states' highest courts as opposed to the previous 8-year period when 16 cases had reached the highest courts in their states. Moreover, during this same 8-year time period only 1 of the cases was decided in favor of the plaintiffs as compared to 7 out of 16 between 1973 and 1980. Faced with less pressure from the courts, legislators and governors were able to turn to issues other than school finance. Events at the beginning of the decade did much to set the tenor for the remaining years. The recession of 1981-82 and the 1983 publication of the report *A Nation At Risk* (National Commission on Excellence in Education, 1983), combined to relegate school finance to the back burner for most of the decade.

By the early 1980s, most states were experiencing fiscal difficulties. The aggregated national balance of state budgets in 1983, for example, was $2.3 billion in comparison to 5 years before, in 1978, when it had been $21.2 billion (Council of State Governments, 1980:275). States like California and Massachusetts had enacted tax and expenditure caps which limited the amount of money available for education equalization aid. Other states, such as Michigan and Oregon, were experiencing severe economic downturns. Most states had dangerously low amounts of economic reserves and experienced decreases in federal funding of education during the first years of the Reagan administration. During these years, the main concern was simply maintaining the overall level of resources for education rather than finding ways to increase resources in order to improve equity.

The 1983 report from the National Commission on Excellence in Education, *A Nation At Risk*, called attention to a perceived crisis in the quality of education in the United States. Governors and legislators responded by shifting their attention from school finance equity to issues of education standards, graduation requirements, teacher certification, and compensation. For some, the equalization efforts of the 1970s had "dealt with" school finance and it was no longer an issue. The courts, the public, and the plaintiffs were either satisfied with or resigned to these initial successes. Therefore, governors and legislators faced less pressure from the courts and the public to equalize school funding, and excellence replaced equity as the focus.

During the excellence reform efforts of the 1980s, governors and legislators expanded the leadership role that they had established for themselves in the 1970s. The sheer volume of legislative activity in education reform issues in the 1980s was unprecedented. By 1985, almost every state had enacted some sort of reform package. For example, over 40 new state testing programs were established and over 1,000 pieces of legislation concerning teacher certification and compensation alone were introduced in state legislatures (Fuhrman, 1994b:31). The diffusion of these policy actions across states was significantly faster than the diffusion rates of school finance reform (McDonnell and Fuhrman, 1985:48).

To some extent the increased legislative and gubernatorial interest in substantive issues of education was an inevitable result of the increased proportion of resources they were providing to education. Since the state share of education funding had increased significantly, it was only natural that governors and legislators, who appropriated these resources, would want to increase accountability and their involvement in the management of these funds. However, the aura of crisis and pressure from the public, especially the business elites, significantly spurred action.

After the recession in 1981-82, the 1980s was generally a decade when state economies were fairly healthy and resources were available to education. Between 1982-83 and 1986-87, state funding for education rose 21.3 percent in real terms (Fuhrman, 1994b:31). This increase, however, financed the general education reforms of concern to the states during this decade rather than equalization efforts. In fact, many of the equity gains that had been made in the 1970s eroded in the 1980s.[10]

As a result, the reforms of the 1970s were not designed to achieve equal educational opportunity, or even equal per-pupil expenditures. The reforms did not account for the fact that poorer districts might choose to tax themselves at a lower rate or for other urban factors that complicate the picture. Urban districts have greater expenditures on public health, transportation, housing, welfare, crime prevention, prisons, and services for the elderly than suburban or rural districts do. These large urban programs create more intense competition for scarce resources and political pressures so that education sometimes can lose out. Although municipal overburden can lead to greater disparities in per-pupil expenditures in urban versus suburban or rural districts, the significance of this type of influence remains in doubt.

Similarly, although the costs of education in urban districts are assumed to be higher than suburban or rural districts, since the cities tend to have more students living in poverty, students requiring at-risk programs, students with limited English proficiency, and students with disabilities, the appropriate weights to compensate for these differences remain uncertain.

By 1979-80, 23 states provided funds to local districts for support services for children at risk and for children with limited English language skills. All 50 states had passed special education programs in keeping with new federal law. However, during the recession of the early 1980s, when there was not enough revenue generated to pay for everything, many of these supplementary programs were the first to be repealed. In addition to reducing the equalizing effects of the 1970s reforms, this circumstance intensified competition among educational interest groups based on which supplementary program (i.e., special education, bilingual education, or programs for impoverished youth) they supported.

Although the reforms in the 1970s had increased the state share of education expenditures to 45 percent in 1979, more than half of school financing remained dependent on local property tax revenues (Fuhrman, 1994a:61). School financing formulas that maintain a local property tax component and do not cap wealthy districts' expenditures, redistribute their local revenues, or set the equalization standard at the highest level of funding in the state are open to growing inequities in per-pupil spending over time.

Circumstances in the 1980s hastened the erosion of school finance equity. The recession of 1981-82 forced some states to cut back on state funding and increase the portion of education expenditures funded through locally raised revenues. Other states, such as New Hampshire, were particularly hard hit by the decrease in federal aid to education and increased local contributions to compensate for these losses. In addition, the real estate boom of the 1980s increased the wide disparities among districts' property values, disparities that were exacerbated as the price of suburban property rose at a greater rate than in the cities.

These factors combined in some states to produce even greater inequities in per-pupil expenditures in the 1990s. In New Jersey, for example, differences in per-pupil expenditures were greater in 1989-90 than they had been before equalization legislation was passed in 1975 (Corcoran and Scovronick, 1995:5). Similarly, in the state of Washington, the share of resources available to school districts with the highest percentage of students living in poverty had declined 4.9 percent between the state supreme court's 1978 ruling and 1991 (Rebell, 1994-95:693). These renewed disparities help explain why plaintiffs have since returned to the courts in six of the eight states which had adopted remedies prior to 1989 to improve equity in their school finance system. This is not to say that the reforms and the litigation of the 1970s did not help. The reforms did help—the disparities in per-pupil expenditures grew at an even greater rate in states that had not passed reform. A recent study using data from over 16,000 school districts over the 1972-92 period found that, on average, court-ordered reform reduced within state inequities in per-pupil expenditures by 16 to 38 percent (depending on the measure of inequity used) while legislated reform without successful litigation did not, on average, reduce inequities by a statistically significant amount (Evans et al., 1997:11, 28). But the efforts of the 1970s did not solve the problem.

SCHOOL FINANCE IN THE 1990S—A DIFFERENT CONTEXT

School finance has reemerged as a major issue in the courts, the statehouses, and the legislatures in this country. The judicial, economic, and political contexts surrounding school finance in the 1990s are, however, somewhat different than those of the previous decades.

The Judicial Context of School Finance in the 1990s

Of the 21 cases considered by the states' highest courts since 1989, 13 have been decided in favor of the plaintiffs.[11] This is a much better success rate than the 1 success in 8 cases or 7 successes in 16 cases during two previous 8-year cycles. School finance cases have expanded from a narrow focus on issues of fiscal neutrality and tax equity in the 1970s to broader considerations of the entire education system and the many variables that affect a child's education in the 1990s. The most dramatic example of the increased scope of courts' decisions is the 1989 Kentucky Supreme Court's decision in *Rose v. Council* by which Kentucky's entire education system was declared unconstitutional.

The Kentucky case exemplifies another trend in the court decisions since 1989: courts are more willing to define the remedies and make concrete requirements for a constitutional remedy than they were in the 1970s. These court-mandated requirements for change often address finance, curriculum, inputs, and student outcomes. In part because plaintiffs rely more on state constitutions' education clauses than on pure equal protection arguments, courts have found it necessary to define their standards more clearly and to explain what qualifies as a "thorough and efficient" education. In Kentucky, as well as in Alabama and Massachusetts, the court listed curricular goals of education and specified student capabilities that should result from a constitutional public school system. Some courts have recommended that state leaders must consider other areas including spending disparities, revenue sources, specific finance and education issues, and deadlines for legislative action.

While in the 1970s and 1980s courts had used the standards of equal revenue for equal tax effort or equal per-pupil expenditures to evaluate the constitutionality of school finance systems, in the 1990s courts have tended to use the standard of equal educational opportunity. Under this standard, claims of inequity and remedies for those inequities are defined in terms of relative availability of educational programs and curricular opportunities. There is also increasing recognition of the fact that achieving equal results may require unequal expenditures. When equity is defined as providing each child with an equal educational opportunity regardless of that child's place of residence, socioeconomic status, race, nationality, native language, or disability, ensuring equity actually requires differences in per-pupil expenditures.

These trends in the courts have encouraged many legal scholars to expect major breakthroughs in school finance reform and important strides toward equity. Although the courts are sending encouraging signals, other political and economic considerations mitigate and in many cases overshadow their effects.

The Fiscal Context of School Finance in the 1990s

Without fiscal slack, enacting school finance reform is difficult and often requires new taxes to create revenue sources for leveling-up policies or the redistribution of revenues from other state programs or districts to education. But increasing taxes has been virtually impossible in the anti-tax climate of the 1990s. Meanwhile, fiscal constraints, an aging population, and growing social problems have intensified competition with other programs for state funds. Some states have adopted what has often been the least politically attractive option of capping education expenditures in the wealthy districts and/or redistributing some of the tax revenues from these districts to the poorer districts.

The incentives for governors and legislators to take leadership roles in increasing equity decrease dramatically in a fiscal environment where reform is possible only through raising taxes or leveling-down. Legislative and gubernatorial leadership on school finance issues has always been dependent on the availability of resources. In the late 1970s, early 1980s, and early 1990s, when there was little fiscal slack, legislators and governors did not maintain the high-profile leadership roles in school finance that they demonstrated during periods of relative fiscal plenty (Fuhrman, 1994b:33). Most states have not had large fiscal surpluses in the 1990s until the last few years (National Association of State Budgetary Officers, 1991, 1993, 1995, 1997).

The Political Context of School Finance in the 1990s

Other political issues made reform particularly difficult and hindered movements toward compliance with court mandates to equalize school finance in the early 1990s. The increased scope and specificity of the courts' mandates for educational reform, which addressed a wider range of educational issues, created a larger, more difficult task for the legislature. Furthermore, in the early 1970s all the successful school finance reforms were passed as part of complex packages that often included multiple issues. Since school finance reform often does not have enough widespread support on its own, packaging it within a broader bill that has something for everyone makes it easier to pass (Fuhrman, 1978:164). But, with courts mandating comprehensive education reforms, the resulting remedies require a great deal of compromise and are difficult to package with other legislation.

The new equal educational opportunity standard used in school finance litigation has also made the politics more contentious in the 1990s. Much of the public support for school finance reform in the 1970s stemmed from dissatisfaction with the local property tax; school finance reform provided tax relief and was therefore politically feasible. In the 1970s, school finance reform often required increases in state taxes, but the existence of fiscal surpluses reduced the amounts that had to come from these tax increases, and reform could be equated with tax relief in the public's minds. That equation no longer exists because any greater state role in equalizing school finance is likely to rely on greater taxation.

The new nature of the court-mandated remedies also calls for increased state monitoring of education spending, state curriculum requirements for minimum standards of education, and minimum and maximum levels of local funding. These reforms, which often accompany equalization efforts, decrease (or at least are perceived to decrease) the amount of local autonomy in education decisions and in setting local tax rates. They are opposed by groups with vested interests in, or ideological commitment to, maintaining local control. Moreover, they directly conflict with increasing voter support for decentralization and deregulation in all aspects of public life (Massell et al., 1997).

Although increasing state taxes and introducing new taxes have never been politically popular moves, the public has had varying degrees of tolerance for tax increases over the years. Currently, an extreme anti-tax mood characterizes the public and their elected officials. An indication of the strength of this anti-tax sentiment is the fact that on the national level, as of October 1996, nearly one-half of all U.S. representatives and 35 U.S. senators had signed a pledge to vote against any tax increases (Rubin, 1996:3058). The 1994 sweeping Republican victory in Congress was largely based on an anti-tax, anti-government platform. Similar results were also observed in the state legislative and executive branches; many newly elected officials fashioned successful campaigns against incumbents by using anti-tax and anti-government themes. In fact, increasing state taxes in the 1990s has proven to be political suicide for many. New Jersey former-Governor James Florio and many of his Democratic colleagues in the legislature learned that lesson the hard way when, in response to *Abbott v. Burke*, they passed reform legislation which included a tax increase. Florio's 1993 defeat by Governor Christine Whitman and numerous Democratic losses in the state legislature during that year were a result of resultant public opposition (Corcoran and Scovronick, 1995).

In addition, general lack of trust in state and local government's use of education funds permeates the politics of school finance today. Many taxpayers have watched their state taxes increase to pay for better education while simultaneously hearing media reports of the decline of the American education system. Increases in education spending have coincided with increases in violence, guns, and drugs in schools. Similarly, Eric Hanushek's studies (1986, 1991, 1996) in which he detected no correlation between the amount of resources invested in education and student achievement received increased attention in the late 1980s and early 1990s. Hanushek and others have pointed to the fact that as per-pupil education expenditures have steadily risen over the past 30 years, average SAT scores have steadily declined (Picus, 1997:35). Of course many factors account for test score stagnation, and recent analyses of educational spending, such as those by Hedges et al. (1994), have questioned Hanushek's econometric techniques and the resulting claim that money does not matter in education. Ferguson and Ladd (1996) used a different econometric model and found a positive correlation between additional resources and student outcomes. Others have used different measures of student outcomes (such as dropout rates and postgraduation wages) and found a positive relationship between spending and increased outcomes (Murray, 1995; Card and Krueger, 1992).

Studies are now underway to identify which types of investments are most likely to improve student outcomes. For example, Krueger (1997) and Monk (1994) conducted studies which demonstrate the importance of teacher education, small class size, and teacher knowledge, respectively, on student outcomes. Despite these other studies, Hanushek's observation of upward trends in spending and downward trends in test scores is enough to raise many questions in the minds of voters about the effectiveness and necessity of increased resources for education.

Few voters have any real understanding of how their education tax dollars are being spent. They often do not appreciate the increased costs of education in the 1990s with higher enrollments, more regulations, and special programs. Each of these trends, especially the increasing enrollments in special education, has significant effects on the distribution of resources and educational opportunity within a state that are generally not sufficiently explained to the public.

Less political will exists to reform school finance systems than there was in the 1970s, especially in states that have had extensive school finance litigation and have enacted multiple remedies. Many people feel that the state has made enough of an effort to equalize school funding and that a lack of results is more a reflection of mismanagement of resources or proof that money does not matter in education than a reflection of incomplete or ineffective state policies. They claim that it makes no sense to invest more money in poorer districts until the local mismanagement problems are solved. In a number of states, these sentiments are complicated by racial prejudices as the poorer districts tend to be cities with high percentages of minorities. Further, antipathy toward unions and tenure among some political factions increases skepticism toward spending more on education.

A symptom of increasing anti-government sentiment and disillusionment with the public schools is the recent tendency to look for solutions outside the public sector. School choice, voucher programs, private management of schools, contracting for services, and charter schools have emerged as new ways to improve education, particularly for students in poorer districts. Such solutions are proposed as cost-effective and efficient ways to improve the quality of education for everyone and are presented as alternatives to pouring more taxpayers' money into schools that do not work. There is no consensus among politicians, education advocacy groups, parents or educators regarding the merits, risks, and viability of these options but the national debate about market-based reforms does call attention to education improvement methods that are not dependent on greater equity among school districts.

Interest Group Politics

Now that school finance reform is increasingly viewed as a zero-sum game where the pie from which all groups must draw is not expected to expand, education groups are even more divided on geographic, programmatic, and philosophical lines than they were in the 1970s. Education interest groups from wealthier districts are threatened by reforms that involve redistribution from particular education services, such as bilingual education or special education programs. The increasing number of students classified as learning disabled has also increased the financial resources, required by federal law, necessary to serve them. Competition between state funding for special programs and for general education aid has divided the education community and, in many states, further strengthened the geographic urban/suburban divide since cities tend to have more students who require additional education services. Education interest groups and educators have not reached a consensus about what constitutes equal or adequate educational opportunity. While a united front from education interest groups might provide legislators and governors with additional incentives to act on school finance reform, the lack of consensus among these groups adds to the public's skepticism that reform is possible or desirable.

Demographics

Demographic trends are eroding voter and taxpayer support for the equalization of school finance. Poterba (1997) observed that an increase in the fraction of elderly residents in a state was associated with a significant reduction in per-child expenditures, especially when the elderly population and school age population were of different races. Finally, the study found that differences in the size of the school-age population do not result in corresponding differences in education spending. Thus, states with larger school-age populations have smaller per-pupil expenditures. This last finding does not bode well for states with increasing enrollments.

Currently, less than 30 percent of adults in the United States have children attending public schools (Crampton and Whitney, 1996:10). The aging of the population has increased the numbers of people who need Medicaid and other programs and strengthened voter interest in these expensive services. In addition, increasing costs of prisons and other crime protection services compete with education for funds. Trends in state budgeting indicate that expenditures on Medicaid and corrections are currently growing at a faster rate than expenditures on education (Crampton and Whitney, 1996).

Changing racial demographics have also contributed to the increased amount of contention surrounding school finance equalization. Many American cities, especially in the Northeast, have experienced substantial white flight in the past 30 years. Black and Latino children are often concentrated in the poorer districts most in need of equalization aid while resources and political influence in the legislature are largely concentrated in the predominantly white suburbs. In many states, while the middle aged and elderly populations are still predominantly white, a rapidly increasing proportion of the students attending public schools are black and Latino. Racial prejudices, such as the idea that all minority school or city officials are corrupt or the idea, reinforced through publications like *The Bell Curve* (Herrnstein and Murray, 1994), that suggest that minority children are less educable than their white peers, strengthen some voters' fears that equalization money will be wasted (Firestone, 1997a,1997b).

Although elementary and secondary school enrollments decreased in the 1970s, enrollments increased in the 1990s, and even larger increases are expected in the near future. The National Center for Education Statistics estimates that in the next decade 6,000 new schools will be needed to accommodate 3 million more children (Crampton and Whitney, 1996:10). Districts need to spend more money just to maintain per-pupil expenditures during periods of increasing enrollments. To the extent that these enrollment increases are concentrated in the poorer districts, they exacerbate disparities in funding and polarize the politics of school finance.

Thus, in the 1990s, the economic and political contexts imply a changed road for school finance reformers. The national trends discussed above provide helpful background, but, since school finance reform is a state-level issue, it is necessary to look at the political, economic, and judicial contexts in each state. In order to understand how these factors affect school finance debates in individual states and to get a sense of what to expect in the future, we now turn to a closer analysis of the politics of school finance in four states.

THE POLITICS OF SCHOOL FINANCE IN KENTUCKY, ALABAMA, NEW JERSEY, AND TEXAS

We chose to study four states that are well known for their school finance histories: Kentucky, where major reform occurred; Alabama, where the lack of political leadership has stymied any response to the court's mandate for reform; Texas, where a solution has brought peace, at least for the time being; and New Jersey, where the school finance reform debate is still raging 25 years after the state's first school finance litigation. The following discussions of each state are based on a review of the literature that focuses on these states and on interviews conducted with academicians, policymakers, and activists who had been involved in reform efforts.

Kentucky[12]

Despite the politically contentious nature of school finance in the 1990s, major school finance reform is possible. Kentucky is often cited as the example of school finance reform that accomplished equalization and comprehensive reform at the same time.

Political incentives for school finance reform in Kentucky included a strong mandate for comprehensive change from the state supreme court, widespread public support, a great need to spark economic development, and relatively low costs. Kentucky had consolidated its school districts in the 1930s and 1950s to county-based districts, reducing the fragmentation and attachment to local control that comes with more numerous, smaller districts. Kentucky has an unusually racially homogeneous population, and minorities tend to be concentrated in the wealthier cities. Thus, equalizing reforms were not perceived as primarily benefiting racial minorities and racial politics did not play a role in the debate. Finally, low investments in education and the need for economic development made it easier for school finance reform advocates to prove the necessity of increased expenditures on education.

The Kentucky Supreme Court decision in *Rose v. Council for Better Education* was key to creating the incentives for legislators and governors to enact reform. Sixty-six school districts (or one third of the state's total) sued the state in *Rose v. Council*, demonstrating widespread support for the idea that something needed to be done. In 1989, the Kentucky Supreme Court was the first ever to declare an entire state education system unconstitutional. Relying on the provision in the Kentucky Constitution that requires "an efficient system of common schools throughout the State," the court determined that each child in the state had a fundamental right to education (Dove, 1991:94) and that this right was violated by the unequal and inadequate nature of the education system. The court declared every piece of legislation related to public schools in Kentucky invalid and charged the legislature with designing a new constitutional education system within a year. The court defined a constitutional system of schools in terms of programs available to students and student achievement results as opposed to per-pupil expenditures. It listed seven goals for education and specified nine minimal standards that the legislature's remedy would have to meet in order to be in compliance.

Within a year, the legislature had passed the Kentucky Education Reform Act (KERA), which had three main components—finance, curriculum, and governance—and a corresponding sales tax increase to fund the bill. KERA created a three-tier system allowing local districts some flexibility in tax rates, capped the wealthiest districts, and leveled-up. There was a hold-harmless provision in the bill which guaranteed that no district could lose money through KERA; everyone won, but the poorer districts won significantly more than the wealthier ones. In order to finance KERA, the state poured an additional $500 million into Kentucky's education system (Reed, 1997:99). KERA remains the law today, having survived for 7 years and three changes in governmental leadership. It has not only survived, it has had impressive results. Kentucky has moved from near the bottom of national rankings in all educational indicators to the middle. In the first 4 years following the passage of KERA, Kentucky's school finance inequities, as measured by the amount of variation in per-pupil expenditures, were cut almost in half (Reed, 1997:99).

Considering the contentious nature of school finance politics, the Kentucky example appears somewhat miraculous. How was such comprehensive reform possible? Who took the lead on KERA, and what factors created the incentives for the legislature to pass it?

Kentucky's educational history had been fairly dismal. For years it had ranked near the bottom of all national education rankings of per-pupil expenditures, measures of equity, and measures of student achievement. During World War II, Kentucky was the number-one state where people were rejected for the draft because of illiteracy. Since then many leaders felt that Kentucky was not getting its fair share of the Southern industrial boom because the state did not have a well-educated workforce.[13] In 1990, Kentucky was still suffering from a lack of economic development and a failing educational system. Predominantly a rural state with coal mining, timber, and agriculture as its main industries, Kentucky's businesses had been satisfied with the level of education of the work force and had typically opposed higher taxes to improve education. But if Kentucky wanted to diversify its economic base and improve the standard of living, that would have to change.

In 1984, Governor Martha Collins was the first governor in Kentucky to talk almost exclusively about education. She argued that improved education would be the key to the future economic development of Kentucky and its survival in the global economy. Governor Collins helped attract a Toyota plant to the state, an event that was critical because it created the need for a more educated work-force.[14]

Governor Wallace G. Wilkinson, the governor at the time of *Rose*, had campaigned on the issue of education reform. Coming from Appalachia with only a high school diploma himself, he was painfully aware of the inadequacies of the education system. He greatly underestimated the cost of reform in his campaign, however, and took a great risk when he backed KERA even though it cost $430 million more than the reform he had promised in his election-winning campaign.[15] Former-Governor Bert Combs, the lawyer for the plaintiffs, also emerged as a powerful political leader in the state at this time.

The grassroots leadership provided by Kentucky's Prichard Committee for Academic Excellence was as important as the political leadership. Founded in 1981, the Prichard Committee consisted of business leaders and other prominent individuals who promoted the idea that education reform was necessary in order to bring economic development to Kentucky. During the 1980s, the Prichard Committee conducted an extensive public education effort, including televised townhall meetings throughout the state that helped create both strong public support for reform and tolerance of tax increases—two components that were necessary in passing KERA.

Consequently, when the Kentucky Supreme Court issued its decision in 1989, legislators were ready and willing to act on the court mandate because they knew that school improvement was an issue that resonated with the people of the state. Legislative leaders appointed a task force on school reform, brought in outside experts and national consultants to help author the bill, and then with the governor's support presented KERA to the legislature. The fact that KERA was a quickly developed, expert-driven reform plan in response to a strong court mandate and that it had strong support from the governor and key legislative leaders made its passage in the legislature possible.

Timing was also key in Kentucky, and some have argued that KERA would not have passed just 2 years later. Although anti-tax sentiment existed in Kentucky at the time, it was overshadowed by the consensus throughout the state that reform was necessary. A few years later, however, especially after the rise of conservative opposition to standards-based reforms, this might not have been the case. Now the school finance portion of KERA is the least contentious part of the bill because it has been the easiest to implement. Most of the hurdles with respect to KERA implementation are in the governance, curriculum, and assessment aspects of the legislation. These components of the reform are difficult to implement because they represent a set of challenges to traditional practices. However, the state continues to make progress on outcome measures and to serve as a model for standards-based reform.

Alabama[16]

Many parallels can be drawn between Kentucky and Alabama's contexts for school finance reform in the 1990s. At the beginning of the decade, these two states were similar in terms of per capita GDPs, poverty rates, and population sizes. Both states were near the bottom in every national ranking of educational indicators. Each state had an active citizen's organization leading a public campaign connecting the problems in the state with the quality of education and building consensus on the need for educational reform to foster economic development. Both states had school finance equity court cases that developed into equity and adequacy cases. In 1993, the Montgomery County Circuit Court declared the state's entire education system unconstitutional in *Harper v. Hunt.* The Alabama court decision was very similar to the *Rose* decision in its verdict, rationale, wording, and remedy requirements. Many of the same school finance experts who had authored KERA also helped write Alabama's comprehensive education reform bill "Alabama First." But, Alabama First was never enacted, and today Alabama's school system is still near the bottom of all national education rankings. Unlike its neighbor to the north, Alabama has not significantly changed its education system or its level of financing during this decade.

What happened in Alabama to make the results of a remarkably similar set of circumstances turn out so dramatically different? Timing played a tremendous role in determining the fate of school finance reform in Alabama. Anti-tax and anti-government sentiments were much stronger in 1993 then they had been in 1990, and by 1993-94 Alabama's political leadership had run into trouble.

School finance reform is inextricably tied to the volatile politics of taxes in Alabama during the 1990s. Alabama has not had the luxury of a fiscal surplus; in fact, a few times education has been pro-rationed when there has been a budget shortfall. Moreover, Alabama is significantly behind the southeastern average in school funding.[17] Thus, in Alabama, even more so than in other places, reform cannot be accomplished without additional tax revenue, and the rise of anti-tax sentiment throughout the country had a great impact on the remedy phase of the Alabama court case. The Christian Coalition, Eagle Forum, and conservative Republicans had significant political power and popularity in Alabama, whereas similar groups had less power in Kentucky 4 years earlier in 1990 during the *Rose* decision. These groups mobilized against education reform in Alabama, viewed the Alabama First bill as social engineering, and did not want to see their taxes rise in order to finance the bill.

When the Montgomery County Circuit Court ruled in *Harper v. Hunt* that the entire Alabama education system was unconstitutional, Governor Guy Hunt did not appeal the case to the highest court in the state both because it appeared to be a losing battle and because he ran out of time. Hunt, a Republican governor, was the only remaining defendant of the five originally named in the suit. The rest had switched over to the side of the plaintiffs. When the court ruling came out, Hunt was facing charges of improper use of public funds and could not afford any more negative publicity. He was found guilty and removed from office shortly after the court decision.

Lieutenant Governor Jim Fulsom Jr., a Democrat, replaced Hunt in office for the remainder of the term. Fulsom supported education reform and worked closely with A+, the Alabama leadership organization that advocated education reform around the state. Governor Fulsom presented Alabama First, along with the corresponding billion dollar tax revenue increase, to the legislature during the session preceding the gubernatorial elections. However, when the general public learned of the high price tag of reform, the consensus that A+ had built around the need for educational reform disintegrated. The Alabama Education Association, led by gubernatorial candidate Paul Hubbart, opposed the Alabama First bill because of its accountability provisions. Hubbart, who was running against Governor Fulsom in the Democratic primary and was vying with Fulsom for the title of "the education candidate," could not allow a Fulsom-backed reform plan to pass. He argued that Alabama could not afford, and did not need, a billion dollars worth of reform. The bill was passed in the Senate but not in the House and was thus postponed until the next legislative session.

The crucial turning point for school finance reform in Alabama was the 1994 election of Governor Fob James. James, a political underdog, ran on a "No New Taxes" campaign platform and rode the national Republican anti-government, anti-tax tide to beat Fulsom, who was hurt by charges of ethical violations. Although he only won the election by a small margin, James has since consolidated his political power in the state. Governor James has taken a strong stand against increased taxes and school reform and fully supports the political philosophy of the Christian Coalition. He has withdrawn from the National Governors' Association and does not support the federal Goals 2000 plan because he considers it to be social engineering. James has characterized the Alabama education system as inefficient and wasteful and has opposed increases in education spending. Governor James has also characterized the *Hunt* decision as judicial intervention, has defied the court order, and has attempted, so far unsuccessfully, to have it overturned. The fact that *Harper v. Hunt* did not make it to the Supreme Court in 1993 has helped James argue that the decision has no authority behind it.

The timing of the elections and political developments in Alabama eliminated the gubernatorial support of comprehensive reform in Alabama, but the effects of these events were compounded by the absence of legislative support for reform. Alabama First had no legislative participation, and former Governor Fulsom was the only political leader with strong stakes in Alabama First. At the same time, the politically powerful Alabama Farmers Association (ALFA) and the Christian Coalition opposed property tax increases and outcome-based education components of Alabama First and presented their own reform bill, Score 2000, which was backed by Republicans in the legislature.

Although A+, which was modeled after the Prichard Committee in Kentucky, had been very active in building consensus around reform, it had only been in existence for a few years. In contrast, ALFA and coalitions with vested interests in maintaining Alabama's property taxes as the lowest in the nation have a long history in the state. Alabama's constitution, written in 1901, favors large property owners and out-of-state businesses and requires a popular vote to raise property taxes. School finance reform in Alabama is further complicated by the fact that a constitutional amendment to the tax system is required to enact many proposed changes to the system.

Race and class considerations also made school finance reform more politically contentious in Alabama than in Kentucky. Racial minorities in Alabama make up a greater proportion of the population and are concentrated in the poorest sections of the state. Therefore, aid that is targeted to the poorest districts is perceived by many to disproportionately assist minorities who have significantly less political power.

Most people in Alabama are discontent with the education system in the state, but they have not been willing to raise revenues in order to improve it. Although incentives exist for the judicial branch to mandate comprehensive reform, as demonstrated by *Harper v. Hunt*, the court decision is an insufficient incentive for the legislative and executive branches to enact reform. The tax, racial, distributive, and ideological implications of comprehensive school reform, along with the perception that Alabama's education problems are rooted in mismanagement rather than lack of funds, have eroded public support.

Texas[18]

School finance litigation and legislative responses are dominant themes in Texas state politics during the 1990s. In 1989, the Texas Supreme Court found the Texas school finance system unconstitutional. The nature of this decision, however, was very different than the decisions in Kentucky and Alabama. In *Edgewood v. Kirby*, the court found that Texas's school finance system violated the state constitution's requirement of an "efficient system of schools" (Fulton, 1997; Fulton and Long, 1993:17). The court ruled that the legislature must devise a new funding system that provided districts with equal access to similar revenues per pupil at similar levels of tax efforts. In addition, the court established that in order to achieve compliance with the *Edgewood* decision, legislators could consolidate school districts and/or tax bases.

After 5 years and four rounds of Texas Supreme Court decisions, a legislated remedy was upheld as constitutional by a 5-4 decision in 1995. This remedy does help to reduce inequities in school finance in Texas. In fact, some predict that by 1999, when the new system is fully implemented, the portion of state revenues excepted from equalization will have decreased from the 1989 level of nearly 21 percent of all state and local revenues to less than 2 percent (U.S. General Accounting Office, 1995). Alterations to the original legislation, however, make it unclear whether or not the present system would be upheld as constitutional if it were challenged again by either the original plaintiffs or the wealthier districts. Moreover, it is uncertain whether equalizing effects will occur and be sustained over time.

Texas has enacted school finance reform in the past, but in the 1990s the politics have become more contentious because it involves redistributing existing resources—not raising new money.[19] The long battle between the court and the legislature, and the threat of the courts closing down the schools, demonstrate the political difficulty of the issue. Without the *Edgewood v. Kirby* ruling and the Texas Supreme Court's continued pressure on the legislature to devise a new constitutional system, reform never would have happened.[20] In fact, the reform legislation of 1993 resulted from frustration with the litigation and the manner in which it obstructed progress on other educational issues. Patience and energy levels wore thin on all sides, and compromises were made in the interest of passing something.

The biggest obstacle to a politically feasible solution that complied with the court order was the fiscal impossibility of leveling-up. The large disparities in property wealth in Texas required an increase in state revenues of an amount close to four times the entire state budget to bring the bottom districts up to the top levels of spending (U.S. General Accounting Office, 1995:31). Responding to the strong anti-tax sentiment in the state and a 10-year record of putting more money into the system in order to help equalize funding, legislators opposed further increases in state taxes in their efforts to comply with the court ruling. Texas's economy has been improving in the 1990s, but business tax exemptions and the absence of a state income tax have reduced the rate by which these improvements transfer to state revenues. Competition for state revenues has been fierce; between 1990 and 1995 Medicaid expenditures increased by 117 percent and criminal justice expenditures by 135 percent (U.S. General Accounting Office, 1995:31). Meanwhile, fiscal surpluses were used to finance a 34 percent increase in total expenditures in education from 1990 to 1994, but much of this increase was used to compensate for the simultaneous 8.6 percent increase in enrollments that necessitated increased expenditures and new facilities in some areas (U.S. General Accounting Office, 1995:31).

Having ruled out state tax increases, and lacking fiscal flexibility to equalize through available revenues, the legislature looked to remedies that would redistribute local wealth. Redistribution is always difficult, but it is more so in a state like Texas with strong racial, class, and urban/rural divides. The initial remedy passed by the state legislature in response to *Edgewood* was ruled unconstitutional because it did not go far enough in guaranteeing equal revenues for equal tax effort. In this ruling the court suggested either consolidating school districts or district tax bases but the public opposed loss of local control over education issues.

The next remedy bill, signed into law in April 1991, consolidated school districts for the purposes of taxation only and provided a mechanism to cap per-pupil property wealth and to redistribute local property tax revenues. This remedy required a constitutional amendment, approved at the polls, allowing the property tax recapture. Although poll data prior to the vote showed significant support for the amendment, it was defeated 63 percent to 27 percent (Reed, 1997:110). Although the debate in the newspapers focused on taxes and education, a recent study suggested that the opposition to the school finance equalization bill was, in many ways, more about racial cleavages over educational opportunities (Reed, 1997:114). The study reported that the racial and economic composition of districts was a better predictor of support or opposition to school finance reform than district wealth. Districts with high percentages of blacks and Latinos were most likely to vote in favor of the amendment, probably because they viewed themselves as the prime beneficiaries of the equity-enhancing reforms. Predominantly white districts, on the other hand, were most likely to oppose the proposal even when their income levels were such that they either would benefit or not suffer significant loss.

After the constitutional amendment and accompanying reform proposal were rejected by the voters, Texas legislators proposed a new remedy to end the long struggle with the courts. This 1993 remedy legislation was finally approved by the court in 1995. It has, for the most part, remained in place and has helped to reduce inequities in Texas school finance. The remedy capped the amount of taxable wealth in a district, limited local property tax rates, and provided districts with taxable wealth above the cap five options for redistributing that wealth to poorer districts. The remedy also included a hold harmless provision that allowed all districts to maintain their 1992-93 revenue levels at least until 1996. The fact that the reform included choices for how the wealthier districts redistribute their wealth and that it did not involve a constitutional amendment changing the state's tax structure made it less threatening to the wealthier districts and therefore easier to pass.

Inequities in Texas still exist, and the remedy may not be the best solution. In May 1998, a group of 126 poor school districts in Texas filed a petition to reopen litigation because of the lack of state compliance with the 1993 finance-reform law (Johnston, 1998). On the other side, a backlash with strong support from the wealthiest districts has been challenging the redistributive nature of the remedy and, in the most recent legislative session, caused some minor concessions. The longevity of this reform thus remains in question.

School finance remains an important issue in Texas state politics, and politicians are wary of disrupting the delicate balance established by the 1993 reform. In the most recent legislative session, Governor Bush and the legislators imposed an unwritten requirement that new policies must not affect the amount of revenue available for education because they did not want to reopen the school finance debate and open the door to further litigation. [21] The 1993 remedy has resulted in significant increases in local property taxes and has sparked a new movement for property tax relief. In 1992-93, state taxes covered 40 percent of education expenditures while local taxes covered 49.6 percent (National Center for Education Statistics, 1995). In 1994, Governor Bush was elected on a platform that the state should assume its fair share of school funding, over 50 percent. Once elected he made local property tax relief one of his main goals and appointed a committee to explore the situation and alternative solutions. A few proposals for property tax reform were debated in the 1997 legislative session, but the school finance revenue neutrality requirement made extensive reform impossible.

New Jersey[22]

In the 1970s, after the 1973 *Robinson v. Cahill* decision, the legislature and the New Jersey Supreme Court engaged in a 3-year struggle, seven rounds of litigation, and a court injunction that closed the schools before a legislated remedy was finally passed, financed, and approved as constitutional. By the 1980s, however, the disparities in per-pupil spending in the cities versus the suburbs were increasing again. New Jersey school finance advocates filed a new suit on behalf of the children in 29 of the state's poorest districts.

The 1990 *Abbott v. Burke* decision in favor of the plaintiffs sparked another round of attempts to equalize New Jersey's school finance system. The court specified that the remedy must ensure that the educational opportunities for the students in the 29 special needs districts equal those of the students in the wealthiest districts in the state. In a later round of the case the court clarified that equal educational opportunity for the students in the special needs districts would require access to all educational and extracurricular activities that were available in the wealthiest districts and funds for supplemental programs to address the special educational needs of urban districts. The decision created an entitlement to equal educational opportunity only for the 30 poorest districts.[23] The court did not hear evidence on, and therefore issued no decision about, the system's constitutionality vis-à-vis the students in the more than 450 school districts remaining. This made it difficult to build a political coalition in support of the decision. On the other hand, the court's use of the standard of equal educational opportunity and recognition of educational overburden in the urban districts boded well for significant equity-enhancing reforms.

New Jersey provides an extremely challenging environment for school finance reform. In 1990, at the time of the *Abbott* decision, the disparities in regular educational spending per student between the richest and the poorest septiles had grown to $2,008 (Firestone, 1997a:5). New Jersey already spent more per pupil on education than any other state in the nation. Thus, while Kentucky and Alabama could point to their low national rankings in per-pupil expenditures as justification for the necessity of increased spending, New Jersey needed other ways to justify increased expenditures.

New Jersey has the second highest per capita income in the nation and yet has four of the country's poorest cities along with a few others that would qualify as the poorest cities in most states. Its predominantly white suburbs have some of the most valuable property in the nation, booming economies, and excellent schools. The cities, on the other hand, are predominantly black and Latino and have little property wealth, stagnant or declining economies, and abysmal education conditions. They also have less than one-quarter of the seats in the state legislature. Blacks and Latinos constitute close to 25 percent of the public school population, yet New Jersey has one of the most segregated school systems in the country.

In contrast with the national trend toward school district consolidation, New Jersey has actually created more school districts and now has over 600. Each has a vested interest in maintaining local control of its own resources and education policies. Although the lack of district consolidation is inefficient, regionalization of school districts is a political taboo because of its racial, class, and ideological implications.

The *Abbott* decision of 1990 was well timed politically. A Democrat, Governor James Florio, a former representative from Camden and an urban schools advocate, had recently been elected and had a Democratic majority in both houses of the state legislature. A general public consensus supported efforts to increase equity and improve the quality of education in the state's poorest districts. In a 1990 poll, out of those who were aware of the *Abbott* verdict, 54 percent agreed with the court and only 38 percent disagreed (Reed, 1997:104).

In response to the *Abbott* decision, a committee of legislators and technical experts authored the Quality Education Act (QEA), a new school finance formula that established a high foundation level of spending for everyone, provided supplemental programs for students in the poorest districts, and slowly phased out state aid to the wealthiest districts. The QEA provided over $1 billion of state aid to education, most of it targeted to the 30 poorest urban districts that educated one-quarter of the state's public school students. Governor Florio backed the QEA and a $2.8 billion tax package that was designed to fund the QEA, address the projected budget deficit, and provide local property tax relief (Corcoran and Scovronick, 1996:6). Within a month, the QEA and the tax package were passed and signed into law. They were never enacted, however, because the legislature rebelled against the Governor's leadership 4 months before the law was to take effect. They passed a revised package called QEAII, which substantially decreased the tax burden and reduced the level of education aid by $360 million (Corcoran and Scovronick, 1996:13).

Widespread public opposition to the QEA proposals, the tax increases, and the prospect of increased spending in urban districts eventually succeeded in derailing these reforms. After the first QEA and the $2.8 billion tax increase were passed, an anti-tax uprising, led by a grass-roots organization called Hands Across New Jersey, caused the governor's approval ratings to drop 19 points (Firestone, 1997a:4). The QEA was criticized for being punitive—punishing the wealthier districts by taking away their state aid. Moreover, it was, and still is, often argued that more money would only be wasted in the poor districts. Perceptions of the urban districts as corrupt, inefficient, and hopeless have been strengthened by the rhetoric supporting choice vouchers and charter schools. These perceptions are further complicated by racial politics; what may lie behind some of the arguments that urban districts are inefficient is the belief that minority children cannot be educated and minority adults cannot run school districts well. Strong opposition also came from a somewhat unlikely source, the New Jersey Education Association (NJEA), which opposed the QEA proposals over pension issues.

In 1991, almost every nonurban legislator who had voted for the QEA and the accompanying tax bill was defeated, and the Republicans gained a majority in the state legislature. Similarly, in 1993, Governor Whitman, running on an anti-tax platform and a promise to reduce income taxes by 30 percent over 3 years, defeated Governor Florio. The Republican legislature and governor have repealed most of the tax increases and much of the QEA spending. In another round of *Abbott* in 1997, the court ordered Governor Whitman and the legislature to provide an additional $130-248 million to the poorest districts (Goodnough, 1997:1). This decision was affirmed in May 1998 when the New Jersey Supreme Court approved a plan for funding and systemic education reform provided by the State Commissioner of Education (*Abbott v. Burke,* N.J. Sup. Ct., May 1998; see Minorini and Sugarman, Chapter 6 in this volume).

Even the combination of a strong court decision, an activist court, and strong gubernatorial and legislative leadership were not enough to pass and sustain reform in New Jersey. Some important lessons can be drawn from the attempts to legislate school finance reform made by Governor Florio and the proponents of equal educational opportunity. First, if the bill had included provisions for accountability, educational standards, and programmatic initiatives, it might have inspired more confidence that the money would be well spent and might have had more support. Second, the QEA was passed too quickly without input from the necessary interest groups. Third, there might have been more support for the reforms if the governor and the legislators had taken more time to build a coalition, to educate the public about the problems, and to explain the reforms to the public. For example, although the middle districts would have benefited substantially from the bill and would only have paid a small portion of the taxes, these aspects were not highlighted in the debate (Corcoran and Scovronick, 1995).

CRITICAL ELEMENTS FOR REFORM

The preceding discussion of four states suggests that the political, economic, and judicial contexts of the 1990s pose a number of challenges for school finance reformers.

Anti-tax and anti-government sentiment has emerged, especially in the 1990s, as a major issue in three of the four cases that we have discussed. The anti-tax message is a simple, clear message that appeals to a widespread audience with offers of concrete benefits. On the other hand, school finance reform is extremely complex; its benefits are more nebulous and are often concentrated in certain areas and populations. In Alabama and New Jersey, the current governors have made repeated promises to reduce taxes and have adopted the issue as a central political priority.

With higher taxes ruled out, revenue to equalize school finance across districts disappears. Economic downturns have similar effects. The current and anticipated fiscal health of each state definitely plays a role in determining the timing, the nature, and the extent of school finance reform. School finance reform is virtually impossible without some sort of fiscal flexibility in the state's budget, whether in the form of fiscal surpluses; public tolerance to raise taxes, as was the case in Kentucky; or the possibility of transferring funds from one district to another, as Texas did.

In Alabama, New Jersey, and Texas, the politics of race have significantly affected reform. In each of these states, respondents pointed to the main role that race plays in education policy, claiming that "We have an unresolved race and class problem in New Jersey that affects everything we do"[24] and "In Alabama, everything comes back to race; there is no public policy in the state that does not come back to race."[25] In each of these three states, the benefits of school finance reform were perceived to accrue mostly, or even exclusively, to racial minorities. The white majority opposed tax increases and redistribution of resources to benefit minorities in part because negative assumptions were made about student ability to learn and about adult competence to lead school systems. In Kentucky, on the other hand, where racial minorities are a smaller percentage of the population and are concentrated in the wealthier districts, racial politics were not salient. It was therefore much easier to organize a community of interest among the white majority and create support for increasing taxes to fund education throughout the state.

These factors pose challenges to school finance reformers. In the states we examined, successful litigation, strong political leadership, and extensive public education efforts proved to be necessary, but not automatically sufficient, conditions for overcoming these obstacles.

In each of the four states we examined above, litigation played a key role in placing and keeping the issue of school finance reform on the state agenda. Without findings in favor of the plaintiffs and orders from the court to reform their systems, none of these states would have undergone school finance reform. A court decision in favor of the plaintiffs can act as a catalyst for reform but it is not sufficient to bring about improvements in a state's school finance system. The nature and scope of school finance litigation, the extent to which the court is willing to define the remedy, and the standards that it uses to evaluate equity all affect the types of incentives created for policymakers and the level of consensus for reform. Court decisions like Kentucky's, which declare the school finance system unconstitutional, define the standard of evaluation as equal educational opportunity, prescribe requirements for reform (including deadlines), and link improvements in finance systems to improvements in both inputs such as teachers and outputs such as student outcomes, appear to inspire legislators to pass significant equity-enhancing reform.

Kentucky's court case opened a window of opportunity for extensive reform. As the comparison of events in Kentucky and Alabama so clearly illustrates however, successful comprehensive litigation is not enough to guarantee reform. An activist court and successful litigation are helpful, but political leadership from the governor and key legislators is essential in passing school finance reform to reduce inter-district inequities. In Alabama, where turnover and corruption severely limited consistent political leadership during the period following legislation, school finance reform efforts had very little chance of succeeding. Now, with the Governor actively opposing school finance reform and challenging the court's authority, there is no hope for success in the near term. As the other states demonstrate, the lack of opposition from the governor and others in positions of leadership is not enough; strong activist political leadership and positive incentives are needed to enact equity-enhancing school finance reform. The benefits of school finance reform need to be clearly articulated to political leaders and the broader public, as does evidence linking equalization of school finance systems with increased quality of educational experiences and improved student outcomes.

In Kentucky these incentives existed and were clearly articulated by the Prichard Commission, the court, legislative leaders, and the Governor. Here the focus was on economic development. A clear argument linking school finance reform and greater investment in education to the future economic health of the state was developed and publicized for many years leading up to the litigation and reform. In other states where there has not been such decisive, repeated articulation of the benefits of school finance reform, it has been hard to identify what politicians and the broader public have to gain from taking on equity issues.

Because the arguments in favor of school finance reform are complex and usually contentious, while those opposing reform are fairly simple and often have more widespread appeal, extensive and prolonged efforts to educate the public and create a community of interest for reform are essential. These efforts are necessary both in building consensus around the need for reform and in garnering support for specific reform bills. In devising a new school finance initiative, governors and legislators must often confront interest groups defending their economic advantages and "a mass public opposition that is, in significant ways, racially based" (Reed, 1997:104). School finance reform is a politically risky initiative for politicians to support unless they can clearly identify and articulate universal benefits, explain where the new money will go, show how it will improve students' experiences and outcomes, and demonstrate how these improvements benefit the wider society. The Kentucky legislators had major advantages by responding to an adequacy argument that framed both the problem and the remedy in terms of substantive education change and not just money.

Such a focus is not sufficient (witness Alabama), but in today's climate it appears at least necessary.

School finance is an increasingly partisan issue in most states as the parties take more sharply defined positions on the issue. A united and broad community of interest can help bridge partisan gaps, especially when remedies that benefit diverse interests can be formulated and presented in ways that attract popular support within the general population. Active coalitions within the educational community can help articulate the need to invest in children and the future and provide arguments that would help push reforms through the political process.

Such coalitions can also examine and illustrate the status of school finance by measuring how the allocation of opportunities and resources changes over time and specifying whether the problem of inequalities exists at a national or state level or is focused only within certain kinds of districts or schools. When courts, legislatures, educators, and the public at large agree on the types of disparities in educational resources that are unacceptable, such agreement helps overcome impediments to reform that are shaped by confusion, uncertainty, and inconsistent or contradictory evidence.

In states where school finance and comprehensive education reform can be billed as a necessary step toward economic development, the politically influential business community can sometimes be united behind reform initiatives and play a very important role in the debate. When the business community and a united education community support reform, as they did in Kentucky, they provide politicians with the incentives that they need to support reform.

As the politics of school finance reform have become more contentious, the issues themselves are also changing. As Allan Odden (1998) has argued, the nature of the school finance equity problem in some states is different now than it was in the past. In the 1970s, for example, inequities resulted from high tax rates in districts with low property wealth and low amounts of per-pupil spending while low tax rates in districts with higher property wealth resulted in high amounts of per-pupil spending. In the 1990s, after an initial round of reforms that attempted to equalize potential revenues, many states are faced with a situation where low-wealth districts have low tax rates and low spending while high-wealth districts have higher tax rates and higher spending. Moreover, in many states, as spending levels have increased in property-poor districts, wealthier districts have increased their local tax rates and maintained spending inequities. Politically, this situation presents a less compelling argument for state intervention because low-wealth districts could improve their situation themselves if they were willing to raise their tax rates.

The shift in school finance reform from tax equity to equalizing educational opportunity creates complex challenges and intricate politics. Many states are attempting to resolve these challenges through the creation of foundation levels and the use of weights to reflect the higher costs associated with serving large numbers of pupils from low-income families, special education, and other special groups, as well as addressing variations in district characteristics such as regional cost differences, size, or enrollment change.

In the current political atmosphere, especially with the public demanding more accountability from its government, it is increasingly difficult politically to sell school finance reform on the equity principle alone. In many cases it has become necessary, though not sufficient, to have an adequacy argument and to explain what the increased or redistributed money will buy. In addition, compelling evidence about the types and levels of investments that are most likely to improve student outcomes can generate public support for school finance reform.

NOTES

1. For a vivid description of the current system's "savage inequalities" that create vastly different opportunities for different children, see Kozol, 1991.

2. Because the authors both reside in New Jersey, the chapter draws heavily on this state's example throughout.

3. However, this was the end result of a series of reforms passed in California. California's highest court required equity in per-pupil spending in its *Serrano v. Priest* case and the legislature passed a remedy consistent with this decision. Not long after that legislation, California voters passed Proposition 13, limiting taxation. The result in California has been a significant increase in school finance equity but a decline in total resources available to education as compared to the national average and a corresponding drop from near the top to near the bottom in the national rankings of many educational indicators.

4. Two state constitutions do not require the legislature to establish free public schools. The Mississippi Constitution simply requires the legislature to establish schools. Under the Alabama Constitution, the state must promote education but theoretically would not be constitutionally required to establish public schools if it did not have adequate resources. In the other 48 states, the constitution requires, at a bare minimum, that the legislature establish a system of free public schools. Fourteen state constitutions require only this minimum standard while 19 state constitutions apply a minimum quality standard to the state system of schools such as requiring that they be "thorough and efficient." Eight states have stronger and more specific quality requirements in their constitutions. The remaining seven states have the strongest category of education clause in their state constitutions, which establish education as the most important duty of the state. See McUsic, 1991.

5. Based on the Education Commission of the States count of legislated school finance reforms between 1971 and 1981 (Fuhrman, 1982:53).

6. The expected rate of diffusion of state preserve policies (not instigated by federal action), as determined by a review of studies of diffusion of innovation, is about 16 years for the first 25 percent and 24 years for the first 50

percent. Thus, the volume of school finance activity in the 1970s is more than twice the expected rate of innovation.

7. These inequity figures come from Table 3-2 of Evans, Murray, and Schwab (Chapter 3) in this volume.

8. California eventually achieved substantial equality of per-pupil spending and of educational opportunity through school finance reform in response to *Serrano* combined with state and local tax capping laws such as Proposition 13 and the Gann Amendment. Equality of spending came at a high price, however, as California's total spending on education declined and the state's education system dropped from one of the best in the nation to one of the worst.

9. The record in the Rodriguez case demonstrated that Edgewood, a poor district in San Antonio, taxed itself at a 24 percent higher rate than neighboring Alamo Heights but still only had a per-pupil expenditure that was 60 percent of Alamo Heights' per-pupil expenditures. In 1967-68 dollars, Edgewood was spending $356/pupil and had a tax rate of $1.05 per $100 of assessed property while Alamo Heights spent $594 per pupil and had a tax rate of only $0.85 per $100 assessed property.

10. As Table 3-2 in Evans, Murray, and Schwab (Chapter 3) in this volume demonstrates with nationally aggregated data, the 95th percentile was spending 2.22 times more than the 5th percentile in 1982 and by 1987 the 95th percentile was spending 2.53 times more than the 5th percentile. Similarly, the other measures of inequality listed in that table all show an increase in inequality from 1982 to 1987.

11. Two of these rulings (Alabama's *Harper v. Hunt* and Missouri's *Committee for Educational Equality v. State*) were decided at the circuit court level in 1993 but were not appealed, and legislative action began in response to the lower court's ruling. In Alabama, the lower court's decision was later upheld by the Alabama Supreme Court in 1996.

12. Much of the information in this section comes from telephone interviews conducted with the following people in May and June 1997: Jacob Adams from Vanderbilt University and Timothy Collins from the University of Kentucky's Appalachian Center.

13. Telephone interview, Timothy Collins, Appalachian Center, University of Kentucky, June 1997.

14. Telephone interview, Timothy Collins, Appalachian Center, University of Kentucky, June 1997.

15. Figure cited in telephone interview, Timothy Collins, Appalachian Center, University of Kentucky, June 1997.

16. Much of the information in this section comes from telephone interviews conducted with the following people in May and June 1997: Wayne Flynt from Auburn University, Kathy Gassenheimer from A+, and Ira Harvey from University of Alabama, Birmingham.

17.   Alabama is $750 million below the southeastern average in school funding, according to Kathy Gassenheimer (in a telephone interview in June 1997).

18.   Much of the information in this section comes from telephone interviews conducted with the following people in May and June 1997: Catherine Clark from the Texas Center for Education Research, Albert Cortez from the Intercultural Development Research Association, and Larry Picus from the University of Southern California.

19.   Telephone interview, Albert Cortez, Intercultural Development Research Association in Texas, June 3, 1997.

20.   In all of the interviews we conducted, people pointed to the court decision and the continued court involvement as the main cause of reform.

21.   Telephone interview, Catherine Clark and Albert Cortez, June 1997.

22.   Much of the information in this section comes from telephone interviews conducted with the following people in May and June 1997: William Firestone from Rutgers University, Herb Green from the Public Education Institute in New Jersey, Nathan Scovronick from Princeton University, and John White from the New Jersey Senate Education Committee Staff.

23.   Although 29 poor districts originally filed suit, an additional one joined and was treated in the remedy phase.

24.   Telephone interview, Herb Green, Public Education Institute in New Jersey, June 1997.

25.   Telephone interview, Wayne Flynt, Auburn University History Department, June 1997.

REFERENCES

Brown, P.R., and R.F. Elmore
   1982   Analyzing the impact of school finance reform. Pp. 107-139 in *The Changing Politics of School Finance*, N.H. Cambron-McCabe and A. Odden, eds. Cambridge, MA: Ballinger.
Card, D., and A.B. Krueger
   1992   Does school quality matter? Returns to education and the characteristics of public schools in the United States. *Journal of Political Economy* 100(1):1-40.
Corcoran, T., and N. Scovronick
   1995   More Than Equal: New Jersey's Quality Education Act. Unpublished paper.
Council of State Governments
   1980   *The Book of the States 1980-1981*, Vol. 23. Lexington, KY: Council of State Governments.
Crampton, F. and T. Whitney
   1996   *The Search for Equity in School Funding*. Education Partners Working Papers. Boulder, CO: National Conference of State Legislators.
Dove, R.G.
   1991   Acorns in a mountain pool: The role of litigation, law and lawyers in Kentucky education reform. *Journal of Education Finance* 17(Summer):83-119.
Evans, W.N., S.E. Murray, and R.M. Schwab
   1997   Schoolhouses, courthouses, and statehouses after *Serrano*. *Journal of Policy Analysis and Management* 16(1):10-32.

Ferguson, R.F. and H.F. Ladd
   1996   How and why money matters: An analysis of Alabama schools. Pp. 265-298 in *Holding Schools Accountable: Performance-Based Reform in Education*, H.F. Ladd, ed. Washington, DC: The Brookings Institution.
Firestone, W.A.
   1997a   Does Court Ordered Funding Equalization "Work"?: The New Jersey Experience. Paper presented at a Conference on Equity Issues in Education at the Woodrow Wilson School of Public and International Affairs on January 17.
   1997b   Telephone interview conducted in June.
Fuhrman, S.H.
   1978   The politics and process of school finance reform. *Journal of Education Finance* 4(Fall):158-178.
   1982   State-level politics and school financing. Pp. 53-71 in *The Changing Politics of School Finance*, N.H. Cambron-McCabe and A. Odden, eds. Cambridge, MA: Ballinger.
   1994a   Governors and education policy in the 1990s. Pp. 56-74 in *The Governance of Curriculum*, R. F. Elmore and S. H. Fuhrman, eds. Alexandria, VA: The Association for Supervision and Curriculum Development.
   1994b   Legislatures and education policy. Pp. 30-55 in *The Governance of Curriculum*, R.F. Elmore and S.H. Fuhrman, eds. Alexandria, VA: The Association for Supervision and Curriculum Development.
Fulton, M.
   1997   Telephone interview conducted in March.
Fulton, M., and D. Long
   1993   *School Finance Litigation: A Historical Summary*. Denver, CO: Education Commission of the States.
Goodnough, A.
   1997   New Jersey's school financing is again held unconstitutional. *New York Times* (May 15).
Hanushek, E.A.
   1986   The economics of schooling: Production and efficiency in public schools. *Journal of Economic Literature* 24(September):1141-1177.
   1991   When school finance "reform" may not be good policy. *Harvard Journal on Legislation* 28(2):423-457.
   1996   Measuring investment in education. *Journal of Economic Perspectives* 10(4):9-30.
Hedges, L.V., R.D. Laine, and R. Greenwald
   1994   Does money matter? A meta-analysis of studies of the effects of differential school inputs on student outcomes. *Educational Researcher* 23(3):5-14.
Herrnstein, R., and C. Murray
   1994   *The Bell Curve: Intelligence and Class Structure in American Life*. New York: Free Press.
Johnston, R.C.
   1998   Frustrated with state, Texas districts back reviving finance suit. *Education Week* May 20, Vol. 17(36): 22.
Kozol, J.
   1991   *Savage Inequalities: Children in America's Schools*. New York: Crown.
Krueger, A.B.
   1997   *Experimental Estimates of Education Production Functions*. Working Paper #379. Princeton, NJ: Princeton University Industrial Relations Section.
Massell, D., M. Kirst, and M. Hoppe
   1997   *Persistence and Change: Standards-Based Reform in Nine States*. Philadelphia: Consortium for Policy Research in Education.

McDonnell, L.M., and S. Fuhrman
  1985   The political context of school reform. Pp. 43-65 in *The Fiscal, Legal, and Political, Aspects of State Reform of Elementary and Secondary Education*, V.D. Mueller and M.P. McKeown, eds. Cambridge, MA: Ballinger.
McUsic, M.
  1991   The use of education clauses in school finance reform litigation. *Harvard Journal on Legislation* 28(2):307-341.
Monk, D.
  1994   Subject area preparation of secondary mathematics and science teachers and student achievement. *Economics of Education Review* 13(2):125-145.
Murray, S.E.
  1995   Two Essays on the Distribution of Education Resources and Outcomes. Unpublished Ph.D. dissertation, University of Maryland.
National Association of State Budgetary Officers
  1991   The Fiscal Survey of the States: October. Washington, DC: National Association of State Budget Offices.
  1993   The Fiscal Survey of the States: October. Washington, DC: National Association of State Budget Offices.
  1995   The Fiscal Survey of the States: October. Washington, DC: National Association of State Budget Offices.
  1997   The Fiscal Survey of the States: December. Washington, DC: National Association of State Budget Offices.
National Center for Education Statistics
  1995   *Common Core Data, 1995.* Washington, DC: U.S. Department of Education.
National Commission on Excellence in Education
  1983   *A Nation at Risk: The Imperative for Educational Reform.* Washington, DC: U.S. Government Printing Office.
Odden, A.
  1998   Improving State School Finance Systems: New Realities Create the Need to Re-Engineer School Finance Structures. Philadelphia, PA: Consortium for Policy Research in Education, University of Pennsylvania.
Odden, A., C.K. McGuire, and G. Belsches-Simmons
  1983   *School Finance Reform in the States: 1983.* Report No. F83-1. Denver, CO: Education Commission of the States.
Picus, L.
  1997   Does money matter in education? A policymakers guide. Pp. 15-36 in *Selected Papers in School Finance, 1995*, W.J. Fowler,. Jr., ed. NCES 97-536. Washington, DC: National Center for Education Statistics, U.S. Department of Education.
Poterba, J.M.
  1997   Demographic structure and the political economy of public education. *Journal of Policy Analysis and Management* 16(1):48-67.
Rebell, M.A.
  1994-95 Fiscal equity in education: Deconstructing the reigning myths and facing reality. *New York University Review of Law and Social Change* 21(4):691-723.
Reed, D.S.
  1997   Court-ordered school finance equalization: Judicial activism and democratic opposition. Pp. 91-115 in *Developments in School Finance, 1996*. Washington, DC: National Center for Education Statistics, U.S. Department of Education.
Rubin, A.
  1996   Time shortens for hard choices on Medicare, social security. *Congressional Weekly* 54(43):3055-3058.

Thro, W.E.
    1989   To render them safe: The analysis of state constitutional provisions in public school finance reform litigation. *Virginia Law Review* 75(8):1639-1679.
    1990   The third wave: The impact of the Montana, Kentucky, and Texas decisions on the future of public school finance reform litigation. *Journal of Law and Education* 19(2):219-251.
U.S. General Accounting Office
    1995   *School Finance: Three States' Experiences with Equity in School Funding.* GAO-HEHS-96-93. Washington, DC: U.S. General Accounting Office.
Weir, M.
    1995   In the shadows: Central cities loss of power in state politics. *The Brookings Review* 13(2):16-19.

6

Educational Adequacy and the Courts: The Promise and Problems of Moving to a New Paradigm

Paul A. Minorini and Stephen D. Sugarman

In 1989, the Kentucky Supreme Court declared the entire state system of public elementary and secondary education unconstitutional and held that all Kentucky schoolchildren had a constitutional right to an adequate education. The decision resulted in a dramatic overhaul of the state's entire public school system, and sparked what many scholars have called the "adequacy movement" in courts, state houses, and education policy circles around the country (Underwood, 1995; Clune, 1993).

That movement has spread rapidly. Since 1989, courts in Alabama, Massachusetts, New Hampshire, New Jersey, New York, North Carolina, Ohio, Tennessee, and Wyoming also have ruled that their state constitutions' education clauses guarantee students an adequate level of educational opportunities that should allow them to achieve certain desired educational outcomes. In addition, claimants in Arizona have won an adequacy case concerning capital costs, and adequacy-based lawsuits are now pending in Louisiana, Minnesota, Pennsylvania, and South Carolina. This new wave of adequacy litigation has not been successful in all states where it has been brought, however. High courts in Florida, Illinois, and Rhode Island recently rejected adequacy-based claims, in part because they viewed such matters as inappropriate for judicial resolution.

Adequacy issues did not come to occupy their current position in courts and state houses overnight. Over the last two and a half decades, the terms of school finance debates in many legal and policy circles have slowly shifted. In the courts, that shift has been away from traditional "fiscal equity" cases (concerned with inequalities in school district per-pupil property tax bases and the per-pupil spending inequalities they yield), toward arguments focused on ensuring that all students have access to educational resources and opportunities adequate to achieve desired educational outcomes (Underwood, 1995; Heise, 1995; Clune, 1993). In the education policy context, the shift has led to efforts to define what educational outcomes all students should attain and what resources are necessary to permit all students to achieve those outcomes (Clune, 1993).

In this chapter we start by going back to the early litigation efforts to elimi- nate racial segregation in public education because we believe that this history sheds interesting light on the school finance litigation that was to follow. We then turn to the legal theories underlying the ultimately unsuccessful legal chal- lenges to school finance inequalities that were brought under the federal constitu- tion. After explaining how that failure turned into something of a success in cases brought in state courts under state constitutions, we explore various reasons why activists and analysts in the mid and late 1980s nonetheless began to look for a new legal approach—one rooted not so much in comparing the poor education some children obtain with others, but rather in comparing the inadequate educa- tion many children receive as judged by some absolute standard. We then trace the rapid success of the new adequacy theory in courts, followed by a more sobering look at the mixed success of this approach in obtaining legislative compliance with judicial decrees. We close with an appraisal of the education adequacy movement to date and its prospects for the future.

EARLY RACE-BASED CASES

In the era before the U.S. Supreme Court decided *Brown v. Board of Educa- tion*, 347 U.S. 483 (1954), black claimants successfully attacked several state educational arrangements as constitutionally inadequate. In those earlier years, the so-called "separate but equal" standard, which had been established by *Plessy v. Ferguson*, 163 U.S. 537 (1896), applied to race-based treatment; this meant that blacks could be forced to accept separate treatment by the government, so long as it was equal treatment. The litigation strategy in the first half of the twentieth century was to show that the segregated schooling provided for blacks was inferior to what was provided for whites and hence in violation of the "equal protection of the law" requirement of the Fourteenth Amendment to the U.S. Constitution.

These early race discrimination cases began with claims that black schools simply did not parallel the white institutions. In *Cummings v. Board of Educa- tion*, 175 U.S. 528 (1899), the plaintiffs' objection was that the district had ceased operation of the black high school but continued to support high school education for white students. (For reasons that seem quite unconvincing 100 years later, the Court found in favor of the school district.) In *Missouri ex rel Gaines v. Canada*, 305 U.S. 337 (1938), the complaint was that Missouri had no black law school but had a law school for whites. The Court ruled that the state's offer to pay the

plaintiffs' out-of-state tuition was an inadequate substitute. *Gaines* was a significant first step in the line of decisions leading to *Brown*.

Anticipating similar litigation, Texas established a black law school, but in
Sweatt v. Painter, 339 U.S. 629 (1950), the Court found it to be unequal to the
University of Texas's white law school. And in *McLaurin v. Oklahoma State
Regents*, 339 U.S. 637 (1950), the Court ruled that it was inadequate for the state
university to admit black graduate students, but require them to sit at separate
desks adjoining the classrooms and separate tables outside the library reading
room, and to eat at separate times in the school cafeteria.

In the course of these decisions, the Court's emphasis moved away from a
comparison of conventionally measured educational resources to an emphasis on
"intangibles." In *Sweatt*, for example, the Court said:

> In terms of number of the faculty, variety of courses and opportunity for spe-
> cialization, size of the student body, scope of the library, availability of law
> review and similar activities, the University of Texas Law School is superior.
> What is more important, the University of Texas Law School possesses to a far
> greater degree those qualities which are incapable of objective measurement but
> which make for greatness in a law school. Such qualities, to name but a few,
> include reputation of the faculty . . . influence of the alumni, standing in the
> community, traditions and prestige. [Moreover, the law school] cannot be ef-
> fective in isolation from the individuals and institutions with which the law
> interacts . . .

Then, in *Brown* itself, the Court directly confronted the question of whether
black elementary and high school students were unconstitutionally denied equal
educational opportunities even though "the Negro and white schools involved
have been equalized, or are being equalized, with respect to buildings, curricula,
qualifications and salaries of teachers, and other 'tangible' factors." Noting first
that "education is perhaps the most important function of state and local governments," the Court then relied on psychological studies to support its conclusion
that to separate the black school children "solely because of their race generates
a feeling of inferiority as to their status in the community that may affect their
hearts and minds in a way unlikely ever to be undone." On that basis the Court
declared that "in the field of public education the doctrine of 'separate but equal'
has no place. Separate educational facilities are inherently unequal."

Put generally, then, although the test of equality throughout this series of
cases was always applied to educational input differentials, over time the inputs
that were compared increasingly included those beyond mere financial resources
and the things money buys directly. In other words, the Court became increasingly concerned not only with the formal educational offering, but also with what
the students were likely to gain from their educational experience, which included, among other things, interaction with other students.

Although it took the adoption of the Civil Rights Act of 1964 to bring about
the beginnings of substantial compliance with *Brown*, once the U.S. Supreme

Court firmly rejected Southern states' neutral-sounding evasion strategies in cases like *Green v. County School Board*, 391 U.S. 430 (1968), and *Swann v. Charlotte-Mecklenburg Board of Education*, 402 U.S. 1 (1971), the dismantling of the official regime of school segregation was finally assured.

But the elimination of schools that were legally open exclusively to white or to black students hardly eliminated racial isolation in America's public schools. As the legal battles moved to the North and the West, it became clear in the 1970s that the Court had not meant that all racially identifiable educational facilities were unconstitutional. Rather, the justices would only strike down regimes that intentionally separated black and white students (*Keyes v. School District No. 1*, 413 U.S. 189, 1973). To be sure, in some Northern and Western school districts, even though segregation had not been the official rule, it could be shown that specific school board decisions (such as where to build new schools) had actually been racially motivated and hence illegal. But if school assignment was based upon neighborhood attendance zones that had been drawn without reference to race, and neighborhoods "happened" to contain concentrations of white or black pupils, the resulting racially isolated schools were not illegal. (Of course, there might have been illegal segregation in the housing market, but that, it turned out, generally had to be attacked in housing cases seeking housing remedies.)

This distinction between de jure and de facto school segregation flowed primarily from the Court's doctrinal interpretation of the Fourteenth Amendment. But it also reflected a subtler interpretation of the "feelings of inferiority" emphasized in *Brown*. It was one thing to say that black children suffered those feelings when they were told by the law that they could not attend school with whites. But it would have been indelicate, to say the least, to contend that they suffered such feelings merely by having black, rather than white, schoolmates.

In the North and West, where one tended to find large urban school districts surrounded by many small suburban school districts, the distinction between de jure and de facto segregation was especially important. Black advocates there faced a difficult legal battle to prove past illegal segregation within the urban center. Moreover, what if more and more whites simply moved to suburbs that were primarily white (assuming one could not prove, as the plaintiffs failed to prove in the Detroit case, that the creation of the suburban school districts was itself intentionally, racially discriminatory; see generally *Milliken v. Bradley*, 418 U.S. 717, 1974)? Southern states tended to have county-wide school districts that were increasingly under order to desegregate. But even there, what if whites moved in large numbers to adjacent counties that historically had few blacks? The Fourteenth Amendment forbade deliberate governmental discrimination on the basis of race; the intentions of individual families as they made their residential choices, however, were outside of the Constitution's reach.

As this scenario (often termed "white flight") was being played out, some people in the civil rights movement began asking other questions. If whites could escape from desegregated city schools by living in outlying areas that were all or largely white, was it legal for them to have "better" schools out there if they were willing to heavily tax their local property tax base to achieve that end? And what about the all-white, or mostly-white, schools within urban school districts in the North and West that weren't going to be ordered to desegregate? Was it legal for those schools to be "better" than the schools in the black neighborhoods?

In the mid-to-late 1960s, some wondered whether advocates for black school children should go back to the "separate but equal" doctrine. That strategy, however, seemed problematic for several reasons. First, if racial imbalance in the student bodies could not be shown to be the result of intentional governmental discrimination, would one be able to show that differences in school quality were intentionally created on the basis of race? (Without such a showing, de facto quality differences seemed no more subject to a racial challenge than were de facto assignment schemes.) Second, despite the special place that had been awarded to education in *Brown*, the Court (and the 1964 Civil Rights Act) soon moved to make intentional racial discrimination generally illegal. In other words, the doctrine of "separate but equal" was broadly overturned—having been made just as inapplicable to public golf courses as to public schooling. Finally, there was the fact that, as one looked around the state, one saw that the apparently excellent public schools that white children attended in some suburbs also seemed markedly superior to public schools elsewhere in the region that also largely enrolled white pupils. Perhaps school-quality differences were not ultimately a race question after all.

These puzzles and concerns forced scholars and activists committed to the idea of equality of educational opportunity for all children to study why it was that some children, both white and black, seemed to be receiving a decidedly inferior education as compared with what other children (mostly white) were receiving. And so, in the late 1960s, while the fight for school desegregation was still in full swing, it was first argued that courts should get involved in the issue of the distribution of school resources quite apart from any question of racial discrimination.

EARLY LEGAL THINKING ABOUT
SCHOOL FINANCE INEQUALITIES

Although in the prior paragraphs describing raced-based litigation we have sometimes phrased the complaints of black students in terms of the "inadequacy" of their educational opportunities, school finance scholars today would probably categorize these lawsuits as "equity" cases. This is because the gist of the complaint was that, although the plaintiffs (blacks) were entitled to treatment that was comparable to what the comparison group (whites) received, they were not receiving it. In other words, "equity" cases are about getting worse treatment than someone else. "Adequacy" cases, as we will see, seem instead to be centrally about getting worse treatment than one is entitled to as determined by reference to some absolute standard and not in comparison with others.

Keeping this distinction in mind, the early advocates for non-race-based judicial intervention into the way school resources were distributed also clearly cast their complaints in equity terms. One group was unfairly getting less than (a worse education than) the comparison group. Moreover, as with the early race cases, the initial attack began primarily with a focus on "tangible" input resources, basically, dollars.

But because the comparison groups were not to be whites and blacks, advocates had to appeal to a different sort of "equal treatment" norm. To some, the basic unfairness arose from the fact that public school finance was really a highly varied, locally funded system (albeit with some state financial assistance thrown in). It was quickly evident to anyone who studied how school finance worked that, because public education was in practice predominantly a local matter, some districts raised and spent a lot of money, while others raised and spent little. As a result, school spending varied enormously from place to place around the state. It also was evident to the casual viewer that many of the high spenders were wealthy suburbs, and that many of the low spenders were communities filled with people of modest means.

If one looked within school districts, sometimes spending per pupil also varied substantially from school to school. Since schools were not revenue raisers, these inequalities arose for other reasons. But because these inequalities were less structural and less easy to document, and because they appeared, on the whole, to be smaller than the inter-district inequalities, the early approaches emphasized district-to-district differences.

If one took a wider view, it was also clear that public school spending per pupil varied enormously from state to state. But this was promptly ignored by the legal scholars, because those differences seemed self-evidently not the result of Congressional decisions that could be attacked under the U.S. Constitution.

The early critics thought that a proper school finance system would be a statewide system that wasn't plagued by local variation. Hence, their objection could most easily be stated in terms of geographical discrimination within the state: children living elsewhere, who were otherwise just like the complaining group, were getting a better education than the complaining group (at least as measured by dollar spending differences) for no reason other than the vagaries of the local financing of education (Wise, 1968; Horowitz and Neitring, 1968).

As a federal constitutional matter, however, it was hard to see why this sort of inequality was impermissible. Where in the federal constitution could the principle be found that educational quality (or spending) had to be roughly equal everywhere around the state? After all, roads, police forces, public transport services, parks, and the like also varied greatly from place to place, and no one at the time seemed to think that was unconstitutional. Wasn't local variation, including variation in public education, a fundamental feature of American history in the same way that variation from state to state has been?

Those seeking a uniform statewide school finance system tended to argue that education was different, noting (as we have seen) that the dismantling of racial segregation in America was litigated around schools and that the U.S. Supreme Court in *Brown* had emphasized the fundamental importance of education. The problem was that those racial desegregation cases had combined education with discrimination on the basis of race. Geographical discrimination just didn't have the same constitutional anchor. Moreover, as noted above, soon the Court also struck down racially segregated swimming pools, train stations, and so on. These later decisions suggested that, at the core, *Brown* was better understood to be primarily about racial equality, a doctrine that was not limited to education.

One could point out that public education was specially aimed at children, but the Supreme Court had given no indication that age (or youth) was to be treated as a category deserving of special judicial attention in the way race (and later gender) was. Moreover, the unequal treatment in education was not against youth (or on the basis of age), but rather among youth.

In *Private Wealth and Public Education* (1970), Coons et al. cast their attack on state school finance systems in a different manner. The constitutional norm they invoked did not insist upon a uniform statewide system. To the contrary, they acknowledged certain possible advantages of a *fair* locally based system that states might wish to embrace. For example, these authors were not offended by arrangements that produced better schools in local communities that in some sense cared more about education—communities such as those that were willing to spend their money on better schools instead of better parks, or that were willing to impose higher taxes on themselves in order to have both better schools and better parks.

The problem, according to the Coons team, was that the existing school finance systems in most states very clearly favored those communities that had more property tax wealth per pupil to finance their schools. Hence the equity case that the Coons team constructed made the comparison groups rich and poor school districts. What was unfair, according to them, was that something so important as education was distributed on the basis of wealth and poverty (albeit wealth and poverty of communities, rather than individuals).

The Coons team hoped that a successful constitutional theory could be created out of the Supreme Court's already-expressed concern about wealth discrimination in the provision of other fundamentally important matters—like the right to vote, the right to obtain a divorce, or the right to mount a criminal appeal. Like education, these other rights were not clearly included in the U.S. Constitution, yet they too were understood to be essential features of the sort of democracy we like to say we have. And when states discriminated against poor people in the provision of these rights (by imposing a financial burden on obtaining access to them) the Court had stepped in (*Griffin v. Illinois*, 351 U.S. 12, 1956, and *Harper v. Virginia Bd. of Elections*, 383 U.S. 663, 1966). Moreover, the Court had also recently acted on behalf of poor people who had exercised their right to travel (from one state to another) but were then denied welfare in their new state of residence (*Shapiro v. Thompson*, 394 U.S. 618, 1969). If restricting the access of the poor to welfare based upon where they lived was illegal, then perhaps the provision of inferior education to the poor based upon where they lived would also be deemed illegal.

The legal theory advanced by the Coons team initially had great success, as both the California Supreme Court and a three-judge federal court panel in Texas held that it was unconstitutional for the state to base school spending on local wealth differences. But when the Texas case reached the U.S. Supreme Court, the wealth discrimination theory was rejected on a vote of 5 to 4 because the Court majority did not see it as a case of discrimination against poor people (*San Antonio Independent School District v. Rodriguez*, 411 U.S. 1, 1973). After all, although the children who were harmed lived in poor districts, they themselves might not have been poor (and some poor children lived in wealthy districts). Moreover, whatever the importance of education, it was by no means being denied to the claimants. Some public education was available to all, and the Court expressed skepticism about whether the extras bought by those districts with more money permitted them to buy anything that was constitutionally significant.

Perhaps the Court would have decided differently if the states charged families tuition to attend public schools and the children of individual poor families were excluded from public education altogether. The Supreme Court hinted at this possibility in footnote 60 of the *Rodriguez* decision. Later, the Court ruled in favor of "excluded" children in *Plyer v. Doe*, 457 U.S. 202 (1982), but not in *Kadrmas v. Dickinson Public Schools*, 487 U.S. 450 (1988). But since local communities everywhere in Texas had pitched in to provide at least some minimum education for everyone, the Court refused to embrace the analogy to those earlier cases about voting, divorce, criminal appeals, and travel that involved outright denials. The defeat in *Rodriguez* spelled the end of federal constitutional litigation with respect to school finance.

But this by no means was the end of school finance litigation. Rather, the venue changed to state courts and, more importantly, the relevant document became the individual state constitution instead of the federal Constitution (McUsic, 1991).

SCHOOL FINANCE LITIGATION AND STATE CONSTITUTIONS

Equity Cases

Just because school finance arrangements are valid under the federal constitution does not mean that they are necessarily valid under state constitutions. To be sure, over the course of the last few decades, legal advocates have generally sought to involve the federal judiciary and the federal constitution in their battles to reform what they have considered to be unfair institutional arrangements. The wrongdoers are generally seen to be state or local governments, and state court judges have not generally been viewed as likely allies in the fight. If nothing else, state judges are often thought to be more cautious because they are politically more vulnerable if they take unpopular stands and because they are understandably more deferential to their co-branches of state government. Indeed, in the early days of the civil rights movement, state courts were viewed as an important part of the problem.

Nonetheless, judicial reform of public schools could be a politically popular thing to do, especially in recent times when our public education system is often criticized as failing on many dimensions. Moreover, as we will see, education has a special place in state constitutions.

In the early years, advocates seemed basically inclined to argue for the Coons team's theory in state court. After all, state constitutions contained their own equal protection clauses, and state judges were not bound to interpret them in the same way as the U.S. Supreme Court had interpreted the Fourteenth Amendment. This line of attack was bolstered enormously by the California Supreme Court, which had initially embraced the Coons team's approach primarily under the federal constitution (*Serrano v. Priest*, 5 Cal.3d 584, 1971—*Serrano I*), but which, after *Rodriguez*, announced that it was sticking with its decision, now squarely resting it on the equal protection guarantee of the California Constitution, which had merited only passing mention in the Court's first decision (*Serrano v. Priest*, 18 Cal.3d 728, 1976—*Serrano II*).

In important respects, from 1971 through 1989 the main battle was over how widely advocates could get the courts to apply the wealth discrimination theory that had been adopted in California. Important equity-based victories were won in several states and continue to be won even in very recent years, for example, in Texas and Vermont (see Minorini and Sugarman, Chapter 2 in this volume). At the same time, however, many cases were lost as state court judges, in effect, found persuasive the view of the U.S. Supreme Court majority in *Rodriguez* and interpreted their own constitutions in the same manner.

The Shift Away from Wealth Discrimination

Starting in 1989, a new legal theory generally called "educational adequacy" moved to center stage in school finance litigation. Before turning to what courts are currently doing in that area, however, it is important to explain the change in thinking of at least some school finance reformers that led to the shift in litigation and judicial focus. Put generally, there was a growing dissatisfaction with the outcomes of school finance "equity" cases, even where they were successful.

First, many advocates began to emphasize a number of issues that the earlier writings had acknowledged but had put aside: (1) some districts (especially urban districts) faced higher costs than others (for example, the higher cost of living in cities required paying higher wages to employees and higher prices for goods); (2) some districts (especially urban districts) had relatively more pupils with exceptional educational needs and so, in some sense, needed more money in order to educate them; and (3) some districts (especially urban districts) had to provide so many other local services that their tax base was not really as available to be drawn on for education as would appear from a simple calculation of local district capacity (e.g., assessed value per pupil). Note that advocates concerned about all three of these factors were centrally interested in the education of poor, inner-city students who were increasingly non-white. In an important sense, these advocates began to doubt whether even successful school finance litigation was doing enough for the pupils they cared most about.

These concerns might be accommodated under the wealth discrimination theory. For example, by adopting the notion of the "weighted pupil" (with extra weight given where the pupil was needier or costs were greater), a district could be deemed to have the equivalent of more pupils; and by adjusting for "municipal overburden" a district could be deemed to have less wealth. Together, these adjustments could reveal a district to be far poorer (and hence entitled to more state financial assistance) than suggested by a simple calculation of its assessed value per student headcount. But making these adjustments (how large should they be?) would get courts into far more perilous territory than was initially promised by the wealth discrimination theory. Moreover, the reality was that these sorts of adjustments would especially benefit urban districts that in many places were already above average both in wealth (if simply measured) and in spending per pupil (if still well below the wealthy suburbs). Hence, these adjustments implied a dramatic reconsideration of which districts were most harmed by the traditional system—which under the simple wealth discrimination theory were the straightforwardly very low-wealth/low-spending districts. In short, those most concerned about poor, minority children in urban centers had reason to cast around for a new approach.

Second, as explained earlier, the Coons team constructed its legal theory around the idea that local variation per se was not impermissible. Of course, the state could have a uniform statewide system if it wished, but that was not to be legally mandated under the wealth discrimination theory. What had to go were local spending differences based on local wealth differences. Although it might have been possible to radically redraw school district boundaries so as to make all the new districts roughly equally wealthy, this was politically unlikely and unnecessary in the view of the Coons team. Instead, through the way it constructed its grant-in-aid program, the state could make each district constructively equally wealthy—essentially by matching the local money raised by poor districts at a much higher rate than that raised by rich districts. They called this option "district power equalizing." District power equalizing would permit local spending differences based upon different tastes, as reflected in differences in local willingness to impose taxes.

Yet, district power equalizing as a legal remedy created dissatisfaction of two highly conflicting sorts. On the one hand, in several states it seemed clear that the courts didn't really accept the implications of the wealth discrimination theory. For them, geographic differences in spending were the central objection. Wealth differences were emphasized as the source of geographic inequalities, but the desired remedy was to eliminate the latter, not merely the former. Perhaps a new legal theory would more logically link the constitutional wrong with the sought-after remedy.

On the other hand, different observers slowly began to realize that to implement the Coons team's district power equalizing solution in response to a victorious school finance case was politically treacherous. This is because district power equalizing typically requires, in a vivid way, taking money from the rich and giving it to the poor. Of course, this is the nature of redistributive taxing and spending policies generally. But the implementation of district power equalizing was viewed as taking local raised property taxes directly away from those districts that had wanted to spend those precise dollars on their children and handing them over to poorer districts to spend on their children (which is, of course, exactly what the wealth discrimination theory required).

Beyond this political difficulty (and inconsistent with the view of those who were pressing hard for ending geographic differences in spending), many reformers began to lose their enthusiasm for even trying to curb relatively higher spending by the rich. Some adopted the view that the rich cannot really be stopped anyway. They can always pull their children out of public schools and put them into pricey private schools. They can add on to what is spent by the public schools—either after school, or on weekends, or in the summer with private lessons, tutoring, and so on. They can raise money to supplement local public schools through local, private, educational foundations that were emerging in many places.

To those who continued to believe in the principle underlying the wealth discrimination theory, these examples were beside the point. Districts should still be prevented from using public powers to take advantage of the greater property wealth that the state had unfairly assigned to their community to tax. (Allowing districts to use this power was also clearly offensive to those, noted above, who sought to transform wealth discrimination cases into a mandate to eliminate geographic differences in spending.) But for others, it began to seem a waste of time and effort to try to prevent the richer districts from spending extra local money from local taxes. This too implied the desirability of a new legal strategy.

Third, the California experience with the wealth discrimination theory unnerved many people, again leading them to search for alternative theories. Soon after the *Serrano* case, California voters passed two initiatives that radically restricted local and state taxing and spending powers. The measure restricting property taxes made it essential, as a practical matter, for the state to take over a much greater share of the school finance load, and this in turn yielded a much greater equalization of spending than had existed before *Serrano*. Yet at the same time these two initiatives sharply curtailed the size of government in California, and rather rapidly California dropped from being one of the states that spent most generously on public schools to one of the lowest spenders.

Research has shown that in other states where courts have ordered school finance reform, school spending has gone up (Evans et al., 1997). Essentially, the judiciary has forced a leveling up of the lower-spending districts. Yet California wound up leveling down. In California, it is generally understood that those taxing and spending initiatives would have passed anyway, because they were responses to forces altogether unrelated to the *Serrano* case (rapidly rising property values that local governments used simply as a way to collect more taxes, and a stubborn Governor Jerry Brown who refused to use a large state surplus to provide tax relief). On this view, California is an outlier that should be ignored when projecting the likely consequences of successful "equity" litigation over school finance.

Nonetheless, it has been argued in the scholarly literature that opposition to the remedy that was called for by the school finance litigation was what gave the initiative sponsors the key support they needed (Fischel, 1989). The theory is that traditional supporters of public education in high-wealth districts turned against the system when they saw that they were no longer going to be able to use it to their advantage as they had in the past. Whether or not the *Serrano* decision was in fact responsible for the passage of the tax and spending control initiatives, these California developments served as a warning: the equality norm is consistent with "equally lousy."

Fourth, because of the ascendancy of other forces, during the 1980s national attention began to turn away from the problem of inequalities in school spending to the shortcomings of public education from top to bottom. Probably the key event was the publication of *A Nation at Risk* (National Commission on Excellence in Education, 1983), and the key message that most people took away from that document was that America's school children were not learning enough— not enough as compared with youngsters in other countries, and not enough for what was becoming needed and surely would soon be widely needed by our contemporary economy. Public schools had to do better by nearly all of our children. Productivity importantly replaced inequality as the salient reform objective.

By 1989, the nation's governors and the federal government began to articulate the goal of high academic standards for all children (see Berne and Stiefel, chapter 1 of this volume; Heise, 1995; Cohen, 1995). While the idea of "education standards" was not new, that "standards" movement hit the national stage with great fanfare at the end of the 1980s and has maintained its presence through the present day. In support of the movement, many states began to design new student achievement tests intended to measure whether students were actually attaining the desired standards. These developments created an atmosphere in which at least some policymakers believed that all children could reach high academic standards if provided with an appropriate level of resources, and that assessments could measure when that had occurred. From this vantage point, an equity-based legal theory that at best promised the plaintiffs schooling comparable to that of other students who also were not learning enough became less attractive.

Finally, the changing landscape of school desegregation litigation has reinforced the desirability of finding a new school finance legal theory. Through the late 1970s and the 1980s, many federal judges were confronted with lawsuits in which the plaintiffs had proven past intentional discrimination on the basis of race, but, because there were relatively few white children left in the school district, the remedy of racially integrating the student bodies of the district's schools appeared largely unattainable. Sometimes the judges sought voluntary metropolitan integration solutions that typically involved black students transferring out to surrounding schools (e.g., St. Louis). Sometimes the judges sought to entice whites back into inner-city schools by making them more attractive through the infusion of new resources (e.g., Kansas City). But often the courts seemed to focus primarily on ordering improvements in the educational enterprise—such as teacher quality, curriculum, facilities, and other support staff—that were in many respects independent of student assignment-related desegregation goals (e.g., Detroit and Kansas City; *Milliken v. Bradley*, 433 U.S. 267, 1977 and its progeny). It was, for many de jure discrimination cases, something of a return to the notion of "separate but equal" after all.

Developments in federal school desegregation jurisprudence in the early 1990s, however, suggest that the litigation era reaching back to *Brown v. Board of Education* is now drawing to a close. Beginning with the Supreme Court's decisions in *Board of Education of Oklahoma City v. Dowell*, 498 U.S. 237 (1991) and *Freeman v. Pitts,* 503 U.S. 467 (1992), and culminating with the Court's decision in *Missouri v. Jenkins*, 515 U.S. 1139 (1995), advocates for poor, inner-city minority communities began to see the doors to federal courts close. These recent Supreme Court decisions essentially relaxed the standard that applied to school districts which had previously discriminated, had implemented a judicially approved remedy, and were now seeking to end federal court involvement in their affairs. But curtailing continuing federal court jurisdiction over a district that had once acted illegally opens the way for the district also to abandon some of the special efforts that had been imposed on it—both programs aimed explicitly at achieving racially balanced student bodies and those aimed more at improving the educational opportunities offered in the often heavily minority schools.

So, if federal desegregation litigation will soon no longer serve as a primary tool for trying to improve educational opportunities for inner-city poor and minority youths, some of their advocates too have concluded that school finance litigation might be a promising substitute (Tatel, 1992). But, as noted earlier, for needy children attending high-cost, urban schools, school finance litigation would be far more attractive if it could be cast more widely than the conventional wealth discrimination approach.

The Embrace of Adequacy

These forces together have brought many school finance reformers around to a new view of what states should do. Rather than the overt "Robin Hood" solution promised by school finance equity litigation, perhaps it would be wiser to direct the main reform effort at getting the states to assure what we believe is best termed a "high-minimum quality education for all."

As spelled out by William Clune (who abandoned the Coons team for this new approach) and others, a state-guaranteed high-minimum is most often what is meant by an "adequate" education (Clune, 1994; see Chapter 2 in this volume). In funding this high-minimum, the system would specifically take into account the varying needs of different types of pupils. It would also recognize that individual schools (or districts) face differing costs. Beyond those based on differences in the cost of living, the high-minimum approach would probably also recognize that some communities will have to pay more to attract equally good teachers to teach their needier and lower-achieving students. It would probably also recognize the benefit some students gain from having higher-achieving classmates and other intangibles that enable their school to provide a good education, and in turn would somehow compensate for the lack of those advantages in other schools. In other words, the high-minimum approach focuses on what would be needed to assure that all children have access to those educational opportunities that are necessary to gain a level of learning and skills that are now required, say, to obtain a good job in our increasingly technologically complex society and to participate effectively in our ever more complicated political process.

In this respect, the adequacy approach decidedly reflects a shift of the sort we saw in the history of the race cases, where the Supreme Court became increasingly concerned with what the real educational opportunity was, and not merely the easily measured input factors. But as noted above, an expanded equity paradigm, at least in principle, could also accommodate these same adjustments.

What is most distinctive about the adequacy approach is that, unlike the traditional school finance cases, it does not rest on a norm of equal treatment. Indeed, the adequacy cases aren't about equality at all, except in the sense that all pupils are equally entitled to at least a high-minimum. In other words, adequacy is not a matter of comparing spending on the complaining group with spending on others. It is rather about spending what is needed (and its focus is in some respects more on the school or the pupil than on the district).

Notice, however, that although educational adequacy is more about outputs than inputs, nevertheless, in the minds of many of its supporters, the achievement of adequacy does not appear to be ultimately judged by actual educational outcomes. It is still an opportunity concept, and as such, compliance with the adequacy requirement is ultimately still a matter of inputs, albeit now more broadly conceived. In other words, at the level of the moral claim, educational adequacy seems to be about what fairly ought to be provided, leaving it in the end to the student to take advantage of that offering.

But if it is neither a matter of comparing inputs with those provided to other pupils nor a matter of everyone's actual outcomes, then how does one decide what inputs an adequate education requires? Would assuring an adequate education for all students cost more than is now spent on elementary and secondary public education, or less? Would it require a great deal more redistribution of money from those living in high-wealth districts than has been required by the equity cases, or less? Just how much extra is to be provided for special needs students and high-cost areas? There are no self-evident answers to these questions.

As we see it, what is "adequate" will come down to a matter of judgment, probably informed by expertise. (There is also an analogy that can be made here to the world of special education, in which each disabled child is now legally guaranteed an "appropriate" education, which, in practice, has tended to amount to what educational experts say will suffice to meet that child's special needs.) Moreover, it seems that in making the judgment about what is fairly required by the educational adequacy requirement, one would want to take into account what outcomes can reasonably be expected from which inputs, even if actually achieving certain outcomes is not required. Indeed, if there are grossly deficient outcomes at present, this may be taken as evidence of inadequate inputs. In these respects, however, the distinction between adequacy as an outcome standard and an input standard becomes blurred.

In any event, because the comparison to be made is with an absolute standard and not in relation to others, most adequacy theorists appear to agree that school districts that can afford to, and choose to do so, ought to be free to offer more than the high-minimum. In this respect as well "adequacy" differs from "equity."

Adequacy as a Legal Requirement?

Do courts have a role to play in trying to achieve educational "adequacy" for all pupils? For the moment the answer is decidedly "Yes." Since 1989 especially, successful state court school finance cases seem to be moving strongly in this very direction (Enrich, 1995).

As a matter of legal doctrine, we hear state courts increasingly saying to their legislatures that the *education clause* of their state constitution gives the state responsibility for education that it may not simply pass on to local school districts. Rather, a *state system* of education is required. That state system, in the most common language of state constitutions, must be "thorough and efficient," and those words are being interpreted by some courts to require what we've been calling "adequacy."

In general, the claimants in educational adequacy cases still tend to be those who live in low-spending districts, although recently many suits have included claims on behalf of larger urban centers that, while at or close to the state average in per-pupil spending, are burdened with educating large percentages and numbers of students living in or near poverty, having limited English proficiency, or otherwise requiring extra educational services.

How have claimants proved that the state has failed to create a system of the sort they claim is constitutionally required? Interestingly enough, an important part of the legal strategy has been to demonstrate that there are large spending and other input differences from place to place—just as in the equity cases. Adequacy plaintiffs also typically point to measures of student performance such as standardized test scores, graduation rates, and the like. Together, this evidence is meant to show that the plaintiffs' schooling opportunities are constitutionally inadequate.

In fact, adequacy cases (like equity cases) usually attack a school finance system that is some version of the "minimum foundation plan" first brought into use in the 1920s. And one basic question is why isn't that "minimum" enough to satisfy the state constitutional command. After all, the foundation plan formula basically assures that each local district has at least some, specified, minimum amount of spending per pupil available to it (provided that it levies the minimum required local tax rate). Beyond that foundation amount, the local districts traditionally can add on out of their own funds if they wish. Recall that under the wealth discrimination theory of the equity cases, the central problem with the foundation plan is the wealth-based local add-ons. But for courts looking for a state "system" in the face of an adequacy suit, the problem has been with the foundation amount itself.

As the judges ruling in favor of the claimants have seen it, a "thorough and efficient" educational system requires that the amount of funding available to districts be set from the perspective of the state deciding what is actually necessary to fund an "adequate" education. This may mean adopting state educational goals and deciding what is needed to achieve them. It may mean taking into account those pupil-need and cost adjustment factors discussed above. At the least, it means self-consciously deciding how much should be spent to provide the statewide education to which all children are entitled by the state constitution. However this is put, what is clear is that almost nowhere could it plausibly be shown that the actual minimum foundation plan level in effect at the time of the lawsuit had been determined as a result of a genuine statewide appraisal of that sort. Rather, the foundation plan level has almost always been determined by the outcome of state politics, i.e., how much redistribution of state tax revenues could be achieved in favor of the poorer districts. In this way we can see how state courts may feel themselves comfortably able to announce that a state system of education is both constitutionally required and clearly does not exist.

What would be enough for the state to meet this conception of the constitutional requirement is a far more complicated matter, however. Indeed, that problem may well explain why some state courts have rejected educational adequacy claims, finding, in effect, that the state constitution's education clause creates no judicially determinable and enforceable standard. But many other courts, at least so far, seem undaunted by this prospect—at least not daunted enough to refrain from condemning the system as it stands.

In thinking about what eventually is to be required by the state constitution, one possibility, of course, is that the courts will identify a substantive standard against which the system will be measured. Assume that, as an abstract matter, the standard will be what we have been calling a "high-minimum"—in the sense that most people would agree that considerable education is increasingly required to become a full participant in today's economic and political life. But that is too abstract. What, more precisely, will be the content, inputs, or outcome goals of that high-minimum? Perhaps the courts will look to what their own legislatures already have said in statutes and regulations that spell out what educational outcomes are expected of students at various levels of their education. Certainly the drive for state standards and assessments geared to those standards will suggest this as a plausible option. Fearful that a recalcitrant legislature might try to thwart the court's efforts by, in effect, "dumbing down" the state goals, the judges might instead look to a national consensus as to what sort of education today's youths need for success. Many adequacy decisions that have ticked off a list of educational goals, in effect, tap into the judges' sense of today's collective wisdom on this matter.

But, of course, under any of these approaches this first step would only help identify the goals of the educational system. Still to be decided would be whether the opportunities provided are fairly calculated to permit pupils to reach those goals. This, it seems, would inevitably put the judges in the middle of a debate between "experts" paraded into court by both plaintiffs and defendants.

Yet, just because the experts will disagree does not mean that they can't provide the judges with helpful insights. For example, James Guthrie and Richard Rothstein have developed a thoughtful methodology for identifying an "adequate" education that they have already applied in more than one state. Simply put, they gather school professionals together to discuss and reach consensus on what inputs are needed for an adequate education and then they price those inputs. If, for example, the professionals decide (based upon research or experience) that elementary school class size of 15 is needed, they plug that in. If the professionals decide that if there are so many disadvantaged kids an extra classroom aide is needed, they plug that in. They also try to adjust for differential wage costs and the like from place to place. In this way they can build up to a total number of dollars that each district (or perhaps even at the level of each school) must have in order to deliver its pupils an adequate education (see Guthrie and Rothstein, Chapter 7 in this volume). (Interestingly enough, once they determine the total per-pupil amount, Guthrie and Rothstein do not insist that schools be required to spend precisely in the way implied by the building blocks that were used in determining the school's total revenue. Instead, schools are to have flexibility in how they use their funds. But they are to be held accountable in some way if the performance of their pupils is not up to par.)

John Augenblick has developed a different approach (Augenblick, 1997). His strategy is to identify the cost structures of districts that are successful. After excluding the outlier districts, both rich and poor, in terms of wealth and per-pupil expenditure, Augenblick scours the remaining districts to see which have been successful in terms of student performance (e.g., 75 percent or more of the pupils meet state minimum competency standards). Then Augenblick looks to see how much was spent per pupil in these successful districts. The basic idea is that if a group of districts with a variety of pupil characteristics can succeed with $X per pupil, then other districts should also be able to do so.

William Duncombe and John Yinger have offered further insights (see Chapter 8 in this volume). They are highly skeptical about whether schools with concentrations of low-income children, especially in urban areas, can realistically succeed with an amount of money that Augenblick's model would provide, and they find arbitrary Guthrie and Rothstein's reliance on the professional model to determine how much *extra* money those schools should have. Instead, Duncombe and Yinger have developed very sophisticated analytical techniques to determine empirically how much extra money schools (or school districts) should be provided when they face high-cost problems that are beyond their control—like needy pupils and high wage costs. For example, if using the Guthrie and Rothstein approach, it was determined that, say, $6,000 per pupil was needed in an ordinary district or school, the Duncombe and Yinger methodology might then suggest that, say, $12,000 per pupil is needed in a district with a great concentration of low-income children—if those children are to perform, on average, as well as children living in the ordinary district. While these numbers are just hypothetical, it is important to note that Duncombe and Yinger do claim that in New York, for example, many upstate urban communities will need more than twice as much money as New York City suburban schools if they are to have any chance of matching the educational outcomes of those suburbs. Moreover, New York City itself, they say, would need perhaps three times what Scarsdale spends. Given the complexity of the Duncombe and Yinger methodology, many will wonder to what extent they really have taken into account only costs that are beyond the school or district's control and not allowed past spending inefficiencies to determine how much future revenue a school or district ought fairly have.

These examples illustrate the sorts of testimony that might be brought forward by the parties. Of course, these various approaches to determining adequacy are likely to yield very different results. Guthrie and Rothstein, for example, are talking about providing something like $500 extra per low-income pupil whereas Duncombe and Yinger are talking about more than $5,000 extra for the same pupils—at least where they are schooled among concentrations of disadvantaged children. If the judges are to make a substantive determination of what is adequate, they will somehow have to resolve this dispute.

If this is too daunting, a different possibility is that courts will ultimately impose more of a procedural test on the legislature. For example, did the legislature reasonably (or in good faith) enact something intended to be what can fairly be called a state system? The state might demonstrate this, for example, by showing that it created a commission, called in experts, adopted educational goals, reasonably priced them out, and provided the needed funding. Of course, reasonable people may well differ on just what those goals should be and, even more so, on how much must be spent in support of them. Under the procedural approach, the court would not insist on a single resolution to the substantive issues. Rather, many schemes could pass constitutional muster. The key thing, again, would be whether the legislature engaged in a process that reasonably related the funding of schools to what had been fairly determined to be their students' actual educational needs.

One might have thought that the state constitutional requirement of a state system of education would mean just that—no local option, at least no local spending add-ons out of local wealth. This indeed may be where some state supreme courts are heading (e.g., Wyoming). It is also consistent with the outlook of those, noted earlier, who are quite unsatisfied with the leeway allowed under the wealth discrimination theory for local add-ons (even if they are wealth equalized).

But other state supreme courts have already gone out of their way to reject this restriction. Several recent opinions have either explicitly or implicitly acknowledged that local add-ons from local taxes would be permissible, but only after a true state system had first been established (*Claremont v. Governor of New Hampshire*, 635 A.2d 1375, N.H. 1997; *Leandro v. State of North Carolina*, No. 179PA96, 1997; *Rose v. Council for Better Education*, 790 S.W.2d 186, Ky. 1989). This latter approach is aligned with that version of the "educational adequacy" theory that rejects trying to hold down higher spending by the rich.

EDUCATIONAL ADEQUACY IN THE COURTS

Adequacy notions first explicitly appeared in school finance litigation in 1976 when the New Jersey Supreme Court in *Robinson v. Cahill* stated that its state constitution required an education system that allowed all students to become "citizens and competitors in the labor market." Similar language was next found in the Washington Supreme Court's 1978 ruling, which declared aspects of the state's school funding system unconstitutional (*Seattle v. State of Washing-*

ton, 585 P.2d 71, Wash. 1978).   The court interpreted the Washington Constitution's education clause as requiring that the state fund schools in a manner that allowed them to "equip our children [to function] as citizens and as potential competitors in today's market as well as in the market place of ideas . . . to participate intelligently and effectively in our open political system . . . to exercise their First Amendment freedoms both as sources and receivers of information and . . . to be able to inquire, to study, to evaluate and to gain maturity and understanding." The court characterized those outcomes as "broad guidelines," noting that "the effective teaching and opportunities for learning these essential skills . . . make up [the] minimum of education that is constitutionally required." The court ordered the state to define what constitutes a basic education and to fund it in all districts.

In 1979, the West Virginia Supreme Court took the notion of adequacy a step further (*Pauley v. Kelly*, 255 S.E.2d 859, W.Va. 1979). Like the New Jersey and Washington courts, the West Virginia Court identified a set of broad goals for a constitutionally adequate education system: "[A] thorough and efficient system of schools . . . develops, as best the state of education expertise allows, the minds, bodies and social morality of its charges to prepare them for useful and happy occupations, recreation and citizenship, and does so economically." Unlike prior courts, the West Virginia court went on to specify what such an education would accomplish in terms of student outcomes:

> Legally recognized elements of this definition are the development in every child to his or her capacity of: (1) literacy; (2) ability to add, subtract, multiply and divide numbers; (3) knowledge of government to the extent that the child will be equipped as a citizen to make informed choices among persons and issues that affect his own governance; (4) self-knowledge and knowledge of his or her total environment to allow the child to intelligently choose life work—to know his or her options; (5) work-training and advanced academic training as the child may intelligently choose; (6) recreational pursuits; (7) interests in all creative arts, such as music, theater, literature, and the visual arts; and (8) social ethics, both behavioral and abstract, to facilitate compatibility with others in this society.

Because procedurally the case arrived in the West Virginia Supreme Court on an appeal from the lower court's dismissal of the action, the court remanded the case back to the trial court for further hearings.

On remand, the lower court declared the state school funding scheme to be inequitable and inadequate, and ordered the legislature to develop a comprehensive plan to bring to the entire education system into constitutional compliance. The trial judge left the design of the plan to the legislature and in 1983 approved the "Master Plan for Education" developed by the legislature and State Department of Education. That plan called for, among other things, the development of standards and curricula geared to those standards, improved facilities, and a revised finance plan.

Fourteen years later, in 1997, a West Virginia lower court ruled that the state had failed to implement all of the requirements of their "Master Plan for Education" (see Minorini and Sugarman, Chapter 2 in this volume), and ordered the state to develop a new plan to bring the system into constitutional compliance in 1998. The court objected especially to the lack of connection between funding levels and actual costs of providing a high-quality education to students in conformity with state education standards.

These early "adequacy" cases were *not* soon followed with similar decisions elsewhere. Indeed, at the time it was not evident that the courts were really doing anything meaningfully different from what was being ordered in school finance equity cases. This thinking was reinforced in subsequent litigation in New Jersey, where the court appeared to have turned back to a more traditional notion of equity.

But, in 1989, the Kentucky Supreme Court explicitly established educational adequacy as a distinct theory in school finance litigation (*Rose v. Council for Better Education*, 790 S.W.2d 186, Ky. 1989). In a sweeping decision, the court found that the entire Kentucky system of education violated the mandates of the state constitution, and ordered the state to overhaul the *entire* system of education to bring it into compliance. In the course of its opinion, the Court emphasized how little Kentucky currently spent for education as compared with neighboring states and in turn how poor was the educational attainment of Kentucky students. While the Court stopped short of ordering specific education reforms, deferring instead to the legislative process in the first instance, it did provide the legislature with broad guidelines about what constitutes an adequate education. Those guidelines defined an adequate education as one that provides students with the opportunity to develop at least the following seven capabilities:

- sufficient oral and written communication skills to enable students to function in a complex and rapidly changing civilization;
- sufficient knowledge of economic, social, and political systems to enable the student to make informed choices;
- sufficient understanding of governmental processes to enable the student to understand the issues that affect his or her community, state, and nation;
- sufficient self-knowledge and knowledge of his or her mental and physical wellness;
- sufficient grounding in the arts to enable each student to appreciate his or her cultural and historical heritage;
- sufficient training or preparation for advanced training in either academic or vocational fields so as to enable each child to choose and pursue life work intelligently; and
- sufficient levels of academic or vocational skills to enable public school students to compete favorably with their counterparts in surrounding states, in academics, or in the job market.

The impact of the Kentucky decision has been felt in many state courts across the country. Since 1989, courts in New Hampshire, Alabama, and Massachusetts have declared their education systems to be constitutionally inadequate, relying specifically on the Kentucky Court's definition of an adequate education when providing guidance to the state legislatures as they craft remedies (*Claremont School District v. Gregg*, 635 A.2d 1375, N.H. 1997; *McDuffy v. Secretary of Education*, 615 N.E.2d 516, Mass. 1993; *Alabama Coalition for Equity v. Hunt*, published as Appendix to Opinion of Justices, 624 So.2d 107, Ala. 1993).

For example, in 1993, the New Hampshire Supreme Court found that the state constitution required the state to create and maintain an adequate education system (*Claremont School District v. Gregg*, 1993). According to the court, such an education "extends beyond mere reading, writing and arithmetic [and] includes broad educational opportunities needed in today's society to prepare citizens for their role as participants and as potential competitors in today's marketplace of ideas."

That 1993 ruling, however, only reversed a trial court's dismissal of the plaintiffs' action prior to a trial on the merits. Following the court's broad articulation of the constitutional right to an adequate education, the trial court held a lengthy trial, after which it ruled that the standard of adequacy set forth by the high court had been satisfied in all complaining school districts. That trial court decision, however, was soon appealed to the New Hampshire Supreme Court, which, in a December 1997 ruling, again reversed the trial court and found that the state system of financing education was unconstitutional because it resulted in many school districts being unable to offer their children adequate educational opportunities.

In that most recent decision, the court further elaborated on what a constitutionally adequate education must accomplish, adopting the seven factors established by the Kentucky Supreme Court. In addition, however, the New Hampshire court went on to note that:

> A constitutionally adequate public education is not a static concept removed from the demands of an evolving world. It is not the needs of the few but the critical requirements of the many that it must address. Mere compliance in the basics—reading, writing, and arithmetic—is insufficient in the waning days of the twentieth century to ensure that this State's public school students are fully integrated into the world around them. A broad exposure to the social, economic, scientific, technological, and political realities of today's society is essential for our students to compete, contribute, and flourish in the twenty-first century.

The New Hampshire court also explicitly recognized that local districts were free to raise local funds to supplement the state-guaranteed high-minimum standard of adequacy.

> We emphasize that the fundamental right at issue is the right to a State funded constitutionally adequate public education. It is not the right to horizontal

resource replication from school to school and district to district. The substance
of the right may be achieved in different schools possessing, for example, differing library resources, teacher-student ratios, computer software, as well as
the myriad tools and techniques that may be employed by those in on-site
control of the state's public elementary and secondary school system.

Other decisions in the 1990s also have adopted broad conceptions of what is
meant by educational adequacy. In 1993, the Tennessee Supreme Court found
that the state constitution required the education system to provide districts with
sufficient funds to permit the attainment of certain broadly defined educational
outcomes: "The General Assembly shall maintain and support a system of free
public schools that provides at least the opportunity to acquire general knowledge, develop the powers of reasoning and judgment, and generally prepare
students intellectually for a mature life" (*Tennessee Small School Systems v.
McWherter*, 851 S.W.2d 139, Tenn. 1993). Similarly, in 1994, the Arizona
Supreme Court ruled that the state's system for funding school facilities was
unconstitutional because certain districts lacked the resources necessary to maintain adequate school buildings (*Roosevelt Elementary School District v. Bishop*,
877 P.2d 806, Ariz. 1994). That decision, while limited to capital funding, also
suggested that similar principles of adequacy might apply to school districts'
operating costs.

In 1995, the highest court in New York held that the state is constitutionally
obligated to create and maintain an education system that provides children with:
"the basic literacy, calculation, and verbal skills necessary to enable [them] to
eventually function productively as civic participants capable of voting and serving on a jury. . .[and] minimally adequate physical facilities and classrooms. . .to
permit children to learn" (*Campaign for Fiscal Equity v. State of New York*, 86
N.Y.2d 307, N.Y. 1995). And in March 1997, the Ohio Supreme Court ruled that
by permitting dramatic deficiencies in facilities, materials and supplies, and class
sizes in some of the poorer school districts, the state had violated its constitutional duty to provide students with a "thorough and efficient" education system
(*DeRolph v. State*, 79 Oh.St.3d 297, 1997). The court's decision did not discuss
any outcome standards of adequacy or a minimum threshold of a basic education,
but rather simply ruled that the conditions in poor school districts around the state
were unacceptable.

Recent adequacy litigation in North Carolina also is significant in several
important respects. First, that litigation was filed in 1995 by a coalition of low-
wealth school districts that had filed and lost a traditional finance equity battle in
the mid-1980s. This recent lawsuit attempts to avoid the precedent of the earlier
decision by focusing the court on adequacy issues, as opposed to the comparative
fiscal equity issues. In addition, this recent lawsuit was joined by a coalition of
relatively high-spending, high-wealth urban school systems, whose claims focused on their inability to serve adequately their high-needs, at-risk student popu-

lations. This suit illustrates the applicability of the adequacy theory to both low-wealth rural districts, as well as high-wealth, high-need urban systems.

The North Carolina Supreme Court ruled in July 1997 that the complaining school systems are entitled to a trial, and that the state constitution does guarantee all schoolchildren a basic, adequate level of educational opportunities. Significantly, the court also ruled that variations in spending that result from local add-ons would be permitted in the system so long as all districts could provide students with the constitutionally guaranteed minimum level of opportunities.

Events in Wyoming over the last decade and a half also have brought the issue of educational adequacy to the political and judicial forefront. In 1980, the Wyoming Supreme Court found that the state education funding system violated the state constitution's equity requirement, noting that "until the equality of financing is achieved, there is no practicable method of achieving the equality of quality" (*Washakie v. Herschler*, 606 P.2d 310, Wash. 1980). In its 1995 decision (*Campbell v. State*, 907 P.2d 1238, Wyo. 1995), the court ruled that the legislature's response to the 1980 decision was deficient and ordered the following:

> The legislature must first design the best educational system by identifying the "proper" educational package each Wyoming student is entitled to have. . . . The cost of that educational package must then be determined and the legislature must then take the necessary action to fund that package. Because education is one of the state's most important functions, lack of financial resources will not be an acceptable reason for failure to provide the best education system. All other financial considerations must yield until education is funded.

Recall that the Kentucky court, for example, had provided the legislature with very broad guidelines as to what constituted the components of an adequate education. But it had left it to the legislature to design a school finance system that fit within those broad guidelines. The Wyoming court, by contrast, did not articulate such broad guidelines. Rather, it specifically directed the legislature to determine what is a "proper educational package" for all Wyoming students. The bite of its order, however, was that once the legislature identified that package, the state had the constitutional duty both to determine how much it would cost and to fully fund it. The court emphasized that the legislature's funding decisions could not be driven by politics or concerns about revenue availability, but must instead make judgments about actual educational goals, needs, and costs.

Significantly, the Wyoming court rejected the notion that local school districts could exercise their local taxing power to supplement the state provision of school finances. Indeed, the court noted that "historical analysis reveals local control is not a constitutionally recognized interest and cannot be the basis for disparity in equal educational opportunity." This approach, however, seems to be more of an exception than a rule in adequacy litigation. Indeed, most states and state courts addressing adequacy concerns have approached the issue more like the New Hampshire and North Carolina Supreme Courts, which would allow for local variation in spending so long as all districts have access to a high-minimum level of adequacy.

Not every state's high court has been receptive to adequacy arguments. In Illinois, where the state constitution's education clause explicitly requires the state to "provide for an efficient system of high quality public educational institutions and services," the Illinois Supreme Court rejected attempts by plaintiffs to evaluate whether the quality of education offered in many plaintiff districts met that constitutional standard. According to the court, "questions relating to the quality of education are solely for the legislative branch to answer" (*Committee for Educational Rights v. Edgar*, 1996). The high courts in Rhode Island and Florida relied on a similar rationale in rejecting adequacy-based claims (*Coalition for Adequacy v. Chiles*, 680 So.2d 400, Fla. 1996: "appellants have failed to demonstrate . . . an appropriate standard for determining 'adequacy' that would not present a substantial risk of judicial intrusion into the powers and responsibilities assigned to the legislature"; *City of Pawtucket v. Sundlun*, 662 A.2d 40, R.I. 1995: "what constitutes an 'equal, adequate, and meaningful' [education] is 'not likely to be divined for all time even by the scholars who now so earnestly debate the issues'").

As we explained earlier, some civil rights advocates see adequacy cases as a way to improve the education of inner-city, minority children even if they attend largely all-minority schools. But now a new twist on the adequacy theory has been proposed in two Minnesota cases seeking, among other substantive education remedies, racial integration. Advocates there have sought to have an adequate education defined in such a way as to include a racially integrated education (e.g. *Minneapolis NAACP v. State of Minnesota* and *St. Paul School District v. State of Minnesota*, both filed 1996). If this approach were to succeed, it would provide a way, through the state constitution's education clause, to remedy nonintentionally created racial isolation, a situation that the federal constitution—through the equal protection clause—would not redress. That the adequacy theory can be advanced on behalf of these two very different educational visions underscores its plasticity. This divergence in approach also exposes the understandable division of opinion within minority communities: some continue to aim for integrated schools even if this means having many children attend school far from home, while others want to concentrate on improving local schools and not risk that precious resources wind up being spent merely for transportation and not education.

LEGISLATIVE RESPONSES TO
EDUCATIONAL ADEQUACY DECISIONS

An important consequence of moving to an educational adequacy-based theory is that it may require legislative solutions that go far beyond matters of school funding. Indeed, in Kentucky the emphasis on providing resources to districts that enable them to afford students opportunities to reach certain outcome standards led to remedies that have required not only the restructuring of funding arrangements, but also a re-evaluation and adjustment of all programmatic aspects of the educational process.

In response to the Kentucky Supreme Court's decision, the Kentucky legislature enacted the most comprehensive statewide education reform package to date: the Kentucky Education Reform Act (KERA) (Trimble and Forsaith, 1995; Heise, 1995). While some question how much that reform has improved student achievement, few deny the sweeping nature of the reforms or the fact that Kentucky has dramatically increased its financial effort for education, going from one of the lowest spending states in 1990 to now being in the middle of the pack. Bringing about these changes is generally considered to be a great litigation success.

On the school funding side, KERA established a new foundation program that substantially increased the guaranteed minimum per-pupil expenditure statewide. Overall, the reforms initially resulted in a 25 percent increase in spending in the poorest districts and an 8 percent increase in the richest districts (Alexander, 1991). Beyond funding reforms, KERA mandated a new statewide performance-based assessment system tied to newly developed education standards, statewide curriculum frameworks, an accountability system with rewards and sanctions for schools tied to the achievement of high academic standards and the new assessments, as well as school-based decisionmaking statewide.

What was it about the Kentucky case that led the legislature to react so boldly and quickly to the court's order? First, the very nature of the court's order—which declared the entire public school system to be inadequate—suggested that minor tinkering with the existing system would not lead to constitutional compliance. Additionally, adequacy's focus on providing students with the opportunities necessary to achieve state-defined educational outcomes caused the state to (1) define such outcomes, (2) develop measures of when students were meeting those outcomes, and (3) create programs to move districts with large numbers of students failing to meet expectations forward. Finally, it appears that Kentucky was politically primed to respond quickly and positively to the court's decision. The governor had campaigned in support of school reform, the still-politically-powerful former-governor had represented the plaintiffs in the litigation, and school improvement had been strongly pushed for some time by a statewide education-reform committee that had the support of both business leaders and other community elites (see Carr and Fuhrman, Chapter 5 in this volume).

How much of a difference these reforms have made in the lives of Kentucky schoolchildren is another matter (see Evans et al., Chapter 3, and Goertz and Natriello, Chapter 4 in this volume). If the reforms are to yield gains in educational achievement, at least some of that should have occurred already. But there is controversy over whether it has. On one set of tests, Kentucky youths seem to be learning more than ever; but as judged by another set, these children are still below average. Whatever the conclusion one draws about the improved learning that Kentucky schoolchildren have experienced as a result of the reforms, it seems clear that opportunities to achieve learning at higher levels are being offered in areas of the state and to schoolchildren who prior to the reforms were not receiving such opportunities.

In Kentucky, the court's pronouncement on educational adequacy at least led directly and promptly to substantial reform. The political response has been far less satisfactory, however, in some other states. In Wyoming, for example, the response to the Wyoming Supreme Court's "adequacy" decision initially got off on the wrong foot. The legislature undertook a serious examination of its obligations, and Guthrie and Rothstein were brought in to apply their approach to determining the cost of an "adequate" education (described above) to Wyoming's situation. Drawing in substantial respects on those expert recommendations, a legislative package was put together that was passed largely as proposed in July 1997. However, although this new school funding plan purportedly met the court's mandates, the governor vetoed several of its key provisions.

In the spring of 1998, the legislative and executive branches of government in Wyoming finally came together and passed a reform that they believe will hold up against judicial scrutiny. The new law increases the state education budget by approximately 10 percent, pumping a new $76.5 million into the system. In addition to the finance reforms, the law also establishes a statewide student assessment system to measure achievement progress in years to come. Based on a "rational" determination of what educational services are needed to provide students with adequate educational opportunities, this new funding scheme stands a fair chance of being upheld should it again be challenged in court.

The story is much more disheartening in Alabama. The judicial order in that state's adequacy case required the legislature to implement specific reforms in the following areas: (1) student performance standards; (2) educator performance standards; (3) accountability; (4) school based management; (5) staff development, teacher compensation, and adequate staff and support services; (6) non-school barriers to learning; (7) early childhood education; (8) infrastructure; (9) technology; and (10) special education. Because the governor at the time supported education reforms, the initial finding of liability by the trial court was not appealed.

Legislation that substantially mirrored the court's remedial order was introduced in 1994 but failed to pass. Indeed, a new governor was elected who took the attitude that no trial judge was going to tell him how to run the state education system. Furthermore, the trial judge who issued the original remedy order no longer presides over the case. The upshot is that the legislature has failed to implement any meaningful reform responding to the court's orders.

Consequently, in 1996 the parties returned to court, but not to argue over the trial court's liability finding. Rather, the state defendants asked the Alabama

Supreme Court to invalidate the trial court's remedial order, in part on the grounds that it represented an unwarranted intrusion into matters reserved for the executive branch. On January 10, 1997, the Alabama Supreme Court rejected the state's appeal and gave the legislature until early 1998 to come up with its own remedial plan. Yet, as of the time of this writing, the state has still failed to come up with a plan. Perhaps the lower court will soon be compelled to order the implementation of the original remedy. If the New Jersey experience is any guide, however, this is not likely the end of the involvement of the Alabama courts.

In New Jersey, where the state supreme court pronouncements over years of school finance decisions have had both equity and adequacy overtones, plaintiff districts have continually returned to court complaining that the legislative response has been insufficient. A first back-and-forth battle was played out in the 1970s, and the court seemed finally satisfied. But in response to a subsequent lawsuit filed on behalf of some of the state's poorest urban school systems, the court in 1994 ordered the state to bring the spending levels in the plaintiff school systems—comprised of 29 poor urban districts—up to the level of the wealthiest school systems by the 1997-98 school year (*Abbott*, 1994). In addition, the court required the state to provide whatever supplemental services and resources are necessary to account for the extra educational needs associated with educating large numbers of students from disadvantaged backgrounds.

In late 1996, New Jersey's legislature adopted the governor's proposed response to the court. At the heart of the new law is the notion that all schools should be funded at a level which allows them (and their students) to meet the state's education standards. The new scheme sets a base per-pupil figure (for regular education only) that claims to be sufficient to meet those standards. At the elementary level the amount is set at $6,720, at the middle school level it is $7,526, and at the high school level it is $8,064. In addition, the law provides supplemental aid to the state's poorest districts to assist them in meeting the needs of their at-risk student populations.

No sooner had the legislation passed, however, than state officials were back in court defending it. Plaintiffs claimed that the new law failed to satisfy the equity components of the court's prior school finance orders and therefore continued to violate constitutional standards. The plaintiffs also questioned the validity of the cost estimates used to set the base and supplemental funding amounts.

In a May 1997 decision, the New Jersey Supreme Court agreed with the plaintiffs. The court faulted the new law primarily on the grounds that there was no "demonstrable relationship" between the amount of funds the state identified as necessary to provide a "thorough and efficient" education, and "the real needs of the disadvantaged children attending school in the special needs districts." Indeed, the court concluded that "[b]ecause the state never conducted [a] study . . . to determine the actual needs of children in the special needs districts, the aid amount provided for by the new plan is necessarily arbitrary and therefore fails to satisfy the court's orders."

The New Jersey court's order to the state legislature reflected great frustration with the compliance efforts exhibited by the state defendants to date. "The legislature is required, as interim remedial relief, to assure by the commencement of the 1997-98 school year, that per-pupil expenditures in the poor urban districts are equalized to the average per-pupil expenditure in the wealthy suburban districts." In addition, the court ordered the state to study, identify, fund, and implement the supplemental programs required to redress the disadvantages of public school children in the special needs districts. Lastly, the court required the state to "assure that all education funding, including and especially the additional funding ordered today, is spent effectively, efficiently, and in furtherance of the achievement of the core curriculum content standards."

This 1997 New Jersey decision reflects something of a blend of traditional finance equity and adequacy approaches. The court required that the state conduct a study of what it would take—in terms of educational services and resources—to provide disadvantaged children in the poorer school districts with opportunities to achieve the state's educational content and achievement standards. As an interim step to moving to that adequacy-based system, however, the court required per-pupil expenditure equality between the poorest and wealthiest districts.

In May 1998, the New Jersey Supreme Court issued what could be the last decision—at least for a few years—in the state's long-running school finance battle (*Abbott v. Burke,* N.J. Sup. Ct. May 1998). The court noted that "this decision should be the last major judicial involvement in the long tortuous history of the State's extraordinary effort to bring a thorough and efficient education to the children in its poorest school districts." The recent decision approves a plan for funding and systemic education reform in the State of New Jersey put forward by the State Commissioner of Education after a long process of expert consultation and review.

In essence, the court ordered that the state implement the following education reforms: (1) whole school reform, namely the "Success for All" model; (2) full-day kindergarten and half-day preschool for 3- and 4-year-olds; (3) a technology, school-to-work, alternative school, accountability, and college-transition program; (4) standards that will enable individual schools to adopt additional supplemental programs and funding to support such programs where a demonstrated need is established; and (5) a comprehensive facilities plan. While these reforms were proposed in the first instance by the State Commissioner of Education, the fact that the Supreme Court has ordered that they be implemented sends a powerful message to the executive and legislative branches about the need for swift compliance.

Indeed, unlike the Kentucky Supreme Court's decision, which only articulated broad guidelines for the intended reforms, the New Jersey court has ordered a comprehensive education reform package that could dramatically change the interaction between teacher and child in the plaintiff school districts. In that respect, the New Jersey decision is another bold step in a direction of the "adequacy" reform movement. As the court said, "Success for all will come only when the roots of the educational system—the local schools and districts, the teachers, the administrators, the parents, and the children themselves—embrace the educational opportunity encompassed by these reforms."

In Arizona, after the high court's 1994 ruling declaring that the state's system of funding capital facilities and costs was unconstitutional, the legislature and governor worked to pass a redesigned system in 1997. However, on October 24, 1997, the Supreme Court sent the legislature back to the drawing board. Facing a lower-court-imposed deadline of June 30, 1998, the legislature and governor were told once again to craft a system of funding school facilities that will ensure that all facilities in the state meet the high court's earlier articulation of adequacy.

In June 1998, the Supreme Court of Arizona for a fourth time declared that the State's recent effort to solve its equity problems with respect to school facilities was unsatisfactory. Under the court's prior rulings, the state was constitutionally compelled to establish minimum adequate standards for school facilities and provide for funding that ensures that no district is unable to meet those standards. Moreover, the state was supposed to ensure that any funding mechanism to achieve that end must not itself result in substantial disparities between districts. Like New Jersey, that decision blends an adequacy and equity component.

The recent legislation fell short of meeting the court's articulated requirements. While the state's facilities standards passed judicial scrutiny, the court found that the funding mechanism that the state adopted created substantial disparities in school districts' abilities to raise revenue for schools. The court gave the legislature 60 days in which to develop an acceptable plan for funding facilities improvements across the state.

The experience in states like Alabama, Arizona, New Jersey, and Wyoming demonstrates that there are real limits on judicial authority over the legislative process. The power of the courts is mainly the power to say no. In the end, it is the legislature (or the state department of education) that must propose and implement the reforms. Courts can threaten individual defendants. They can even threaten to close down the entire public school system, although were it necessary to carry out this threat, it would probably have a perverse impact on the objectives the courts are seeking to achieve. In any event, because of the nature of the adequacy theory, it currently seems unlikely that many courts will take over the educational system and impose their goals, their implementation strategies, and their funding mechanisms on the people of their state. It isn't so much that the courts could not turn to educational policy experts to help them make these decisions. Rather, it is that making those choices would seem to force the courts to get into issues that are too much a matter of political judgment.

Still, one should not unduly despair about the limits of judicial power. For one thing, courts imposing equity remedies on states in wealth discrimination cases have also not had smooth sailing. In Texas, for example, the Texas Supreme Court had to reinsert itself into the problem several times as the legislature continually failed to enact a reform that met the court's standard. Indeed, this is the same lesson to be learned from the first two decades of public school desegregation litigation. Faced with "massive resistance" by Southern states, the courts had to endure seemingly endless legal battles before the regime of school segregation finally fell.

Of course, many today believe that the fight to obtain true equality of educational opportunity for blacks has never been won. Now some hope that educational adequacy litigation can be harnessed, at least in part, in furtherance of that goal. If so, this new wave of court-ordered reform could turn out to be, through a very convoluted route, the real legacy of *Brown*.

It remains to be seen, however, just how insistent the courts that have handed down educational adequacy decisions will be. Perhaps, as in the race area, the judges will turn out to be more effective at striking down blatant violations of clear norms of fairness than they are at bringing about genuinely equal educational opportunities that satisfy the original victim class.

CONCLUSION

Educational adequacy has strengths and weaknesses both as a legal theory and as a principle for guiding educational policy. By exposing the shortfall between what students now receive and what they really need, it can lay bare the gap that the states must fill if they are to have a chance to match reality with their own common rhetoric—that all children (or at least most children) can genuinely be taught to the high standards that will be critical for success in the twenty-first century. Because the adequacy notion aspires to ambitious educational outcomes across the board, inherent in it is the necessity that school finance arrangements take into account the special needs of some children, the high costs some schools face, and so on. Moreover, although we are doubtful that lawyers will win a *national* commitment to adequacy in the courts, the more that states embrace the concept, the more pressure there is likely to be on the federal government to assist children in those states that have insufficient fiscal capacity to provide sufficiently for their own pupils.

Furthermore, at least in its predominant view, educational adequacy does not stand in the way of some communities providing, and thus some children attaining, even more than the high-minimum sought for all. Although this inequality is apparently acceptable—even welcome—to most supporters of the educational adequacy theory, it is a glaring unfairness to those who cling to the principle underlying the equity cases. To school equity devotees, such inequalities could only be fair if education beyond the high-minimum is the equivalent of frivolous extra frosting on an already well-frosted cake. For that to be true, of course, the high-minimum would need to be genuinely very high.

On that score, however, supporters of the school finance equity cases are likely to be skeptical about how capable or persistent courts in adequacy cases can or will be in demanding a genuinely high-minimum that delivers results. They fear that, in the end, wealthier school districts will succeed in making sure that their greater fiscal capacity may be used to purchase advantages that are well worth having. For equity supporters, therefore, the best hope still lies in forcing the rich and the poor into the same educational boat.

But this appraisal of what is both politically and judicially possible under the adequacy approach may be too pessimistic. A few more litigation successes like that in Kentucky, and most recently in New Jersey, could generate considerable optimism and courage among state supreme courts. As a result, state constitutional provisions with respect to education, despite their ambiguity, could become truly powerful sources of children's rights.

In the end, technical developments may play a key role in resolving this matter. If reliable and agreed-upon measures of what children should learn and have learned at various stages of their schooling could be developed, that would be an important first step. Although some people think we are well down that road already, one must be at least somewhat skeptical of that conclusion in view of the firestorm of opposition that has greeted President Clinton's proposals for national education testing.

In any event, having measurable standards is only a part of the job. It is not enough merely to aspire to teach all children to those standards. We also need the technology to bring that off. Money, perhaps a lot more money in some schools, may be necessary—or maybe not. And at the moment there is no consensus as to just how much more, if any, is needed in just which schools. But, this is a new area of research and perhaps before long some agreement will be reached on an approach that draws the best from the Guthrie and Rothstein, Augenblick, and Duncombe and Yinger approaches.

Even then, we note that those methodologies tend to be backward looking— seeking to identify what would it cost to enable all schools to achieve X result, given the way successful schools have been run to date. But many think that there are new, much more highly productive, educational solutions out there waiting to be discovered, or perhaps already discovered and just waiting to be identified. One thing these solutions tend to have in common is a belief that the focus of reform should be at the school level.

For example, several prominent educational innovators like Robert Slavin, Henry Levin, Theodore Sizer, James Comer, and Chris Whittle (and his Edison

Project) say they know what school changes are needed to achieve success for all, even though each relies on quite a different strategy. Other reformers insist that we need school-site management as a prerequisite for any improvement, or that we need rebuilt schools that are now in physical disarray, or that the rules be changed with respect to hiring and firing of school employees, including school principals. Some insist that we "reconstitute" failing schools, putting them into some kind of receivership. Yet others point to successful "high performance" organizations in other fields as examples for schools to emulate. Still others see the main hope in market competition brought about through large-scale school choice schemes (such as widespread charter school and/or school voucher plans). It is not inconceivable that all (or most) of these approaches could work. Indeed, some of them would cost little or no new money, although they might change considerably the way that money is spent. We doubt that courts will insist upon any single one (or combination) of these reforms. Yet, legislatures, school districts, and schools might well be moved to try out many of them in response to educational adequacy litigation—and from that experience we might get a better idea about which, if any, really do work on a large scale.

Whatever hopes there may be for the future, at present, alas, certainly in our large urban school districts, it is widely perceived that we are nowhere near having success for all. Moreover, some fear that, given the amount of money that can plausibly devoted to elementary and secondary education, having most children achieve high standards is an unattainable goal. Indeed, some pessimists believe not only that extra money (even if it were available) won't bring about success for all, but also that no education reform, at least by itself, is capable of yielding high educational attainments by most big city schoolchildren. For some of these critics, school finance litigation is wasting our time, money, and attention. Instead, as they see it, dramatic changes must first be made in the lives of the parents of these children; whether the parents need good jobs or moral rearmament may be in dispute, but the common notion is that the child's home life needs improving first.

But educational adequacy supporters are unlikely to be dissuaded by this pessimism about the role of the schools. Not only are they unwilling to give up on another generation (or more) of children while awaiting other social changes, but also they find it politically and practically more attractive to begin by seeking directly to improve the lives of children. Hence, whether or not educational success for most children is really attainable in the short run, lawyers are likely to continue to press courts to say that educational adequacy is a judicially enforceable state constitutional objective. And if the claimants continue to win in court, the judges may at least function as a spur to more innovation and experimentation than our existing public education system would undertake on its own. Therein, perhaps, lies the main promise of the new educational adequacy paradigm.

REFERENCES

Alexander, K.
  1991   The common school ideal and the limits of legislative authority: The Kentucky case.
          Harvard Journal of Legislation 28:341-346.
Augenblick, J.
  1997   Recommendations for a Base Figure and Pupil-Weighted Adjustments to the Base Figure
          for Use in a New School Finance System in Ohio. Report presented to the School
          Funding Task Force, Ohio Department of Education.
Clune, W.H.
  1993   The shift from equity to adequacy in school finance. *The World and I* 8(9):389-405.
  1994   The shift from equity to adequacy in school finance. *Educational Policy* 8(4):376-394.
Cohen, D.
  1995   Standards-Based School Reform: Policy, Practice and Performance. Unpublished paper
          presented at the Brookings Conference on Performance-Based Approaches to School
          Reform, April 1995. Washington, D.C.
Coons, J., W. Clune, and S. Sugarman
  1970   *Private Wealth and Public Education.* Cambridge, MA: Harvard University Press
Enrich, P.
  1995   Leaving equality behind: New directions in school finance reform. *Vanderbilt Law
          Review* 48:101-194.
Evans, W., S. Murray, and R. Schwab
  1997   Schoolhouses, courthouses, and statehouses after *Serrano*. *Journal of Policy Analysis
          and Management* 16(1):10-31.
Fischel, W.A.
  1989   Did *Serrano* cause Proposition 13? *National Tax Journal* 42:465-473.
Heise, M.
  1995   State constitutions, school finance litigation, and the "third wave": From equity to ad-
          equacy. *Temple Law Review* 68:1151-1176.
Horowitz, H., and D. Neitring
  1968   Equal protection aspects of inequalities in public education and public assistance pro-
          grams from place to place within a state. *UCLA Law Review* 15:787-816.
McUsic, M.
  1991   The use of education clauses in school finance reform litigation. *Harvard Journal on
          Legislation* 28(2):307-341.
National Commission on Excellence in Education
  1983   *A Nation at Risk: The Imperative for Educational Reform.* Washington, DC: U.S.
          Government Printing Office.
Tatel, D.
  1992   Desegregation versus school reform: Resolving the conflict. *Stanford Law & Policy
          Review* Winter:61-72.
Trimble, C.S., and A.C. Forsaith
  1995   Achieving equity and excellence in Kentucky education. *University of Michigan Journal
          of Law Reform* 28(3):599-653.
Underwood, J.K.
  1995   School finance adequacy as vertical equity. *University of Michigan Journal of Law
          Reform* 28(3):493-519.
Wise, A.
  1968   *Rich Schools, Poor Schools: The Promise of Equal Educational Opportunity.* Chicago:
          University of Chicago Press.

7

Enabling "Adequacy" to Achieve Reality: Translating Adequacy into State School Finance Distribution Arrangements

James W. Guthrie and Richard Rothstein

INTRODUCTION

This chapter addresses the financial consequences of an evolving concept—that of an "adequate" education. A growing number of state court decisions suggest that "adequacy" is challenging "equity" as the standard to which state school revenue distribution plans should be held (see Minorini and Sugarman, Chapter 6 in this volume). Parallel school finance developments in states without such court mandates suggest that a commitment to provide an "adequate" education to all students is part of a broader national political consensus.

However, consensus about this goal may be outpacing our understanding of how to define and achieve it. *Equity* itself is more complex than it first appears, because nominal equity takes account neither of differences in student need nor of geographic differences in costs. The concept of *adequacy* adds an additional complexity, requiring us to link cost calculations to decisions about minimally appropriate resource input levels and schooling outcomes. While defining equity is essentially a technical enterprise, moving to adequacy requires policy and value judgments about which achieving consensus, ultimately, may be more difficult.

Following a brief history of the evolution of adequacy as a school finance concept, this chapter has five principal parts:

• First, we examine definitional challenges associated with translating an abstract term, "adequate," into a practical school finance distribution formula, and survey three distinct approaches to the problem—statistical, empirical, and judgmental. Each of these methods has a different strategy for anchoring the concept of "adequacy" in some sense of educational accomplishment, some goal to be achieved. This approach establishes baselines such that "inadequate" can be identified.

• Second, this chapter concentrates on one of the alternative strategies (the professional judgment method) and describes means for assembling instructional components capable of delivering whatever outcomes—educational content or pupil performance levels—are deemed "adequate." Here, we also discuss how policy decisions must be made about whether, and to what extent, school districts receiving a dollar value of resources deemed capable of producing adequate outcomes should be required by law or policy actually to utilize those dollars in ways research determines are most effective for achieving those outcomes.

• Third, we discuss how to assign dollar values to such instructional components.

• Fourth, we illustrate how, as in the search for equity alone, a determination of the cost of an adequate education for typical students can then be adjusted, to ensure financial "adequacy" for all pupils, by taking account of varied pupil characteristics, school scale and district characteristics, and differences in educational costs in different geographic regions of a state.

• Finally, we briefly note some additional questions which remain unresolved in the calculation of adequacy. Chief among these is the additional policy debate regarding test and measurement means for appraising pupil progress toward whatever is legislatively specified as adequate academic performance (Carlson, 1996).

The authors recently participated in a commission from the state of Wyoming to respond to these challenges. We are currently engaged in refining our approach in other states as well. In what follows, we utilize these experiences to illustrate our themes.

We discuss only problems related to how to *spend* adequate funds for education; this chapter does not discuss how to *raise* these funds, i.e., revenue sources and related taxation matters. It does not concern itself with physical facilities and other large capital outlay considerations. It only lightly touches on the role of federal government regulations or revenues in contributing to state efforts to achieve adequacy. Likewise, it barely references the non-finance components of a comprehensive education policy system, such as testing and accountability provisions or teacher training and staff development requirements, which might necessarily have to be joined with a revenue distribution plan to ensure what Clune refers to as "true adequacy" (Clune, 1994).

Historical Context

In response to court decisions, several states, e.g., Alabama, Mississippi, New Hampshire, North Carolina, Ohio, Vermont, and Wyoming, are presently attempting to construct practical definitions of an "adequate" education. These efforts take place against an historic backdrop. Table 7-1 utilizes a categorization of states-by-litigation status developed by Alan Hickrod, and then calculates real changes in education spending for each state from 1970 to 1995.

School spending has been increasing in virtually every state, and we make no claim here that it is a concern for "adequacy" alone which is propelling the change. Our contention is more simple. A national pattern of growing elementary and secondary expenditures in states with or without a history of "equity" and/or "adequacy" litigation is apparent. With the exception of California, all states have increased average per-pupil spending in the last quarter century, and most have increased it dramatically. In some states without litigation, spending has increased to avoid litigation. In other states where courts have upheld previous financing schemes, spending has still increased at rates similar to those where litigation had an opposite result. Thus, we contend that the national "adequacy" debate can be seen, in part, as an effort to evaluate whether this spending growth has been sufficient and to ensure that the new money is distributed within states in a fashion that will produce desired outcomes.

Historic "Adequacy": Politically Determined Inputs

Despite recent interest, "adequacy" is not a new concept in school finance. Charles Benson explained it as early as 1978 (Benson, 1978). Kirst and Garms explored the term in a chapter on the evolving context of education reform in the initial American Education Finance Association yearbook published two decades ago (Kirst and Garms, 1980).

But although the term "adequacy" has been used for 20 years, the concept has had a practical school finance meaning for much longer because many states have politically determined "adequate" levels of inputs to support the schooling process. The "foundation" distribution formula approach has existed since the beginning of the twentieth century, with elucidations by early school finance scholars such as Cubberley (1919a, 1919b), Mort et al. (1960), and Johns et al. (1983). Their "foundation plans" had "adequate" as an assumed condition. The "foundation" was, and in most states still is, a per-pupil dollar floor below which a state does not permit a district's spending to fall.

When the "foundation" finance distribution concept was originally adopted by states, and as it continues in most states today, governors and legislatures define "adequate" by determining how much state revenue is available, or how much additionally they are willing to generate through added taxation. This aggregate revenue amount has then been embedded in a minimum "foundation"

TABLE 7-1 Increased State Spending on Elementary and Secondary Education[a]

State[b]	Year of Final Decision in First Court Case	Nominal Spending Growth 1970-95 (in percent)	Real Spending Growth[c] 1970-95 (in percent)
States Where Court Decisions Required School Finance Reform[d]			
West Virginia	1979	837	105
Arkansas	1983	802	97
Connecticut	1977	827	94
Kentucky	1989	787	94
New Jersey	1973	795	87
Texas	1989	691	73
Ohio	1979	658	66
Tennessee	1993	632	60
Maryland[e]	1997	625	58
New Hampshire	1997	652	58
Wyoming	1980	631	53
Massachusetts	1993	620	51
Vermont	1997	619	51
Washington	1978	576	42
Arizona	1994	543	35
Montana	1989	469	19
California	1971	384	1
States Where Court Decisions Upheld Existing School Finance System and Required No Reform[f]			
Georgia	1981	782	93
North Carolina	1987	739	83
Alaska	1997	766	81
Nebraska	1993	726	81
Maine	1992	751	78
Michigan	1973	707	77
South Carolina	1988	692	73
Rhode Island	1992	687	65
Virginia	1994	658	65
Pennsylvania	1979	666	60
Wisconsin	1989	629	60
New York	1992	604	47
Colorado	1982	594	45
Idaho	1975	593	45
Minnesota	1993	557	44
Oregon	1979	567	40
North Dakota	1993	492	30
Illinois	1996	461	23

TABLE 7-1 (*continued*)

State[b]	Nominal Spending Growth 1970-95 (in percent)	Real Spending Growth[c] 1970-95 (in percent)
States Where Litigation Is Pending		
Alabama	761	88
Florida	654	65
South Dakota	610	56
New Mexico	608	48
Louisiana	571	47
Missouri	548	42
States Without School Finance Litigation[g]		
Indiana	788	95
Kansas	651	64
Mississippi	652	64
Oklahoma	591	51
Nevada	549	36
Hawaii	540	34
Delaware	486	28
Iowa	455	22
Utah	459	17

[a]State and local spending only; federal funds not included.

[b]States listed by spending growth.

[c]Real spending growth calculated by using regional services indices of the Consumer Price Index, adjusted by the CPI-U for 1970-78. (There is considerable scholarly controversy regarding the most appropriate deflator to use in the historical analysis of school spending. It is not appropriate to engage that debate here, but for purposes of this analysis, some deflator must be utilized. Our reasons for preferring a services deflator are discussed briefly under "Adjusting Adequate for Pupil, School, and Regional Characteristics" and are described in greater detail in the references cited in that section. However, regardless of which deflator is utilized, the point made by this table, that spending growth experience has been similar in states categorized differently by litigation status, would be unaffected. If this table had been adjusted utilizing the more conventional consumer price index, real spending growth would appear to be greater, but the diversity of states' growth, and the similarity of experiences within litigation status groups, would be similar.)

[d]In some of these states, a reformed school finance system was also challenged in a subsequent court case.

[e]While plaintiffs lost a court case, the state eventually signed a consent decree, agreeing to reform its system.

[f]In some of these states, new cases have been filed; in some, plaintiffs have lost a second time, while other cases are pending.

[g]Includes states where litigation was withdrawn or is dormant.

SOURCE: For litigation status, Hickrod et al. (1997), updated by author; for Nominal Spending Growth, authors' calculations from the National Center for Education Statistics (1997); for Services Index, 1978-95, from the Bureau of Labor Statistics (BLS; 1997); 1970-78, authors' estimates based on regional changes in CPI-U from BLS (1997). Table reproduced from Rothstein (1998).

distribution formula. Whatever this per-pupil minimum spending amount, it has then been presumed to be adequate. As Minorini and Sugarman (see Chapter 6, page 190, in this volume) note, "almost nowhere could it plausibly be shown that the actual minimum foundation plan level . . . had been determined as a result of a genuine statewide appraisal [of what is actually necessary to fund an 'adequate' education]." Some states, however, have relied on alternative definitions of adequate inputs, such as teacher certification requirements, state textbook selection, and class size or pupil-teacher maxima. The "foundation" has been intended to ensure that there is no systematic underinvestment in schooling within a state.

Foundation-related, per-pupil revenue levels have been questioned politically and legally for three decades, since Coons et al. and Wise formulated legal challenges based on the United States Constitution's Fourteenth Amendment equal protection clause (Coons et al., 1970; Wise, 1968). However, it was initially a foundation program's statewide per-pupil revenue distributional equity which came under scrutiny, not the adequacy of that spending level. The legal assaults of the last three decades were mostly intended to ensure that state-authorized spending levels, be they adequate or inadequate, were at least equally accessible to local school districts. But recently, the focus has broadened.

Modern Adequacy: Technically Defined and Outcome Oriented

The evolving concept of "adequacy" suggests that something beyond equity is at issue. The "something else" is a notion of sufficiency, a per-pupil resource amount sufficient to achieve some performance objective. Thus, adequacy is increasingly being defined by the outcomes produced by school inputs, not by the inputs alone. Clune contends that as the nation increasingly debates means for obtaining higher levels of student academic performance, the policy debate is beginning to shift away from "equity" and toward means for ensuring that students receive resources enabling them to learn to higher standards. Thus, adequacy deliberations sometimes are bundled with quests for "opportunity standards" (Porter, 1993). "Delivery standards" is another related idea asserting that pupils and schools cannot fairly be held accountable for performance unless there is first an assurance that the levels of available resources are adequate and that students are appropriately exposed to the knowledge they are expected to master.

**DEFINITIONAL CHALLENGES:
IDENTIFYING ANCHORS FOR "ADEQUATE"**

If adequate is to have a meaning beyond what is assigned to it via a set of political decisions about revenue availability, then a judgment has to be made about expected ends to be achieved, some level of accomplishment or performance. *Adequate to do what? Adequate how? Adequate for what purpose?*

Responding to these queries necessitates at least a twofold policy judgment about (1) learning or performance levels to be attained and (2) resource levels likely to permit schools to accomplish these learning purposes with students. This section is concerned principally with the first of these policy objectives, determining what students should know and be able to do. Only by specifying such an objective can calculations be undertaken to facilitate the second objective, specifying that the resource level involved is sufficient.

Specifying learning is difficult, more difficult than it first appears. While we have an apparent national consensus that student outcomes are currently inadequate, this consensus extends only to the vaguest of generalities when it comes to specifying the extent to which this is the case.

Consider one of the early attempts by a state court to define adequate outcomes, that of the West Virginia Supreme Court in *Pauley v. Kelly* in 1979. The Court required the legislature to fund a school system that would develop "in every child" these capacities; see Box 7-1.

Other state courts and legislatures have required funding adequate to develop similar collections of competencies; in at least one case (Kentucky, in *Rose v. Council for Better Education*, 1989) an additional, relative, capacity was added: "sufficient levels of academic or vocational skills to enable public school students to compete favorably with their counterparts in surrounding states."

The Wyoming Supreme Court (in *Campbell County v. The State of Wyoming*, 1995) required resources sufficient to provide each student with a "proper education," and the legislature subsequently defined a basket of education goods

---

BOX 7-1
West Virginia Supreme Court Definition of an Adequate Education

(1) literacy;
(2) ability to add, subtract, multiply and divide numbers;
(3) knowledge of government to the extent that the child will be equipped as a citizen to make informed choices among persons and issues that affect his own governance;
(4) self-knowledge and knowledge of his or her total environment to allow the child to intelligently choose life work—to know his or her options;
(5) work-training and advanced academic training as the child may intelligently choose;
(6) recreational pursuits;
(7) interests in all creative arts, such as music, theater, literature, and the visual arts;
(8) social ethics, both behavioral and abstract, to facilitate compatibility with others in this society.

SOURCE: *Pauley v. Kelly*, 255 S.E. 2nd 859 (W.V., 1979).

and services that comprise such a proper (in our terms, "adequate") education. The basket consisted of some 30 courses and kinds of knowledge, designed to achieve a group of broader outcomes similar to those specified in West Virginia, Kentucky, and other states. The legislature deliberated upon these outcomes in great detail. For example, one Wyoming goal in the basket of expected outcomes and courses specified that every child should learn cardiopulmonary resuscitation. This objective was subsequently altered in favor of learning to balance a checkbook and manage a retirement portfolio. Boxes 7-2 and 7-3 display the Wyoming "Basket of Education Goods and Services."

Even a cursory glance at these "baskets" suggests that few of these outcomes can be, or are, measured by the standardized reading and math tests that most uninformed discussions of school finance assume can measure adequacy. Whether, for example, the same resources that produce mathematical competency also, without augmentation, produce adequate performance in the fine and performing arts, is a question which analyses of finance adequacy cannot ignore, but which has yet barely been addressed by education finance theorists.

Despite the difficulties, however, the adequacy litigation and legislation in Wyoming suggest a range of achievement levels and exposure to knowledge and skills that can serve as ends toward which to orient a practical school finance distribution system. Any of these outputs or ends can serve as an anchor around which to design particular components of an overall instructional system. Once an acceptable instructional system is in place, it should then, in principle, be possible to assign costs to the components.

Designing an Instructional Delivery System

Designing a state school finance system, even one oriented toward "adequacy," inevitably creates a tension between the dictates of a "system" design and the characteristics of individual students. State policymakers cannot easily prescribe the nature of instruction and the levels of resources for each of a state's literally thousands or millions of individual students. Hence, the necessity of designing a "system." Such a system should attempt to provide local school districts, local schools, and even classroom teachers with resources and inducements to tailor instruction to the characteristics of students. Ultimately, though, state-level policymakers must design a school finance system; they cannot now design a resource allocation program for each individual student. Because current policy tools are often clumsy, the needs of school finance systems on occasion may appear insensitive to the needs of individual students. Tailoring school finance to individual student characteristics is a research frontier where far more knowledge is needed.

Given the above-mentioned complexity, policy analysts and researchers have been pioneering three approaches to calculate the costs of adequacy: (1) inference from outcomes by statistical analysis, (2) inference from outcomes by em-

BOX 7-2
The Wyoming Basket, 1990-1997

Regulations adopted by the State Board of Education in 1990 required that:

Section 7. *Common Core of Knowledge.* All public school students shall meet the student performance standards at the level set by the school and district in the following areas of knowledge:

  (a) Language Arts;
  (b) Social Studies;
  (c) Mathematics;
  (d) Science;
  (e) Fine Arts and Performing Arts;
  (f) Physical Education;
  (g) Health and Safety;
  (h) Humanities;
  (i) Career Options;
  (j) Foreign Cultures Including Languages;
  (k) Applied Technology

Section 8. *Common Core of Skills.* All public school students shall meet student performance standards at the level set by school and district in the following skills:

  (a) Problem Solving;
  (b) Interpersonal Communications;
  (c) Keyboarding and Computer Applications;
  (d) Critical Thinking;
  (e) Creativity;
  (f) Life Skills, including Cardiopulmonary Resuscitation (CPR) training.

Section 11. *At-Risk Students.* The district shall have policies and procedures for every school in the district to identify and intervene with at-risk students. In addition, all schools shall provide instruction as appropriate through the school curriculum directed at the prevention of at-risk behavior.

Section 12. [High School] *Graduation Requirements.*

  (a) A student shall master the student performance standards within the common core of knowledge and skills at the levels set by the district and the schools, including alternative schools.

Section 13. *Services.* All districts shall provide the following support services for all students:

  (a) Health Services;
  (b) Media Services;
  (c) Guidance Services

SOURCE: Catchpole (1996).

BOX 7-3
The Wyoming Legislative Enacted 1997 Basket

In 1997 the Wyoming Legislature adopted these requirements into law and made the following modifications:

Common Core of Knowledge.
Changed "Language Arts" to "Reading/language arts" and required that reading writing and mathematics be emphasized in grades 1 through 8.
Changed "Career Options" to "Career/vocational education."
Added "Government and Civics (including state and federal constitutions)"

Common Core of Skills.
Changed "Life Skills, including Cardiopulmonary Resuscitation (CPR) Training" to "Life skills, including personal financial management skills."

Added [High School] *Graduation Requirements.*
Four school years of English
Three school years of Mathematics
Three school years of Science
Three school years of Social Studies
(including history, American government and economic systems and institutions)
Mastery of the common core of knowledge and skills

SOURCE: Catchpole (1996).

---

pirical observation, and (3) professional judgment. The first and second of these approaches usually depend upon states having sophisticated student achievement testing systems which provide standardized statewide measures of student performance, with data linking this performance to student background characteristics.[1] In states where such testing systems do not exist, then the third approach, professional judgment, seems to be the only alternative, where "getting to adequate" necessitates building an instructional resource model to which costs can subsequently be assigned. As we note below, however, we regard the professional judgment method as preferable in many respects, even where testing systems do exist.

Each of these three alternatives results in an estimate of the cost of an adequate education for a presumed or hypothetical typical student. Having made this calculation, each alternative must then adjust this cost (or perhaps redefine the goal of adequate outcomes) for students in different socioeconomic circumstances and locations. With these results—estimates of the cost of an adequate education for each category and location of students in a state—policymakers must then determine whether and how districts may be required to spend the funds in an efficient manner likely to produce the desired adequate outcomes. Here, again, is the tension between the design of a "system" and the possible different characteristics of individual students.

Inference from Outcomes by Statistical Analysis

Statistical analysis is one way to relate observed student outcomes to resources, in hopes that adequate resource costs can then be inferred. This method, in effect, conflates into a single step the challenges of inferring adequate resource levels and pricing those levels. Rather than identifying specific instructional components deemed necessary to achieve adequate outcomes, and then pricing these components, this statistical method infers total value of the components by associating total school district spending with adequate outcomes.

In this "black box," or raw correlational approach, the policy system, after determining an acceptable level of pupil performance or proficiency, then determines a delivery system dollar amount associated with it. This strategy bypasses any effort to construct or deduce a desired instructional delivery system. Such a bypass also obviates the need to determine costs of instructional components. Under this correlational approach, the "cost" of attaining "adequacy" is whatever agencies that achieve adequate outcomes happen to spend, after accounting for any identifiable inefficiencies in these agencies' operations.

While the statistical methods are complex, the principle behind them is relatively simple. With a sufficiently large database, each factor contributing to school costs can be examined and its unique relationship to another factor determined, distinct from the influence of other factors. For example, we may want to know how much more it "costs" to hire a teacher in an urban community than in a non-urban one. If we have sufficient data on teacher salaries and community characteristics, we can separate the common relationship between salary and urbanicity in all communities from the factors that may vary from community to community—like teachers' experience or training, community climate, community housing costs, etc. The result is the statistical generation of an abstract urban community where teacher salaries are uninfluenced by variations in these other costs, or by the choices districts may make in the type of teacher they hire.

If adopted as a basis for policy, this correlational strategy would derive a unit cost (per classroom or per pupil) amount found to be associated with adequate levels of pupil academic achievement and recommend allocation of such resource levels to school districts or other operational agencies. This approach could include statistical controls for social and economic characteristics of students. How available revenues were translated into an instructional delivery system would be of no policy consequence in such a "black box" approach. Presumably, districts or schools would be free to undertake whatever operational translation they desired, knowing that assigned per-pupil revenue amounts had been found sufficient to elevate their mix of pupils to the specified level of performance.

This statistical approach to estimating adequacy has won increasing favor among academic econometricians in recent years. The methodology has recently been applied to New York data by Duncombe and Yinger (see Chapter 8 in this volume), and to Wisconsin data by Reschovsky and Imazeki (1998). Ladd and Yinger (1994) and Downes and Pogue (1994) have made important theoretical contributions on which the Wisconsin and New York studies build. These analyses, in turn, build on the path-breaking work of Chambers (1998), whose efforts of the last two decades have now culminated in a "GCEI," or geographic cost of education index. While Chambers, and econometricians who have followed him, usually claim only to provide a method for calculating how costs of education differ for students with varying needs and in varying locations, it is but a small additional step to link these indices to an outcome measure so that the indices calculate the cost of achieving a given educational outcome for students with varying needs and in varying locations. Indeed, outcome measures are implicit in a cross-sectional index, even where the index makes no claims about adequacy. In the case of Chambers's GCEI, for example, no test scores or other outcome measures are utilized. Nonetheless, differences in student need are considered an external cost imposed on school districts. Thus, coefficients in the GCEI describe how much more it costs a district to educate children from minority families, or in districts with high crime rates. However, this measure can describe only how much districts actually spend, over and above their regular spending, on the education of children in these districts, once other factors influencing spending are controlled. The measure does not determine whether this additional spending is the correct amount to generate outcomes for at-risk children (defined in this way) that are comparable to outcomes for other children. Without an implicit assumption that outcomes are thereby made comparable, it is unclear what relevance these coefficients might have.

In principle, if a decision is made regarding acceptable achievement levels, then the per-pupil spending level related to such pupil performance can be inferred. Duncombe and Yinger's New York studies relate student achievement to a variety of schooling and school district characteristics, including per-pupil spending levels. They necessarily rely on a limited number of outcome (achievement) measures in the construction of their equations, assuming that "outcomes often are highly correlated with each other" (Duncombe et al., 1996). Their equations include controls for 3rd- and 6th-grade math and reading test scores, graduation rates, and the percentage of students who receive the more rigorous New York State Regents Diploma. Incorporating additional achievement measures would not only increase the complexity of the calculations but also, if the extent of collinearity is unknown, inject unknown errors into the results. Further, many of the desirable outcomes (as defined, for example, in the Wyoming basket or in the West Virginia *Pauley v. Kelly* decision) are not presently measured and cannot be quantified for use in such a statistical model.

Because these indicators (test scores, graduation rates, and Regents Diploma awards) may not accurately measure the totality of school outcomes, Duncombe and Yinger prefer an alternative "indirect" control for school district performance. They assume that average school district performance is one where voters likely to have children in the public schools vote for average property tax rates in communities with average incomes. These (abstract) communities can then be used to observe how much per-pupil spending is necessary to achieve average educational outcomes, again while controlling for other cost or discretionary factors.

Using this preferred "indirect" measure, Duncombe and Yinger conclude that average school performance in New York City costs 7 percent more than the cost of this performance in the average district statewide. Yet when they calculate education costs using the "direct" performance measures (test scores, graduation rates, and Regents Diplomas), they find that New York City's costs are 262 percent more than average. These widely divergent results discourage confidence in either measure. Statistical sophistication has, in this case, outpaced ability to explain the relationship between spending and school performance.

Reschovsky and Imazeki also utilize a statistical methodology to estimate the cost of adequacy in Wisconsin districts. They measure outcomes by 10th-grade test scores, controlled for 8th-grade scores of the same students. By this means, they attempt to isolate the "value added" by school districts, reasoning that the 8th-grade score may reflect students' social capital and instruction in other locations as well as the effectiveness of instruction in the present district. "Adequate" outcomes are defined as the average 10th-grade value-added throughout the state; Reschovsky and Imazeki conclude that the cost of achieving this adequacy, before adjusting for student need and geographic differences, is $6,331 per pupil. They truncate their cost index, however, and reduce the adjustment called for in the case of Milwaukee, believing that "no district could have costs that were more than twice the average." (Recall that the Duncombe-Yinger direct approach yielded a result for New York City that was 3.5 times the state average.) Reschovsky and Imazeki also find that education costs in the Milwaukee suburbs were 11 percent below the state average, while Chambers found that teacher costs in these suburbs were 17 percent above average. These substantial differences between models with seemingly similar plausibilities suggest that statistical methods cannot soon be expected to command authority as a way actually to adjust state education expenditures.[2]

Even if it were possible to quantify all outcomes, such models could at best tell us what resource levels were generally associated with acceptable achievement (with inefficient practices removed, to the extent known), not what resource levels would be necessary, if used efficiently, for this achievement. To reach this level of analysis, the statistical controls would have to include alternative pedagogies and curricula, something beyond our sophistication. If the policy goal is for a legislature to adopt (or a court to mandate) the minimum level of resources necessary to achieve acceptable outcomes, this becomes a crucial distinction.

Statistical methods, like those of Chambers, Duncombe-Yinger, and Reschovsky-Imazeki, appear to have a greater level of precision than the judgments of professional educators about what spending is necessary to achieve acceptable results. (Duncombe and Yinger, Chapter 8 in this volume, refer to professionals' judgments as "ad hoc, with no demonstrated connection between the environmental factors and educational costs"[p. 271].) Yet in reality, the precision implied by statistical modeling may be misleading because each of the definitions of data used in these equations, and rationales for their use, requires assumptions and judgments that are not necessarily more precise than those of professionals operating without statistical models. For example, the Duncombe and Yinger control for "efficiency" assumes that districts are more efficient to the extent they rely on local, rather than state funds, but this assumption requires greater examination than the authors can give it. As we discuss below, the percentage of students receiving free or reduced price lunches is a very poor proxy for at-risk children, yet most modelers must use this indicator because none other is available. Most models control for teacher experience in defining what a teacher "costs," yet few education researchers believe that there is a simple relationship between teacher quality and experience. (To the extent the relationship is not simply linear, then pay for experience may incorporate some inefficiency, not a cost of adequacy.) Similarly, Chambers's analysis shows that teacher salaries are higher where more teachers graduated from colleges whose entering freshmen had higher SAT scores, yet few professional educators would be willing to conclude that such teachers are necessarily higher quality teachers, and so the higher prices paid for them might be an inefficient expenditure rather than a district choice to purchase higher quality.

Or consider the assumptions implicit in the Duncombe and Yinger attempt to estimate adequacy by an "indirect" voter preference-tax price methodology. In effect (to paraphrase Justice Stewart's oft-repeated observation about pornography), the indirect method acknowledges that we can't define the elements of an adequate education, but insists that, nonetheless, voters know it when they see it. While this is an interesting hypothesis, and worthy of extensive empirical investigation, it is itself as imprecise as professional judgment. Even if tax-price behavior reflects something about the value of education, voters may value education based on incomplete or inaccurate information. Indeed, one of the dilemmas confronting advocates of school choice as a competitive means of improving school quality is that, when choice has actually been implemented, parents have chosen schools for a wide variety of reasons, quality not necessarily being paramount. Some parents choose schools from inadequate information or unequal access to it (Carnegie Foundation, 1992); some because they wish to associate with others from their racial or ethnic subgroup (Wells, 1993); some because they believe schools are of better quality if they enroll children from more affluent neighborhoods (Willms and Echols, 1993). Yet the "indirect" method of postulating outcomes must assume, if it is to be used as a basis for calculating true costs, that voters are rational and well informed about educational quality. If not, we can't utilize voting behavior to define adequacy.

Because assumptions of this kind are so necessary before modeling can be interpreted, the seemingly precise results of the models reflect the imprecision of the assumptions. Unless we can become more satisfied with the precision of the assumptions, we cannot conclude that statistical modeling is a more precise means of estimating the cost of adequacy than is the informed judgment of policymakers and professionals. This should not be surprising. While econometric modeling of the costs of education is relatively new, this aid to policymaking has long been used in other social policy fields. And while econometricians plausibly defend the validity of their conclusions, they have not been able to persuade policymakers that particular models can effectively predict, for example, whether a minimum wage increase will cause unemployment, whether trade agreements cause job relocation, whether higher welfare benefits reduce poverty, or whether interest rate reductions are inflationary. In each of these cases, conclusions from modeling may challenge commonsense misconceptions and may help to inform debates, but cannot resolve them.

We do not mean to suggest that these modeling exercises in education are not important or useful. Quite the contrary. They hold great academic and theoretical interest, and may suggest insights that would stimulate productive further research into the relationship between spending and student achievement. We consider, for example, the Duncombe and Yinger findings of widely different costs for New York City using direct and indirect methods of estimating achievement to be a particularly provocative call for further investigation.

Because the technology of calculating "adequacy" is so primitive, it can be very useful to compare, for a given state, the costs of adequacy determined by these statistical methods with the costs determined by alternative approaches described below (empirical observation and professional judgment). If the results of the three approaches differ significantly, this should cause policymakers to reexamine the assumptions in each of the models to determine, if possible, which variations in assumption are driving the differences. There is no state, however, where such an exercise has been conducted.

At the most practical level, because of its technical complexity, there is little chance that statistical modeling can be proposed to any state as the primary means of calculating the cost of an adequate education or as the primary way of estimating how the costs of education may vary from place to place or from student to student. Ultimately, when courts demand or legislatures determine that an adequate education be funded, they will require a calculation of this adequacy that seems intuitively reasonable, that is understandable to reasonably well-educated policymakers, and that can be explained to constituents. For such calculations, other methods are required. These other methods must rely upon assumptions about educational productivity that are no less intuitive than the assumptions made by modelers, but in these other methods, the assumptions are more explicit, and so the focus of debate can more easily concentrate on the assumptions themselves, not the calculations flowing from them.

An Empirical Search for What Is Instructionally "Adequate"

This strategy determines a level of acceptable pupil performance or proficiency specified as adequate, and then identifies school districts or schools which achieve the desired goals. The level of resources expended by such school districts is then deemed to be adequate. "The underlying assumption is that any district should be able to accomplish what some districts do accomplish" (Augenblick, 1997:4). Skeptics may contend that such deductive strategies are based upon past and existing expenditure patterns which may themselves be products of unfair and perhaps unconstitutional school finance plans, and thus these strategies lead to recommendations for the underfunding of education. However, the actual spending levels determined by research to be associated with desired levels of pupil performance seem to achieve the goal in mind. In effect, what successful districts spend, however unconstitutional or inadequate they may appear when examined without reference to outcomes, has sufficed to obtain the performance ends desired. Hence, these dollar amounts must be presumed to be "adequate," provided their statistical derivation has fully controlled for the non-school resource factors (like student family background characteristics) that are also known to affect academic achievement. In reality, as with the statistical model discussed previously, this strategy runs a greater danger of leading to over-funding of education, because it relies on data from all districts that produce adequate outcomes, including those that produce adequate outcomes inefficiently.[3]

The empirical approach is described in detail in a 1995 investigation undertaken by Augenblick, Alexander, and Guthrie for the state of Ohio, and then revised in a report by Augenblick in 1997 (Augenblick et al., 1995; Augenblick, 1997). It initially involved constructing a representative pool of Ohio school districts, comprised of all Ohio districts save those which were characterized by high and low extremes of property wealth and per-pupil spending. Once such outliers had been removed, remaining districts were ranked by a composite of student performance measures in reading, mathematics, writing, and science. Districts whose average student performance was at the 70th percentile or higher on most measures were defined as providing a minimally adequate education.

Augenblick et al. (1995) next examined instructional arrangements of the districts which met the performance criteria. These districts' mixes of instructionally related components such as ratio of professionals to pupils, class sizes, school sizes, and course offerings were distilled and taken to be instrumentally exemplary for districts attempting to reach specified levels of achievement. These exemplary conditions and practices can be taken as a model instructional program, one empirically verified by student performance. It then becomes possible to assign costs to these empirically derived instructional components.

A problem with this approach is its suggestion that the identified instructional components and mixes are highly desirable. A local school district deviating from such resource norms would be at risk, unless it produced higher-than-expected student academic achievement. A revenue distribution program that funds specific instructional components, whether derived empirically, as in the 1995 Ohio study, or through professional judgment, as we describe (below) for Wyoming, can restrict local school district discretion and, thus, initiative. Because a state identifies a collection of resources as adequate, and funds that collection, it does not mean that districts should be prevented from organizing resources and instructional delivery differently to achieve the same objective. There is an inherent tension between the state's interest in guaranteeing to each school district an adequate level of resources, and the state's interest in assuring that local initiative, creativity and sense of control are mobilized to deliver those resources.

These criticisms were leveled against the 1995 Augenblick et al. report. In response, Augenblick's 1997 report revised the earlier approach by eliminating any empirical observation of school inputs, only observing the average per-pupil spending level that was correlated with acceptable outcomes. In addition, and in response to other criticism, the more recent report abandons a norm-referenced outcome measure (the 70th percentile of the statewide district achievement distribution) and adopts a criterion-referenced measure (percent passage of minimum competency levels).

Augenblick, therefore, now identifies 102 (out of 607) Ohio school districts whose students meet 17 of 18 performance thresholds, or output criteria (outlier high and low property wealth and/or high- and low-spending districts were again eliminated from consideration). In addition to a dropout rate of 3 percent or less and an attendance rate of at least 93 percent, the remaining 16 criteria consist of specified passage rates on the state's minimum proficiency tests. (For example, four of the criteria are passage rates of 75 percent on the 4th-grade proficiency tests in reading, mathematics, writing, and citizenship, and another four are passage rates of 60 percent on the comparable 12th-grade proficiency tests.) Once having identified a pool of districts which did not exhibit extremes of wealth or spending and in which students had met these state measured performance criteria, Augenblick constructed a weighted per-pupil revenue amount from among eligible district expenditure patterns. The per-pupil dollar amount derived from this process was $3,930, based on 1996 Ohio spending levels (Augenblick, 1997). This, then, is the Augenblick definition of "adequacy" for Ohio school districts (before additional resources are added for students with special needs and other factors).

A similar approach was used by Illinois Governor James Edgar's Commission on Education Funding in 1996 to estimate the cost of the foundation of an adequate education. The Commission retained Fordham University Professor Bruce Cooper, acting on behalf of the Coopers & Lybrand accounting firm, to carry out the calculations of a foundation level for Illinois schools. To establish this foundation level, Cooper grouped schools by poverty (defined by the percentage of students receiving free or reduced-price lunches) into those where eligibility was less than 20 percent, those where it was 20-40 percent, and those where it was greater than 40 percent. In each poverty grouping, schools were then identified where composite (grades 3, 6, and 8 for elementary schools, grade 11 in high schools) scores on the Illinois Goals Assessment Program were in the top quartile of all schools' scores. Of these high-performance schools, per-pupil expenditures were averaged only for those schools whose per-pupil expenditures were below average for the state as a whole. Presumably, these criteria resulted in average expenditures calculated from only efficient high-performance schools. With this procedure, the 1995-96 average (i.e., the cost of adequacy) was calculated to be $4,225 per pupil. (Not all expenditures were intended to be covered by this foundation; costs of special education, bilingual education, categorical programs, transportation, school lunch, and certain other services were excluded.) The Commission recommended that this foundation level of adequacy then be adjusted for regional cost of living differences and for student poverty rates. The Commission's report, however, was not adopted by the state legislature, despite the governor's endorsement.[4]

Augenblick, Myers, and Anderson (1997) also report that a similar empirical approach has now been adopted by Mississippi, which has identified 30 successful schools where test scores are satisfactory and concluded that the costs of operating these schools is "reasonable." This cost of education in these 30 schools is being defined as the cost of adequacy, with adjustments made to this necessary cost for districts with varying costs of living, student poverty rates, etc. As of this writing, however, the Mississippi method has not been described in the published education finance literature.

A limitation of the Ohio and Illinois (and presumably, the Mississippi) approaches, as with similar approaches discussed above, is that the minimum proficiency tests measure only certain cognitive outcomes, not the full range of cognitive, value, and behavioral outcomes we (and the courts) regard as adequate. As we noted above, it may be that further study will determine that all outcomes are positively related, i.e., a district in which most students pass proficiency tests in reading, mathematics, writing, and citizenship is also likely to be a district that adequately develops student "interests in all creative arts, such as music, theater, literature, and the visual arts" or a district most of whose students have adequate "social ethics, both behavioral and abstract, to facilitate compatibility with others in this society." However, with no available research on these relationships, it would be premature to jump to such conclusions.

Another limitation of the Augenblick et al. (1997) approach is that the proficiency test passage data utilized are uncontrolled for student characteristics. It is assumed, for example, that districts with large proportions of economically disadvantaged and/or racial minority youth can produce passage on proficiency tests utilizing basic resources with the same resources as districts with smaller proportions of such youth.[5]   Recent work by Grissmer analyzing student achievement by the "value added" in schools demonstrates that analyses of test scores without such controls can be misleading (Grissmer et al., 1994). As noted above, statistical "black box" approaches to adequacy attempt roughly to control for the additional costs of educating students who bring less social capital to schooling, although the success of such controls is open to question.

Full controls for student characteristics, leading to sufficient resources for each demographic category of student to achieve the same adequate outcomes, are consistent with an apparent national consensus that identical minimal competency (in our terms, minimally adequate outcomes) should be achieved by all schools, irrespective of their students' socioeconomic characteristics. The state of Texas, for example, categorizes schools by race/ethnicity and income levels, but requires schools in each category to have a minimum 35 percent passage rate on the Texas Assessment of Academic Skills (Olson and Hendrie, 1998). We tend to believe that this is an unreasonable approach to adequacy, but reserve final judgment pending additional data. It could be an important exercise to determine whether the resources required to achieve this minimum passage rate were the same in each socioeconomic category, and if not, whether full funding of the differences is a realistic goal. As we described in an earlier section, one statistical study concludes that a combination of geographic cost and student needs differences results in an adequacy funding definition for New York City that is two to three times the state average; another concludes that costs in Milwaukee are over twice the state average. We suspect that, at least for the foreseeable future, legislatures are unlikely to fund such a wide range of variation.

There are two difficulties facing analysts who attempt to fine tune the relationship of student social and economic circumstances to the acquisition of specified achievement levels, difficulties shared in common by those who utilize either of the three approaches (statistical, empirical, judgmental) to adequacy.

First, obtaining data and gaining professional agreement on the best way statistically to control for student socioeconomic status is difficult. Many education researchers use the percentage of children who receive free or subsidized meals under the Federal school lunch program as a proxy for the economic status of a school. Nationally, about half of all schoolchildren benefit. But participation rates provide only bifurcated data: a child's family is either poor enough to qualify for the lunch program, or it is not, yet the most important distinctions between children's readiness to learn occur within each of those groups. Stable lower-middle-class families (with incomes up to 185 percent of the poverty line, now more than $30,000 a year for a family of four) are eligible, as well as welfare recipients; stable middle-class families earning more than about $30,000 a year are ineligible, along with the affluent.

A more important deficiency of school lunch data is the wide range of participation, even among schools that may be socioeconomically similar.

Schools often forfeit an effort to encourage older children to enroll in the program; adolescents often do not consider it "cool." How many elementary school children enroll is also related to the extent to which school administrators and teachers aggressively promote it. Changing policy priorities of federal, state, and district officials can affect how well documented eligibility must be. In some schools, eligible children may be denied participation because applications were not properly completed; in others, ineligible children participate because of lax administration. If we compare test scores between schools in different communities that may have the same percentage of children eligible for free and reduced-price lunches, we still cannot be confident we are comparing children who are similar.

Second, even if these data and modeling challenges can be overcome, the endeavor is fraught with moral and political difficulty. If we abandon Texas's one-standard-fits-all approach, do we specify, for example, that in most districts, 75 percent of students are expected to pass a proficiency test, but it is somehow acceptable for districts with mostly low-income families to have a 35 percent passage rate? Ohio, Illinois, and Texas calculate adequacy with methods that answer this question firmly in the negative. Regardless of student socioeconomic status, all schools must achieve the same average proficiency to be considered to have adequate outcomes.

We are not persuaded that this answer is satisfactory. If it were possible to specify what resources would be needed to ensure that even low-income students achieved at 75 percent proficiency, this almost certainly would be more resources than are necessary to achieve an "adequate" (i.e., 75 percent) result in districts with more advantaged students. At the moment, however, the science of determining adequacy does not permit us even to begin discussions with such precision.

The Augenblick approach controls for efficiency in another regard: it excludes from consideration districts above the 95th or below the 5th percentile in spending for administration, operations and pupil support (counselors, librarians, etc.), even if these districts' outcome criteria meet the thresholds.[6] This definition of efficiency should also be examined further; resources for pupil support and those for instruction may, to some extent, be substitutable; a district that achieves minimum outcomes by using more counselors and fewer teachers might not necessarily be doing so inefficiently.

A "Professional Expert" Strategy for Identifying Instructional Components

An alternative strategy for determining the instructional components undergirding an "adequate" education is to rely upon professional judgment to construct an ideal-type delivery system, without either statistical or empirical inference from actual measured outcomes. The components of such a system can then be identified and costs assigned to them. While, at first glance, such an approach may seem unscientific, the approximations inherent in professional judgment may be no less precise than those embedded, though more hidden, in statistical or empirical methods. It is possible that professional judgment, if carefully exercised, may be better able to adjust for the vast multitude of factors involved than a statistical or empirical approach.

A school finance system in which the state funded, or guaranteed funding, for a defined set of resources in each district (including class sizes, teacher salary levels, a specific number of administrators and clerical staff, etc.) was once common, particularly in Southern states (Augenblick and Myers, 1994). It is no longer widely used, however, and this system predated a concern to link these resource models to a notion of "adequacy." The notion of input adequacy, however, was implicit in these systems. Once adequacy became an explicit concern, a "professional judgment" approach was developed by Jay Chambers and Thomas Parrish in proposals they made for funding adequate education systems in Illinois in 1992 and in Alaska 2 years later (Chambers and Parrish, 1994). Because they recognized that no precise technology exists for linking resources to outcomes in education, they declined to term their goal "adequate," using the term "appropriate" instead. Calling their method the "Resource Cost Model" (RCM), Chambers and Parrish convened committees of teachers, administrators, and public officials to deliberate and determine what resources were necessary to deliver an appropriate education. They toured facilities across the states and met with local educators and policymakers. They concluded in Illinois, for example, that teacher staffing resources should be provided so that a regular grade 1-3 class should have 22 pupils, that a speech therapist should have a caseload of 62 pupils, and that schools insulated to a proper standard should have resources to purchase energy to maintain a year-round building temperature of 70 degrees.

The charge of these committees was not entirely to specify the resources of an appropriate education, because they were also told they must "keep a balance between the resources they would like to see specified for each educational program and what they believed to be affordable" (Chambers and Parrish, 1994:53) given the states' fiscal and political realities. Operating under these guidelines, the process resulted in a recommendation for an appropriate funding level that was 2 percent greater than present total funding in Illinois, and 16 percent greater than present total funding in Alaska. However, the Chambers-Parrish specifications of appropriateness, developed through this process, would have required substantial redistribution of resources from district to district within these states.

Having specified appropriate level of resources by this consultative process, employing professional judgment, Chambers and Parrish utilized a statistical analysis to estimate the costs and the intra-state cost differences of providing these resources. The result, however, was that "policymakers [in both states] tended to find the overall system somewhat incomprehensible and complex"

(Chambers and Parrish, 1994:72). The RCM was not, therefore, ultimately adopted as a basis for policy in these states.

While Chambers and Parrish relied on the professional judgment of Illinois and Alaska educators in specifying resource levels required for an adequate (i.e., appropriate) education, it may now or soon be possible to specify adequate resource levels based on a distillation of national empirical research about effective schools and judgments of professional researchers regarding effective practices. Such specifications might be based on "whole school designs," off-the-shelf school blueprints intended for adoption in their entirety by schools (Odden, 1997; Odden and Busch, 1998). The New American Schools organization has adopted seven of these designs for promotion to schools, including "Roots and Wings (Success for All)" developed by Robert Slavin's team at Johns Hopkins University; "Atlas Communities," based primarily on the School Development Program (SDP) developed by James Comer; the "Audrey Cohen College System" developed at the college of that name in New York City; "Co-NECT," a school design developed by a Cambridge (Massachusetts) consulting firm; the "Expeditionary Learning" program affiliated with Outward Bound; the "Modern Red Schoolhouse," designed by the Hudson Institute; and the "National Alliance for Restructuring Education" that cooperates with schools (e.g., in Kentucky) to restructure their resources to meet higher academic standards. Other "Whole School Design" models are those of the Edison Project, the E.D. Hirsch "Core Knowledge Curriculum," "Accelerated Schools" developed by Henry Levin at Stanford, and the "CMCD" (Consistency Management and Cooperative Discipline) program now being disseminated in Texas, Chicago, and Norfolk (Fashola and Slavin, 1998).

None of the above listed designs can yet be said to be firmly established by research, in the sense that the achievement of students in schools following these models has been proven superior in replicated controlled empirical or experimental studies. However, many education policymakers are impressed with anecdotal evidence concerning the success of some or all of these programs, and with some limited empirical data that tends to confirm it. These designs will become more formidable if research continues to accumulate regarding their effectiveness. The resources specified by each of these designs (with the exception of the National Alliance for Restructuring Education, which does not promote a single design as such, but tailors its recommendations to individual affiliated schools) could be priced, and the sum might be considered the cost, at the school level, of an adequate education. One preliminary effort to estimate the costs of some of these programs was undertaken by Jennifer King (1994).

A professional judgment approach that utilizes both consultation with local experts (as did Chambers and Parrish) and reliance on national research and whole school designs, was adopted in 1996 by a consulting group led by James W. Guthrie to calculate an adequate level of resources to be distributed to Wyoming school districts (Guthrie et al., 1997). The Wyoming approach differed from the earlier work of Chambers and Parrish in three important respects. First,

Guthrie et al. had been retained by the state legislature to design a system to fulfill a mandate of the Wyoming Supreme Court in *Campbell v. Wyoming*. The court prohibited the legislature from considering the total cost of a new education funding system, requiring that the "best" (i.e., adequate) system be funded regardless of cost: "lack of financial resources will not be an acceptable reason for failure to provide the best education system." Therefore, unlike the Alaska and Illinois experts for the RCM, the Wyoming professional expert groups were not asked to balance adequacy with expense in making their recommendations. Second, in defining adequacy, Guthrie et al. consulted with professional expert groups in Wyoming and nationally, but did not rely exclusively on the opinions of practitioners. Rather, these opinions were used to inform the consultants' views, based on national research and prior experience, regarding the resource elements necessary to produce adequate outcomes. In this respect, the Guthrie et al. approach is consistent with the "whole school designs" analysis as described by Odden.

Third, learning from the Illinois and Alaska experiences, Guthrie et al. did not use a complex statistical method (regression models) to calculate resource costs or cost adjustments, believing that they would be unlikely to be able to explain how these calculations were made in a manner that would be understood and accepted by nonprofessional policymakers, educators, and citizens. Rather, less sophisticated but more easily understandable methods, still based on economic theory, were employed.[7]

Fourth, because the Wyoming legislature was ordered by the court to produce recommendations for adequacy on very short notice, Guthrie et al. calculated the costs only of the main elements of an adequate education, using less precise methods to estimate other costs. (For example, cost of utilities was calculated by taking the average cost of Wyoming districts in the prior year, with no attempt to specify resources necessary to reach a target temperature for classrooms when controlled for building insulation standards.)

Guthrie et al. also adopted the professional judgment approach (as opposed to the Augenblick approach of inferring resources from observed adequate outcomes) not only because of concerns, described above, about poorly specified outcome measures in education generally, but because the state of Wyoming did not utilize a standardized achievement test like that in Ohio, Illinois, Mississippi, or Texas, even for narrowly defined academic outcomes, and so even poorly specified outcome data were not available. In many states without adequate assessments, the professional judgment method may be the only alternative available, without resorting to the sorts of indirect voter preference models suggested by Duncombe and Yinger.

We prefer the professional judgment approach, not because we believe it is more precise than statistical or inferential methods (it may not be more precise), but rather because its imprecision is more transparent. When one econometric model finds a great difference in cost between two districts, while another model finds a much smaller difference, policymakers are at a loss to understand what assumptions inside the "black box" create these conflicting results. But when prototypical resource models of adequacy have different costs, it is clear what the reasons for this difference are: one professional judgment model may propose a 3rd-grade class size of 15 students, for example, while another may propose a class size of 20. Policymakers, educators, and voters can then enter this debate, exercising their own best judgments about whether the research evidence on the benefits of smaller class sizes in the early grades is sufficiently persuasive to justify the additional cost. As this research evidence advances, the professional judgment method will be able to improve the precision of its results.

For now, the professional judgment method makes explicit what more statistical methodologies tend, unwittingly, to hide: As the Rhode Island Supreme Court stated in a recent adequacy decision, "what constitutes an 'equal, adequate, and meaningful' [education] is 'not likely to be divined for all time even by the scholars who now so earnestly debate the issues'" (quoted in Minorini and Sugarman, Chapter 6 in this volume).

Nevertheless, even after having expressed our preference for the professional judgment approach, principally because of limitations inherent in black box statistical approaches and the limitations of many standardized measures of student outcomes, we acknowledge that the professional judgment approach is itself imperfect. It suffers from the possibility of not being reliable. Will double panels arrive at similar conclusions when provided with similar information? In the Wyoming circumstances described below, two panels, operating 6 months apart, did arrive at similar judgments. However, this is a sample size far too small to arrive at a conclusion regarding the utility of the professional judgment process in every setting.

Also, when professional panels make judgments, there is always the risk of conflicts of interests. This would be so whether the panels include physicians, attorneys, engineers, or educators. "Adequate" may be defined by panel members with an eye toward their own circumstances and the personal consequences for them of arriving at particular "adequate" revenue levels. And, of course, one cannot be absolutely sure of the basis of their professional judgment in such matters. In effect, each professional panel participant is his or her own "black box," the internal machinations of which are not immediately transparent.

In the following pages, we describe the Wyoming professional judgment approach, to illustrate how our methods unfold in practice.

ESTABLISHING A DEFINITION OF ADEQUATE BY
PROFESSIONAL JUDGMENT IN WYOMING

Guthrie et al., the Wyoming consultants, operated with two waves of independent panels of education experts. The first wave was comprised of Wyoming education experts. Its principal objective was to identify the components of an instructional system which could deliver an adequate education. These expert panels were assembled multiple times to develop and verify "prototypical" schools and the instructional components within such schools capable of delivering the Wyoming legislature's specified basket of education services and knowledge. The second wave of expert panels was comprised of regional educational experts. Included were principals, superintendents, and other practitioners from states surrounding Wyoming and exhibiting similar economic and geographic profiles—rural, agricultural, and extractive mineral-intensive. It was subsequently convened to verify that the delivery components in the prototypical schools designed by the initial expert panels could indeed achieve the instructional objectives specified by the legislature in its "basket" of education goods and services.

The first wave of experts assembled was comprised of three educator panels, one each for elementary, middle, and secondary schools. These were selected from among experienced and qualified teachers, pupil personnel professionals, and administrators employed in Wyoming's 49 local school districts.[8]

Instructional Strategies and Their Implications for Resource Allocation

Panelists were informed repeatedly that consultants would not restrict their creativity or decision-making freedom. However, experts were also informed that consultants, at least preliminarily, were predisposed toward a seven-pronged instruction and resource allocation strategy for elementary schools. (Similar exercises, not discussed here in detail, were carried out for middle and high schools as well.) The seven-pronged elementary strategy, which was adopted and refined by the expert panels, included the following:

(1) *Early grade resource intensity improves student outcomes.* Guthrie and his associates contended to the expert panels that inverting the conventional resource allocation pyramid was strategically important. Conventionally, a substantially greater amount is spent by public schools on secondary than on primary school students. In 1997, the national public school pupil-teacher ratio was 14.9 in secondary schools and 19.0 in elementary schools (National Center for Education Statistics, 1998:Table 64). This spending pattern is principally a product of smaller classes and a more specialized set of course offerings in high school. Also, high school students usually have available to them a wider range of higher cost extracurricular activities. The Guthrie team believed that, within reasonable boundaries, this imbalance could and should be redressed, and that additional elementary level school resources, appropriately distributed, would be a better investment. By spending more, appropriately, early on, consultants believed that (1) a better learning foundation could be constructed from which students could then benefit in the remainder of their schooling and (2) more intense resources, in the particular form of smaller regular classes for elementary students, would

enable their teachers more productively to identify and cope successfully with exceptional students.

Consultants in Wyoming took the Tennessee class size experimental results to be among the most powerful and credible research results available in education (Mosteller, 1995; Krueger, 1997). The fact that small class sizes (15 and 16 students per instructor) utilized in the Tennessee experiment resulted in higher and sustained levels of student achievement in the early elementary grades, particularly for low-income students, was a finding that the consultants forcefully brought to the attention of the Wyoming expert panels. The panels found this theory persuasive, and the result was a prototypical elementary school instruction model based upon average class sizes of 16, and overall pupil/teacher ratios of 14.4 per professional. These are among the most favorable pupil/professional ratios to be found anywhere in the nation, even among states spending substantially larger amounts of money per pupil.

(2) *Small classes can more productively accommodate exceptions.* The conventional pattern by which American public schools cope with exceptional students is through categorical aid programs which provide additional resources for differential treatment. Disabled students, low-income students, gifted students, and those whose proficiency in English is lacking are often pulled from classrooms and provided with some variety of specialized instruction. Wyoming consultants were unconvinced that this model is the most effective. Certainly, for severely handicapped students, it may be necessary. However, in other instances it can be stigmatizing to the child to be identified as exceptional and it may be instructionally inefficient to depend upon pull-out programs. The small class sizes contained in the Wyoming prototypical model, particularly in the primary grades, were intended to enable a classroom teacher, with appropriate professional training, to identify students in need of extra assistance and provide such assistance herself or himself. Additional school-wide resource teachers were funded as a supplement to regular classroom resources, but without specific categorical designations. The Wyoming instructional prototypes depend upon the classroom as the first bulwark against exceptional children either falling through the instructional cracks or obtaining stigmatizing and inappropriate treatments.

(3) *Small elementary schools are generally better than large schools.* The Guthrie team also suggested to the Wyoming panel participants that, all things being equal, elementary schools of approximately 200 to 400 students were more conducive to learning than larger schools (Guthrie, 1979). Experts concurred, and the Wyoming elementary prototypes are constructed around an abstraction of 288 pupils in grades K-5. This number results from having a total of six (conventional) grade levels with three classes per grade level. Class sizes are assumed to be 15 for grades K-3 and 18 for grades 4 and 5. Multiple sections at each grade level were thought to be important in the event parents wanted to have a choice among instructors at any grade level, and to allow school administrators to assign

teachers to children with some flexibility to match complementary teaching and learning styles.

(4) *Professional development enhances teacher effectiveness.* Deriving maximum benefit from small classes and small schools necessitates that individual teachers possess sophisticated professional knowledge and, in many cases, different training from that possessed by many regular classroom teachers today. To take advantage of the small-class model effectively, a teacher must be informed not only about instruction, but also about how to diagnose early signs of learning disability or language deficiency and about how to tailor appropriate instruction to special needs. Because of the added demands in this model upon elementary classroom teachers, the prototypical model is rich in resources for the in-service staff development of teachers.

(5) *Remote identification of exceptionality is imprecise.* Policymakers understand that some children are disabled, gifted, non-English speaking, at-risk, etc. However, practical decision tools for identifying such students are blunt and imprecise. Those at a school or in a classroom are best suited to make such judgments. This poses a challenge for policymakers. If those close to students are responsible for the identification, how can policy avoid incentives for such professionals to over-identify special needs children, generating more categorical revenue than is needed to constitute an adequate resource level?

Wyoming consultants' answer to this challenge was, in the first instance, to eliminate categorical funding procedures to the extent possible, and instead to rely upon a "census based" pupil identification system. Here the statewide frequency of "high incidence" categories of exceptional students is assumed to hold for any particular school district. For example, in Wyoming, 3 percent of students are assumed in the consultant-recommended model to be gifted. All school districts then receive a small amount of additional resources for extra supplies, field trips, etc., for 3 percent of their enrolled students. Beyond this small amount of additional resources, however, the small class sizes funded in the model ensure that gifted children receive the specialized instruction they require in the regular classroom. Actual identification of individual gifted students, and the eventual prescription of more intense services for them, is left to the discretion of local educators, with classroom teachers having primary responsibility.

A similar approach was recommended by Wyoming consultants for the funding of low-cost disabled student services. The recommendation to the legislature is that a uniform percentage of children with mild disabilities be funded in each district as part of an expanded regular program. (However, because some districts in Wyoming are so small that an expected uniform percentage of children with mild disabilities might not apply, in the event a district believes it has a greater proportion of students than the state-funded figure in any exceptional student category, it should have the right to appeal to the State Education Department for additional funds.) In the case of severe disabilities, which occur in school districts with unpredictable regularity, it was recommended that the traditional categorical funding approach be retained, with the state reimbursing the full costs of these low-incidence, high-cost services, once the disabilities were identified.

(6) *Concentrations can provoke added costs.* As noted, a final recommendation has not yet been made regarding the amount of additional resources, if any, districts should receive for a normally expected incidence of mildly learning disabled students. Because funding was provided for exceptionally small class sizes and intense professional development, we anticipate that these resources would be less than are traditionally allocated for special services. Also, we anticipate that a normally expected incidence (in Wyoming) of other special needs students (for example, at-risk students) can also be provided for without additional resources—small class sizes, school-wide resource teachers, and intense professional development being sufficient. But whereas the overall strategy assumes that small classes and well-trained professionals can cope with the conventional incidence of exceptional students, disproportionate concentrations of such students can result in challenges beyond the capacity of classroom teacher and individual school officials to cope. Hence, a concentration or threshold funding strategy was devised to compensate districts or schools in which the proportion of Limited English Proficient (LEP) or Economically Disadvantaged Students (EDS) exceeded the statewide average by more than 150 percent.[9] Only where such thresholds are breached was a categorical program recommended, in which each identified student earns for the district involved a higher per-pupil revenue amount.

In an important respect, however, this method unavoidably funds education in excess of an adequate level. This is because of the role played by federal funding, a role that must be addressed if states, for the first time, begin to require that school districts provide an adequate education using state and local resources alone. The Wyoming Supreme Court, for example, required that money be allocated to districts based on the actual costs experienced by these districts, including the greater costs which may be entailed in the education of economically disadvantaged or racial minority students. The court required the legislature to guarantee to districts full reimbursement for these additional costs.

However, this requirement (and, in consequence, the consultants' model) conflicts with the federal Title I requirement that federal funds supplement, but do not supplant, state and local funds. If the Wyoming adequacy funding formula prescribes state-guaranteed resources necessary to educate disadvantaged children, and if Title I funds then supplement these amounts, districts with disadvantaged children will receive more than their actual costs of educating these children, once Title I funds have been added to the state-guaranteed adequate amounts. If, on the other hand, the amount of Title I funds available in any year is deducted from the state guarantee to districts, this will conflict with the "supplement-not-supplant" language of the federal program.

Clearly, the most desirable policy, and the policy most in accord with the spirit of the Title I requirement, is, paradoxically, the alternative that conflicts with the literal requirements of federal law. If a state formula that guarantees adequacy truly compensates districts for the higher costs of educating disadvantaged children, the state will accomplish the Congressional purpose of Title I when it applies its Title I allotments toward this compensation. The Congressional "supplement-not-supplant" language was clearly designed to prevent districts from applying Title I funding toward the regular cost of education and thus negating the supplemental intent of the law. The "supplement-not-supplant" language was not written in anticipation of a state's assumption of responsibility for the extra costs entailed by a disadvantaged student population. Permitting a state that assumes this responsibility to apply Title I funding to its own commitment would be fully in accord with the spirit and intent of the "supplement-not-supplant" provision, provided the state defines this new commitment consistent with minimal federal standards for Title I funding.

To resolve this dilemma, the best public policy for a state implementing an adequacy formula would be to obtain a waiver from the U.S. Department of Education that would permit the state to apply Title I funds to the state's commitment to districts, based on a demonstration by the state to the Department of Education that disadvantaged students are being given resources that supplement and do not supplant the resources given to regular students, and that these supplemental resources are at least equal to the resources provided by Title I funding. In other words, in the Wyoming case discussed here, the state should be able to show that class sizes and professional development resources were funded at levels that took account of the needs of Title I-eligible children. In the absence of such a waiver, the model provides a more-than-adequate funding level.

(7) *Those closest to students should make most instructional decisions.* Whereas the prototypical model is comprised of instructional components constructed by education experts, it is still an abstraction constructed by individuals remote from the day-to-day circumstances of teachers who interact with particular students. Out of a belief that those who actually instruct students should have maximum professional discretion in determining strategies and tactics, the funding model recommended by the consultants in Wyoming deliberately places the prototypically generated resources into a "block grant." This mechanism attempts to restore as much conventional local control to Wyoming school districts as a Supreme Court decision will permit, but also is intended to enhance the professional discretion of local officials and professional educators.

Thus, the prototypical models created by the Guthrie group with its expert panels were created only for the purpose of pricing each resource in the model so that a total per-pupil spending level, deemed sufficient to produce the adequate basket of educational outcomes, could be allocated to school districts for the number of children they enrolled. The consultants frequently emphasized, and the legislature subsequently endorsed, the principle that no district should be required to spend the per-pupil funds it receives in a manner that reproduces the prototypical school models. Nothing in the legislation based on the consultants' report, for example, restricts schools in their grade groupings or in their class sizes. Individual schools can create classes which are larger or smaller, depending upon how they choose to allocate their block grant resources. Because these choices will not affect the total size of the block grant, districts must exercise choices and determine priorities. A district choosing to pay higher salaries than the model recommends will probably be required to have larger classes to offset the cost of higher salaries, and a district choosing even smaller class sizes in selected grades than the model recommends will probably have to increase class sizes in other settings in order to stay within its total block grant. However, while districts are not required to spend block grants as the prototypical models recommend, it would not be unreasonable to expect state regulators to scrutinize especially carefully those districts whose performance appears to be notoriously low while spending resources in radically different ways from the prototype.[10] And, of course, while the finance block grant carries no requirements for particular spending strategies, the state department of education may have other rules and regulations (about course offerings, curriculum, etc.) that, in effect, restrict the freedom of districts to spend money as they please.

Tables 7-2 through 7-4 display the elementary, middle, and high school prototypes recommended by Guthrie et al. to the Wyoming legislature.

DIRECTLY (AND INDIRECTLY) ASSIGNING
COSTS TO ADEQUACY

Once prototypical models were specified, Wyoming consultants had to attach costs to each of the model's components. This procedure can be extraordinarily difficult in education. There is not a large and active market to assist in establishing costs. In other spheres where there are multiple suppliers and purchasers, more active agents of supply and demand, and greater competition, determining cost is more straightforward.

Though great public attention has been focused lately on efforts to expand the private education sector to compete with public education, private education remains small relative to public education, and there is little immediate prospect that this relationship will change significantly. About 12 percent of U.S. elementary and secondary students are enrolled in private schools, a share substantially unchanged for half a century (National Center for Education Statistics, 1998). Even though the U.S. Supreme Court (*Pierce v. Society of Sisters,* 1926) countenanced private education as a means of meeting compulsory attendance statutes, states have chosen to provide education publicly and to subsidize it with public revenues. In most communities, the overwhelming share of the education supply is controlled by a single agency or a very few agencies. These local public school districts dominate the market for purchasing education components. For someone wishing to be a teacher, there are few prospective purchasers of that

TABLE 7-2   Wyoming Prototypical Model: Elementary School, K-5;
Preliminary Costs[a]

Description	Units	Salary Cost	Salary-Driven Benefits[b]	Health Benefits	Total Cost
A. Personnel					
1. Teachers	20.00	$31,758	$6,034	$3,641	$828,660
2. Substitute teachers (5%)	0.90	$10,500	$803		$10,173
3. Aides (FTE)	3.00	$10,080	$1,915		$35,986
4. Pupil support	1.50	$31,758	$6,034	$3,641	$62,150
5. Library/media	1.00	$31,758	$6,034	$3,641	$41,433
Certif. librarian					
Media assistant					
Technician					
6. School administration	1.00	$50,877	$9,667	$3,641	$64,185
7. Clerical/data entry	2.00	$16,000	$3,040	$3,641	$45,362
8. Operations	2.50	$20,000	$3,800	$3,641	$68,603
B. Supplies and					$61,950
Instructional Materials					
C. Equipment					$37,837
D. Food Service (varies by district)					
E. Categorical Aid					
1. Special education(current expenditure placeholder)					$152,514
2. Limited English speaking(varies by district)					
3. Disadvantaged youth(varies by district)					
4. Gifted					$1,296
F. Student Activities					$2,167
G. Professional Development					$26,352
H. Assessment					$7,200
I. District Expenditure					
1. Maintenance and operations					$93,064
2. Administration and miscellaneous expenditures					$159,323
3. Transportation					$77,180
Total Enrollment:	288		Total cost		$1,775,433
			Adj.$/ADM		$6,165

[a]Assumptions: 288 students; class size 16; pupil/teacher ratio 14.4.
[b]Salary Driven Benefits: Social Security, Medicare, Workers Comp, Unemp Ins, State Pension.

SOURCE: Guthrie et al. (1997:92).

TABLE 7-3   Wyoming Prototypical Model: Middle/Jr. High, 6-8; Preliminary Costs[a]

Description	Units	Salary Cost	Salary-driven Benefits[b]	Health Benefits	Total Cost
A. Personnel					
1. Teachers	19.5	$31,758	$6,034	$3,641	$807,944
2. Substitute teachers (5%)	1.00	$10,500	$803		$11,021
3. Aides (FTE)	3.00	$10,080	$1,915		$35,986
4. Pupil support	3.00	$31,758	$6,034	$3,641	$124,299
5. Library media					
Certificated librarian	1.00	$31,758	$6,034	$3,641	$41,433
Media assistant	1.50	$18,000	$3,420	$3,641	$37,592
Tech. assistant					
6. School administration	1.00	$50,792	$9,650	$3,641	$64,083
7. Clerical/data entry	2.00	$16,000	$3,040	$3,641	$45,362
8. Operations	3.00	$20,000	$3,800	$3,641	$82,323
B. Supplies and Instructional Materials					$56,887
C. Equipment					$43,880
D. Food Service (varies by district)					
E. Categorical Aid					
1. Special education(current expenditure placeholder)					$158,869
2. Limited English speaking(varies by district)					
3. Disadvantaged youth(varies by district)					
4. Gifted					$1,350
F. Student Activities					$16,179
G. Professional Development					$27,450
H. Assessment					$7,500
I. District Expenditure					
1. Maintenance and operations					$112,500
2. Administration and miscellaneous categories					$165,961
3. Transportation					$80,396
Total Enrollment:	300		Total cost		$1,921,014
			Adj.$/ADM		$6,403

[a]Assumptions: 300 students; class size 20; pupil/teacher ratio 15.4.
[b]Salary Driven Benefits: Social Security, Medicare, Workers Comp, Unemp Ins, State Pension.

SOURCE: Guthrie et al. (1997:93).

TABLE 7-4   Wyoming Prototypical Model: High School, 9-12; Preliminary Costs[a]

Description	Units	Salary Cost	Salary-Driven Benefits[b]	Health Benefits	Total Cost
A. Personnel					
1. Teachers	41.18	$31,758	$6,034	$3,641	$1,706,066
2. Substitute Teachers (5%)	1.70	$12,250	$937		$22,418
3. Aides (FTE)	6.00	$10,080	$1,915		$71,971
4. Pupil support	5.00	$31,758	$6,034	$3,641	$207,165
5. Library media					
Certificated librarian	1.00	$31,758	$6,034	$3,641	$41,433
Media assistant	2.00	$18,000	$3,420	$3,641	$50,122
Tech. assistant					
6. School administration	1.00	$53,071	$10,083	$3,641	$66,795
	1.00	$47,675	$9,058	$3,641	$60,374
7. Clerical/data entry	5.00	$16,000	$3,040	$3,641	$113,405
8. Operations	5.00	$20,000	$3,800	$3,641	$137,205
B. Supplies and Instructional Materials					$164,765
C. Equipment					$97,266
D. Food Service (varies by district)					
E. Categorical Aid					
1. Special education(current expenditure placeholder)					$317,738
2. Limited english speaking(varies by district)					
3. Disadvantaged youth(varies by district)					
4. Gifted					$2,700
F. Student Activities					$100,203
G. Professional Development					$58,500
H. Assessment					$15,000
I. District Expenditure					
1. Maintenance and operations					$342,600
2. Administration and miscellaneous categories					$331,923
3. Transportation					$160,792
Total Enrollment:	600		Total cost		$4,066,441
			Adj.$/ADM		$6,781

[a]Assumptions: 600 students; class size 17; pupil/teacher ratio 17.
[b]Salary Driven Benefits: Social Security, Medicare, Workers Comp, Unemp Ins, State Pension.

SOURCE: Guthrie et. al. (1997:94).

individual's instructional services in most communities. If teachers are union-ized, there may be even less of a market. Not only can one purchaser, a school district, dominate a local teacher market (a condition known technically as "monopsony"), but one labor supplier, a teachers' union, can influence the price of teachers as well (a condition of monopoly). In the absence of a market, therefore, it is not possible to assume that actual costs of education inputs are equivalent to what school districts actually spend for those inputs. Expenditures may be too high, or too low, for adequacy.

Teacher compensation typically comprises at least 50 percent of a school district's expenditures, and other professional compensation (for school adminis-trators, counselors, librarians, etc.), tightly linked to that of teachers, comprises another 10 percent (Protheroe, 1997). When so major a portion of an industry's technology falls outside the boundary of an active market, assigning costs can be especially difficult. It is for this reason that, in translating "adequacy" to rev-enues, it is necessary to rely upon inferences from expenditures, not on expendi-tures themselves.

As discussed earlier in this chapter, there is an increasingly important body of literature arguing that the number of statistical observations available in educa-tion is sufficiently large and varied that economic costs of school inputs generally and teacher salaries in particular can be calculated using statistical regression techniques (Chambers, 1995). However, as we suggested above, we are not persuaded that this approach can overcome the monopolistic and monopsonistic conditions common to almost all of the observations, that the number of observa-tions is, in fact, sufficiently large in a state like Wyoming, or that statistical techniques can control for other characteristics (e.g., teacher quality) with suffi-cient precision (Rothstein and Smith, 1997; Mishel and Rothstein, 1997). Conse-quently, other methods of inferring real costs from observed expenditures must be utilized.

In Wyoming, Guthrie et al. assigned costs to prototypical school instruc-tional components through two principal strategies. One, where there was no market immediately in operation, they inferentially linked market cost to a proto-typical component. Second, where a supply and demand situation could reason-ably be determined to be operating, they took school-incurred prices for such items to be an accurate expression of market costs.

Salaries of education professionals were the principal prototypical instruc-tional components to which market costs could not easily be assigned. This condition was resolved by disaggregating teacher and other professional educator remuneration into four component categories: entry-level salaries, payments for college courses in excess of a bachelors degree, payments for seniority status, and fringe benefits.

Guthrie et al. identified an appropriate level for entry-level teacher salaries by examining teacher salaries in the metropolitan communities where it was presumed conditions approaching labor market competition for college-educated workers were more likely to prevail. In these communities, entry-level teacher salaries may be more influenced by market forces. Teachers may have few options in offering their services to school districts, but if teacher salaries fall too low, potential teachers can seek employment in other services in these communities that typically employ college-educated labor. Conversely, a larger supply of college-educated labor can tip the district-union bargaining relationship in the district's favor. But because even these conditions can only make teacher labor markets more competitive, but not fully competitive, the teacher salary level in more developed professional labor markets must still be examined for reasonableness.

For Wyoming, Guthrie et al. began by identifying the entry-level teacher salary in the most metropolitan region of the state, the Laramie-Cheyenne corridor, where relatively large numbers of professionals are employed in the state university, state government, and private professional business services. (Professional salaries in this corridor are also influenced by market conditions in nearby Fort Collins, Colorado, another university community with high-tech services.) This entry salary was then compared to the Wyoming statewide mean and median entry salaries, and all three were found to be nearly identical. The salary level was then compared to typical entry salaries in the seven states surrounding Wyoming, and the Wyoming entry salary was found to be higher than salaries in each of these states. Professional experts were then consulted to determine if the teachers attracted by this entry salary were sufficiently well qualified to deliver the required basket of educational services. After determining that this salary level was adequate to attract qualified personnel, it was then possible to assume this figure as a cost base for further salary adjustments. Such adjustments were calculated for the remaining three categories.

In the case of payments for education credits beyond the bachelors degree, Wyoming's consultants concluded that it was the consensus among education researchers that payment for these credits (typically reported in "columns" on a salary schedule) had, in American education, ceased to be related to teacher quality. Districts rarely monitor the courses teachers take to earn these credits, and little or no effort is made to ensure that the knowledge and skills gained in these courses are those most needed to improve professional performance. Therefore, the column increments for taking courses had become a ritual in which teachers take courses in order to qualify for salary increments expected in a teacher-career path. The increments teachers are paid for taking courses are, in effect, a form of deferred compensation, added to the teacher entry-level salary. Therefore, Wyoming amounts currently paid for these credits were added to the entry-level teacher salary to create a prototypical model teacher salary. School districts were allocated per prototypical teacher the statewide mean amount for units in excess of a bachelors degree. Thus, there was no implicit recommendation in the model about whether school districts should use these funds in the traditional way (requiring teachers to take additional courses to earn salary points), should use them to fund an additional automatic salary progression (without course taking required), or should increase the starting salary and flatten the progression. (Of course, as noted above, the block grant philosophy of the model would not require districts to spend their resources as prescribed, even if the model in this case did make an implicit recommendation.)

The adjustment made for teacher experience (seniority) was similar, but with an important difference. Research has found that there is additional quality gained from teacher experience (Guthrie et al., 1970), but these gains typically are realized within the first 10 years of teaching, and there is no evidence that teacher seniority increments (i.e., "steps" on a teacher salary schedule) are, on the whole, meaningfully related to gains in teacher quality. Thus, most teacher salary increments for "steps" are also a form of deferred compensation for beginning teachers. This conclusion, by itself, would have led to a recommendation only slightly different from that for credits. However, an additional consideration came into play with respect to salary "steps." While a district could affect the course-taking of its teachers by changing its compensation system, to a large extent the seniority distribution of teachers in a district is beyond the district's control. If districts are simply allocated per prototypical teacher, as in the case of course credits, the statewide mean amount paid for steps (years of service) on salary schedules, districts with unusually senior teachers would be penalized and districts with unusually junior teaching forces would receive more than that required to provide children with an adequate education. Because regional variations in economic conditions were the main cause of atypical seniority distributions (districts hire large numbers of teachers during periods of economic growth, and hire few during slowdowns), the model for Wyoming holds that teacher seniority is a condition beyond the control of districts and thus deserving of a district-by-district adjustment. Because the principle of this adjustment was that boom-and-bust economies (not unusual in mineral-dependent areas of Wyoming) can create abnormal distributions of teacher seniority, districts were not given an adjustment if they chose to hire more experienced teachers for openings (i.e., by hiring out-of-state teachers and crediting prior experience on their salary schedules) rather than beginning teachers. Rather, adjustments were only granted based on in-state teacher experience, dated from the teacher's initial hire date, regardless of prior experience.

The model also prescribed a fringe benefit package (retirement, health insurance, etc.) and added the cost of this package to the model salary. Revenue amounts for other categories of professional personnel (counselors, librarians, and school and district administrators) were indexed to beginning teacher salaries via a scale developed from statewide expenditure data for each personnel category.

Classified personnel salaries were assumed to be more market-sensitive than teacher salaries. Skills of custodians, bus drivers, clerical staff, cafeteria workers, etc. are similar to those sought by many private-sector employers. Hence, an assumption of market cost appears reasonable in such instances. The quantity of resources specified in the prototypical model was therefore multiplied by the average salary currently paid for each type of classified employee, to generate a cost for such personnel.

Because of the limited time available to deliver a final product to the legislature by the Supreme Court's deadline, the remaining costs of a prototypical school (approximately 15 percent of the total) were estimated based primarily on current averages, modified by input from the professional expert panels. This included instructional materials and other supplies; operations, maintenance and repair, and administrative (i.e., district) overhead. Thus, Wyoming statewide mean figures for these items were taken as initial estimates of both need and costs. In principle, however, an adequacy model could create a defined basket of such materials and supplies, a maintenance schedule, and an administrative model, and cost it. This, in fact, had been done by Chambers and Parrish for Alaska and Illinois in the early 1980s.

For the Wyoming model, however, in the case of instructional materials and supplies, the current average amount was validated (and then adjusted somewhat) by consultation with professional expert groups. A more fully developed cost-based adequacy model would also require validation of operations and maintenance costs by, for example, a survey of the conditions of existing plant and equipment. Because school districts typically cut back first on necessary maintenance activities in response to fiscal stress, validation of these costs should be a priority for further study. Similarly, Guthrie et al. assumed that a statewide average ratio of administrative (district) overhead to other expenditures was a valid reflection of overhead costs. However, a study of Wyoming districts' administrative efficiency would also be necessary to gain greater confidence that current average expenditures reflect actual costs. The manner in which these personnel and nonpersonnel quantities and costs were allocated for a prototypical model is displayed in Tables 7-2 through 7-4.

To recapitulate, following (while modifying) a method first developed by Chambers and Parrish in the early 1980s for establishing appropriate resource levels in Alaska and Illinois, Guthrie et al. designed an education system for Wyoming by positing absolute quantities of classroom and resource teachers, aides, support staff, supplies and materials, operations and maintenance, school administrators, and district administrative overhead deemed by Wyoming professional educators (and supported by national research) to be sufficient to provide an adequate education (in Wyoming terms, a legislatively determined "basket of educational goods") to Wyoming children. In the case of some of these inputs, however, necessary quantities were estimated by utilizing existing expenditures because there was insufficient time to fully investigate the adequacy of resource quantities or the efficiency with which they are currently used. Once the resource quantities were specified, prices were attached to each input. In the case of teachers and other professionals, a model compensation level was established by taking into account labor market competition for college-educated labor, relative compensation levels in surrounding states, and professional opinion about compensation levels necessary to attract teachers of sufficient quality to deliver the "basket." In the case of most other inputs, prices were attached to the model by assuming that actual prices paid were market-determined and therefore reflected actual costs.

These procedures resulted in a basic per-pupil cost of an adequate Wyoming education of about $6,580 (for 1995-96), excluding capital expenditures.[11] It was the recommendation of the Wyoming consultant team, as well as the policy of the state, that this Wyoming per-pupil cost be distributed as a "block grant" to Wyoming school districts. By constructing prototypical models, Guthrie et al. determined that an adequate education could be delivered to Wyoming children by utilizing these specific quantities and combinations of resources, and it was the consultants' professional judgment that these quantities and combinations of resources were probably the best way to deliver the basket of educational goods. However, Guthrie et al. and the state also recognized that there may be other equally effective resource strategies that might deliver the basket. Permitting school districts to deploy resources as they see fit not only preserves the possibility that school districts may develop equally, or even more effective delivery systems, but also preserves a Wyoming tradition of local control in education, which is a political value that Wyoming wishes to maximize for its own sake. Therefore, while the prototypical model cost is calculated utilizing, for elementary schools for example, an average class size of 16 and an average teacher compensation cost of $41,433, districts may pay teachers more or less in compensation, offsetting these choices by increasing or decreasing class sizes or by trading salaries for benefits. While the model implies a recommendation that special needs children be integrated in regular classrooms where possible, districts can use the block of resources granted to them to increase regular class sizes in order to fund more individualized instruction for special needs children (except to the extent, of course, that this option is limited by federal law, as in the case of special education).

ADJUSTING ADEQUACY FOR PUPIL, SCHOOL, AND REGIONAL CHARACTERISTICS

Once the Guthrie team had calculated a basic per-pupil block grant dollar amount for Wyoming districts, individual district circumstances required further adjustments in order to achieve true adequacy.

Regional Cost Differences

In the most important respect (professional salaries), the model's cost is based on prices in one metropolitan corridor (Laramie-Cheyenne), chosen because these communities have more competitive professional labor markets than elsewhere in the state. In other respects, model costs are based on statewide average prices.

Yet the per-pupil costs so derived may not be applicable everywhere in the state, because the real costs of delivering the basket may vary from place to place. Therefore, a regional cost index must be applied to the model per-pupil amount before revenues are distributed to districts.

If Wyoming had fully developed competitive markets throughout the state, Guthrie et al. would have recommended that this index be based primarily (to the extent of professionals' relative importance in the model) on professional salary relationships across the state. If the salaries of managers, accountants, engineers, and other professionals with college degrees are consistently higher in one of the state's communities, it should be expected that a teacher of comparable quality would be proportionally more expensive to attract and retain in that community. And the revenues to a school district in that community should then be adjusted to reflect that higher cost of professionals, in proportion to their relative importance in the prototypical model.

This approach was not available, however, because there are few Wyoming communities with professional labor markets. In other states, where developed professional labor markets are more widespread, the approach may still not be available because data are generally unavailable on salaries by community and by occupation.[12]

Because relative data on professional wages were not available, the Guthrie team could not estimate what it should cost to hire a teacher in one community, relative to another. As a second-best alternative, therefore, an attempt was made to determine what it would cost districts to provide teachers with comparable standards of living in different communities. And because there is no direct measure available of standards of living, a third-best alternative was attempted: How can districts provide teachers with an ability to purchase a comparable market basket of goods and services? A cross-sectional consumer price index was needed to make these comparisons.

Fortunately, the state of Wyoming had in existence an official consumer price survey, designed for the purpose of specifying different poverty lines in different communities so that the state could forgive property taxes for homeowners whose incomes were below the poverty line. This survey, conducted every 6 months (and using product and service weights adapted from the Consumer Price Survey [Bureau of Labor Statistics, 1997]), resulted in a Wyoming Cost of Living Index (WCLI) which provided index numbers that could be applied to each school district in the state.

Guthrie et al. proposed two controversial modifications to this WCLI before applying it to model per-pupil district allocations. First, medical care prices were eliminated from the index (and the remaining items were reweighted). This is because (1) the recommended cost-based school financing model fully funded health insurance as a benefit for school district employees; (2) insurance company premiums, which reimburse the bulk of employee health care consumption, did not vary from region to region within Wyoming; and (3) many Wyoming districts were too small for insurers to adjust premiums for regionally affected experience. (The Bureau of Labor Statistics Consumer Price Survey prices only the administrative costs of insurance companies, and treats all medical care as though it were directly purchased by consumers without intermediaries.) Therefore, there was no reason to increase (decrease) a school district's block grant because medical care prices in its community were higher (lower) than elsewhere, since the prices teachers faced would be relatively unaffected; teachers, if fully insured, would have as a relatively small share of their health care consumption the cost of deductibles, copayments, and other incidental payments that would be paid at prevailing community prices. The consultants' judgment was that the lesser inaccuracy was introduced by eliminating the medical care component than by including it.

The second controversial modification was the failure to include the full cost of "housing" in the price index used to adjust education expenditures. Rent of shelter (or the rental equivalence of home ownership, or in Wyoming, mobile home ownership) represents a relatively large weight in consumer price indices. Nonetheless, this component was eliminated because it was felt that regional differences in rental prices primarily reflected differences in regional amenities, not differences in amortized costs of construction. This was one of the most difficult decisions to explain to the satisfaction of Wyoming policymakers, because it made common sense to many of them that if it costs more to rent housing in a community, a school district should compensate teachers for these higher housing prices.

In Wyoming, the problem was reflected most starkly in the community of Jackson, located in Teton County, one of the nation's most beautiful resorts. Housing prices in Jackson are much higher than elsewhere in the state: with housing prices included, the Teton school district would have had an index number of 134.4; without rental housing equivalence prices, its index number was 117.9 (with Laramie-Cheyenne = 100, no other district had a with-housing index number higher than 107.1). Teton school district administrators complained that the high price of housing made it difficult if not impossible for them to hire and retain teachers, that teachers accepted positions only to quit after finding they could obtain housing only in trailer camps far away, and that only a regional cost adjustment that fully compensated the district for the higher housing prices its employees must pay would permit Teton to compete fairly with other districts for teachers.

In response to this challenge, Guthrie et al. reviewed Teton school district data. To their surprise, they found that, with salaries not significantly higher than those paid elsewhere in the state, Teton had a lower teacher turnover rate than was typical in Wyoming. Remarkably, while Teton had experienced more rapid enrollment growth than the state as whole in recent years, the Teton district had a smaller percentage of junior teachers than the statewide average. Guthrie et al. have no firm explanation for these phenomena, but the possibility remains that the amenities of this community are so strong that they overcome the high costs of housing. Because prices generally are higher in Teton, even with rental housing removed from the WCLI, Teton will receive a geographic cost adjustment from the Guthrie et al. model that will entitle the district to about 20 percent more revenue than the typical Wyoming district will receive (compared to 34.4 percent more if calculated with rental prices included in the index). The Guthrie team remains concerned that this 20 percent bonus will further enhance Teton's ability to attract and retain teachers, and that the imprecision of this method of calculating geographic cost adjustments will have the perverse result of increasing the inequality of real resources available to Wyoming districts. This, however, is the opposite of the concern most frequently expressed by Wyoming policymakers who instinctively feel that Teton teachers should be fully compensated for higher prices in their community. The Guthrie et al. recommendation, however, was adopted by the legislature.

Four other states (Colorado, Florida, Ohio, and Texas) presently distribute revenues to school districts after adjusting these revenues for estimated differences in geographic costs. Each utilizes a different method for calculating the adjustment, based on the state's geographic characteristics and data availability (Rothstein and Smith, 1997). However, nowhere, to our knowledge, has a state undertaken a systematic study of teacher quality to determine whether a geographic cost adjustment succeeds in equalizing resources available to students. This is a high priority for future research.

Adjustment For Inflation

Guthrie et al.'s calculation of prototypical model costs in Wyoming was based on data in the year prior to the model's implementation. For the model's recommendations to reflect the actual costs of adequacy in future appropriations for K-12 education, the legislature must adjust each of the inputs in the model for inflation.

The WCLI could be used for this purpose as well, but Guthrie et al. recommended against this use, for two reasons. First, since William Baumol first explained the concept of the "cost disease" in labor intensive services, it has been widely accepted that school input inflation proceeds at a different rate from consumer price inflation (Baumol, 1967; Baumol et al., 1991; Rothstein and Miles, 1995). While it may not be the case in every year, school inflation will generally be more rapid than consumer price inflation, because manufactured products benefiting from technological improvements have greater relative importance in consumer purchases than in school purchases. On the other hand, a high proportion of school purchases are for professional labor, where opportunities for technological improvement are relatively limited (although not nonexistent, as attested by the use of aides for the less professional portions of teacher workloads during the last 20 years).

Secondly, the WCLI would be unsuitable even if consumer price inflation were applicable to schools. This is because the WCLI, administered by a small Wyoming administrative department, is relatively unsophisticated in its price gathering. This is inevitable, given the budget and professional resources available to the state. Any consumer price survey requires numerous decisions about quality change and substitutability that are subject to error. In the case of a geographic cost adjustment, the WCLI provided the only available data, and so its use was recommended for this purpose. However, more sophisticated alternatives are available for estimating inflation.

Guthrie et al. recommended that inflation in the professional compensation component of the prototypical model be estimated by using the Bureau of Labor Statistics Employment Cost Index (ECI) components for professional/technical and managerial labor; that inflation in nonprofessional compensation be estimated by using the balance of the ECI; and that inflation in the nonpersonnel items be estimated by using a regional consumer price index produced by the Bureau of Labor Statistics. As an alternative method of estimating non-personnel inflation, Guthrie et al. recommended that Wyoming explore the possibility of contracting with Research Associates of Washington to produce a nonpersonnel school input index tailored to the particular needs of the Wyoming model. Research Associates (Kent Halstead, principal) annually publishes a school price index comprised of separate indices for each input weighted by that input's relative importance in a 1975 base year (Research Associates of Washington, 1997). Guthrie et al. recommended not using this index for anything other than the limited purpose described (purchases of nonpersonnel goods and services) because of the dangers implicit in estimating actual inflation in the price of a service (i.e., teachers) when the prices are based on actual payments in a noncompetitive market.

One reasonably can speculate regarding the extent to which Wyoming, as a state, represents anything but Wyoming. The state is among the nation's least populous. It has only 100,000 school children, a population which is stable to slightly declining. It has only 48 school districts. It has an unusual proportion of school children in remote and sparsely populated areas. We could go on and describe more unique characteristics of Wyoming. However, we make no case that Wyoming or, for that matter, any state, is representative of the nation as a whole. In fact, even among heavily populated, mixed economy states such as California, Illinois, or Texas, the intense developmental and political history of school finance renders each a policy-unique situation. Rather, our point is that the features of the school finance system designed for Wyoming anticipate most of the characteristics and conditions that analysts and researchers will face in other states. Wyoming had to develop a "basket of expected educational outcomes," a prototypical delivery system had to be designed, the characteristics of district and pupil variation had to be taken into account, and cost adjustments of all kinds had to be undertaken. In other state situations, solutions may be different depending upon state characteristics. These solutions will almost inevitably be more complex in more diversified states. We contend, nevertheless, that the dimensions on which solutions are sought are likely to be similar to the dimensions pursued in Wyoming.

UNSOLVED MYSTERIES

Attempting to define an "adequate' education and thereafter to translate such a definition into the reality of school finance has begun. No doubt, the beginning efforts described in the above sections of this chapter will appear unusually crude to twenty-first century education and finance experts who plow this ground. However, a contemporary decisionmaker, be it a judge or elected official, should understand fully that this translation is still a primitive endeavor, still far more of an art than a science. We do not yet have full consensus on the objectives of the education system, and in the unlikely event we ever do, we do not know how to measure our progress toward those objectives with complete precision. Further yet, we are unsure of a foolproof technology that will enable a school to instruct in a manner which will result in a guarantee of desired student performance. Finally, we are woefully short of the data regarding spending which will enable us accurately to assign costs to whatever instructional models emerge as sensible.

While most Americans agree that public schools should provide students with knowledge and skills, our understanding of educational technology is undeveloped when it comes to linking necessary resource inputs to desired outcomes. Consider these issues, touched on very briefly in previous pages, to which we presently have few satisfying answers:

• Defining adequacy must entail specifying resource levels minimally necessary to produce desired outcomes, not a level that wastes resources unneeded for this production. Yet even if we could determine resource levels that generally produce adequate outcomes, this level may be too generous if the resources are utilized inefficiently. For example, recent results from the Third International Mathematics and Science Study (TIMSS) reveal that American 4th graders perform, on average, at least as well, if not better than 4th graders in most comparable nations. The International Association for the Evaluation of Educational Achievement (IEA) confirmed in 1991 that American 9-year-olds read better than 9-year-olds almost anywhere in the world. But, according to the TIMSS, American 8th and 12th graders perform increasingly worse than their counterparts in math, and the IEA shows that American 17-year-olds' reading is also not up to par. Is this condition because, on average, we provide adequate resources to teach math and reading to 4th graders, but the resources for later grades are inadequate? Or is it because, with adequate resources, our pedagogies and curricular designs for 4th graders are superior to those for older children? Or is it neither of these, and simply a case of the TIMSS being flawed, for example, being better aligned with the outcomes we seek in the 4th grade than the outcomes we seek for older children?

• Do we assume, in funding an adequate education, that the level of resources necessary to produce adequate outcomes in reading are the same as those necessary to produce adequate outcomes in math? Are they the same as those necessary to produce an adequate quality of "social ethics to facilitate compatibility with others in this society"?

• To what extent should schools be held responsible for the specified outcomes, as opposed to other institutions? Educational policymakers have become aware of the need for more school resources to produce acceptable outcomes for children from economically disadvantaged families, but this awareness is still unsophisticated. Almost entirely unexplored are the relationships between school outcomes and the economic institutions that provide school graduates with economic opportunity. These relationships cannot be ignored if courts wish to require schools to enable graduates "to compete favorably with their counterparts in surrounding states." The competitiveness of a state's high school graduates is affected not only by these graduates' academic, social, and citizenship skills, but also by the state's economic infrastructure. A state with better-educated students may have more difficulty than surrounding states in attracting job-generating investments because its highways are inadequate or even because its climate does not provide the amenities sought by highly educated workers. Clearly, the adequacy of schools' resources cannot be measured solely, or even primarily, by the competitiveness of state industry, although educational preparation for work cannot be ignored either.

• Public, and even scholarly debate about "standards" (i.e., adequate outcomes) suffers from a confusion between minimum and average goals, and between relative and absolute goals. This confusion becomes especially important if "adequacy" is defined as the resources necessary to produce "average" outcomes. Yet because it is so much easier to specify "adequacy" in norm-referenced terms, relatively little consensus exists regarding criterion-referenced adequacy, even in the basic skills of reading and math.

These problems make it difficult, if not impossible, to derive an understanding of resource adequacy from the outcomes we posit as minimally acceptable. The following examples illustrate why our understanding of outcomes is still too primitive to permit inferences about resource adequacy from this understanding. President Clinton has stated a standard that "all" 9-year-olds should read at a 4th-grade level. But a "4th-grade level" is the mean for today's 4th graders. There is invariably a distribution around this mean, so that if resources are adequate for the average 4th grader to read at a 4th-grade level, then these resources will still generate some 4th graders reading at the average level for 2nd graders, while some 4th graders will read at the average level for 6th graders. If what President Clinton means is literally that all 4th graders should read at least as well as the average 4th grader reads today, this probably means, given the inevitable distribution of outcomes, that the average 4th grader will have to read as well as today's average 6th or 7th grader (and even this standard will leave some 4th grade students, at the far left tail of the distribution, not meeting the minimum standard of today's average 4th grade level.)

Norm-referenced standards, therefore, are ultimately disconcerting for calculation of adequate resources. And the efforts of the education policy community to develop criterion-referenced standards, which in principle are necessary if resource levels are to be attached, are still relatively undeveloped. Great attention has been paid to the analyses of NAEP scores by the National Assessment Governing Board (NAGB). According to NAGB, for example, in reading, only 30 percent of 4th and 8th graders, and only 36 percent of 12th graders are "proficient." In math, only 21 percent of 4th graders, 24 percent of 8th graders, and only 16 percent of 12th graders are "proficient." Yet authoritative analyses of the NAGB performance standards have found them technically flawed and misleading. This makes them unsuitable for links to resource levels. The General Accounting Office found that considerably more students were probably "proficient" than the NAGB standards implied (U.S. General Accounting Office, 1993:31-32). A National Academy of Education panel concluded that the procedures by which these achievement levels had been established were "fundamentally flawed" and were "subject to large biases" and the achievement levels by which few American students had been judged proficient were set "unreasonably high" (National Academy of Education, 1993:xxii,148). The panel recommended to the Department of Education that NAEP Achievement Levels should not be used. In fact, the panel stated, continued use of these standards could set back the cause of education reform because it would harm the credibility of the NAEP test itself.[13]

The logical problems inherent in attempting to develop an outcome standard from norm-referenced rather than criterion-referenced assessments are also implicit in Richard Murnane and Frank Levy's widely cited proposal that our standard be the ability to do math and to read at a 9th-grade level, among other competencies (Murnane and Levy, 1996). By definition, however, the average 9th-grade student now does math and reads at a 9th-grade level. What Murnane and Levy must mean is that schools must be reformed so that *no* high school graduate or dropout reads below the level that is now average for 9th graders. They cannot mean this in a literal sense, but unspecified is precisely what the left tail of the distribution must look like to be acceptable.

In the absence of an inventory of occupational projections and related academic requirements, can outcome standards be inferred statistically? We think not. Card and Krueger have shown that investment in education is positively related to earnings (Card and Krueger, 1996), but their approach cannot deduce an adequate level of earnings from which correlated academic achievement can be observed. As noted, absolute earnings levels are related to a wide variety of macroeconomic and labor market policies, of which educational investment is only one. While we know that better-educated adults have higher earnings than less-educated adults, this may be partly because education is used as a sorting mechanism.

These difficulties in defining adequate outcomes are logically prior to the challenges of attaching input prices to these outcomes. Yet we know very little about how to address them. Meanwhile courts, legislators, and the public will continue to demand that we "put the cart before the horse" and estimate the price of adequacy before we truly know what it is.

None of the preceding is intended to choke debate or impede the efforts of policymakers and analysts to design adequacy-based systems of school finance. Rather, these caveats are extended to those who might otherwise believe that determining what is adequate is a simple task of finding an able cost accountant and thereafter placing the numbers in the correct columns.

NOTES

1.   As we note below, however, the second approach has been utilized without controls for student background characteristics. And one statistical analysis illustrative of the first approach (Duncombe and Yinger, Chapter 8 in this volume) utilizes a "voter preference/tax price" model to estimate adequate outcomes, without reference to tests or other measures of student performance.

2.   How substantial are these differences? Let's make the simplistic assumption that the only important resources in education were teachers and other classroom inputs. Then, if a typical district in Wisconsin required resources for an adequate education sufficient to fund class sizes of 20, and if Reschovsky-Imazeki's analysis were correct, then Chambers's adjustment would give Milwaukee suburbs 28 percent more resources than needed, or resources sufficient for class sizes of about 14 students. If Chambers's analysis were correct, then Reschovsky-Imazeki's adjustment would give Milwaukee suburbs 28 percent fewer resources than needed, and would only give these suburbs resources sufficient for class sizes of about 26 students.

3.   This methodology, based on an empirical search for districts with adequate outcomes, is the implicit theory of the New Jersey Supreme Court in *Abbott v. Burke* (1990), in many ways the most radical of state court adequacy decisions. The Court's reasoning suggested a requirement that (poor) districts with low outcomes (including test scores) must be able to achieve high outcomes by spending what (rich) districts with high outcomes spend.

4.   Personal communication, R. Greenwald, March 19-20, 1998.

5.   Although the Augenblick method in Ohio and the Cooper method in

Illinois adjust the calculation of adequate resources to be distributed to high-poverty districts, the adequacy level itself is initially calculated in both methods by observing high-scoring districts in an investigation where all districts, regardless of student poverty intensity, must score at the same proficiency level, on average, to be considered.

6. There is too great a probability of unusual circumstances to justify inclusion beyond these distribution points.

7. Intra-state costs adjustments were the most controversial of consultants' recommendations, and citizens, legislators, and the court were eventually persuaded of the appropriateness of these adjustments only because they did not rely on mathematical manipulations beyond the skill of policymakers.

8. Wyoming districts were subsequently reduced to a statewide total of 48, as a consequence of district consolidation.

9. In 1995 in Wyoming, 11 percent of children 5-17 years old were in poverty (National Center for Education Statistics, 1998: Table 20), and fewer than 2 percent were identified as having Limited English Proficiency (U.S. Commission on Civil Rights, 1997: Table 2.3). A 150 percent cut-off might not be appropriate in other states where the base percentages of at-risk students were higher.

10. And, as Andrew Porter (1995) has noted, as performance standards become more sophisticated, it will become more difficult to separate them from "opportunity to learn" standards, even in high-performing districts. It is one thing to say that a state can spend resources however it wishes, provided its scores on standardized tests are adequate. However, it will not be so simple for a state to separate a requirement for adequate performance (assessed with portfolios and projects) from the way resources are arrayed to deliver instruction to fulfill such standards. "The more structure required of a portfolio, the more intrusive the portfolio becomes" (p. 23).

11. Because in each state, different expenditures were excluded for consideration from an adequacy model, and because of inter-state cost differences, this adequacy level cannot be compared to the $3,930 Augenblick deems adequate in Ohio, or the $4,225 Cooper deems adequate in Illinois, or to whatever amount is eventually deemed adequate in Mississippi, as calculated by an inferential model; or to the $6,331 Reschovsky and Imazeki deem adequate in Wisconsin, as calculated by the statistical model. (Duncombe and Yinger do not state a dollar figure for adequacy in New York, but presumably it would be whatever the district with an index number of 100 spends.)

12. In many states, the only relative wage data available are those required to be reported by the U.S. Department of Labor, and these data display average wages by industry sector, but not by occupation. Thus, reported wages in the finance sector aggregate wages of banking executives, tellers, and janitors, for example. In some states, where broad regional occupational wage data are available, they are not provided at the community level, do not include total com-

pensation (including benefits), and mix average wages of full-time, part-time, and seasonal employees.

13.   As this chapter went to press, a panel of the National Research Council of the National Academy of Sciences issued a report reiterating these earlier conclusions of the GAO and NAE. According to the NRC report, cutoff points between NAEP achievement levels are "consistently set too high," leading the public to draw inappropriate conclusions about America's schools. "The current process for setting achievement levels is fundamentally flawed," the panel states. "If left unaddressed, NAEP's effectiveness and future prospects for success will be undermined" (Pellegrino et al., 1998:167 and Executive Summary).

REFERENCES

Augenblick, J.
   1997   *Recommendations for a Base Figure and Pupil-Weighted Adjustments to the Base Figure for Use in a New School Finance System in Ohio.* Report presented to the School Funding Task Force, Ohio Department of Education.
Augenblick, J., and J. Myers
   1994   *Determining Base Cost for State School Funding Systems.* Denver, CO: Education Commission of the States Issuegram.
Augenblick, J., K. Alexander, and J.W. Guthrie
   1995   *Report of the Panel of Experts: Proposals for the Elimination of Wealth Based Disparities in Education.* Report submitted by Ohio Chief State School Officer T. Sanders to the Ohio State Legislature.
Augenblick, J.G., J.L. Myers, and A.B. Anderson
   1997   Equity and adequacy in school funding. In *The Future of Children: Financing Schools.* 7(3):63-78.
Baumol, W.
   1967   Macroeconomics of unbalanced growth: The anatomy of urban crisis. *American Economic Review* 57:415-426.
Baumol, W., S.A. Batey Blackman, and E.N. Wolff
   1991   *Productivity and American Leadership.* Cambridge, MA: Massachusetts Institute of Technology.
Benson, C.
   1978   *The Economics of Public Education.* Boston: Houghton Mifflin.
Bureau of Labor Statistics
   1997   Consumer Price Index homepage. In *Bureau of Labor Statistics* homepage [Online]. Available: http://stats.bls.gov/cpihome.htm. [June 16, 1998].
Card, D., and A. Krueger
   1996   Labor market effects of school quality: Theory and evidence. Pp. 97-140 in *Does Money Matter? The Effect of School Resources on Student Achievement and Adult Success,* G. Burtless, ed. Washington, DC: The Brookings Institution.
Carlson, D.
   1996   *Adequate Yearly Progress: Issues and Strategies.* Washington, DC: Council of Chief State School Officers.
The Carnegie Foundation for the Advancement of Teaching
   1992   *School Choice.* Princeton, NJ: The Carnegie Foundation for the Advancement of Teaching.

Catchpole, J.
  1996   *Accreditation Guide, November, 1995.* Cheyenne, WY: Wyoming Department of Education.
Chambers, J.
  1995   *Public School Teacher Cost Differences Across the United States.* NCES Working Paper 95-758. Washington, DC: U.S. Department of Education, Office of Educational Research and Improvement.
  1998   *Geographic Variations in Public Schools' Costs.* NCES Working Paper 98-04. Washington, DC: U.S. Department of Education, Office of Educational Research and Improvement.
Chambers, J., and T. Parrish
  1994   State level education finance. In *Cost Analysis for Education Decisions: Methods and Examples. Advances in Educational Productivity, Volume 4*, W.S. Barnett, ed. Greenwich, CT: JAI Press.
Clune, W.H.
  1994   The shift from equity to adequacy in school finance. *Educational Policy* 8(4):376-394.
Coons, J.E., W.H. Clune, and S.D. Sugarman
  1970   *Private Wealth and Public Education.* Cambridge, MA: Harvard University Press.
Cubberley, E.P.
  1919a   *Public Education in the United States; A Study and Interpretation of American Educational History; An Introductory Textbook Dealing with the Larger Problems of Present-Day Education in the Light of Their Historical Development.* New York: Houghton Mifflin.
  1919b   *State and County School Administration.* New York: Macmillan.
Downes, T.A., and T.F. Pogue
  1994   Adjusting school aid formulas for the higher cost of educating disadvantaged students. *National Tax Journal* 47(1):89-110.
Duncombe, W., J. Ruggiero, and J. Yinger
  1996   Alternative approaches to measuring the cost of education. Pp. 327-356 in *Holding Schools Accountable*, H.F. Ladd, ed. Washington, DC: The Brookings Institution.
Fashola, O.S., and R.E. Slavin
  1998   Schoolwide reform models: What works? *Phi Delta Kappan* 79(5):370-379.
Grissmer, D.W., S.N. Kirby, M. Berends, and S. Williamson
  1994   *Student Achievement and the Changing American Family.* Santa Monica, CA: RAND.
Guthrie, J.W.
  1979   Organization scale and school success. *Educational Evaluation and Policy Analysis* 1(1):17-27.
Guthrie, J.W., H.M. Levin, and R.S. Stout
  1970   *Schools and Inequality.* Cambridge, MA: Massachusetts Institute of Technology Press.
Guthrie, J.W., G.C. Hayward, J.R. Smith, R. Rothstein, R.W. Bennett, J.E. Koppich, E. Bowman, L. DeLapp, B. Brandes, and S. Clark
  1997   *A Proposed Cost-Based Block Grant Model for Wyoming School Finance.* Sacramento, CA: Management Analyst & Planning Associates, L.L.C.
Hickrod, G. Alan, Larry McNeal, Robert Lenz, Paul Minorini, and Linda Grady
  1997   Status of school finance constitutional litigation, 'The boxscore': In *Illinois State University, College of Education* [Online]. Available: http://www.coe.ilstu.edu/boxscore.htm [April 25, 1997].
Johns, R.L., E.L. Morphet, and K. Alexander
  1983   *The Economics and Financing of Education.* Englewood Cliffs, NJ: Prentice-Hall.

King, J.A.
    1994   Meeting the educational needs of at-risk students: A cost analysis of three models. *Educational Evaluation and Policy Analysis* 16(1):1-20.
Kirst, M., and W.I. Garms
    1980   The political environment of school finance policy in the 1980's. Pp. 47-78 in *School Finance Policies and Practices: The 1980's A Decade of Conflict.* Cambridge, MA: Ballinger.
Krueger, A.B.
    1997   Experimental Estimates of Education Production Functions. Working Paper #379. Princeton, NJ: Princeton University, Industrial Relations Section.
Ladd, H.F., and J. Yinger.
    1994   The case for equalizing aid. *National Tax Journal* 47:211-224.
Mishel, L., and R. Rothstein.
    1997   *Measurement Issues in Adjusting School Spending Across Time and Place.* Paper presented at the Annual Data Conference of the National Center for Education Statistics, Washington, DC, July. Washington, DC: Economic Policy Institute.
Mort, P.R., W.C. Reusser, and J.W. Polley
    1960   *Public School Finance: Its Background, Structure, and Operation.* New York: McGraw-Hill.
Mosteller, F.
    1995   *The Tennessee Study of Class Size in the Early School Grades.* Somerville, MA: American Academy of Arts and Sciences
Murnane, R.J., and F. Levy
    1996   *Teaching the New Basic Skills.* New York: Martin Kessler Books, The Free Press.
National Academy of Education
    1993   *Setting Performance Standards for Student Achievement. A Report of the National Academy of Education Panel on the Evaluation of the NAEP Trial State Assessments: An Evaluation of the 1992 Achievement Levels.* Stanford, CA: National Academy of Education.
National Center for Education Statistics
    1998   *Digest of Education Statistics 1997.* NCES 98-015. Washington, DC: U.S. Department of Education, Office of Educational Research and Improvement.
Odden, A.
    1997   *How to Rethink School Budgets to Support School Transformation.* Arlington, VA: New American Schools.
Odden, A., and C. Busch
    1998   *Financing Schools for High Performance. Strategies for Improving the Use of Educational Resources.* San Francisco: Jossey-Bass.
Olson, L., and C. Hendrie
    1998   Pathways to progress. In *Quality Counts 98. The Urban Challenge. Public Education in the 50 States.* In collaboration with the Pew Charitable Trusts. *Education Week*, January 8.
Pellegrino, J.W., L. R. Jones, and K. J. Mitchell
    1998   *Grading the Nation's Report Card: Evaluating NAEP and Transforming the Assessment of Educational Progress.* National Research Council. Washington, DC: National Academy Press.
Porter, A.C.
    1993   Defining and measuring opportunity to learn. Pp. 33-72 in *The Debate on Opportunity to Learn Standards: Supporting Works,* S.I. Traiman, ed. Washington, DC: National Governors Association.

Porter, A.
  1995   The uses and misuses of opportunity-to-learn standards. *Educational Researcher* Jan./
          Feb.:21-27.
Protheroe, N.
  1997   ERS—Local school budget profile study. *School Business Affairs* 63(10):42-49.
Reschovsky, A., and J. Imazeki
  1998   The development of school finance formulas to guarantee the provision of adequate edu-
          cation to low income students. Pp. 121-148 in *Developments in School Finance 1997*.
          Washington, DC: U.S. Department of Education, National Center for Education Statis-
          tics.
Research Associates of Washington
  1997   *Inflation Measures for Schools, Colleges, & Libraries. 1997 Update*. Arlington, VA:
          Research Associates of Washington.
Rothstein, R.
  1998   *A Race to the Top? How States Have Hustled to Spend More on Schools: Some New
          Ways of Looking at Data on School Spending, 1970-1995*. Paper presented at the annual
          conference of the American Education Finance Association, Mobile, AL, March.
Rothstein, R., and K.H. Miles
  1995   *Where's the Money Gone: Changes in the Level and Composition of Education Spend-
          ing*. Washington, DC: Economic Policy Institute.
Rothstein, R., and J.R. Smith
  1997   *Adjusting Oregon Education Expenditures for Regional Cost Differences: A Feasibility
          Study*. Sacramento, CA: Management Analysis & Planning Associates, L.L.C.
U.S. Commission on Civil Rights
  1997   *Equal Educational Opportunity and Nondiscrimination for Students with Limited English
          Proficiency: Federal Enforcement of Title VI and Lau v. Nichols. Equal Educational
          Opportunity Project Series, Volume III*. USGPO 1997-431-645/80294. Washington,
          DC: U.S. Government Printing Office.
U.S. General Accounting Office
  1993   *Educational Achievement Standards. NAGB's Approach Yields Misleading Interpreta-
          tions*. GAO/PEMD 93-12. Washington, DC: General Accounting Office.
Wells, A.S.
  1993   The sociology of school choice: Why some win and others lose in the educational market-
          place. Pp. 29-48 in *School Choice: Examining the Evidence*, M.E. Rasell and R. Rothstein,
          eds. Washington, DC: Economic Policy Institute.
Willms, J.D., and F.H. Echols
  1993   The Scottish experience of parental school choice. Pp. 49-68 in *School Choice: Examin-
          ing the Evidence*, M.E. Rasell and R. Rothstein, eds. Washington, DC: Economic Policy
          Institute.
Wise, A.
  1968   *Rich Schools, Poor Schools: The Promise of Equal Educational Opportunity*. Chicago:
          University of Chicago Press.

8

Performance Standards and Educational Cost Indexes: You Can't Have One Without the Other

William D. Duncombe and John M. Yinger

INTRODUCTION

Performance standards and educational adequacy have been at the center of recent debate on educational reform. Many states have implemented new performance standards, often based on student test scores, and a district's state aid is sometimes linked to its success in meeting the standards (Clotfelter and Ladd, 1996). National politicians have debated the merits of a nationwide testing program, which is a way to obtain comparable performance indicators across states. In addition, several state supreme courts have ruled that their state constitution requires a system enabling all school districts to reach an adequate performance level (see Minorini and Sugarman, Chapter 6 in this volume), and state aid programs can be used to provide all districts with the funds they need to reach a performance level that is thought to be adequate—or some higher standard.

Performance standards are designed to encourage more effective educational practices, particularly in school districts that are currently not performing well, by holding school districts accountable. The trouble is that a district's performance is influenced not only by the actions of its administrators and teachers but also by factors outside of its control, such as the nature of its student body. A recent article in *The New York Times* expresses this concern very clearly. In a discussion of report cards and school rankings, now used in 35 states, this article points out that "because such rankings are often based exclusively on test scores, which give only a partial snapshot of a school's performance, some educators worry that schools may be unfairly blackballed, especially those with high populations of poor children" (Steinberg, 1998).

Thus, a focus on performance is inevitably unfair unless it can somehow account for the impact on performance of factors that are outside the control of school officials. Without such an accounting, some schools get credit for favorable conditions that were not of their making and other schools get blamed for unfavorable conditions over which they have no control. In order to be fair, school report cards and performance-based state aid systems must distinguish between poor performance based on external factors and poor performance based on school inefficiency.

Similarly, a state aid program that brings districts up to a minimum spending level, which is called a foundation program, cannot ensure that a performance-based adequacy standard will be reached in all districts unless this spending level is much higher than the amount a typical district needs to reach an adequate performance. This problem reflects the fact that school district performance is also influenced by the cost of education, which varies widely from district to district based on wage rates, student characteristics, and other factors that are outside the control of district officials. Existing state aid formulas either ignore these factors altogether or else use ad hoc corrections, such as "weighted pupil" counts, that account for them only partially at best. As a result, a foundation program that provides enough revenue for an average district to meet an adequate performance standard leaves a high-cost district short, often far short, of the revenue it needs.

In this chapter, we explain in detail why a performance standard, whether it is set at a level that defines an adequate education or at some other level, must go hand in hand with an educational cost index; we discuss the alternative methods for estimating educational cost indexes, and show how high-cost districts can be brought up to a performance-based state adequacy standard by incorporating these costs indexes into a foundation aid program. Our analysis is illustrated with data from New York State. We find, for example, that the large central city districts must spend two to three times as much as the average district to reach the same performance standard.

THE CONCEPTUAL FOUNDATIONS OF
EDUCATIONAL COST INDEXES

An educational cost index is designed to measure how much a school district would have to spend, relative to the average district, to obtain any given performance target. Some scholars, including Guthrie and Rothstein (see Chapter 7 in this volume), have used the term "cost index" to refer only to differences in input prices across districts. However, we use the term to refer to a comprehensive accounting of the reasons why some districts must spend more than others to achieve any given performance level—a definition that, as we will show, involves far more than just input prices. After an introductory example, this section explains the relationship between educational performance measures and cost indexes, and discusses, in general terms, the factors that influence educational costs. The following section reviews alternative methods for estimating educational cost indexes.

An Introductory Example

Before turning to educational performance and costs, it may prove helpful to explore an example from everyday life that involves the same concepts. The example is the service of providing comfortable shelter. A natural measure of performance for this service is the indoor temperature. This is not, of course, the only dimension of comfort. In some contexts, one might want to know about the extent to which rain leaks in; in others, humidity might be a concern. As with any performance standard, however, some simplification is necessary, and the indoor temperature appears to measure the dimension of comfort that is of most concern to most people in this country. Thus, we will focus on a temperature as a measure of performance.

Now suppose some national consumer group interested in comfortable shelter sets a standard for adequate performance at 72 degrees. A natural question to ask is: How much would it cost to achieve this standard in different parts of the country? To answer this question, one must consider the technology with which comfort is provided. This technology is straightforward: a household must purchase various inputs, such as a furnace and natural gas and insulation, that can deliver or preserve heat or cold and thereby provide an indoor temperature that is different from the outdoor temperature. The impact of these inputs depends, of course, on the outdoor temperature, as well as on other environmental factors, such as the wind.

The cost of achieving the comfort standard therefore depends on two factors. First, it depends on the prices of inputs. The price of natural gas is not the same in all parts of the country, for example, and people in high-price places must pay more to obtain the same amount of natural gas. Second, it depends on the environment. During the winter, people in Minneapolis face much lower outdoor temperatures than do people in San Diego, so it costs them more to bring the indoor temperature up to the standard. To put it another way, people in Minneapolis must purchase more inputs to reach the standard. In another season (or for other cities), one obviously would have to consider the cost of bringing down the indoor temperature when the outdoor temperature is above 72 degrees. A comfort cost index that reflected only gas price differences could be developed, but it obviously would provide an incomplete accounting of costs because it would ignore the outdoor temperature.

It follows that a comprehensive comfort cost index must consider both the prices of inputs and the harshness of the environment. As we will see, these are exactly the factors at work in determining the cost of education.

The factors discussed so far are all outside a household's control; the same cannot be said for everything that influences comfort. Households may, for example, buy an inefficient furnace, use a relatively expensive type of fuel, neglect to have their furnace maintained properly, or neglect to install the proper weatherstripping. These decisions all affect how much a household spends to obtain comfort but they should not influence a measure of the cost of comfort, which, as we use the term, is based solely on factors outside a household's control.

This leads us to another concept, namely efficiency, which is the extent to which a household uses best-practice methods to achieve comfort. In some contexts, it may be helpful to measure inefficiency and to separate its impact on comfort spending from the effect of cost factors. However, it would be inappropriate to let household choices influence a cost index, so any method to obtain a cost index must be insulated from the effects of household choices, including those that determine efficiency.

The key question for our purposes is: How could one determine the cost of meeting the performance standard in various locations? One way to proceed would be to select a certain type of house with certain heating and insulation characteristics as a standard and then use engineering studies to determine the amount of fuel it would take to keep this house at 72 degrees under the average weather conditions that are experienced in each location. The cost of meeting the standard is the amount of fuel required multiplied by the cost of fuel in that location. This approach has the advantages that it directly accounts for household choices (by using a standard house) and that it can be based on extensive information on weather conditions. This approach also has the major disadvantage, however, that it requires a detailed engineering study that is usually not available.

An alternative approach, which is analogous to the educational cost indexes discussed below, is to gather information for a sample of locations on (1) average household fuel bills, (2) actual indoor temperatures obtained by households, (3) a few key measures of weather conditions, such as average temperature or heating degree days, (4) the cost of the main input, namely fuel, and (5) average household choices that might influence fuel efficiency, such as whether they maintain their furnace annually and whether they use the appropriate weather stripping. An analysis of this information using regression analysis, which is a standard statistical procedure, can then reveal the extent to which input costs and weather conditions affect spending for fuel, holding constant both actual temperatures and household choices. This analysis leads directly to a cost index, which is defined as the amount a household would have to spend in each location, relative to a household in the average location, to obtain a given indoor temperature, under the assumption that the household makes efficient choices about its heating/cooling system. If, for example, Minneapolis has a cost index of 200, households there would have to spend twice as much as households in the average city to obtain the same level of comfort. This approach is more abstract than the previous one in the sense that it does not consider all the details of heating technology, but it captures the main features of the problem and has the great advantage that it can be implemented with readily available data.

In combination, a comfort standard and a cost index reveal how much households in each community would have to spend to meet the standard, based on factors outside their control. In principle, this information also could be obtained from a production study conducted in each community, which would reveal the set of inputs needed to achieve the standard, along with information on each community's input prices. The regression approach provides the same information at much lower cost by determining how spending varies with input costs and environmental conditions, controlling for actual comfort outcomes.

Measuring Educational Performance

With education, as with home comfort, one cannot set a performance standard without selecting a way to measure performance. To put it another way, one cannot determine whether a school has met a performance standard unless its performance can be observed and measured. Policymakers may wish to avoid this choice, because selecting a standard is inevitably somewhat controversial. No set of performance standards can capture all aspects of learning, and schools may respond to specific standards by "teaching to the test" or otherwise shifting their resources to meet the standard at the expense of other legitimate objectives. Nevertheless, this choice cannot be avoided. Any policy to enhance school performance involves, either explicitly or implicitly, a specific performance measure. The trick is to select performance measures that are rich enough to capture success in a range of educational activities. For the most part, the selection of a performance measure is based on the judgement of politicians and educational policy officials, perhaps with some input from scholars. The most common measure is based on some kind of test score, such as an average elementary reading or math score. A dropout rate is another widely used measure at the high school level.

To set a performance standard, policymakers must select both a measure of performance and the level of performance school districts are expected to meet. For example, all school districts might be expected to achieve a certain average test score or to ensure that a certain percentage of their students score above some standard reference point on a certain test. Standards of this type can be set for a single indicator or for a set of indicators. For example, school districts might be expected to have a certain average test score and a certain graduation rate.

We have developed an alternative approach, which selects performance indicators on statistical grounds. In particular, this approach determines which performance indicators are valued by voters, as indicated by their correlation with property values and school spending. This approach, which is explained in detail in Duncombe et al. (1996) and Duncombe and Yinger (1997), results in an index of educational performance. This index is a weighted average of the performance indicators that are found to be statistically significant, where the weights reflect the value voters place on each indicator.[1] In the case of New York State, this approach leads to an educational performance index based on three performance indicators: the average share of students above the standard reference point on the 3rd- and 6th-grade Pupil Evaluation Program (PEP) tests for math and reading, the share of students who receive a more demanding Regents diploma (which requires passing a series of exams), and the graduation rate. These indicators reflect a wide range of school district activities, including both elementary and secondary teaching and programs designed to promote student retention, and reflect the degree of success at both the high and low ends of the student performance distribution.

Although these indicators are identified by an objective, statistically based procedure, they do not, of course, summarize all educational activities by a school district. Like all other approaches to measuring performance, this approach makes the problem manageable through some simplification. Moreover, this approach results in a performance yardstick, but it cannot determine the point on the yardstick that school districts should be expected to meet or that defines an adequate performance. As with other approaches, the selection of the performance target must be based on the judgment of public officials.

Separating Factors In and Outside the Control of School Officials

Either indirectly, as in the case of district report cards, or directly, as in the case of a performance-based aid system, performance standards are intended to boost a school district's incentive to use effective educational policies. The problem, however, is that actual performance is influenced not only by the decisions of school officials but also by factors outside their control. Thus, some districts find it easy to meet a standard even if they are very inefficient, whereas others find it impossible to meet a standard even if they are more efficient than other districts. It is neither fair nor effective for a state to reward districts that achieve high performance (or to punish districts that perform poorly) based on factors that are outside their control. A fairer approach is to reward districts that perform well despite external obstacles, such as concentrated poverty, and punish districts that do not perform well despite favorable circumstances.

The indoor-temperature example presented earlier may help to make this point because it explains how external factors work. Just as some communities face relatively high oil prices and harsh weather, which raise the cost of meeting any comfort standard, some school districts face relatively high input prices (such as teacher salaries) and relatively harsh educational environments, which raise the cost of meeting any educational performance standard. Thus, the key to removing external factors is to calculate an educational cost index; as we use the term, such an index measures the impact of input and environmental costs, not just input prices. This cost index plays a key role in public policy; it is not fair to expect a high-cost district to achieve the same performance as other districts unless it is given enough resources to compensate for high costs.

The Role of Input Prices

In the case of education, the most important input is teachers, so in constructing a cost index, it is vital to account for teachers' salaries. Secondary inputs, such as school facilities, also play a role in delivering education, but data on the prices of these inputs are generally not available. In some cases, data on administrators' salaries are available, but these salaries are so correlated with teachers' salaries that they add little to the analysis. Like almost all the literature, therefore, we will restrict our attention to the role of teachers' salaries.

A cost index is designed to measure the impact of factors outside the control of school officials. It is not appropriate, therefore, to directly use actual teachers' salaries in constructing a cost index because those salaries reflect both the generosity of the school district, a factor over which they have control, and the underlying labor market conditions, which cannot be influenced by school officials. A cost index should reflect the fact that some school districts are located in high-wage labor markets, where they must pay high salaries to attract people away from other school districts or away from the private market; and it should reflect the fact that the external conditions in some school districts are so harsh that teachers will not come there without receiving "combat pay"; but it should not reflect the fact that some school district administrators pay higher salaries than necessary to attract their teachers, because they are poor negotiators or for any other reason.

A cost index should not be affected by school districts' choices, so the influence of school officials on teachers' salaries poses a challenge to anyone who wants to construct a cost index. Fortunately, however, well-known statistical procedures can separate the impact of school officials on teachers' salaries from the impact of external factors and produce a cost index based only on factors outside the control of school officials. These procedures are discussed in a later section.

The Role of Environmental Factors

The home comfort example reveals that the cost of meeting a performance standard depends not only on input prices but also on the environment in which the relevant services are provided. This lesson carries over into education, as school districts with a harsher educational environment must pay more to obtain the same educational performance as other districts. This section explains the impact of environmental factors on educational costs and shows how this impact can be estimated using widely available data.

The key role of environmental factors, also called fixed inputs in the literature, was first identified in the Coleman Report (Coleman et al., 1966), which showed that a student's performance on standardized tests depended not only on his or her own characteristics and family background but also on the characteristics and backgrounds of the students in his or her class. All else equal, for example, a student's performance is likely to be lower if she comes from a poor family or if a large share of her classmates come from poor families. This finding translates into a statement about educational costs. If performance declines as student poverty increases, then a district with a high poverty rate cannot achieve the same performance as a district with a low poverty rate without running programs (which, of course, cost money) to offset the impact of poverty.

The important role of environmental factors in educational production has been verified by dozens of studies. A review of many early studies is provided by Hanushek (1986). Good recent studies, such as Ferguson (1991), Ferguson and Ladd (1996), and Krueger (1997), use school and student-level data, and provide a more detailed analysis of the relationship between the student/family characteristics and student performance. The study by Ferguson and Ladd, for example, finds that a student's 4th-grade educational performance (on reading and math tests) is affected by, among other things, the share of students receiving a free lunch (a measure of poverty), the share of adults in the district with a college degree, a measure of student turnover, and district enrollment. These studies are analogous to engineering studies that link detailed weather conditions and indoor comfort in each type of house.

Production studies focus on the impact of environmental factors on a measure of performance, such as a test score, holding-constant inputs selected by the school, such as the student/teacher ratio. These studies imply that costs are higher in school districts with a harsher educational environment, but do not estimate cost differences directly. Moreover, the results of these studies vary significantly, depending on the methodology, the quality of the data, and other factors, so that even if the results were translated into cost differences across districts, these differences would vary widely from one study to the next.

Another set of studies shifts the focus to educational costs. These studies, which are analogous to a study of spending for home heating across a sample of communities, determine the extent to which districts with a harsh educational environment, as measured by the characteristics of their students, must pay more to achieve the same performance as other districts, where performance is measured by a set of performance indicators. These studies include Bradbury et al. (1984), which looks at all local spending, including spending on education, as well as studies by Ratcliffe et al. (1990), Downes and Pogue (1994), Duncombe et al. (1996), and Duncombe and Yinger (1997). These studies build on a well-known general treatment of environmental factors by Bradford et al. (1969).

At one level, these cost studies are equivalent to production studies; any statement about production can be translated into a statement about costs and vice versa. In practice, however, the cost approach has several advantages over the production approach as a tool for informing state education policies. First, cost studies focus on school districts, which are the focus of state policy, instead of on individual students.[2] Second, the cost approach makes it possible to examine a range of performance indicators simultaneously instead of one performance indicator at a time. Third, the data required to implement the cost approach are widely available. This does not imply, of course, that the cost approach resolves all the controversies about the nature of educational production that have been debated in production studies. It does imply, however, that the cost approach is a practical alternative to the production approach that makes it possible for state officials to design an educational finance system that accounts, in a reasonable way, using up-to-date data, for key features of educational production in their state.

Perhaps the most crucial feature is variation in the educational environment across school districts. Existing cost studies all demonstrate that a harsher educational environment, as characterized by high rates of poverty and single-parent families, for example, results in a higher cost to obtain any given performance level. Just as the harsh weather "environment" in Minnesota ensures that people who live there must pay more during the winter time than do people in San Diego to maintain their houses at a comfortable temperature, the harsh educational "environment" in some school districts, particularly big cities, ensures that those districts must pay more than other districts, sometimes much more, to obtain the same educational performance from their students.

State educational officials are often aware that environmental factors matter. For example, a report on the status of the state's schools by New York State Education Department says that "Five indicators, each associated with poor school performance, are useful for identifying students at risk of educational disadvantage: minority racial/ethnic group identity, living in a poverty household, having a poorly educated mother, and having a non-English language background" (State University of New York, 1997:3). However, states' performance standards and state aid programs do not take account of these environmental factors in any systematic way. As a result, these programs do not provide sufficient revenue to high-cost districts to allow them to meet the same performance standard as other districts.

The role of environmental factors also is widely ignored in the debate about the relative effectiveness of public versus private schools. Existing studies focus on whether differences in the performance between students in private and public schools, if any, can be explained by the possibility that students who attend private schools (or their parents) are more motivated than students who attend public schools (or their parents) (see, for example, Witte, 1996; and Rouse, 1997). This is, of course, a vital issue, but for policy purposes an equally important and largely ignored issue is whether existing differences in the performance of students in private and public school are due to environmental factors or to school policies. If, for example, performance in city public schools is lower than in private schools because those public schools have more concentrated poverty among their students, then sending all city public school children to private schools would only export their poverty, undermine the educational environment in private schools, and, perhaps, have no impact on student performance. To put it another way, a finding that some private schools perform better than some public schools even after accounting for differences in student motivation gives no insight whatsoever into the impact on performance of a massive move away from public schools toward private schools, which would dramatically shift the educational environment in both types of schools. Thus, more research is clearly needed on the impact of environmental factors on the cost of private education.

ALTERNATIVE METHODS FOR CALCULATING EDUCATIONAL COST INDEXES

Several different methods for calculating educational cost indexes have been proposed by scholars. This section explores the strengths and weaknesses of several key methods, and it compares the indexes that result when each method is applied to data for New York State.

Input Prices

Some scholars have proposed that educational costs be measured with an index of input prices, usually just teachers' salaries. Because teachers are by far the most important input in producing educational performance, teachers' salaries do, indeed, have a major impact on educational costs. However, a teacher salary index, by itself, has three major flaws as a measure of educational costs.

First, teachers' salaries reflect differences in teachers' experience and education, which are associated with quality differences across teachers. One cannot claim that a school district has high costs whenever it decides to hire teachers with extensive experience or with graduate degrees. Ideally, salaries that apply to teachers of comparable quality should be compared.

Second, as noted earlier, teachers' salaries at a given quality level can be influenced by the decisions of school officials. A cost index is intended to measure factors outside the control of school officials, so it should not reflect their bargaining skill or their generosity to teachers. A cost index based solely on teachers' salaries will provide the misleading impression that generous school districts are forced to pay more than other districts to obtain the same performance, when in fact their higher spending is entirely of their own making.

Finally, a teacher salary index ignores the role of the environment altogether. A school district with a harsh educational environment must spend more than other districts to obtain the same performance, even if teachers' salaries are the same everywhere. Thus, an index based on teachers' salaries leaves out one of the key sources of variation in educational costs across districts, namely environmental factors, and therefore understates educational costs in districts with a relatively harsh educational environment.

Adjusted Input Prices

Some scholars have recognized the first two problems with a cost index based solely on teachers salaries and suggested an alternative approach based on predicted salaries (Chambers 1978, 1995; Wendling, 1981). This approach uses regression analysis to separate the impact on teachers' salaries of internal factors under district control from the impact of external factors, and then predicts salaries holding the internal factors constant. In a typical study, the internal factors include teacher experience, education, and certification, as well as the district's salary structure, and the external factors include the wage level in the surrounding labor market and the classroom environment that confronts teachers in each district. This approach explicitly recognizes that conditions in some schools are so harsh that teachers must receive "combat pay" to work there. In other words, equally qualified teachers will not come to those schools unless they are paid more than they would be paid at other schools where the private wage scale is the same.

This approach solves the first two problems by constructing an index of predicted teachers' salaries.[3] One might at first conclude that it also solves the third problem because it accounts for the impact of environmental factors on teachers' salaries. As explained earlier, however, environmental factors affect not only the price of inputs but also the quantity of inputs required.

This point can be illuminated by returning to the nonschool example at the beginning of this chapter. A notion similar to "combat pay" could arise in the provision of home comfort if the price of the key input, namely natural gas, depends on the weather.[4] Suppose, for example, that colder weather requires more maintenance of natural gas pipelines and hence leads to a higher price for gas in colder places. A cost index for comfort based on the price of natural gas would clearly capture this phenomenon. However, such a cost index would not capture the fact that, to obtain any given comfort standard, households in a colder climate not only must spend more per unit of gas but also must purchase more gas than households in a warmer climate. Similarly, to achieve any given performance standard, school districts with a harsh educational environment not only must pay more to attract teachers, but also must hire more teachers (or spend additional money on other educational programs) than schools with an average educational environment.

In short, a cost index based on teachers' salaries, even if it is predicted on the basis of external factors, including environmental ones, ignores an important source of variation in educational costs and understates costs in districts with a harsh educational environment.

Ad Hoc Cost Adjustments for Environmental Factors

Many state aid formulas include ad hoc adjustments for environmental factors. This type of adjustment is also proposed in the Wyoming context by Guthrie and Rothstein (see Chapter 7 in this volume). States may pay more for transportation in less dense districts, for example, or compensate for a concentration of students with disabilities or whose native language is not English. Some programs also provide more money to districts with more children in poverty. However, these programs inevitably are ad hoc, with no demonstrated connection between the environmental factors and educational costs.[5]

The 1996 New York State aid programs, for example, include several provisions that could be interpreted as cost adjustments.[6] Operating aid, which provides 53 percent of the total aid paid to school districts, is based on the number of "weighted" pupils in a district. Pupils with extra weights include pupils in secondary school and pupils with "special education needs," defined as students who score below the minimum competency level on the 3rd- and 6th-grade reading or math PEP tests. The first of these weighting factors is supported by some studies of school spending in other states (Ratcliffe et al., 1990), which find a higher cost for high school than for elementary school students. However, it is not supported by our analysis of data for New York State, which finds no cost differences by grade.

The second weighting factor is undoubtedly correlated with cost variables, but we believe it is inappropriate to include a performance measure based on PEP scores in an aid formula. This approach rewards districts for poor performance and gives them an incentive to perform poorly in the future. Aid formulas should be based on factors outside a district's control, such as concentrated poverty, that make it difficult for the district to reach a high performance standard, but not on performance indicators that are influenced by the district's actions. New York also has a relatively new program, called Extraordinary Needs Aid, which gives more aid to districts with lower incomes and higher poverty concentrations. The program provides less than 5 percent of the total aid budget, however, and the formula is not based on any estimate of the relationship between educational costs and poverty.

Comprehensive Cost Indexes with Indirect Controls for Performance

To move beyond input prices, a cost index must consider the impact of environmental factors on a school districts' costs after accounting for teachers' salaries and for the district's performance. This step requires a statistical procedure based on data describing a district's spending and teacher's salaries, along with measures of relevant environmental factors, such as the district's poverty rate. In addition, it requires information that makes it possible to control for performance. One approach is to control for performance indirectly by controlling for factors that are known to influence performance and that are outside the control of school district officials. This method has been employed by Bradbury et al. (1984) and by Ratcliffe et al. (1990), and is illustrated by Downes and Pogue (1994) and Duncombe et al. (1996).

This approach draws on a large literature concerning the demand for public service outcomes, such as school district performance (Inman, 1979; Ladd and Yinger, 1991). In particular, dozens of studies have shown that public outcomes depend, in part, on income, tax price, and measures of voter preferences, such as the percent elderly. In this context, the tax price is the cost to a voter of raising performance by one unit. It is analogous to a private price; if the tax price goes up, voters select a lower public outcome. By controlling for a school district's income, tax price, and voter characteristics, therefore, one is indirectly controlling for school district performance.

This method builds on a regression analysis in which the level of public spending is a function of income, tax price, and voter characteristics (to control for performance) and of teachers' salaries and environmental factors (to account for costs). The regression results can be used to determine how much each district would have to spend if its income, tax price, and voter characteristics (and hence its performance) were average, given its teachers' salaries and environmental factors. A cost index is simply this spending amount relative to the spending amount in the average district. In other words, the cost index indicates how much each district would have to spend, relative to the average district, to achieve an average educational performance. Because it is derived from a statistical procedure, this index is not influenced by politics or by guesses as to the role of various environmental factors.

Three features of this approach should be emphasized. First, like the salary-based indexes discussed earlier, it can be implemented without any decision about the appropriate way to measure school district performance. However, it implicitly defines school district performance using the set of school performance measures that are highly correlated with income, tax price, and voter characteristics. Because this correlation is never observed directly, this definition is hidden from view. One might say that this is an advantage, because a potentially divisive debate about the appropriate performance measures can be avoided, but it is also a disadvantage because the performance measures that are selected implicitly might not, if identified, be reasonable. Moreover, even though it may be possible to avoid selecting performance standards in constructing a cost index, such a choice is, as shown below, unavoidable in the design of a performance-based aid program; the implicit standards in a cost index based on this indirect method cannot match the explicit standards in an aid program.

Second, this approach has the disadvantage that it is relatively abstract; policymakers may not find it easy to understand why controlling for income and tax price is equivalent to controlling for educational performance. Moreover, many studies have shown that cost factors are part of the tax price, that is, they influence the willingness of voters to vote for higher educational performance. Thus, variables, such as poverty, that increase educational costs, also raise the tax price and lead to a decrease in educational performance. The dependent variable, namely spending, picks up these two offsetting effects. Strictly speaking, therefore, one cannot determine the impact of teachers' salaries and environmental factors on costs without first accounting for their impact on tax price and hence on the demand for public services. This problem can be solved (Ladd and Yinger, 1991), but the solution is complex and difficult to explain to public officials. Fortunately, however, the tax-price effect appears to be relatively small, so the studies that apply this approach to education ignore the tax-price effect. This implies that these studies understate the variation in costs across school districts, but probably not to a large degree.

Third, this approach does not avoid the problem that teachers' salaries are influenced by school officials. The best way to handle this problem is to use techniques for estimating what are called simultaneous equations. In this case, unobserved school district characteristics, such as bargaining skill, generosity, or managerial competence, might simultaneously influence both the dependent variable, spending, and one explanatory variable, teachers' salaries. If so, the teachers' salary variable is said to be "endogenous," and its estimated coefficient—and hence cost indexes based on it—will be biased. To eliminate this bias, a researcher must identify at least one variable that influences teachers' salaries but is not affected by unobserved school district characteristics. With such an "instrumental" variable in hand, a researcher can use a well-known technique called "two-stage least squares" to eliminate the effect of unobserved school district characteristics on teachers salaries—and hence to eliminate the bias. Two such instrumental variables available to us in our New York data set are the average wages of manufacturing production workers and the population of the county in which the school district is located. The first of these variables measures one dimension of the private wage scale against which a school district must compete, and the second recognizes that wages tend to be bid up in larger metropolitan areas.

Comprehensive Cost Indexes with Direct Controls for Performance

Because many measures of educational performance, such as test scores and dropout rates, are available, a more direct approach is to include each district's actual performance level in the cost equation. Under this approach, a regression analysis of educational spending uses performance measures as explanatory variables instead of income, tax price, and voter characteristics. This approach has now been used by several scholars, including Downs and Pogue (1994), Duncombe et al. (1996), and Duncombe and Yinger (1997). This approach makes explicit the selection of performance standards and leads directly to an educational cost index, defined as the spending a district is required to make (relative to the average district) to meet a selected value of the performance variables, given its own input prices and environmental factors.

By controlling for performance directly, this approach avoids the complexity of the tax-price effect, which was discussed earlier. No fancy algebra is needed to obtain the correct cost index. However, this approach runs into another problem, namely, that unobserved school district characteristics might affect both school spending (the dependent variable) and measures of performance (explanatory variables). This simultaneity problem, like the one associated with teachers' salaries, requires the use of two-stage least squares. Fortunately, instruments for this procedure are readily available and are, in fact, defined by the indirect method just discussed. The indirect method is based on the well-established result that school performance depends on income and tax price, so income and tax price are natural instruments.[7]

As first pointed out by Duncombe and Yinger (1997), this approach also leads to a school district performance index. This index is a weighted average of the performance measures included in the regression, where the weights are the regression coefficients. Duncombe and Yinger also explain that these weights can be interpreted as demand weights; that is, they reflect the weight households place on each of the performance measures. With this approach, the performance measures used in a final regression are those that prove to be statistically significant; under this demand interpretation, this approach allows a researcher to identify the performance measures that play a significant role in households' demand for educational performance.

In addition, this performance index, with its statistically determined weights, makes it possible to set a single performance standard that covers a wide range of performance indicators. Instead of setting performance standards separately for several different indicators, such as test scores and a dropout rate, policymakers could set a standard based on this index. They could, for example, set the standard at the median of the index's current distribution.

Comprehensive Cost Indexes with Direct Controls for Performance and Efficiency

One might criticize the approaches in the two previous sections because they could confuse high cost and inefficiency: large districts may not have higher costs, for example, but may instead just be inefficient. This problem is analogous to the problem of controlling for household choices, about furnace maintenance for example, in the case of home comfort. In technical terms, ignoring inefficiency could lead to "omitted variable bias" in estimating the effects of environmental factors on costs. In this section we will discuss a method for measuring district inefficiency and including it in an expenditure regression. Inefficiency is, of course, difficult to measure, and the approach we will present is not the final word on the subject, but it does provide one tractable method to control for efficiency and thereby to minimize, if not eliminate, the effect of omitted variable bias on cost indexes.

The approach we have in mind measures efficiency using what is called a "best-practice" technique (Ruggiero, 1996).[8] With this technique, a district is said to be inefficient if it spends more on education than other districts with the same performance and the same educational costs. The degree of inefficiency is measured by the extent of this excess spending. Although the "best-practice" technique we use, called data envelopment analysis (DEA), is well known in some circles, Duncombe et al. (1996) were the first scholars to use it as a way to control for school district efficiency in an analysis of school district spending. It has the advantage that it requires the same data as the expenditure regression in the previous section and the disadvantage that it involves mathematical programming techniques and is therefore difficult to implement—and to explain. Moreover, it is possible that all districts in a state are inefficient relative to best practices in other states or relative to available management practices that are not used anywhere; however, no existing empirical method can shed light on inefficiency of this type.

This best-practice technique, like the regression approach in the previous section (and like any performance standard), requires a researcher to select specific performance measures. When the two methods are combined, that is, when a best-practice measure of efficiency is included in an expenditure regression that directly controls for performance, the same performance measures appear in the regression and in the calculations that yield the efficiency measure. Hence the choice of performance measures influences the efficiency measure, just as the inclusion of the efficiency measure in the regression might influence which performance measures turn out to be significant (and hence are included in the final regression). This linkage could be a source of contention when the focus is on a single, arbitrarily selected performance indicator; districts found to be inefficient in this case may simply be concentrating on other types of performance. This problem can be minimized by using statistical criteria, such as the ones described earlier, to select a range of performance measures for inclusion in the cost and efficiency analyses.

Strictly speaking, the DEA approach does not lead to a measure of efficiency alone but instead to a measure of the extent to which one district spends more than other districts to achieve the same performance. As a result, our best-practice variable picks up variation in educational costs as well as in efficiency. Thus, including both this variable and cost variables in an expenditure regression might, in principle, make it difficult to sort out the role of input and environmental cost factors. With our New York data, at least, this does not turn out to be the case. Even when the best-practice variable is included, the cost variables behave as expected and are statistically significant, and the best-practice variable itself has the expected impact on spending and is statistically significant, too (see Table 8-1).

TABLE 8-1 Education Cost Models (with and without New York City and Yonkers), New York School Districts, 1991[a]

Variables	Estimates Without New York City and Yonkers[c]		Estimates With New York City and Yonkers	
	Coefficient	t-statistic	Coefficient	t-statistic
Cost Equation[a]				
Intercept	-4.9550	-1.53	-4.3542	-1.44
3rd- and 6th-grade PEP scores (average % above standard reference point)[b]	5.1106	2.50	5.6171	2.86
Percent non-dropouts[b]	4.4757	1.62	4.2826	1.55
Percent receiving Regents diploma[b]	1.3449	3.19	0.9231	2.09
Efficiency index (percent)[b]	-1.1670	-4.87	-1.1429	-4.81
Log of teacher salaries[b]	0.6487	1.57	0.7211	1.72
Log of enrollment	-0.5680	-3.54	-1.1823	-2.67
Square of log of enrollment	0.0345	3.44	0.1171	2.32
Cubic of log of enrollment			0.0035	-1.85
Percent of children in poverty	1.0109	3.93	0.9526	3.73
Percent female-headed households	2.2260	3.85	2.0751	3.61
Percent of students with severe handicap	0.8584	1.29	0.7137	1.10
Percent of students with limited English proficiency	4.0525	2.68	4.2940	2.82
SSE	34.58		33.45	
Adjusted R-square	0.32		0.34	

[a]The cost models are estimated with linear 2SLS regression. The dependent variable is the logarithm of per-pupil operating expenditures. The sample size for both models is 631 districts.

[b]These variables are treated as endogenous. See the text for a discussion of the instruments.

[c]These regression results are those presented in Duncombe and Yinger (1997). Besides not including NYC and Yonkers, there are some differences in the data and measures between this regression and the regression reported in columns 3 and 4.

The best-practice variable, and indeed any measure of school district effi-ciency, could be influenced by unobserved school district characteristics that also influence spending. As a result, this variable, like the performance measures and teachers' salaries, must be treated as "endogenous." To find the required exog-enous instruments, one can turn to the large literature on the determinants of governmental efficiency. As discussed in Duncombe and Yinger (1997), for example, scholars have argued that a school district's efficiency is influenced by the state aid it receives and by the education and income of its voters.

The process of identifying these instruments can be thought of as an analysis of the determinants of school district efficiency. Duncombe and Yinger (1997) also show that these instruments, along with controls for educational costs and for performance indicators that are not considered in deriving the best-practice effi-ciency index, can explain a large share of the variation in this index. For the most part, these instruments affect the best-practice measure in the direction predicted by the literature on efficiency and are statistically significant. These results provide some evidence that this approach is indeed a reasonable way to account for school district efficiency in an expenditure regression.[9]

Relationship Among Various Approaches

In this section we present a comparison of educational cost indexes using all of the above methods. Using data from 631 school districts in New York State in 1990-91, we show how input prices vary, why it is so important to account for environmental factors, how direct and indirect controls for performance compare, and what happens when one accounts for inefficiency.[10]

The key analytical tool in these calculations is a regression analysis of school spending. In our preferred regressions, the explanatory variables are several performance measures, teachers' salaries, environmental cost factors, and a best-practice control for efficiency. Table 8-1 provides regressions results when the cost model is run without (columns 1 and 2) and with (columns 3 and 4) New York City and Yonkers. The estimates of cost indices presented in this chapter are based on the model with New York City and Yonkers. Two performance measures prove to be statistically significant: the average share of students above a standard reference point on a set of elementary math and reading tests and the share of students who receive a relatively demanding "Regents diploma," instead of a regular one. A third performance measure, the graduation rate, is close to significant at conventional levels and is also included. These three measures cover a wide range of school district activities both for students who are doing well and for students who are doing poorly. Input prices and the efficiency control are statistically significant (at the 10 percent and 1 percent level, respec-tively) with the expected sign. Moreover, four environmental variables play a statistically significant role, namely, district enrollment, the percentage of chil-dren in poverty, the percentage of households headed by a single female, and the percentage of students with limited English proficiency. We find, as do many previous studies, that the impact of district enrollment on costs is roughly U-shaped, with relatively high costs in both the smallest and largest districts.[11] Finally, because expenditures for students with disabilities are so high in some districts, this regression includes a disability variable, namely the percentage of students with a severe handicap, even though it is not significant at conventional levels.[12]

Table 8-2 describes cost indexes calculated with each of the above methods. This table shows how the cost indexes vary by region and type of district, by number of pupils, by income, and by property value. The regions in New York are downstate, for the New York City region, and upstate, for the rest of the state. The first column indicates the number of districts in each class.

Results for the most comprehensive approach, which we believe to be the most accurate, are presented in the second column. According to this approach, upstate suburbs have the lowest costs, with an average index of 90.8. In other words, the average upstate suburb must spend $0.908 to achieve the same performance that the average district obtains for $1.00. In contrast, New York City, with a cost index of 386.9, must spend almost 4 times as much as the average district to achieve the same performance.[13] Costs are also relatively high in the three large upstate cities (Buffalo, Rochester, and Syracuse), which have an average index of 189.6, and in Yonkers, which has an index of 191.9. The results in this column also reveal that costs are relatively high in the smallest and largest districts and that costs tend to increase slightly with income and with property value—except at the bottom of the distribution.

These results provide striking testimony to the magnitude of variation in educational costs particularly between large central cities and suburban districts. Recent estimates of cost indices in Wisconsin (Reschovsky and Imazeki, 1998) and Michigan (Courant et al., 1995) show similar large differences in costs between large central cities and their suburbs. Even if state aid offsets all differences in district capacity to raise revenue, it is unlikely that a city with a cost index of 200 or 300 will be able to provide the same performance as a district with a cost index of 75 or 100.

An educational cost index that does not account for efficiency, which is presented in the third column of Table 8-2, leads to a higher apparent variation in costs because it inappropriately treats inefficiency as a cost factor, at least to the extent that inefficiency is correlated with cost variables that are included in the analysis. The key problem in New York State is a positive correlation between the wage rate and inefficiency; with no control for inefficiency, the impact of wages on costs is exaggerated and the cost index for high-wage districts is too high while the cost index for low-wage districts is too low. Compared to our preferred index, therefore, this approach drops the average cost index to 83.4 in the low-wage upstate suburbs, and boosts the cost index in downstate districts where wages are relatively high. In particular, the index goes up to 396.5 in New

York City and jumps by over 20 percent in Yonkers and in the downstate small cities and suburbs. Excluding a control for efficiency also magnifies the U-shaped relationship between costs and enrollment and the positive relationships between costs and both income and property value. Because this cost index exaggerates the variation in costs across districts, it would, if used in an aid formula, overcompensate districts with high wages or enrollments at either end of the distribution.

The fourth column of Table 8-1 controls for efficiency, but does not treat efficiency as endogenous. This index moves in the opposite direction compared to our preferred index by having less variation in costs, particularly by district enrollment size. Perhaps the biggest change is in the index value for New York City, which is 40 percent lower than our preferred index. Treating efficiency as endogenous reduces the estimated importance of most cost factors in New York, particularly limited English proficiency, thus underestimating the cost index in large cities.

Results based on the indirect method of controlling for service quality are presented in the fifth column of Table 8-2. These results exhibit considerably less variation across type of district, and in fact lead to the rather startling result that costs in New York City are only slightly higher than average. However, this approach, like the previous ones, does indicate relatively high costs in other large cities. Compared to earlier approaches, this approach also leads to less variation in costs with district size, except in the case of the smallest districts.

This approach does not provide a very compelling alternative to the approaches with direct controls for district performance. Not only does the indirect approach require more stringent assumptions than the direct approaches, but when our control for efficiency is introduced into the regression, none of the regression coefficients is statistically significant. In applying this approach, therefore, we must choose between results that are biased because they exclude a control for efficiency (the ones presented in column five of Table 8-2) or results from an equation that cannot untangle the roles of cost factors and inefficiency.

A cost index based on New York State's official weighted pupil measure is presented in the sixth column of Table 8-2. This index exhibits little variation across districts; indeed, only one category of district, namely under 100 pupils, has costs more than 3 percent away from the state average. Moreover, the variation that does exist appears to miss the strong tendencies observed in the more comprehensive indexes, namely, the high costs in large cities, the U-shaped relationship between costs and enrollment, and the increase in costs with district income and property value. In short, the ad hoc procedures used to determine weighted pupils in New York State bear little systematic relationship to costs, as estimated with either the direct or indirect methods.

Finally, a cost index based on teacher salaries is presented in the last column of Table 8-2. This index adjusts (as do the regression-based indexes) for the fact that higher salaries must be paid to attract teachers of given quality to harsher

TABLE 8-2   Comparison of Education Cost Indices for New York State
School Districts in 1991

Socioeconomic Characteristics	Number of Districts	Direct Cost Indices		
		Endogenous Efficiency	No Efficiency Index	Exogenous Efficiency
Region Type				
Downstate small cities	7	132.16	171.21	120.65
Downstate suburbs	130	108.20	129.10	103.83
New York City	1	386.89	396.49	226.87
Yonkers	1	191.91	276.81	156.42
Upstate large cities	3	189.64	188.95	171.25
Upstate rural	212	98.92	93.54	99.43
Upstate small cities	47	109.05	103.74	111.63
Upstate suburbs	231	90.75	83.42	93.66
Number of Pupils				
Under 100 pupils	1	172.87	304.45	133.58
100-500 pupils	61	107.26	115.13	103.93
500-1,000 pupils	113	99.49	98.16	99.55
1,000-1,500 pupils	131	93.07	86.80	95.55
1,500-3,000 pupils	181	96.24	94.86	97.55
3,000-5,000 pupils	80	96.64	96.99	98.16
5,000-10,000 pupils	54	111.46	118.58	108.65
10,000-50,000 pupils	10	149.30	168.13	135.69
Over 50,000 pupils	1	386.89	396.49	226.87
Income Class (percentile)				
Under 10th	63	101.51	95.05	101.52
10th to 25th	95	98.14	91.82	99.88
25th to 50th	158	96.63	90.24	98.41
50th to 75th	158	99.29	98.29	100.03
75th to 90th	94	105.23	114.55	101.93
Over 90th	64	103.65	123.98	99.69
Property Values (percentile)				
Under 10th	63	99.56	90.35	101.33
10th to 25th	95	97.06	88.13	99.25
25th to 50th	158	96.50	89.95	98.74
50th to 75th	158	100.55	99.62	99.80
75th to 90th	94	103.69	115.96	101.02
Over 90th	64	106.67	129.44	101.91

NOTE: All indices are relative to the state average, which is set at 100. Sample size for the analysis
is 631 school districts. The indirect cost index in the fifth column is a reduced form model where the
demand instruments—income, taxshare, and households with children—are substituted into the cost
model for outcome measures. The weighted pupil index in the sixth column is based on a ratio of

Indirect Cost Index (No Efficiency Index)	Cost Index Based on Weighted Pupils	Teacher Salary Cost Index
111.53	102.65	108.90
100.90	101.61	103.57
111.83	98.11	125.36
130.14	98.69	113.78
135.72	100.31	110.92
103.83	99.90	98.68
102.44	100.52	102.64
94.49	99.02	98.08
199.21	120.35	96.94
116.47	101.16	97.74
103.31	99.43	99.13
96.26	98.55	98.90
95.57	100.73	100.30
94.81	99.59	100.70
100.94	101.11	103.26
116.66	100.67	107.21
111.83	98.11	125.36
105.53	99.68	99.47
102.03	100.49	98.93
99.46	99.39	98.89
98.68	99.45	99.89
97.89	99.92	101.80
99.23	102.57	102.49
102.09	100.19	99.78
99.74	99.38	99.04
98.20	100.28	99.19
98.63	99.57	100.11
100.08	100.17	101.51
106.03	100.85	101.15

weighted pupils over total enrollment. Extra weight is given to secondary, handicapped, and special needs pupils. The index in the last column is based on the relationship between teacher salaries and family and student characteristics. Income is based on estimated per capita adjusted gross income in 1991 and property values are per capita market value for all property in 1991.

educational environments. This approach, like the direct and indirect methods, picks up the relatively high costs in New York City and in other large cities, although the magnitude of the difference between city and other districts is much smaller. This approach also indicates that costs increase with district income and property value, although the differences along these two dimensions are very small. However, this approach fails to pick up the relatively high costs of small districts and finds only modestly higher costs in the large districts than in districts of average size.

Another way to compare these cost indexes is to look at the extent to which they are correlated across districts. Our correlation results are presented in Table 8-3. Not surprisingly, the highest correlation, 0.95, is between the direct cost index with endogenous efficiency and the direct cost index with efficiency treated as exogenous. Leaving out the efficiency controls altogether drops the correlation to 0.92. The correlations are considerably smaller between our preferred index and both the indirect cost index (0.73) and the cost index based on weighted pupils (0.12). This, of course, reinforces the message from Table 8-2. The weighted-pupil approach, in particular, appears to have little to do with costs based on a comprehensive analysis. Finally, there is a moderately high correlation between our preferred index and the teacher salary cost index (0.80). Although the teacher salary cost index exhibits relatively little variation compared to the direct index with endogenous efficiency, it appears that districts with relatively high costs according to one index also tend to have relatively high costs according to the other.

COST INDEXES AND STATE FOUNDATION FORMULAS

Educational cost indexes are important largely because they make it possible to design fairer and more effective educational funding policies. This section explores the link between educational costs and one important state policy, namely, a foundation aid program. We show how to bring educational cost indexes into a foundation aid formula—and what happens when cost indexes are ignored. The issues discussed here also arise in programs designed to reward districts that meet performance standards or to punish districts that fall short. As several states have discovered, rewards or punishments that focus exclusively on performance, with no adjustment for costs, end up helping the districts that need help least and punishing the districts that are, through no fault of their own, stuck with the harshest educational environments (Clotfelter and Ladd, 1996).

How to Include Cost Indexes in a Foundation Formula

About 80 percent of states use some form of a foundation grant system, which is designed to ensure that all districts meet some minimal performance standard set, in principle, at a level deemed adequate, if not higher. For the most

TABLE 8-3 Correlations Between Education Cost Indices for New York State School Districts in 1991

Socioeconomic Characteristics	Direct Cost Indices			Indirect Cost Index (No Efficiency Index)	Cost Index Based on Weighted Pupils	Teacher Salary Cost Index
	Endogenous Efficiency	No Efficiency Index	Exogenous Efficiency			
Standard Deviation	22.04	38.19	14.31	11.53	8.88	4.17
Maximum	386.89	396.49	226.87	199.21	264.07	125.36
75th Percentile	104.39	107.38	103.96	104.56	102.90	101.71
25th Percentile	88.90	78.97	92.38	92.48	97.01	97.23
Minimum	75.52	61.92	80.60	82.55	44.69	92.51
Correlations						
Direct cost indices						
Endognous efficiency index	1.00					
No efficiency index	0.92	1.00				
Exogenous efficiency index	0.95	0.85	1.00			
Indirect cost index (no efficiency index)	0.73	0.76	0.76	1.00		
Cost index based on weighted pupils	0.12	0.15	0.14	0.15	1.00	
Teacher Salary Cost Index	0.80	0.78	0.80	0.46	0.16	1.00

NOTE: All indices are relative to the state average, which is set at 100. Sample size for the analysis is 631 school districts. The indirect cost index in the fourth column is a reduced form model where the demand instruments—income, taxshare, and households with children—are substituted into the cost model for outcome measures. The weighted pupil index in the fifth column is based on a ratio of weighted pupils over total enrollment. Extra weight given to secondary, handicapped and special needs pupils. The index in the last column is based on the relationship between teacher salaries and teacher, family, and student characteristics.

part, however, these systems use spending as a measure of "performance," and therefore do not bring many districts up to any given performance standard defined on the basis of test scores or other reasonable performance measures. This need not be the case: cost indexes make it possible to design a foundation formula that provides sufficient revenue to enable all well-managed districts to reach an adequate performance level. We will illustrate our analysis with results from New York State.

A foundation plan is designed to bring all districts up to a minimum spending level per pupil.[14] Let V_i stand for the property tax base in district i. Then an *expenditure-based* foundation grant per pupil is defined by

$$A_i = E^* - t^*V_i = E^* (1 - v_i)$$ (1)

where E^* is the expenditure standard, t^* is the minimum tax rate set by the state, $V^* = E^*/t^*$ is the property value above which a district receives no aid, and $v_i = V_i/V^*$ is a property value index. A foundation aid program is designed to provide every district with enough resources to provide the foundation level of spending per pupil at the minimum tax rate specified by policymakers.

If taken literally, Equation 1 implies that districts with tax bases above V^* actually receive negative aid. This formula is usually modified in practice, through minimum aid amounts or hold-harmless clauses, so that all districts receive some aid, thereby reducing the equalizing power of the formula. Moreover, a foundation grant usually is accompanied by a requirement that each district levy a tax rate of at least t^*; otherwise, some districts might not provide the minimum acceptable spending level, E^*. New York and Illinois are notable exceptions (Miner, 1991; Downes and McGuire, 1994).

Because they do not systematically account for cost differences across districts, these plans may not provide the funds that a high-cost district needs to reach a minimum performance level. In particular, districts with relatively high costs cannot reach the standard unless they set a tax rate that is above the required minimum.

To make the switch from spending to performance, one must incorporate educational costs into the aid formula. This step can be done using one of two equivalent methods. The first method begins by selecting a performance standard, say S^*, based on a performance index derived from a cost equation, such as the one described earlier. As noted earlier, policymakers must determine which index value is the appropriate standard for their state. They could, for example, set the standard at the 25th percentile of the current performance distribution, as measured by the index. The cost equation then indicates how much each district would have to spend, say C_i, per unit of S, given its input prices and environmental factors. Because they come from the same equation, the performance index and the cost index are consistent, that is, they involve the same performance measures. Note also that this cost measure is not the same as a cost index because it is not divided by the costs in the average district, say $\overline{C}$. The second method focuses on the amount the average district must spend to achieve the standard, E^*, which is equal to S^* multiplied by $\overline{C}$. The amount any individual district must spend to achieve the standard, then, is simply E^* multiplied by c_i, which is the cost index for district i. These two approaches are equivalent because, by definition, $S^* C_i$ equals $E^* c_i$.

Based on these concepts, we can now see that a *performance-based* formula that brings all districts up to the selected performance standard, S^*, at an acceptable tax burden on their residents is as follows:

$$A_i = S^* C_i - t^* V_i = E^*(c_i - v_i) \tag{2}$$

where the amount each district must spend to reach the standard replaces the fixed amount of spending in Equation 1 (Ladd and Yinger, 1994). The amount of aid this district receives equals the spending level required to reach S^* minus the amount of revenue it can raise at the specified tax rate t^*. As with Equation 1, raising S^* to an extremely high level would, at great cost, result in an equal educational output in every district, and allowing negative grants would boost the equalizing impact of the grant.

In short, one cannot switch to a performance-based aid program without replacing the notion of the foundation spending level, which does not recognize cost variation across districts, with an estimate of the spending that is required to achieve the performance standard in a district with average costs. In principle, this new spending standard, E^*, could be obtained using the method described by Guthrie and Rothstein (see Chapter 7 in this volume), which aggregates the cost of typical input bundles, so long as the calculation is based on the inputs employed by a district with average input and environmental costs.[15] Returning to the home comfort example, our approach is analogous to a regression-based approach, whereas this input-aggregation approach is analogous to an engineering study. Our approach provides an alternative to the approach in these other studies because the cost equation reveals how much a district with average costs would have to spend to meet any performance standard, so long as this standard is set at some percentile of the performance index. In other words, this approach employs a statistically based calculation of the required spending in the district with average costs instead of pricing the set of inputs that experts believe are needed for a district to meet an adequacy standard. Reasonable people may disagree about which approach is to be preferred. Whichever approach is taken, however, the use of a cost index in the aid formula is crucial.

Because some districts are inefficient, a program based on Equation 2 will not bring all districts up to the foundation level (and implicit performance standard) even with a required minimum tax rate. In fact, virtually all districts fall short of the best-practice efficiency level. As a result, it seems reasonable to design a foundation formula so that every district will have enough revenue to achieve the foundation performance level at some efficiency level, say the 75th percentile of the current efficiency distribution across districts, which we call the baseline efficiency level. If it falls short of this level, it will not achieve the foundation level of performance unless its tax rate is above the specified rate.

In addition, switching to a performance-based aid system undoubtedly would not immediately bring high-cost districts up to the performance standard. Even if the resources needed to meet the standard were available to them, these districts would have to alter some existing practices, design new programs, and hire at least some new teachers, administrators, and counselors. These steps would take time. A reasonable approach, in our view, would be for a state to move to a performance-based aid system over a period of several years, providing along the way both management assistance and new research evidence about the effects of various educational programs. In combination with these extra steps, moving to a performance-based aid system would allow a state to say that it had provided each district with the resources it needs to meet the performance standard, as determined by the best available information and the current state of knowledge about educational costs.

Simulating the Effect of a Performance-Based Aid Program

Using data from New York school districts, excluding New York City (which otherwise would dominate the aid program),[16] Duncombe and Yinger (1997) simulate the effect of different aid systems on student performance in each district. These simulations employ not only the performance and cost indexes discussed here, but also analyses of voter demand for educational performance and of the determinants of school district efficiency, which are not presented here. The key results are reproduced in Table 8-4.[17] This table shows the average performance, as measured by the performance index described earlier, in each class of district under foundation aid programs based on various ways of accounting for educational costs. In this table, performance is expressed relative to the actual 1991 performance level in the average district, not, as in Equation 2, in terms of required spending. Thus, an index of 39.7, the current value for upstate large cities, indicates a performance that is almost 60 percent below the state average. All of the aid programs have the same overall state budget and impose a minimum-tax-rate requirement, and each type of aid system (a column) is examined for three different performance standards or foundation levels (the panels), namely, the 25th, 50th, and 75th percentiles of the 1991 performance distribution in New York, as measured by the performance index. As indicated in the table, these percentiles fall at 76.2 percent, 97.4 percent, and 120.4 percent, respectively, of the current performance in the average district.

The first column of Table 8-4 indicates district performance under the existing aid system, which includes several small lump-sum programs plus a founda-

TABLE 8-4 Comparison of Predicted Performance Under Different Foundation Formulas Relative to State Average Performance in 1991 for New York School Districts

Class of District	Actual Outcomes	Performance-Based Aid System with Direct Cost Indices			Expenditure-Based Aid System
		Endogenous Efficiency	No Efficiency Index	Exogenous Efficiency	
S*=25th percentile	76.2				
Average	100.0	104.1	102.1	100.6	103.0
Downstate					
Small cities	83.0	85.4	90.1	90.0	78.4
Suburbs	118.5	123.7	125.7	126.0	120.0
Upstate					
Large cities	39.7	68.7	59.7	71.0	40.9
Rural	89.4	95.4	89.2	91.5	93.1
Small cities	82.2	90.1	83.0	86.3	86.1
Suburbs	104.1	104.8	101.5	102.4	107.4
S*=50th percentile	97.4				
Average	100.0	122.7	117.6	117.7	118.9
Downstate					
Small cities	83.0	99.2	104.6	103.1	87.1
Suburbs	118.5	146.4	149.4	148.7	135.8
Upstate					
Large cities	39.7	87.0	80.9	89.3	47.6
Rural	89.4	115.8	106.4	108.1	110.9
Small cities	82.2	110.8	101.2	103.3	100.7
Suburbs	104.1	119.4	114.1	113.0	122.4
S*=75th percentile	120.4				
Average	100.0	155.9	150.8	149.0	153.3
Downstate					
Small cities	83.0	138.2	141.9	139.2	123.3
Suburbs	118.5	195.6	198.4	197.4	180.3
Upstate					
Large cities	39.7	104.7	100.0	106.5	64.2
Rural	89.4	145.1	135.7	135.0	142.3
Small cities	82.2	136.7	128.3	127.2	128.7
Suburbs	104.1	148.6	143.6	139.9	155.4

NOTE: All grants require approximately the same state budget to fund as the aid system in 1991, $3.65 billion. S* is the student performance target that defines the aid system. Student performance is expressed relative to the state average performance in 1991. A value of 100 equals this average. All aid plans in this table require districts to assess the minimum tax rate set by the state.

tion plan with the minimum expenditure (not performance) level set at approximately the 25th percentile of the 1991 expenditure distribution and with various hold-harmless and minimum-aid provisions. The second column of Table 8-4 presents results for a performance-based foundation plan with a required minimum tax rate and endogenous efficiency. The performance increases above their existing levels are most dramatic for large, upstate central cities. The average performance for these three cities with the most generous plan, 104.7, is slightly more than 2.5 times as large as their current performance, 39.7. This new performance level falls short of the target S^*, 120.4, because the increased aid drives the efficiency level in these districts below the baseline level. This performance-based foundation plan also boosts performance in all other classes of district, although not by such dramatic amounts.

Implementing this aid plan requires an understanding of cost indexes, an explicit decision about the acceptable level of inefficiency, and the estimation of cost indexes controlling for efficiency. Existing state plans do not take any of these steps, so Duncombe and Yinger (1997) also simulate three alternative foundation plans based on less complete information.

The simplest foundation plan follows Equation 1, with no recognition of costs or efficiency. The results for such a plan are presented in the last (fifth) column of Table 8-4. Because the implicit expenditure target in the current New York foundation plan is set at about the 25th percentile of the current expenditure distribution, a comparison of the first and last columns in the first panel of these tables largely reflects the impact of eliminating hold-harmless and minimum-aid provisions and pooling all lump-sum aid into a foundation formula. These steps would modestly increase aid (and performance) in upstate cities, both large and small, and decrease aid substantially (with little impact on performance) in downstate cities and suburbs. The average impact on rural districts and downstate suburbs would be minimal.

Bringing in the results in the second column, we can see that a performance-based foundation goes much farther than an expenditure-based foundation in shifting aid toward large cities and thereby boosting their performance. It does not go nearly as far, however, in shifting aid away from downstate small cities and suburbs, a result shown by their high performance. Largely because they face very high labor costs, these downstate districts tend to have high costs, a fact that is missed by an expenditure-based plan. The current system of hold-harmless and minimum-aid provisions serves some of the same purpose as a cost correction by boosting aid to these districts, but it goes too far in this direction and does not ensure fair treatment either within these districts or between these districts and others.

Table 8-4 also reveals that even the most generous expenditure-based foundation plan leaves large cities far short of any performance target, even with a required minimum tax rate. In fact, the most generous such plan, in the last panel of Table 8-4, helps large cities but still leaves them at an performance level well below the 25th percentile of the current distribution!

Related simulations in Duncombe and Yinger (1998b) make the key point here in a different way. Consider, the notion of a "performance gap," defined as the sum across districts of the amount by which actual district performance falls below the performance standard, weighted by the number of students in the district. Duncombe and Yinger show that with the foundation level (and implicit performance standard) set at the 25th percentile of the 1991 performance distribution and a required minimum tax rate, an expenditure-based foundation plan would close only 36 percent of the current performance gap in New York. In contrast, a comparable, and equal-cost performance-based foundation plan would close 84 percent of performance gap (and would close 100 percent of the gap if all districts met the baseline efficiency standard). The point should be clear: expenditure-based foundation plans, which are used in most states, leave many high-cost districts short of even a minimal performance standard.

A state cannot implement a performance-based aid program without estimating a cost index. As noted earlier, an aid program for municipal services, including education, based on an estimated cost index was implemented in Massachusetts (Bradbury et al., 1984), and school aid programs based on estimated cost indexes are presented in Ratcliffe et al. (1990) and Downes and Pogue (1994). However, the cost indexes estimated in these cases do not control for efficiency. Thus, we now examine performance-based foundation programs that incorporate a cost index estimated without controlling for efficiency and that implicitly assume, following Equation 2, that all districts are efficient. A cost index estimated in this way is biased, because the omission of an efficiency variable biases the coefficients of the included cost variables, but it takes a large step toward recognizing the role of input and environmental cost factors.

Results for these programs, presented in the third column of Table 8-4, reveal that in most cases adding a cost index closes a large share of the gap between the expenditure-based foundation in the fifth column and the complete performance-based foundation in the second column. Under the most generous plan (75th percentile), for example, adding a biased cost index raises performance in upstate large cities from 64.2 (column 5) to 100 (column 3), compared to the complete-information performance (column 2) of 104.7.

In contrast, the foundation plan based on a biased cost index leads to higher aid and higher performance for downstate small cities and suburbs than either the expenditure-based foundation or the complete-information foundation in the second column. As explained earlier, this result mainly reflects the large, negative correlation between efficiency and wage rates; because of this correlation, leaving efficiency out of the cost equation biases upward the coefficient of the wage variable and hence biases upward the cost index in places, like downstate districts, with high labor costs.[18]   In effect, therefore, an aid program based on a biased cost index rewards the downstate districts for their inefficiency. This is, of course, an inappropriate outcome.

This result poses a serious challenge to policymakers and researchers. Aid formulas based on simple cost indexes of the type that have been presented in the literature appear to be a big step in the right direction, but this step has a price. To the extent that efficiency is correlated with cost factors, a standard cost index will reflect inefficiency as well as costs, and an aid formula based on it will favor inefficient districts as well as high-cost ones. In New York, this effect does not boost aid to big cities, which despite their reputation are relatively efficient, but instead boosts aid to downstate small cities and suburbs, which tend to be inefficient by our measure.

Obviously the relevant correlations could vary from state to state, so these results cannot determine whether this type of plan would reward the same types of district for inefficiency in other states. Nevertheless, the possibility that the plan rewards inefficiency clearly undercuts its appeal.

As noted earlier, one simple step a state can take to recognize the role of efficiency is to bring in the concept of baseline efficiency. All this step requires is identifying an efficiency level that is regarded as acceptable. This approach recognizes that virtually no districts will be able to achieve perfect efficiency so that spending greater than S^*C_i is needed to bring district i up to the S^* performance target. Compared to the previous approach, therefore, this approach focuses more aid on higher-need districts. The fourth column of Table 8-4 shows the impact of a foundation plan with a biased cost index but with a baseline efficiency level set at the 75th percentile of the current efficiency distribution. This plan takes another small step toward the complete-information plan in the second column. In the downstate districts, the entry in column 4 generally falls between the entry in column 3, which has no correction for efficiency, and the entry in column 2, which is based on an unbiased cost index. Moreover, performance in large cities would actually be slightly higher with this plan than with our preferred plan because the biased cost index exaggerates the cost impact of high wages in these districts.

The simulations in Table 8-4 all involve the same state budget, namely, the actual New York State educational aid budget in 1990-91. A natural question to ask is: What would happen if the budget increased? In the case of foundation plans without a minimum tax rate, the effect of a higher state budget can be dramatic. With a foundation plan of this type, many districts set tax rates below the level needed to achieve the foundation level of spending (and, in the case of performance-based foundation plans, of performance), that is, they use some of their state educational aid to fund noneducational programs or to cut taxes. Some portion of any additional state aid will be devoted to education and will therefore boost districts' educational spending and performance. In the case of performance-based foundation plans with a minimum tax rate, however, additional state aid has no such effect. Somewhat ironically, in fact, additional state aid leads to a small decrease in performance (Duncombe and Yinger, 1998a). The minimum tax rate requirement ensures that all districts raise enough revenue to fund the performance standard if they meet the baseline efficiency standard. Additional state revenue is therefore not needed to meet the standard. However, a district's efficiency is influenced by the amount of aid it receives, and higher aid generally leads to lower efficiency. As a result, the increase in the state budget shifts the burden of financing education from local governments to the state, with no change in the amount of revenue available for education and, in the process, makes school districts a little less efficient. This drop in efficiency results in a small drop in performance.[19]

CONCLUSIONS

An extensive literature establishes that both school district and student performance depend not only on factors that school officials control, such as the student/teacher ratio, but also on factors that are outside their control, including input prices, such as regional wage rates, and environmental factors, such as concentrated poverty. It follows directly that the cost of education is not the same in every district, with higher costs in districts in higher-wage labor markets or with a harsher educational environment. A shift to educational performance standards, whether these standards are simply targets or are imbedded in a foundation aid program, can be neither fair nor effective unless it recognizes this variation in the cost of education. This shift cannot be fair to districts that, through no fault of their own, face harsh educational environments, and it cannot be effective because it hands out rewards and punishments that are not related to the contributions of school personnel.

Scholars have identified a variety of methods for measuring the cost of education, all of which have limitations. The simplest reasonable methods, which are indexes of teachers salaries predicted on the basis of conditions in the local labor market and in a district's schools, fail to recognize that districts with a relatively harsh educational environment must hire more teachers (or purchase more of other inputs) than other districts to achieve the same performance. The most comprehensive methods, which recognize the role of environmental factors and control for school district efficiency, involve some complex, hard-to-explain steps. Nevertheless, the literature demonstrates that cost variation across schools is very large and cannot be ignored. Policymakers and scholars need to continue the search for sensible, practical ways to measure educational costs and incorporate them into performance-based educational policies.

NOTES

1. Strictly speaking, this interpretation of the weights depends on the assumption that educational performance is provided at constant cost (Duncombe

and Yinger, 1997). This assumption cannot be avoided without very complex statistical procedures, and it is employed in virtually all the educational finance literature, even though it has not been adequately tested. One implication of this assumption is that a district's cost index does not depend on its level of performance. The performance indicators we selected had an adjusted R-squared of at least 0.10 with variables typically found in an education demand equation, including income and tax share. In addition, we ran a factor analysis on an array of performance indicators measures, and the scree plot indicated three distinct performance dimensions, which are very similar to the three measures we actually use.

2. In principle, the methods discussed here could be applied at the school level and perhaps even at the classroom level. Cost studies at the school level might prove to be helpful for understanding performance disparities within districts, which is an important issue in many large cities. However, the data for such applications have not yet become available and, even if available, would not yield district-wide cost indices because they could not consider some elements of cost, such as the salaries of administrators and counselors.

3. This statement may be a bit too strong, because this method cannot adjust for teacher quality differences that are known to school officials (and reflected in salaries) but unknown to the researcher. For example, school officials may be able to judge teacher quality through letters of recommendation or the interview process; however, such qualitative data about teachers are generally not collected on a consistent basis. As a result, this approach, along with the more general approaches in later sections, may overestimate the generosity of some districts with relatively high-quality teachers (based on unobserved factors).

4. An analog to the first problem with using teachers' salaries could arise in this example if households could select different grades of natural gas. There is no analog here to the second problem with using teachers' salaries, however, since households do not negotiate over natural gas prices.

5. During the 1980s, a state aid program for municipalities in Massachusetts incorporated a regression-based cost index (Bradbury et al., 1984). This program has since been discontinued.

6. The 1996 New York State aid formulas are described in *State Aid to Schools* (State University of New York, 1996).

7. One might be concerned that income and preference variables, such as average education, are themselves endogenous. If so, using these variables as instruments could lead to biased coefficients and biased cost indexes. With our New York State data, however, leaving out these instruments has virtually no effect on the cost indexes. The correlation between the index we report and either an index without the income instrument or the preference instruments is 0.99 or above.

8. Applications of this technique to education typically ignore environmen-

tal cost factors, and therefore incorrectly conclude that high-cost districts are "inefficient" (Bessent and Bessent, 1980). Ruggiero (1996) shows how to incorporate environmental factors into the DEA calculations, but also shows that the technique breaks down if more than one or two such factors are introduced. Several other approaches to efficiency estimation use various ad hoc statistically based adjustments for multiple environmental factors (Ray, 1991; Grosskopf et al., 1997; Duncombe and Yinger, 1997).

9. Two new instruments are included to account for the endogeneity of efficiency: (1) a dichotomous variable for whether the district is a city district (city districts are not required to use an annual budget referendum); and (2) percent of district employees that are executives, managers, or professionals. The first of these variables is clearly exogenous since rules regarding referendums are set by state law, and there has not been any change in the city classification in decades. The second instrument, like the instruments discussed in note 7 might not be exogenous. However, if this instrument is excluded from the regression, the estimated cost index is hardly affected; its correlation with our preferred index is 0.99.

10. Because we rely on the 1990 census data, we cannot determine the stability of these cost indices over time. This is a good issue for future research.

11. The enrollment in a district is influenced, of course, by district consolidation or district splitting. The U-shaped relationship we estimate implies that it may be possible to lower educational costs by consolidating small districts and splitting up large ones. We do not consider these possibilities here, but consolidation is examined in Duncombe et al. (1995). In the long run, enrollment in a school district may also be influenced by the decisions of school officials, as parents make residential choices and choices about private school based on school quality and property tax rates. We know of no study that considers this possibility, and it is an important topic for future research.

12. We do not attempt a full analysis of spending on students with disabilities and in fact our dependent variable, approved operating expenditure as measured by the state, does not include all such spending. For an analysis of the cost of special education, see Chaikind et al. (1993). Broader measures of students with disabilities also complicate the analysis because they may be influenced by the way a school district determines which students have disabilities (Lankford and Wyckoff, 1996). We restrict our analysis to environmental variables, such as the poverty rate and the share of students with severe disabilities, that appear to be, for all practical purposes, outside the control of school officials.

13. These results are not driven by New York City. A regression analysis that excludes New York City and Yonkers (columns 1 and 2 of Table 8-1) results in cost indexes, both for New York City and for other districts, that are similar to those in Tables 8-2 and 8-3.

14. Historically, New York has used a modified foundation formula, but the current formula mixes elements of a foundation formula and a power-equalizing

formula. In effect, the current formula appears to act as a power-equalizing formula for districts with spending levels in the middle of the spending distribution. The state aid formulas are described (State University of New York, 1996).

15. The key problem with this approach is that it does not provide researchers with a method for identifying this average-cost district. This problem is not recognized by Guthrie and Rothstein (see Chapter 7 in this volume).

16. As noted earlier, New York City has the highest costs in the state, but it also now receives below average aid per pupil. New York City also has a very high share of the pupils in the state, so if it is included in the simulations, it receives a very large share of any performance-based aid program and little is left over for other districts. Results for other states are unlikely to be so dominated by one district, so we focus on simulations without New York City. The cost index used in these simulations is based on the regression results reported in columns of 1 and 2 of Table 8-1. Besides being estimated without New York City and Yonkers, this cost regression differs from the one reported in columns 3 and 4 (which was used for our preferred cost index in this chapter) because of several data modifications made since publication of Duncombe and Yinger (1997).

17. Table 8-4 is a revised version of Table 6 in Duncombe and Yinger (1997). The revisions were necessary to correct a minor programming error. This error did not affect any other tables, nor did it affect any of the substantive conclusions in the original Duncombe and Yinger paper.

18. All cost coefficients are biased when efficiency is left out of a cost model, but in our equation the bias in the wage variable is particularly dramatic.

19. This analysis ignores tax distortions. A shift to more state aid (and, in New York at least, a more balanced education finance system) could result in efficiency gains in the form of less tax distortion that are large enough to offset the efficiency losses in education.

ACKNOWLEDGMENTS

This chapter was originally prepared for a conference sponsored by the Committee on Education Finance, National Research Council, Irvine, California, January 30-31, 1998. The authors are grateful to Janet Hansen, Sunny Ladd, Bob Schwab, Steve Sugarman, and other participants in that conference for comments on the original draft.

REFERENCES

Bessent, A., and E. Wailand Bessent
    1980   Determining the comparative efficiency of schools through data envelopment analysis. *Educational Administration Quarterly* 16:57-75.

Bradbury, K.L., H.F. Ladd, M. Perrault, A. Reschovsky, and J. Yinger
  1984   State aid to offset fiscal disparities across communities. *National Tax Journal* 37:151-170.
Bradford, D., R. Malt, and W. Oates
  1969   The rising cost of local public services: some evidence and reflections. *National Tax Journal* 22:185-202.
Chaikind, S., L.C. Danielson, and M.L. Brauen
  1993   What do we know about the costs of special education? A selected review. *Journal of Special Education* 26(4):344-370.
Chambers, J.
  1978   Educational cost differentials and the allocation of state aid for elementary and secondary education. *Journal of Human Resources* 13:459-481.
  1995   Public school teacher cost differences across the united states: Introduction to a Teacher Cost Index (TCI). Pp. 21-32 in *Developments in School Finance, 1995*. Washington, DC: National Center for Education Statistics.
Clotfelter, C., and H.F. Ladd
  1996   Recognizing and rewarding success in public schools. Pp. 23-64 in *Holding Schools Accountable: Performance-Based Reform in Education,* H. F. Ladd, ed. Washington, DC: The Brookings Institution.
Coleman, J.S, E.Q. Campbell, C.J. Hobson, J. McPartland, A.M. Mead, F.D. Weinfeld
  1966   *Equality of Educational Opportunity.* Washington, DC: U.S. Department of Health, Education and Welfare.
Courant, P., E. Gramlich, and S. Loeb
  1995   A report on school finance and educational reform in Michigan. Pp. 5-33 in *Midwest Approaches to School Reform*, T.A. Downes and W.A. Testa, eds., Chicago: Federal Reserve Bank of Chicago.
Downes, T., and T. McGuire
  1994   Alternative solutions to Illinois' school finance dilemma: A policy brief. *State Tax Notes* February 14: 415-419.
Downes, T., and T. Pogue
  1994   Adjusting school aid formulas for the higher cost of educating disadvantaged students. *National Tax Journal* 47:89-110.
Duncombe, W., J. Miner, and J. Ruggiero
  1995   Potential cost savings from school district consolidation: A case study of New York. *Economics of Education Review* 14:356-384.
Duncombe, W., J. Ruggiero, and J. Yinger
  1996   Alternative approaches to measuring the cost of education. Pp. 327-356 in *Holding Schools Accountable: Performance-Based Reform in Education*, H.F. Ladd, ed. Washington, DC: The Brookings Institution.
Duncombe, W., and J. Yinger
  1997   Why is it so hard to help central city schools? *Journal of Policy Analysis and Management* 16(1):85-113.
  1998a   An analysis of two educational policy changes in New York: Performance standards and property tax relief. Pp. 99-136 in *Educational Finance to Support Higher Learning Standards*, J.H. Wyckoff, ed. Albany, NY: New York State Board of Regents.
  1998b   School finance reform: Aid formulas and equity objectives. *National Tax Journal* 51:239-262.
Ferguson, R.
  1991   Paying for public education: New evidence on how and why money matters. *Harvard Journal on Legislation* 28:465-498.

Ferguson, R., and H.F. Ladd
   1996   How and why money matters: An analysis of Alabama schools. Pp. 265-298 in *Holding Schools Accountable: Performance-Based Reform in Education*, H.F. Ladd, ed. Washington, DC: The Brookings Institution.
Grosskopf, S., K. Hayes, L. Taylor, and W. Weber
   1997   Budget-constrained frontier measures of fiscal equality and efficiency in schooling. *Review of Economics and Statistics* 79:116-124.
Hanushek, E.
   1986   The economics of schooling: Production and efficiency in public schools. *Journal of Economic Literature* 24:1141-1177.
Inman, R.
   1979   The fiscal performance of local governments: An interpretative review. In *Current Issues in Urban Economics*, P. Mieszkowski and M. Straszheim, eds. Baltimore: The Johns Hopkins University Press.
Krueger, A.B.
   1997   *Experimental Estimates of Education Production Functions*. Working Paper #379. Princeton, NJ: Princeton University, Industrial Relations Section.
Ladd, H.F., and J. Yinger
   1991   *America's Ailing Cities: Fiscal Health and the Design of Urban Policy*. Baltimore: The Johns Hopkins University Press.
   1994   The case for equalizing aid. *National Tax Journal* 47:211-224.
Lankford, H., and J. Wyckoff
   1996   The allocation of resources to special education and regular instruction. Pp. 221-257 in *Holding Schools Accountable*, H.F. Ladd, ed. Washington, DC: The Brookings Institution.
Miner, J.
   1991   *A Decade of New York State Aid to Local Schools* Metropolitan Studies Program Occasional Paper No. 141. Syracuse, NY: Syracuse University, Center for Policy Research.
Ratcliffe, K., B. Riddle, and J. Yinger
   1990   The fiscal condition of school districts in Nebraska: Is small beautiful? *Economics of Education Review* 9:81-99.
Ray, S.C.
   1991   Resource-use efficiency in public schools: A study of Connecticut data. *Management Science* 37:1620-1628.
Reschovsky, A., and J. Imazeki
   1998   The development of school finance formulas to guarantee the provision of adequate education to low income students. Pp. 121-148 in *Developments in School Finance 1997*. Washington, DC: National Center for Education Statistics, U.S. Department of Education.
Rouse, C.E.
   1997   *Private School Vouchers and Student Achievement: An Evaluation of the Milwaukee Parental Choice Program*. Unpublished manuscript, May 1997.
Ruggiero, J.
   1996   On the measurement of technical efficiency in the public sector. *European Journal of Operational Research* 90:553-565.
State University of New York and The State Education Department
   1996   *State Aid to Schools: A Primer*. Albany, NY: The State Education Department.
   1997   *New York: The State of Learning, Statewide Profile of the Educational System*. Albany, NY: The State Education Department.

Steinberg, J.
  1998   Underachieving schools are shamed into improvement. *The New York Times* (January 7):B7.
Wendling, W.
  1981   The cost of education index: Measurement of price differences of education personnel among New York state school districts. *Journal of Education Finance* 6:485-504.
Witte, J.F.
  1996   School choice and student performance. Pp. 149-176 in *Holding Schools Accountable: Performance-Based Reform in Education*, H.F. Ladd, ed. Washington, DC: The Brookings Institution

Biographical Summaries
of Contributors

ROBERT BERNE is vice president for academic development at New York University, where he has been a faculty member since 1976. His primary research interests involve educational policy research issues, such as school finance equity and school-level budgeting. In addition to numerous published articles, he is the co-author (with Leanna Stiefel) of *The Measurement of Equity in School Finance* and the co-editor (with Lawrence Picus) of *Outcome Equity in Education*. Dr. Berne chaired the Outcome Equity Study Group for the New York State Commissioner of Education, served as executive director of the New York State Temporary Commission on New York City School Governance from 1989 to 1991, and was the director of policy research for New York State's Temporary Commission on the Distribution of School Aid in 1988. Currently, he is a member of the National Research Council's Committee on Education Finance. He received an M.B.A. in finance and a Ph.D. in business and public administration from Cornell University.

MELISSA C. CARR received her master's degree in public affairs at the Woodrow Wilson School of Public Affairs, Princeton University. Formerly director of programs in the former Soviet Union for Project Harmony, she has worked with government ministries, partner schools, and nongovernmental organizations to develop international educational and cultural programs. Her research interests include educational equity and adequacy across gender, race, income, and geographic regions; the role and nature of nongovernmental organizations in emerging democracies; and the role of educational and curricular reforms in societies in transition. She has a B.A. in political science from Amherst College.

ROSEMARY CHALK *(co-editor)* is senior program officer with the Committee on Education Finance. She has served as a study director for several projects within the National Research Council since 1986, including studies on family violence, child abuse and neglect, and research ethics. Prior to that time she was a consultant for science and society research projects in Cambridge, MA. She was the program head of the Committee on Scientific Freedom and Responsibility of the American Association for the Advancement of Science from 1976-86. Ms. Chalk has a B.A. in foreign affairs from the University of Cincinnati.

WILLIAM D. DUNCOMBE is associate professor of public administration at The Maxwell School, Syracuse University. He is also a senior research associate at the Center for Policy Research. He has written numerous articles related to school finance issues, and his fields of specialization include the analysis of school costs, consolidation, and efficiency, and the distribution of state school aid. He has also conducted research in public budgeting and finance of state and local governments. He has an M.P.A. and Ph.D. in public administration from Syracuse University.

WILLIAM N. EVANS is a professor in the Department of Economics at the University of Maryland, a research associate of the National Bureau of Economic Research, and a senior research associate at the Project HOPE Center for Health Affairs. Professor Evans has spent the past 19 years in the Atlantic Coast Conference, joining the Maryland faculty in 1987. His principal research interest is in applied microeconomics and he has worked on topics in public finance, labor economics, industrial organization, and health economics. His current research centers on the impact of education finance reform, the effects of family structure on mothers and their children, and the economic control of tobacco and alcohol. He has a Ph.D. in economics from Duke University.

SUSAN H. FUHRMAN is professor of education and dean of the Graduate School of Education, University of Pennsylvania. She is also chair of the management committee of the Consortium for Policy Research in Education. Her research interests are in education policy finance, including state policy design, accountability, deregulation, and intergovernmental regulation. She is author of numerous papers on education policy, the editor of *Designing Coherent Education Policy: Improving the System* and *The Governance of Curriculum*, and co-editor (with Jennifer A. O'Day) of *Rewards and Reform, Creating Educational Incentives that Work*. She has served on national and state task forces and commissions, including the U.S. Department of Education's Independent Review Panel for Title I, the National Research Council's Committee on a National

Educational Support System for Teachers and Schools, the Standards Task Force of the National Council of Education Standards and Testing, and the New Jersey Task Force on Educational Assessment and Monitoring. Dr. Fuhrman is currently a member of the National Research Council's Committee on Education Finance. She holds a Ph.D. in political science and education from Columbia University.

MARGARET E. GOERTZ is professor of education and co-director of the Consortium for Policy Research in Education at the University of Pennsylvania. Previously, she was executive director of the Education Policy Research Division of the Educational Testing Service in Princeton, NJ. She is currently a member of the National Research Council's Technical Panel on Special Education, and a former member of the National Research Council's Committee on Goals 2000 and the Inclusion of Students with Disabilities. Her research activities include studies of standards-based reform in education and allocation of school-level resources. She has an M.P.A. and Ph.D. in social science from The Maxwell School at Syracuse University.

JAMES W. GUTHRIE is professor of education and public policy at Peabody College, Vanderbilt University. Prior to his Vanderbilt appointment, he was co-director of Policy Analysis for California Education (PACE) and professor of education at the University of California at Berkeley. He has worked for the California and New York State Education Departments, served as an education specialist for the United States Senate, and was a special assistant to the Assistant Secretary of the U.S. Department of Health, Education, and Welfare. He has been honored as an Alfred North Whitehead postdoctoral fellow at Harvard University, visiting fellow at the department of educational studies of Oxford University, and in 1990 was named as the American Education Research Association's first senior fellow. Dr. Guthrie is president of a private management consulting corporation, Management Analysis and Planning Inc., which specializes in education finance and litigation support. He is a member of the National Research Council's Committee on Education Finance. He has a Ph.D. in education policy from Stanford University.

JANET S. HANSEN *(co-editor)* is the study director for the Committee on Education Finance. As a senior program officer at the National Research Council, she has managed several projects related to education and training, international comparative studies in education, and civilian aviation careers. Prior to joining the NRC staff, she was director for policy analysis at the College Board. She wrote and lectured widely on issues relating to higher education finance, federal and state student assistance programs, and how families pay for college. She also served as director for continuing education and associate provost at the Claremont College and as assistant dean of the College at Princeton University. She graduated from the University of North Carolina and received a Ph.D. degree in public and international affairs from Princeton.

HELEN F. LADD *(co-editor)* is professor of public policy studies and economics at the Terry Sanford Institute of Public Policy at Duke University and co-chairs the National Research Council Committee on Education Finance. Her research expertise involves state and local public finance, and she has published extensively in the areas of education finance, property taxation, state economic development, and the fiscal problems of U.S. cities. Among her numerous publications, she is the editor of *Holding Schools Accountable: Performance-Based Reform in Education* and the co-author (with John Yinger) of *America's Ailing Cities: Fiscal Health and the Design of Urban Policy.* She has been a visiting scholar at the Federal Reserve Bank of Boston, a senior fellow at the Lincoln Institute of Land Policy, and a visiting fellow at the Brookings Institution. She holds a Ph.D. in economics from Harvard University.

PAUL A. MINORINI is a director of Boys Hope Girls Hope, a national residential and college preparatory program for at-risk, yet academically capable, youth, headquartered in Bridgeton, Missouri. Previously, he was a senior program officer at the National Research Council for the Committee on Education Finance. Prior to joining the NRC, Mr. Minorini was an attorney at Hogan & Hartson in Washington, DC, where he represented school districts in efforts to obtain greater education funding equity and program adequacy through policy reform and litigation. He has published several articles related to school finance equity and adequacy legal cases. Mr. Minorini has a J.D. from the University of Pennsylvania Law School.

SHEILA E. MURRAY is a National Academy of Education/Spencer Foundation Post-doctoral Fellow and a Visiting Scholar at the Northwestern University/University of Chicago Joint Center for Poverty Research. She is on leave from the University of Kentucky where she is an assistant professor at the Martin School of Public Policy and Administration and the Department of Economics. Her fields of specialization include public finance, econometrics, and the economics of education. Her current research interests are in education finance reform and policy, the distribution of education resources, and the centralization of public school finance. She has an M.A. in economics from the University of Pennsylvania and a Ph.D. in economics from the University of Maryland at College Park.

GARY NATRIELLO is professor of sociology and education at Teachers College, Columbia University. He is also a senior research scientist at the Institute for Urban and Minority Education and editor of the *Teachers College Record.* His current research interests include the impact of evaluation processes on students and the needs of at-risk students. He has worked with the at-risk students projects at The Johns Hopkins University National Center for Research on Effective Schooling for Disadvantaged Youth. Among his numerous publications, he is co-author of *Schooling Disadvantaged Children: Racing Against Catastrophe* (with Edward McDill and Aaron Pallas) and *From Cashbox to Classroom: The Impact of Quality Education in New Jersey* (with William Firestone and Margaret Goertz). Dr. Natriello is a member of the Committee on Education Finance of the National Research Council. He has a Ph.D. in the sociology of education from Stanford University.

RICHARD ROTHSTEIN is a research associate of the Economic Policy Institute, an adjunct professor of public policy at Occidental College, and a contributing editor of *The American Prospect*. He is the author of numerous publications in education finance including: *The Way We Were?* and *Where's the Money Gone? Changes in the Level and Composition of Education Spending, 1967-91* (and its update *Where's the Money Going?*). He also co-edited (with Edith Rasell) *School Choice: Examining the Evidence*. Mr. Rothstein was formerly a program analyst for the Los Angles School Board.

ROBERT M. SCHWAB is professor and director of graduate studies at the Department of Economics, University of Maryland, College Park. His fields of specialization are in public and urban economics. He has published numerous articles on education finance, and his most recent research focuses on education finance reform, the distribution of education resources, and education productivity, with a particular emphasis on the relative efficiency of public and private schools. Dr. Schwab is a member of the Committee on Education Finance of the National Research Council. He has a Ph.D. in economics from The Johns Hopkins University.

LEANNA STIEFEL is professor of economics at the Robert F. Wagner Graduate School of Public Service at New York University where she is director of the public and nonprofit program for M.P.A. students. Her published work includes many articles on school finance equity and school finance reform. Her current research activities include studies of the efficiency and equity of school-level resource allocation and school-based financing. She is author of *Statistical Analysis for Public and Nonprofit Managers* and co-author (with Robert Berne) of *The Measurement of Equity in School Finance*. She has a Ph.D. in economics from the University of Wisconsin-Madison.

STEPHEN D. SUGARMAN is Agnes Roddy Robb Professor of Law at the University of California at Berkeley where he is also director of the Family Law Program of the Earl Warren Legal Institute. Professor Sugarman is a member of the National Research Council's Committee on Education Finance. His published scholarship in the field of educational policy and the law covers topics such as school finance reform, school choice, and the legal rights of public school children. Among his many publications, he is co-author (with John Coons and William Clune) of *Private Wealth and Public Education* and (with John Coons) of *Education by Choice* and of *Scholarships for Children.* He has participated in school finance litigation in several states and, on behalf of children from low-wealth school districts, argued the case of *Serrano v. Priest* before the California Supreme Court. He has a J.D. from the Northwestern University School of Law.

JOHN M. YINGER is professor of economic and public administration at The Maxwell School, Syracuse University. He is also associate director for the Metropolitan Studies Program at the Center for Policy Research. Previously, he was associate professor at the John F. Kennedy School of Government, Harvard University. He has published numerous articles in his fields of expertise, which include state and local public finance, discrimination in housing, and urban economics. He is co-author (with Helen Ladd) of *America's Ailing Cities: Fiscal Health and the Design of Urban Policy.* In 1995, Dr. Yinger was awarded the Gustavus Meyers Center Award for the Study of Human Rights in North America for his book *Closed Doors, Opportunities Lost: The Continuing Costs of Housing Discrimination.* He has a Ph.D. in economics from Princeton University.

Index

Alabama
    adequacy standard, 22, 23, 149, 175, 200
    constitution, 169
    context for reform, 157-158
    legislative response, 200-201, 204
    litigation, 22, 42, 149, 159, 167, 170, 175
    politics of school finance reform, 157-160,
        166, 167
    property taxes, 159-160, 166
    reforms, 73, 159-160, 200-201
    spending, 163, 171
Alaska
    cost of education, 229, 231, 245
    litigation, 44, 212
    reforms, 84
    spending on education, 212
Analysis of school finance equity
    alternative groups of special interest, 12
    child perspectives, 10-11, 24
    conceptual distinctions, 9-13
    ex ante and ex post concepts, 12-13
    inputs, 11-12, 24
    methodology, 103-104
    outcomes, 11-12
    outputs, 11-12, 24
    processes, 11-12
    taxpayer perspectives, 10-11, 24
    units of analysis, 11, 15, 17, 20, 22, 24
Arizona
    legislative response, 204
    litigation, 42, 175, 197
    reforms, 73, 204
Arkansas
    litigation, 42, 56, 69
    reforms, 73
Assessment. See Student outcome assessments
Atlas Communities, 230
Audrey Cohen College System, 230

B

Barro index, 84-85
Benefit principle, 10
Block grants, 61-62, 237, 238, 246
Bureau of Labor Statistics, 250

C

California
    definition of equality, 75, 144

impact of reforms, 49-50, 63, 74-75, 90-92,
        93, 101, 186
    litigation, 3, 8, 39, 42, 47, 48-50, 56, 69,
        72, 74, 75, 81, 82, 91, 92, 93, 95, 143,
        145, 169, 170, 183, 185, 212
    private school enrollments, 92-93
    Proposition 13, 3, 49, 74, 75, 81, 94, 169,
        170, 185-186
    reforms, 49, 73, 146, 169
    spending on education, 74-75, 81, 82, 93,
        95, 101, 169, 170, 211, 212
    student performance, 90-91
    teacher salaries, 102
    voluntary donations to local schools, 91-92
Cases. See Court cases
Categorical grants, 101, 104, 130, 234, 235,
        236, 239-241
Center for Education Policy Analysis—New
        Jersey, 103
Chambers' Teachers' Cost Index, 84-85
Charter schools, 27, 153, 164
Child/student equity, 10, 11, 28
Christian Coalition, 158, 159
Civil Rights Act of 1964, 14, 177-178
Class size, 234, 238-241. See also Teacher/
        pupil ratios
Coefficient of variation, 19, 76, 85, 110-111,
        114
Colorado
    cost of education, 212, 249
    litigation, 45, 212
Concepts. See Equity concepts
Co-NECT, 230
Connecticut
    litigation, 42, 67, 69, 212
    reforms, 73, 80-81
    spending on education, 80-81, 212
Consistency Management and Cooperative
        Discipline (CMCD), 230
Consortium for Policy Research in Education,
        103
Consumer Price Survey, 247
Contracting for services, 153
Core Knowledge Curriculum, 230
Cost functions, 21, 29
Cost indexes, education, 221
    adjusted input prices, 270-271
    Barro index, 84-85
    calculation, 269-282
    Chambers' Teachers' Cost Index, 29, 84-85
    comparison of, 277-282